Every Good Boy Does Fine

Every Good Boy Does Fine

A LOVE STORY, IN MUSIC LESSONS

Jeremy Denk

RANDOM HOUSE | NEW YORK

Published in the United States by Random House, an imprint and division of Penguin Random House LLC, New York.

RANDOM HOUSE and the HOUSE colophon are registered trademarks of Penguin Random House LLC.

Hardback ISBN 978-0-8129-9598-5
Ebook ISBN 978-0-8129-9599-2

Printed in the United States of America on acid-free paper

randomhousebooks.com

9 8 7 6 5 4 3 2 1

FIRST EDITION

Book design by Simon M. Sullivan

To György Sebők,
who deserves much more than this book, but it's
something

And to all the other people who save us from
ourselves

Contents

PART THREE: *Rhythm*

Prelude

When I was twelve, I went to the record store in the new mall and smeared what was left of my slice of Sbarro's pizza all over every last item in the classical aisle. I had to hold albums to know if I truly wanted them. After ten minutes, my mother yelled from the mall concourse—"Hey bub, time to go." So I grabbed a cassette of Mozart's *Sinfonia Concertante* with the Cleveland Orchestra. It wasn't clear what "Sinfonia" meant, much less "Concertante," but I knew the Cleveland Orchestra was legendary.

Back at home, I shut my door, wrestled off the cellophane, put the tape on, and heard a story unfold. *Ah, yes, Mozart.* The music was lovely, fine, elegant: just what I expected. As you will discover, I was the kind of kid who thought he'd already figured out Mozart but could barely tie his shoelaces. A couple minutes in, something odd happened: a few buzzing trills. Possibly nothing, a side idea branching off the piece's tree, climbing a few notes. But then there were a few more. I was sure they must be done now—but then, again, there were more, louder, higher. Had Mozart lost his mind? I'd been practicing trills at the piano, and as far as I could tell, they were charming decoration, a detail, like a turned leg on a chair, or molding around the ceiling of a room. But not here. Mozart was letting the detail take over and outgrow itself. He was creating a massive imbalance in his balanced world, for reasons unknown.

A trill is the closest you can get at the piano to the vibrato of the human voice, and that's what I felt: the notes were *vibrating* with energy. They climbed a major scale. Now, I was also practicing scales, of course. Scales were the ultimate joyless task, an endless and recursive tedium. But at this moment it seemed like I was the scale. The growing, climbing notes were mapping onto me, everywhere, rising in my chest, changing my breath, and in the balls of my feet, making me stand on my toes. I was no longer receiving music from without, but being filled from within, like a balloon. This feeling was so intense that for once I didn't have time to overthink.

At last, these trills found a thrilling, marching climax: *Here we are,* the music seemed to say, *striding on top of this hill we've climbed.* The violins syncopated against the march in the violas, grooving on all the excitement. I danced around my tiny square of shag carpet for a few seconds, imagining this was the point. I said to myself, *Yes, I get it now!* But as I lifted my foot to come down on the next chord, the music shifted from loud to soft, creating an unusual paradox: a shock of gentleness. I looked over at my cassette player, nestled between all my childhood books and one sex-crammed novel that I'd stolen from my father's shelf.

A second of amazement, halted mid-dance, like Wile E. Coyote when he realizes he's gone off a cliff. Normal musical time stopped. Most of the orchestra went into holding mode. The only exception was the violin section. They were still syncopating, even though they had no beat to syncopate against. (The reason for their rhythm had vanished, but the urge remained.) I didn't realize that the violins were descending the same scale we'd just climbed. I only knew that the notes were beautiful, but also dissonant, and I wanted to hold on to them, to every one—but (such is life) each kept sliding on to the next.

In that bizarre, melting moment, one of Mozart's greatest inspirations, I was eager to be brave. I wanted to throw open my door and share the moment with my parents. I might have taken the unusual step of being nice to my brother. But I worried my father would make a joke, or my brother would think I was showing off, or my mother would ask why I hadn't dusted the living room. So I sat on the floor next to my bed and played the same bit over and over, stirring the air like a stew, keeping the joy to myself even though the essence of it was feeling as though you wanted to embrace the whole world.

}

Thirty-eight years later, I was in my kitchen writing, and that passage from the *Sinfonia Concertante* came to mind. To be honest, I'd been avoiding it. It was too holy, too radioactive, a precious memory that made me feel vulnerable and again twelve years old, or again a college student falling in clueless love and not knowing what to do with a feeling that was too big. But I decided to be braver than the old days. I ventured into my cobwebbed closet, pushed past neglected cookbooks and abandoned humidifiers, and in a little leatherette case, there it was—my old cassette. The previous owner of the house had left behind a tape player. It worked, against all odds. Fifteen minutes later, I found myself staring at a salt shaker on my kitchen table, not sure where I'd been.

I tried to analyze my way out of the emotion. I dissected its structure. Section One—of course, the trills. This section depended on repetition, a repetition you couldn't possibly expect, that lasted way too long. It inched toward an unknown goal at the risk of being ridiculous. Section Two was a moment of savoring, where all the energy and work found a satisfying outlet. Section Three was by far the best—but meaningless without the previous two. Here, Mozart let his magnificent edifice dissolve. Accomplishment fell away.

And it hit me. This passage was the perfect metaphor for the very thing I was writing, the story of piano lessons: obsessive repetition, climbing toward an unknown goal that rewrites itself, once achieved. The truest realizations aren't at the peak, but are discovered almost by surprise, and through release, by passing back down the old, same steps. If you forced me to sum it up, I'd tell you that is the point of this book: a love for the steps, the joys of growing and outgrowing and being outgrown. And—just as in the Mozart—how time seems to stop, or even go in reverse, when you are learning.

But first, I'm afraid, we have to talk about my parents.

PART ONE: *Harmony*

1. *The Earliest Lessons*

PLAYLIST

SAINT-SAËNS: Symphony no. 3 in C Minor (*Organ*), second movement
MAHLER: Symphony no. 1 in D Major (*Titan*), first and fourth movements
CLEMENTI: Sonatina in F Major, op. 36, no. 4 (as much as you can stand)

My father was a monk. It's fun to drop this into conversation and watch for the double take. "Before I was born!" I add with a wink. When I was a child, Dad loved to tell stories about his decade with the church. One elderly brother refused to walk down the hall to the toilet and kept a pail in his room—he was dubbed "Thunderbucket." He dumped the pail out his window one morning, spilling its contents on a painting in the chapel below; this came to be known as "The Miracle of the Weeping Madonna." Dad went on and on about his roommate, Frater Lawrence, a brilliant thinker who didn't bathe, who "looked like an ape and smelled worse." Lawrence tutored my father on Dante, until he and his odors were mysteriously spirited off to Rome. My favorite characters were the spunky nuns Dad met when the abbey sent him to Notre Dame, cussing up a storm at the football games.

Because of these stories, my brother and I found the monastery intriguing. We assumed it was somewhere you went for kicks, like a theme park or resort. "Why'd you leave?" we'd ask, not knowing we were questioning our own right to exist. Though he always gave the same answer, he made us wait for it. All those devotional years had made him desperate to perform, and no audience was too small or gullible. He hammed it up, frowning, sighing, appearing to shake off searing memories and shadows of existential doubt, until at last he said: "I just couldn't stand the fried chicken."

We didn't know why this was funny, and Dad always followed his favorite lines with a stern, almost-furious face, so that you didn't know if laughter was allowed. I remember seeing that same expression years later, just after I'd moved my parents into assisted living. We were sitting around at lunch. An ambulance pulled up in the parking circle, lights flashing. "Here comes the meat wagon," Dad said, letting his gaze fall on a nearby resident, slumped in a wheelchair, hooked up to an oxygen tank. We all felt we had to laugh, but he kept at the frown, sustaining it like a pedal tone in music, insisting on the truth behind the punch line.

}

In assisted living, Mom made Dad go to writing class with her. That's how my brother and I finally got serious answers about the past. The main class assignment was a memoir. Dad complained, but you could tell he loved it. He squirreled himself away in his room, keyboard clicking madly, like a journalist on a deadline. The resulting autobiography*—"The Demythologization of Uncle Joe"—is written in a curious hybrid style, somewhere between Boswell's *Life of Samuel Johnson* and a Rodney Dangerfield routine. The elevated sentences are often too elevated ("As will be seen coloring the following barely historical and no doubt somewhat unavoidably fictional life chapters, the writing of which I now find to be inescapable, my life has been far from being epical"). The jokes have a way of circling back and making fun of themselves. There are lengthy factual passages where he seems to take special pleasure in boring you. But every so often, a sincere descriptive sentence slips through the cracks and breaks your heart.

---

*Coincidentally, around that time, I had just gotten my book deal—a contract for the book you are currently reading—which was mentioned, to considerable hubbub, in *The New York Times*. This prompted from my parents a great deal of "Oh, so who's the big man now" and "Are you sure you'll deign to have dinner with us?" etc. And then, in a truly hilarious development, my father managed to finish his book in the time it took me to choose a file name for mine. He emailed it to me, smugly, with two words: *Done. —Dad*

The first chapter alludes to tremendous guilt and refuses to specify a cause. Guilt for guilt's sake. Dad grew up in the Chicago suburbs: Irish mother, Bavarian father. The patriarch is mentioned least, but you sense he is the villain: grasping, disciplinary, severe. My father found his family escape in science: college in DeKalb, then a job as a chemical engineer in New Jersey. This lasted for a number of years. If you don't like the smell of the New Jersey Turnpike, you can blame him.

But at this point in the memoir, without explanation, a new thread emerges: an interest in the theater, poetry, literature. Facts paled before beauty. Dad started venturing into New York City, frequenting bohemian cafés, far from his vacuum tubes. And there, in that den of iniquity (where I now live), surrounded by actors (whom I avoid), seemingly in search of adventure and freedom, he met the last thing you would expect: a nice Catholic girl, Mary Elise Rafferty, of East Orange, New Jersey. The dream of a creative life retreated. They got married a year later: "what they call love at first sight, but more accurately ought to be called an act of desperation on both our parts." But Mary Elise had asthma, which became pneumonia on their honeymoon, and later chronic bronchitis, of which she died on December 3, 1955, three years after their wedding. They weren't able to consummate their marriage.

After her death, science lost what remained of its volatile luster. Dad began Bible study classes. They weren't enough, and so: off to the monastery he went, for ten years. Nothing in my life to date approaches this act of selling everything you own, surrendering self and ambition. Yet I feel that his choice wasn't one hundred percent faith. It had an aesthetic element. He craved to perform a moral act that was also beautiful. Dad and I eyed each other warily because we shared that underlying bias: overflowing tenderness for art and ideas; cautious irony toward people. If the boat was sinking, and the choice was between saving more passengers or the last copy of Bach's *Saint Matthew Passion*, we would both hesitate.

And so, while the Sexual Revolution upended the nuclear Beavers, and the civil rights struggle raged, and Vietnam escalated, Dad was immersing himself in the Bible, studying Dante and Homer, finishing a doctorate in chemistry so he could teach at Belmont Abbey College, becoming ordained, learning rituals. But his guilt found a cunning new avenue of attack. As the world's arc bent toward justice, he felt he was engaged in a form of escapism—devotion to God was a moral failing greater than all the rest. He drove away from Catholicism in May 1969, and was stopped for speeding in Tennessee. I was born in May 1970. Dad gave me the middle name Martin, for Luther King Jr., a symbol of what he had missed.

≀

My mom's memoir portrays a stark but hilarious family split: prudent *Prairie Home Companion* types on one side; wild gumbo wastrels on the other. Her mother's ancestors were Swedish Lutherans, but father Orville came from New Orleans. Orville's aunt Zelda was fired from a department store for theft. Mom describes the moment Zelda was forced to move in with them:

> Zelda arrived jobless, and overweight, with high blood pressure, diamond rings, furs, fancy clothes, her love of parties, booze, rich New Orleans food, and a shiny black grand piano.

Notice how she slips the piano in, at the end of a list of decadent, unnecessary, and dangerous things.

Orville had a series of decent jobs in the auto industry, and so they lived in prosperity through the Depression, with money to share:

> A steady stream of men and women [rang] our back doorbell asking for handouts. Millie or Mother would answer the ring and shove me behind the door. Sandwiches, coffee, water, leftovers from last night's dinner were regularly doled out as the people sat on the back steps. They were never invited in.

"They were never invited in": a classic Mom line. You can't tell if she approves of this boundary drawn on generosity, but she wants you to know about it.

This way of life evaporated when cigar-smoking Orville, ignoring doctors' warnings, collapsed of a heart attack, leaving the family with no resources. I think it made it harder for my mother that they weren't victimized by world events, but by personal failing. Mom's response to fate was to worry about every action, freezing everything in place, a strategy that worked all too well. It made her more physically immobile, year by year, until even the three-inch step to her front door was a challenge. I try to make light of my mother's anxieties; but every so often I feel this paralysis creep up on me onstage, in front of thousands of people.

After Orville's death and a few scrappy years, Mom married a police officer named Fran. There is no portrait of Fran in her memoir. She explains only the pragmatic: how they acquired a car, fixed up a bathroom, and produced three kids. The tone of her prose doesn't change—if anything, it becomes even more objective—when a note appears on the kitchen table, saying that Fran has decided to leave and won't be back. A pair of vanishings: her father from a heart attack, her husband from a different failing of the heart. In music, the return of a theme is often a comfort or delight, but in real life not so much.

≀

I guess I'm the convergence of these plot lines: my mother, adrift with three kids; my father, confused and (one presumes) spectacularly horny in the monastery. They'd known each other growing up in Chicago, and had been writing to each other. Were they in love? The memoirs don't say.

There was no time for dating. They were both broke, and fortyish. They married in Chicago but by the fall of 1969 were settled in North Carolina, far from family disapproval. My dad was then wiry, with a nice full head of hair and intelligent eyes. My mom's hair, despite her losses, had not yet turned white. She had huge, hilarious glasses, and some memory of a young girl's style. In his time at Notre Dame, Dad had acquired computer savvy, and he was hired at North Carolina Educational Computing Services. An interesting career path for a recovering priest—shepherd of souls, now an administrator of soulless machines.

Those North Carolina years, a fresh start for my parents, are mostly a haze for me. My brother Josh arrived in May of 1972, and my mom's previous kids started fleeing. Cathy and Chris went off to college and marriage. Jimmy was still in high school; I only remember him shirtless, wandering around the yard. My strongest memories are TV-related: watching *All My Children* and *The Price Is Right* in the mornings, while Mom drank a mysterious clear glass of brown liquid (not coffee). My first words were "bad Erica"—meaning Erica Kane, one of the most popular characters in soap opera history, and one of *TV Guide*'s 60 Nastiest Villains of All Time.

My parents enrolled me and Josh in an experimental preschool, a satellite program of Duke University. I drew an elaborate, Seussian robot that got featured on the cover of an education magazine. One day, researchers at the school dyed our lunch green to see if we would eat it. Josh refused to be a guinea pig; he brought his fist down on the tray, spattering everyone in verdant mashed potatoes. A teacher recommended Dad take me to a Suzuki school, to try the violin. We drove for an hour. I was led into a room with a row of children playing "Twinkle, Twinkle." I remember this with absolute clarity. Their bows moved back and forth together as they faced a wall of mirrors—each child duetting with a diabolical backward twin. I threw a tantrum almost as dramatic as Josh's potato storm, and that was that, for a while.

Two other important events of the North Carolina years: The first was that my dad built a stereo from a kit. He purchased an album called *The One Hundred Greatest Hits of Classical Music*, with cute drawings for each piece. My favorite was the "Hallelujah Chorus." I sang it at a grocery store and impressed (or freaked out?) a clerk. The second big event was that Mom slipped on some ice and broke her leg. A couple pins and she was on her feet, but the feeling of being able to stand on her own never returned.

≀

We left North Carolina in 1975 because Dad got an offer—a big career upgrade—to oversee a chain of university computer networks in New Jersey. We ended up in Englishtown, a bedroom community not far from Manhattan but not close either. Mom lost her circle of friends and the ability to attend college classes. Dad threw himself into his high-stakes job. Life was crowded—traffic, surrounding homes—yet lacked community.

Here, my memories sharpen. In the den we had a couch facing a TV, a big Formica table, and an old upright piano. The piano had no meaning at first—just a brown dusty heirloom. At the opposite end of the house was a formal living room with two lofty bookshelves. For me this was the heart of things, a shrine. The books were surrounded by icons: crouching onyx kings, a picture of my grandmother, a dinosaur egg, a crucifix. The titles included historical epics, a few classics, a Bible, an unabridged dictionary, and a trove of '70s philosophy, straddling devout religion and hippie new age—*Jonathan Livingston Seagull, Zen and the Art of Motorcycle Maintenance.*

My happiest time was spent cross-legged on the living room floor, in my pajamas, immersed in the bottom shelf with all the records. I worked my way through the *One Hundred Greatest Hits.* I air-conducted the *Air on the G String, Ride of the Valkyries,* and *Peer Gynt.* Venturing farther into the stack, I found two Freudian orchestral discs, my Dad's favorites: Saint-Saëns's *Organ* Symphony and Mahler's *Titan.*

One unusual day, Dad beckoned me away from my spot on the floor. He wanted us to listen to the Saint-Saëns on the couch together. I snuggled into the cushions. I heard deep bass notes circling, aspiring, giving up again. A theme in doubt. Music losing steam, searching for an exit. My dad murmured—"Keep listening." We lay in wait like hunters. After a dark and foreboding silence, the wooden speakers vibrated with a massive C-major chord, rocking the house with triumph.

"Holy crap," Dad said. I consider that to be my first real music lesson. He seemed so happy. There was no trace of his default grumpiness.

That organ chord gave him pleasure, a dopamine burst, but Mahler brought a deeper satisfaction. He often sang the big, brassy finish of the *Titan* faintly to himself on Sunday afternoons, while balancing his checkbook at the table in the den.

Mom didn't like the Mahler, especially the end; she found it bombastic, even silly. While Dad was (still!) looking for transcendence,

Mom was content with survival. She preferred lighter or wistful music. She had no patience for heroism. I can only guess what Josh wanted in those days. Probably nurturing companionship—but he was in the wrong family for that.

I kind of agreed with Mom, a rare occurrence. Even at six years old, I thought Mahler's triumphant ending was too much. I liked the beginning, though. I played and replayed that opening, feeling like a grown-up as Dad helped me lay the needle on the vinyl, and I tried to keep my hands from shaking. A second or two of silent glide; a bit of crackle; and then, the reward: a single note in the strings. It didn't feel like an orchestra yet. That note didn't even feel like music—it was just sound. Over that sound were laid darker sounds. But then it came back to the original blankness, even more haunting now because it contained absence, an afterimage of what it had lost. My mind was often drawn to that opening note, a thing representing nothing. It terrified me and yet I couldn't get enough.

{

I was now in elementary school. At recess, someone stole my lunch money and so when the lunch hour arrived I ran up to the cafeteria lectern to deliver a tearful, vengeful soliloquy to the entire student body. I implored them to search their hearts and give my dollar back. The principal came and talked me down from the microphone. This was just one of several incidents, my teacher explained at a conference with my parents. I read all the time and didn't socialize. (To me this made perfect sense. Books were less likely to hit you than other kids; reading was a refuge and an activity that Mom and Dad wouldn't complain about.) The teacher said she'd seen kids like me get into emotional trouble—I needed to be occupied.

At this point (according to my parents) I asked for piano lessons. They were surprised because of my passionate rejection of the violin, but I'd been banging away at the spinet here and there. As it happened, a teacher lived right down the street: Mona Schneiderman. (Has a more perfect piano teacher name ever been invented?) And so a new weekly routine began, in lieu of medication or therapy. Mom was relieved it didn't involve more driving. I have unreliable memories of Mona's face—just a general kindness, light brown hair, glasses. Her upright piano stood just off the kitchen, sharing space with a formal dining room.

Mona gave me a book of sheet music: *Very Easy Piano Pieces for Children.* On the cover, I scrawled in my loopiest script: "Love the piano." I got assigned my first piece, "Wonderful World," on March 10, 1976 (I was five and three-quarters). It had lyrics:

I'm so happy, I'm so happy,
For the world is full of things,
Birds and flowers and sunny hours,
My heart just sings and sings!

Under all the flowery words, Mona started to lay down physical laws: she wanted flat hands, curved fingers, a low and quiet wrist. I remember sitting at her spinet, raising one knuckle at a time, keeping my back straight, kicking my feet against the soundboard.

Then Mona sent my parents to a music store in a strip mall, next to Eng's Chinese restaurant. We purchased a book called *Theory Is Fun.* The book asked me to come up with an acronym for the five lines of the treble clef, for example "Every Good Boy Deserves Fun." I suggested "Eating Good Berries Delights Freddie." Learning to read music was a frenzy of flash cards, the sort of code-breaking work I enjoyed beyond reason. I devoured the new language and spat it back out.

Mona's next task was to impose rhythmic order. At the top of one piece she marked *one, two, three, four,* showing me exactly how long each note was supposed to last. For the next piece she told me to mark time myself, and chaos ensued:

I can totally empathize with my six-year-old self. I marked time as I understood it. Long notes were slow and boring and therefore a low priority. I love how the last 3 and 4 are squished at the end, ruefully realizing those beats had to go somewhere—an approach I still apply to housecleaning.

I thought of Mona twenty years later, in a dorm lounge in Marlboro College, when I had a lesson trying to undo her early discipline, all that insistence on the invisible grid of time. It was a coaching session with the American composer Leon Kirchner. He was—again, but differently—frustrated with my rhythm, and, to conjure what was lacking, he began to sing rhythms as gestures, using nonsense syllables, *tee tee TAAAAAHHH taaaa ta tee,* gesticulating to the nondescript and dingy drop ceiling as if it were the spire of a cathedral. There was no hint in his singing of a quarter note or eighth note, or counting; all that was back in the past, assumed animal knowledge, not even worth mentioning. Each note in a phrase, as he told it, was like a bumper in a pinball machine, sending its energies off to the next. If there was a longer note, it had to be justified by gravity, by the forces against it or within it. There was depth to waiting. Quicker notes were like impulses, whims, the skips of stones, skimming a surface. For him rhythm was meaning, and the grid existed to vanish.

❧

Piano lessons accelerated a general nerdy awakening. I got obsessed with chess, for instance, when Dad taught me the moves. A corner of the den acquired a hand-painted chess table. My father played with me and was remorseless, beating me game after game, leaving me teary and emotional in the face of his reasoning. Then he came home from work lugging a huge object. "What the hell is that, Joe?" Mom asked. Dad clunked it onto the table. "A computer," he said, as we gathered round. It was grayish blue, and resembled a cash register. Instead of a screen, it had a roll of paper. Dad showed me some BASIC commands, and I created the following—

```
10 PRINT "HELLO WORLD!"
20 GOTO 10
```

—at which point the computer kept printing hello, clicking and humming, until Mom shouted that dinner was ready. This process pleased me. I created all sorts of looping, talking programs, and some games, and I played against the computer, which was great, since I knew exactly how to beat my own creation.

When programming got boring, there were books. I'd conquered *Wind in the Willows, The Chronicles of Narnia,* and, best of all, *Finn Family Moomintroll,* which resonated with my Nordic genes and premature nostalgia. So I convinced Dad to bring down *The Source,* the thickest book on the shelf. "Eight hundred and seventy-three pages left to go," I'd say to Mom, to prevent her from asking if I'd done my chores. She'd ask me what the plot was, but I couldn't tell her.

Around this time, as I got more certain of my passions, family life became less certain. If I asked Dad about going for miniature golf, he might smile, but more likely he'd lose his temper. Mom would take us out to Carvel for soft serve, one of her favorite treats, but she screamed at other drivers en route. Once home, she'd lean on the kitchen counter for a smoke, staring out the window at the backyard. It was impossible to talk to her then. She poured herself drinks (which Josh and I still didn't know were drinks). Both my parents smoked. I remember Dad saying he was proud to be down to two packs a day. So much self-medication! When Dad took us grocery shopping on Saturday mornings, I remember sensing his relief as the car pulled out of the garage.

New Jersey days had only one dependably carefree moment. At night, after the bathing and toothbrushing, Dad would come to our shared bedroom, sit on a bedraggled armchair, and launch into the next installment of an ongoing saga, the adventures of his latest superhero (Sir Snigglepuss, Masterful Mervenpoop) swashbuckling through the high seas or wielding a machete in South American jungles. Chapters always ended with a cliffhanger. We fell asleep in the to-be-continued. I remember the light from the hallway, the dark of the room, the edgy sound of his voice, the flow of the story leading me on.

§

After six months, Mona referred me to a well-regarded area teacher named Lillian Livingston. "Mona said he was too hot to handle," Mom bragged on the phone to friends and relatives. To me, though, they said: "You have a talent—now you have to get serious." I liked the word "talent" and hated the word "serious." It was great to hear I had a musical gift, but it felt like too much, piled on. At school, teachers praised my writing and told me I was astonishingly quick at math. Abilities brought responsibilities, my parents said, over and over. Excellence meant a few moments of praise, and countless more hours of work.

My new teacher, Lillian, had a sizable studio and a proper and intimidating setup: a dedicated music room with two grand pianos (!) and a dark waiting room, like at the doctor, where you overheard the last moments of preceding lessons. Lillian also had a dog. When we met years later, she told me how much I loved that dog and cuddled with it after my lessons, and how hard it was for me to be dragged away. It's true, after my Lillian lessons I always felt as if I'd barely survived; I needed time and space before I could go home to my parents' different demands.

Lillian had a powerful personality. She outlined standards and promised consequences when they weren't met. It was no longer Mona's kindly, other-motherly world. Once I brought in the "Moonlight Sonata," because what could be better than that? Lillian launched into a tirade: the edition I was using was bad, and I had no business playing music like that yet, I had to be serious and respectful. I thought about how beautiful the piece was, as tears streamed down my face.

Sonatinas—Classical 101—were the focus of my work with Lillian, music so transcendentally mediocre that it is thought a child cannot ruin it. They follow a formula: You start with a cheerful tune and then play some scales, wrapping things up with the classical equivalent of "jazz hands." At the beginning of the second half, you get one semi-surprising shift, as if the piece were about to become interesting. This is just a decoy—soon you have to play the same dippy tunes and scales all over again. Sonatinas could be considered instruments of torture, despite and because of how happy they seem.

I worked for months on Clementi's Sonatina, op. 36, no. 4 in F Major. *Con spirito,* it says; "with spirit!" My score gathered markings, each week, until the things I was supposed to do gradually got hidden behind all the things I wasn't supposed to do.

Somewhere in that riot of scribbles, you can find "Remember fingering." Lillian was tenacious about this. Every week, she said I had to decide which finger went with which note, and stick to it. I felt this was anal at best and stifling at worst. Couldn't your fingers be free? Another sore spot with Lillian was rests. They got circled in multiple inks. When my left hand finished playing a phrase, it had a tendency to remain on whatever note it had just played—much like me on a typical concert afternoon, thinking I should get out of the hotel and see a bit of the town I'm in, but instead lying in bed with Netflix.

Most important, Lillian introduced me to a new word: *phrasing*. "Avoid sudden lunges in dynamic," the Clementi score says. You had to connect the notes so that they felt like toothpaste squeezed out of a tube, not a series of arbitrary lumps. At the end of the first phrase, Lillian made me write out a bedrock principle:

Loud/Soft—dissonances stronger, resolutions less. This quintessential classical way of ending—the musical equivalent of a curtsy—hides a contradiction. The "wrong" chord is played with emphasis, but the "real" chord is played quietly, as an afterthought. Lillian marked this nuance everywhere. It was her mission in life to teach thirty or so New Jersey kids, raised on *The Brady Bunch* and *Happy Days* and *The Loveboat,* the importance of elegance.

𝄐

Toward the end of second grade, a major life choice was made. My parents enrolled me in a new, advanced class. The class had only thirteen students. We ended up together for three years. We weren't tied to the district's curriculum, and could learn at our own pace. Dad explained that he wanted me to find my potential.

At first, this changed my concept of school. My new teachers were less hassled, more attentive, more like I wished my parents were— patient, capable of extended listening. They walked me through the unfamiliar, even advising me as I tried to be social. I managed to make my first real friends. There was black-haired and dark-eyed David Soloshatz, with impeccable handwriting and a quiet way. I was jealous of how organized he seemed to be. Occasionally he wore an exotic yarmulke. My other great friend was Colin, whose last name I don't recall. Colin's hair was a brown moppy mess and his face a morass of freckles, and he already played the guitar and a couple other instruments, and wrote songs, and threw himself into one implausible precocious endeavor after another: playwriting, pottery. His grades were uneven. My father didn't like Colin. He said, "Jack of all trades, master of none"— projection, obviously. But Colin seemed a lot happier than Dad, or Mom, or me.

⟨

Lillian told my parents that I needed and deserved a grand piano. Money was still tight. My parents hemmed and hawed. Lillian put us in touch with a piano technician who, for a thousand dollars (in 1977), sold us a reconditioned Behning. It arrived with a few caveats. There were no wheels—the legs were nestled in wooden blocks, painted an unmatchable and sullen white. Once in place, there was no moving it. The black case was covered in graffiti (*TK hearts RF, LADIES LIKE IT*), and the ivory keys were yellowed and chipped, like eighty-eight British teeth. Eventually it came out that the piano had been in a burlesque house in Atlantic City. Dad explained to me that burlesque was a different kind of *Muppet Show*. Mom chuckled.

Now that I had my grand taking up prime real estate in our family den, Lillian demanded I practice an hour a day. I was stunned. Piano was now a work camp. Was it too late to get off this moving train? My pieces were at most a few minutes in duration. I'd go through them once, then twice. By the third Sisyphean time the music seemed a million percent less charming, and harder than when I started. Luckily, my music books were crammed with distractions. Next to one of my favorite pieces—a minuet by Mozart, from *Don Giovanni*—was a picture of a banquet table topped with a candelabra, a story about Mozart and his father, a summary of the plot of the opera (soft-pedaling the rape angle), and a definition of the minuet. I read those paragraphs thousands of times to fill the hour, and to avoid worrying about the things Lillian told me were wrong.

Dad didn't like my Mozart—too frilly. He preferred a Bach chorale in a different book. But it had no explanatory note or pictures, just a strange and morbid title. "Jeremy, 'Come Sweet Death,' please," he'd say.

"Dad, not again."

" 'Come, Sweet Death,' for me," he'd beg.

When I didn't play it slowly enough, Dad would make me do it again: "Come on, give it some feeling."

One day I refused: "Dad, I'm a serious pianist now, that's what you said."

"Yes . . ."

"If I'm a serious pianist, I shouldn't have to perform for you on command."

Dad turned to Mom. Eloquent silence, a volley of rolled eyes, then the phrase "too big for his britches." But I remember thinking: *It's their own fault.*

For a while, I developed a brilliant trick to pad out my required practice hour. I'd sit at the piano in the afternoons after school and improvise melodies. "I already practiced!" I'd say. My parents caught on to this ruse after a couple weeks. If it sounded like I was enjoying myself, they didn't consider that practicing. But I kept returning to a little lilting tune in 3/8, which they loved; they were convinced I was now also a composer. My tune was in C major—sharps and flats were too much work!—but plaintive and bittersweet.

It was Dad's idea to name it "Ode to an Irish Grandmother." I'd never met either grandmother. Dad explained, his eyes glistening, that she

drank condensed milk straight out of the can. Why was condensed milk so emotional? (And what was condensed milk?) Recently I realized that the tune of the ode is only somewhat subtly stolen from the theme for *Star Wars*.

My other masterpiece I named myself:

In the middle, I wrote a fanfare that went up to a high C—as if the piece were summoning itself for some great task—but then the music falls, exhausted, in a disheveled scale, back to the same place as before. Clever text-painting or compositional desperation—you decide.

One evening, my parents said I should write out my pieces. It was the news hour, and the piano was in the den with the TV, so I trudged upstairs to my room. Notating music was a drag, especially away from the piano. There were so many hidden rules about stems going up or down. I had a complicated, vexed relationship with the quarter note rest—even today I couldn't draw one for you if my life depended on it. I kept making mistakes, crossing them out, and when I brought the score downstairs for my mom, she said:

"No, you have to do a neat version. No mistakes."

If only I'd known what I know now! I would have shown my mother a copy of Beethoven's manuscript for op. 111, with its illegible clouds of notes and scratches and maniacal fervor. Instead, I went back upstairs. I started over ten times, at least. I was in tears (not an infrequent occurrence) by the fifth time, and I thought the task impossible—how did any composer ever write music?—until my mom allowed me to use Wite-Out. Painting out the errors, I slowly created an acceptable version, but the process was so removed from what I loved about music that I refused to write any more pieces, and I stuck to my pledge until college. I also stopped improvising. My dad blamed my mom for destroying my creativity and ruining my compositional career. He brought it up often, over subsequent years, perhaps not the most helpful way to handle it.

≀

Lillian made me play in group recitals in her home, and then I began to take auditions run by the National Guild of Piano Teachers, where you got complex report cards on various parameters of music. Music was becoming a class, like any other. To help me perform under pressure, Lillian introduced me to her foolproof system of "memory stations."

She'd make me put numbers at key junctures scattered through the music. Then I had to learn to start from memory at each. In my lesson, as if it were a form of bingo, she'd call out a number and I'd jump. "Five!" she'd bark, and I'd skip to a theme halfway down the page. "Three!" sent me back over what I'd just played. I couldn't get into any particular mood. The music was ruined. But at least I wouldn't be sitting onstage trying to think what comes next, heart racing, while my parents sweated and someone in the audience coughed and Lillian regretted the moment she took me on. I'd always have some reliable place to skip to; I'd never stammer to a halt.

My mom loved memory stations. Need I say more?

On my score of Clementi's Sonatina in F, memory stations are referred to five times, in various scripts and deranged capitals, until at last—who knows what threats were issued?—I put them in. They are circled in unmissable brown Magic Marker. There is a hilarious number 11 on the last measure. If disaster struck, the nuclear option was to head for 11, play the wrap-up chords, *plop plop,* and rise for undeserved applause—a bit like the captain of the *Titanic* saying "Hey, at least we saved some rowboats."

Thirty or so years later, I had a memorable memory slip at Carnegie Hall in my debut with the Philadelphia Orchestra, playing Liszt's First Piano Concerto with Charles Dutoit. There's a beautiful, serene, arching solo piano passage at the beginning of the slow movement; I got through it reasonably well. Then comes a freer passage, a recitative: the strings quivering, the pianist emoting up and down the keyboard. There are two outbursts, with slightly different harmonies, and somehow I mixed up the first and second. For a blank moment I had no idea what the harmony was, where it was going, there on the stage of Carnegie Hall; all my years of study and theory and preparation were for nothing. Non-performers can't perhaps associate with this species of moment: it's not just that you're screwing up then and there, but that your whole life is pointless. The only delicious part of the heart-stopping panic was to see Dutoit panic also. His hands flapped through the beats, frantic and cartoonish; he didn't know where I was or what I was about to do. And somehow his confusion saved me; somebody had to rescue this sinking ship. I played some gobbledygook, and muddled through to familiar ground.

Lillian's memory stations would have been completely useless with an orchestra: a hundred people can't skip around with you. Upon reflection—you always spend a lot of time analyzing these mistakes, like a coach after a defeat—I realized I had no emotional attachment to that section of the Liszt. The passage just before it is one of the most beautiful things ever written for the piano, but this recitative seemed overdone, false, flailing about in imitation angst. A moment I never found interesting enough to love.

ᘒ

In my advanced school program, the teacher let me sail ahead in math. I got heavy into algebra, five years in front of the normal curriculum.

Solving for x was much simpler than piano problems. The quadratic equation became my calling card. I'd try to dazzle people with it—but aside from Colin and David, the other kids seemed more annoyed than dazzled.

As my parents were realizing, this school experiment had drama and disaster baked into it; it was just a matter of time. The small class created long-standing attachments and resentments. One day the teacher taught us how to build cubes out of construction paper. I loved the pattern, the delicate scissors-work, how the miracle of Scotch tape made a T three-dimensional. I assembled a family—Papa, Mama, adorable teensy babies—and set them on my desk. This family had no issues; it was pure cubic comity. Enter Jennifer, my nemesis, the most streetwise of all the "advanced" kids. (She and I had a history. She had given me a Valentine's Day card that I opened to find a brown blob, labeled with the word "doody.") The teacher left the room for a moment, and Jennifer didn't hesitate: she ran over and crushed the whole lot. I struck out in revenge, but was outmatched in both strength and tactics. I ended up on the floor amid sticky remnants of construction paper. First I had to go to the nurse for triage, then the therapist—the class had a dedicated therapist, did I mention?—and many things came out, all the levels of stress and the feeling that I had to perform well in every possible way and how could she do that to my cubes and my parents and . . .

The bearded psychiatrist was comforting. I liked him more than any adult I'd ever met. He wasn't as judgmental as my parents, or my piano teacher. He also didn't seem worried. But in his memoir, my father recalls the psychiatrist explaining that they categorized gifted children into two groups: disturbed and not disturbed.

༄

Toward the end of the seventies, home life got worse. My father's job stress, in tandem with my mom's drinking, manifested for me and Josh in the form of an unavoidable and senseless anger, a kind of autopilot screaming that inhabited the late afternoons. We tried a vacation once—a cheap one, driving to the Jersey Shore for a production of

Godspell and some swimming—but it backfired. Mom pestered Dad about something, and he shoved her back in a chair. All of us were in shock for a few days. Dad's devotion and intelligence and monastic past and sense of culture—all gone in a spasm of violence and weakness. I'm sure his guilt haunted him. Mom nourished a new fear, the last thing she needed.

Our best family time was in front of the TV. The boob tube brought a truce. We would have missed church rather than *The Muppet Show*. Kermit at least knew something about irony and timing, while our priest earnestly droned on. To counter the anti-culture of sitcoms, my parents also gave us a steady diet of PBS, especially *Live from Lincoln Center*. One memorable night we all sat through a performance of Luciano Pavarotti and Joan Sutherland. My brother was miserable, twisting his curly hair in the corner. I was bored at first, but got drawn in. Dad, in ecstasy, ordered the record at one of the commercial breaks.

The PBS opera album—mostly Verdi, some Donizetti—became my new life soundtrack. I felt this music was both more true and more sweeping than Dad's big orchestral blowouts. I memorized many of the words, for instance:

Parigi, o cara
noi lasceremo

Parigi ("Paris") is sung to a nice rocking rhythm, like a lullaby. *Cara* ("dearest") is sung to the exact same. The music lilts, bar by bar. But the third phrase rises, as the singer speaks of leaving, of freedom. One measure suddenly spans over to the next. When Pavarotti climbed there, from a C to an F, his voice had a new quality—as if trying to find or open something. This moment grabbed on to me, and still does, despite all that I've come to know about Pavarotti and singers in general. You feel the possibility of strain in the voice, but before the strain becomes real he's jumped the hurdle and converted it into beauty.

I sang along with Pavarotti in mangled Italian. The other thing I loved was the catchiness. No matter what happens in Italian opera—tenderness, desperation, anger, jealousy—everything eventually surrenders to a sway. Feelings morph into a musical impulse, and once you are in its spell—the spell of the Italian tune and the roll of its syllables—it returns the feeling to you like a gift, wrapped in special paper—as if to say yes, these emotions are shared, they belong to all of us, and even the deepest sadness comes with a side of pleasure.

But I couldn't stay long in the living room, swept up in Verdi. I had to return to the den to practice, now an endless hour and a half every day. This location made it impossible for me to work without commentary. My parents got ever more involved. Was my talent the thing that might balance the scales, and redeem their collapsing marriage? My mother developed a two-tier grading system for anything I played. Either it danced—or it didn't dance. She would make this assessment from the kitchen while I was in the middle of my Mozart minuet, or my Chopin waltz (her favorite)—"It's not dancing, try it again." And I'd scream back at her, "You don't know anything about music!" "I know what sounds good," she'd say. "I've never seen you dance," I'd retort. That was true, and unkind—since the broken leg, even her walk was shaky.

One day, Lillian made me perform one of my sonatinas at a school recital—in a classroom in front of my classmates, on a clunky spinet with several sticking keys. I rushed in the last movement. My mom came, and her postmortem was brief. "You rushed, bub," she said, in front of everyone. "It didn't dance." And that was that. It was bad enough to have my teacher pass judgment every week. But to have my mom chime in, after all I suffered for my art!

The afternoon after that recital, I ignored the piano and my parents, and sat on the couch watching my least favorite show, *Andy Griffith*.

"Time to practice," Mom warned.

I refused to move.

"It's time," Dad said. He'd just gotten home.

"Soon," I grunted, "I'm busy now."

Then the real fight began. "If you don't want to practice," Dad asked, "why don't you just quit?" I stared at them, eyes misting.

"What do you think, Joe, should we call Lillian right now and cancel his lessons?"

"Maybe we should, Jackie."

They did this out of love, I assume, but it boggled my mind—how could they be so cruel? I dreaded my lessons, but I never wanted them to stop. This piano now seemed inseparable from me, immovable as the Behning on its blocks. I wasn't sure how this had happened. Part of it was my love for music, whatever that means, but part of it was less selfless—piano was the only way I'd found to express myself, a shelter and a persona. Some childhood fears are tangible, but most are absences, losses of frame, like when my parents talked about getting divorced, or when I dreamed one night that the universe had nothing in it. If I had to quantify how I felt about quitting the piano, it was somewhere in the middle of those two losses—worse than my family splitting up, but not quite as bad as the vanishing of the entire universe.

2. *Harmony* LESSON ONE

PLAYLIST

RAVEL: Piano Concerto for the Left Hand
MOZART: Concerto in F Major, K. 459
MOZART: Sonata in C Major, K. 545, second movement
SCHUBERT: Impromptu in F Minor, D. 935, no. 1
SCHUBERT: Sonata in B-flat Major, D. 960, second movement
BEETHOVEN: Sonata in C Major, op. 53 ("Waldstein"), third movement

I was sitting in the Chili's at O'Hare, studying some Beethoven. My neighbors were yelling at a row of hanging television sets. A waiter came over. I was forced to prevent him from taking the last of my chicken wings, and while we scuffled, he noticed my reading material.

"Are you a musician?" he asked, his face friendlier than moments earlier.

"Yes, a classical pianist," I said.

"Wow! You, like, tour and stuff? That must be amazing. I took lessons for a while but gave it up."

He appeared to be momentarily sad, and the fingers of his right hand wiggled as if remembering a scale. He added: "It just *sucks* that I didn't keep with it."

I hear this a lot, and still haven't figured out how to respond. But I knew what was coming next. "How do you get your hands to do different things at the same time?" he asked, with total innocence, as if he felt sure the question could be answered in a Chili's. This is by far the most common reason people give me for quitting. Two simultaneous tasks are too many, which is to say: having two hands makes the piano impossible.

⁊

I know my hands pretty well. I know these halves better than myself as a whole. My right hand is more agile, more Fred Astaire, willing to throw itself into a flurry of fast notes at a moment's notice. It has a tendency to try too hard and tire itself out. My left hand is better at solid notes, things that require cushioning, weight, gradation. It can play louder than my right, and more smoothly, but prefers not to move fast; it believes in patience and preparation. You could say that my left hand is older than my right, and wiser, and so much lazier.

This works out, mostly: these tendencies are suited to the jobs the two hands typically have. But when it doesn't, my pianist friend Evelyne Brancart taught me a trick. Let's say my left hand won't execute a little pirouette of notes. I force it to hang loosely by my side, like a child sent to the corner with a dunce cap, and bring up my right hand to play the same passage, perfectly, elegantly, lightly. Then I lift my left hand to do the exact same thing. It will not, cannot. At this point I will literally talk to my left hand: "Why can't you do that? The right hand can." Evelyne told me that wasn't a healthy part of the process—but I like being a terrible parent to my hands. It goes both ways. My right hand will jab into the keys, too fast, too eager. I shift my body to the right, and bring my left hand up to play four gorgeous legato notes in a row. My right hand hangs there, sheepish and shocked at how much more beautiful it sounds.

It's a curious feeling: one half of you can do something that the other half cannot. There's a clog, an inability to transfer excellence from side to side. I find I have to physically look at each hand, and mirror the motion off an axis running down my middle. When it works, it's quite a reward: you become a whole person again.

⁊

I was booked to play Ravel's *Piano Concerto for the Left Hand* with the National Symphony Orchestra. Now, there's a special case of the hands—a masterpiece born of amputation. Paul Wittgenstein's right arm was a casualty of World War One, but he had the means to commission one of the leading composers of his age. In place of two cooperating hands and ten fingers, you have five, which feel like much less than half.

Ravel's approach is *not* to do the best he can to approximate a "real" piano concerto, given the limitations. He deals with the one hand he's dealt like you'd deal with an animal you can't outrun, so you have to just stand there and stare it down. The orchestra starts deep in the bass, invoking the very idea of left-handedness, the lower-than-low region of the piano where the pitches approach indistinguishable noise. The cellos and basses play undulating notes, like waves of a subterranean sea, and on top of that a contrabassoon solo appears. The contrabassoon is both iconic and rare, specific and bizarre. Its unmistakable sound comes with sampled-sounding, gravelly overtones—a sound partly about its own unlikelihood.

Gradually, inevitably, Ravel builds from this dark beginning, assembling the full forces of the orchestra one by one. Adding frequencies, adding colors to the palette. You'd think he'd take pity on the poor pianist who will have only half the volume he normally would, half the notes; you'd think he'd compensate with a lighter texture, meet the soloist halfway. But no. The orchestra begins an almost unfathomable crescendo. It's glorious and gorgeous. But what on earth? You sit there waiting to play, as the impossibility of what you are about to do becomes ever more evident. There you are with one nervous and one superfluous hand, pretending to be a person whose arm was blown off in a terrible civilization-destroying war, and on your left is the Western Orchestra, a magnificent, luxurious, superfluous instrument at the peak of its glory and on the edge of its decline, a veritable symbol of civilization itself, towering over you, and Ravel keeps piling on delicious instruments, colors, layers. Even a pianist pounding with both hands could never compete with this. You would be drowned in that sea of sound, a pantomime.

It is perverse at its core, or at least it would be, except for the genius of the piano's first cadenza. The orchestra trembles, hits a huge chord, and stops. Into the void Ravel sends the piano's lowest octave, setting free overtones, getting the whole instrument to ring. With the help of the pedal, this makes a shattering effect. Ravel makes the instrument itself do the work of the missing hand.

As this cadenza continues, and the left hand careens over the keyboard, trying to be everywhere at once, I hear defiance: this limb, so often subjugated, saying *No, all the territory of the keyboard is mine*, taken back from the tyrannical right hand and rightly conquered in the name of the bass line, and especially in the name of harmony, which governs all the beautiful melodies.

{

People know what a melody is. It's a sort-of object. You hum it to yourself, and possess it; you feel it in your mind like you feel your wallet in your pocket. But if you mention harmony to a non-musician, best of luck. I've watched many eyes glaze over. Maybe the person knows there's such a thing as a D-minor chord, but he/she can't hum it. You explain: that's because it doesn't exist consecutively but simultaneously, or, really, abstractly—then you get flustered, realizing everything you just said is kind of wrong. Meanwhile they feel you are lecturing them, and rightly so—what does all this have to do with the joy and raw feeling of music?

It's interesting how this powerful parameter of music, in many ways the beating heart of the Western classical canon, is seen as an insider thing. When I went to the Marlboro Music School, and rehearsed with some of the most gifted young musicians of my generation and some of its wisest elders, I'd say, "Let's play the dominant chord louder than the tonic" and people would make fun of me for being a nerd. It was socially acceptable to play harmonies—it couldn't be helped—but not to label them.

Melodies belong to specific pieces, but harmonies are shared—across a style, across a culture. They belong less to individuals than to periods of time. Mozart, Haydn, and Beethoven, between 1770 and 1820 or so, all built off the same basic set of chords, like a starter set of Legos. There are extensions, excursions, extenuations, but basically they work from good old one, four, and five, the fundamental trio. Harmonies are a vehicle, a stage, a backdrop. There are endless famous melodies ("Ode to Joy," "Mary Had a Little Lamb," "Like a Virgin") but it is incredibly, world-historically rare when a harmony is so original that it attains the celebrity of melody. The Tristan Chord is really the main one I can think of, and it precipitated an apocalypse, the dissolution of harmony itself. Some harmonies appear to be special because they have legacy regional names—the Neapolitan Sixth Chord, for example, which must have been popular in Naples but spread over time and became common currency, in the same way that Bolognese ragù now belongs to every two-bit Italian restaurant in the world. For the most part, no individual creates a harmony. They are there for all of us, a common good, a common resource.

For the pianist, this division of melody and harmony, with all its symbolic overtones, becomes part of your body. The left hand tends to the harmony, and acts as the backup band, the mass; the right gets the good tunes and much of the credit. From earliest childhood, you shape yourself around these tendencies, and organize your mind into two zones, or "ways." It's not just that you're executing two tasks at once, but two different impulses. One half, the soloistic individual; the other, the accompanying world. One half specific, discrete accomplishment; the other half the common, discreet good.

{

When the pianist first enters in Mozart's Concerto in F Major, K. 459, you hear a textbook version of melody and harmony. So textbook, in fact, that it's almost a joke. As if Mozart is saying, *This is the simplest possible way to start a piece,* while hiding all the complexities of the world up his sleeve. The tune sits in the right hand, as usual, while the left hand politely remains in the background, tracing chords. But then, for one second, the melody stops for air. In that tiny gap, the left hand plays a witty bit of melody, to hide the seam. A magician's redirect, distracting you from the fact that the melody has run out of gas, that the singer has to breathe.

Even in this rudimentary example there is play, a hint of competing roles, of one-upmanship. Are harmony and melody friends or enemies? I can't help noticing that the left hand is ready exactly at the right moment to step in and take over, like an overeager understudy waiting in the wings. It is dying to be clever, and not "just" accompany.

Much of piano playing has to do with negotiating this perpetually changing labor-sharing agreement. The piano is expected to be as full and self-sufficient as an orchestra, in many ways, but composing for piano is quite different. In an orchestra, you can give all the chords to the strings or the winds when another section is busy, or gets tired. But two hands are the pianist's whole world, our northern and southern hemispheres. We have to fill everything in; otherwise the melody will be naked and alone, and the piano's weakness as an instrument will be exposed.

The most convenient piano setup is an array of chords in the left hand and a free and separate melody in the right. Many of the Chopin nocturnes, for instance, are in this format, and boy does it work. The left hand lays the foundation and gets the overtones of the piano ringing, and the melody floats in the web of those overtones, like a work of art set in its perfect frame. Mozart had a predilection for this too, like in the slow movement of the famous Sonata in C Major (K. 545) that every child plays. The left hand lays down an Alberti bass, in which the harmony ("just" G major) is translated and transmuted into a kind of river of notes, and the melody floats above (a boat, if you will, sailing on the harmony's river), and part of the hypnotic miracle of that movement is that the texture never changes, that the hands stay in their roles, while the harmonies change from toddler-innocent to old-man-complicated and back.

But of course the world would be impoverished if the left and right hands always kept to themselves. Composers are constantly devising stratagems. In the middle of Schubert's Impromptu in F Minor, one of my favorite pieces, the right hand sticks to the middle of the keyboard and does all the river-filler, while the left hand leaps over, in every bar, back and forth from bass to treble, playing a few notes of melody. It resembles a love duet—with a similar premise to a schmaltzy Mendelssohn Song Without Words I used to pull out for parties—but Schubert's calling melodies are all in bits; neither treble nor bass can really complete a thought; they depend on each other and constantly question each other, but never seem to find an answer, and the right hand is never allowed to help.

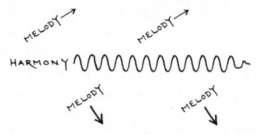

The slow movement of the last Schubert sonata (D. 960) has the opposite setup. The melody sits in the middle of the piano, in the right hand.

When I perform it, I feel this melody like a bull's-eye, a spot that I keep trying to focus on. The left hand leaps over and under to create a texture, or more precisely an aura or halo, around the melody—at once a web of sound and a (ghostly, ethereal) funeral march.

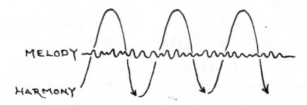

My left hand is often exhausted by the end—it's hard to be an aura, constantly leaping but almost always quiet—and despite all this effort, it doesn't quite solve the "problem" of the right hand, which wants to sustain. Often the division of the hands is just juggling, a logistical question of which hand is available to pick up the notes, like which parent is able to pick up the kids from soccer practice. But sometimes, as in these Schubert examples, the logistics become poetry.

The greatest example of this dance of left and right that I can think of happens in the third, final movement of Beethoven's "Waldstein" Sonata. The first movement is all energy, virtuosity, and drive. The second movement is mostly waiting: a series of hushed questions. The underlying question, compositionally and emotionally, is: How will the last movement respond to the incredible force of the first movement—how do you balance it out? I suppose I hear another question in there: How, in life, do you find something deeper than your youthful enthusiasm?

Beethoven makes it clear: he won't try to compete directly with the explosive force of the first. He begins as far as possible from that world, with a ravishing hush. The right hand, king of the treble, is demoted and relegated to the middle, where it rustles away, as quietly as possible. The left hand becomes the star. It plays a low bass note, telling us *we are in C major,* and leaps over the rustling right hand for a gorgeous group of notes, which sounds to me like a call. (I always think of "the call in the wilderness.") It does it again. And then again, back down, plucking a different bass note (*now we are in G major*), and back up to call. Many pianists play as if the melody begins with the high notes. But Beethoven's idea is far more profound: a melody about the gesture of leaping, about the transfer of meaning from left to right, about taking nourishment from the depths, as if drawing water from a well.

This luminous melody—not just the notes, but also the physical act of playing them, the sensation of crossing over—tells us that melodies arise from the bass, and take their inspiration (you might say) divinely from below, from deep correspondences of harmony, from patterns that generate events, that create sense, and give melodies their reason for being. Deaf Beethoven tells *(and tells) us to listen, to respect this fundamental relationship of music, to understand that harmonies are the source. But, as we said, most people love melodies and couldn't give a crap about harmonies. They prefer to imagine they're enjoying a melody, while they're really enjoying chords. This delusion isn't a problem. People are happy to take the blue pill, and anyway this is a common and inescapable encounter in life, with a beauty of its own: something you think you understand, governed by something you don't.

3. Forty Days and Forty Nights

My father, connoisseur of regret, decided the whole move to New Jersey had been a mistake. Mom was self-destructing; my schooling was tense; his job had shifted from problem-solving to unresolvable politics. So he sent out his résumé. He got an eager response from an implausible place: New Mexico State University, in a small town called Las Cruces. We were surprised to learn that New Mexico was a state.

Dad flew off for a first interview, and came back a few days later with a shard of pottery, a can of enchilada sauce, and some postcards of adobe buildings around historic squares. "There are rattlesnakes—and tumbleweeds," Dad said with a showman's smile, while Mom smoked, not in the atmospheric fashion of some of my later piano teachers, but as if her life depended on it. I don't remember her expressing strong opinions about this move. Hatred of New Jersey had become her great theme; anywhere else would suffice.

Dad liked the place and people, and so he took the job: Director of Computing at NMSU. We had family pronunciation lessons—"*Las Crrrrruces.*" I enjoyed rolling r's, but it took a while to get my tongue going, and once it got going it was hard to stop, not unlike learning to trill at the piano (a process that I was just beginning). It all was falling into place, except for one intractable thing: the Piano Teacher Problem. My parents agonized about transporting me far from culture, and from my future. So Dad gathered intel. Everyone he talked to said there was only one option in Las Cruces: a woman named Audrey Brown, who had all the best piano students, judging by all the competitions they'd won. I didn't like the sound of that. My father wasn't satisfied either. To assuage his guilt, he had to have better than the best in town. He pulled some strings and got someone to put him in touch with the university's piano professor, a man named William Leland.

I'm sure Leland was thrilled to hear from a computer guy in New Jersey whose kid was the next Arthur Rubinstein. He told my father that he didn't take private students, especially not ten-year-olds. He didn't know anything about teaching children! But he kindly agreed to hear me when we arrived, and offer advice.

"So you have to practice," Mom said. As always.

We didn't fly to New Mexico, because my parents didn't want to part with our Volare station wagon, *MotorTrend*'s Car of the Year in 1976. Dad was proud of this award, as if he'd won it himself. So we set off in this least-sexy-of-all-vehicles, while the burlesque piano and other belongings shadowed us in a moving van, and after a long day arrived at my half brother Jimmy's house in White Bluff, Tennessee. Jimmy had left New Jersey just a few years earlier. He took a job making trucks on an assembly line, and discarded his Northern European heritage with glee. He cultivated an impenetrable Southern accent, grew abundant brown hair to his shoulders, and still refused to wear a shirt.

We kids played on the lawn while Mom and Dad tried to understand what Jimmy said. Josh got sick from the potato salad. But we pressed on westward, impatient pioneers. We counted Stuckey's and played license plate games. Josh staged a miraculous intestinal recovery and ordered quail at a roadside restaurant. Let the record show that he ate it all, while our parents kept saying "Quail!" and shaking their heads.

In Texarkana, a fierce thunderstorm. Water flooded under the door of our cheap hotel room; we grabbed towels from the bathroom to stop the flow. The world already seemed to be getting wilder, less controllable. Another interminable day, crossing the plains in the Volare, which despite its award-winning whiteness succumbed to the heat on the side of the road in Abilene. At last, on day four, having counted forty-six Stuckey's in all, approximately the same number of times Mom asked if Dad was lost, we pulled up at the Best Western Mission Inn of Las Cruces.

Behind the town, a backdrop of mountains, almost suspiciously laid out, like a stage set. It had an unusual rock formation, a series of vertical jutting boulders, which the early Spanish explorers thought looked like organ pipes.

After all that time in New Jersey, with so little that wanted visual attention, here there was nothing but things to see. Opposite the organ boulders, at quite a distance, rose a long mesa with a few tiny outcroppings that gave a sense of place and scale and serration, like identifying marks on someone's face, and at sunset the sky above the mesa went into a frenzy of orange and yellow, while the outcroppings got blacker and sharper. Communities of mountains sat at other corners of the horizon, saying *Visit me, I'm the middle of nowhere you've always been waiting for.* But you didn't need the big sweep to find magic. Across from the hotel were stretches of unused space, which had reverted to or never left the state of being desert, with sand and gravel that glinted in the intense sun, and leggy green creosote plants, a plague of them, except that they smelled nice after the rain, and there were *literally* tumbleweeds, as promised, blowing across the road at the behest of various miniature dust tornados, which Dad had to avoid because Mom in her eternal worry explained to him that they were bad for the engine, and so we'd be driving and Mom would scream "Joe!" and Dad would laugh and pretend to steer right at them and we kids in the back were loving it all, let me tell you.

We stayed in the hotel for a week or two, while Dad went to work. The three of us passed long days in the tiny room (plus "kitchenette") with a duet of smells: burning coffee, Mom's cigarettes. We'd head out to the pool every so often and lie on deck chairs and pretend we were celebrities, ignoring trucks careening by, semis full of hay or pecans or manure. My father soon located a rental house not too far away, in an old neighborhood down by the Rio Grande. This house had rusty metal porches and inexplicable extra bits of roof, and in every corner and nook you found black widow spiders. Actual desert danger, not the pretend kind from Road Runner cartoons. The piano came off the moving van and got dumped in the middle of the living room with the sofa and TV. Conflicts ensued between daytime television and my artistic genius. Bach vs. *One Life to Live*. I had to start practicing again, furiously, to be ready for my future.

}

After a couple weeks I had my audition with Professor Leland, soon to be known as Bill. I remember driving over to his house, in a little development near the university, two minutes from a highway off-ramp. The street was modest, a long row of one-story stucco ranch houses, and it was always difficult to pick Bill's out. His house had no garage, just a carport that seemed made of cardboard; but as you walked in, there it was: an enormous, shiny Bösendorfer grand.

Dad and Bill launched into a chummy conversation.

"Wow, that's really something . . ." my dad said about the piano, comparing it to the graffiti-covered monster in our living room. The German name, just like on my Behning, was printed in gold Gothic script. It reminded me of a Bible.

"Yeah, when I was in Vienna I started looking around at these," and Leland began to explain how Bösendorfers were better than Steinways. A different tonal range, he said. He explained the process of ordering one and getting it shipped over, which seemed to fascinate my parents, while I eyed the keyboard: it had extra keys on the bottom, painted in sleek sinister black, which made this more piano in every sense than any I had ever played. I didn't realize at the time what percentage of a professor's salary this piano represented, how much love and devotion.

The room had no embroidered musical puns, no busts of Beethoven or Mozart, no framed programs or pictures of Bill playing concerts. Aside from the piano, it had a chair, a little music cabinet, and a metronome. Bill said "Wait a minute" and pulled chairs from another room for my mom and dad. Dad said later that the room reminded him of the monastery. Music was the main, if not the only, thing. Bill almost never dressed up; he usually looked like he was about to repaint his house. I cannot remember seeing him eat, or hearing him talk about food or other sensual pleasures. He did have a pilot's license, though, as I would eventually learn; and so he did like the idea of soaring over the normal world.

I had prepared my Chopin Waltz in A Minor—a melancholy ditty, not much of an audition piece. I also had one of my sonatinas and a fast, fingery piece from my beloved anthology *The Joy of Bach*. That was it. I sat down to play. My parents must have been on the edges of their seats at this moment of truth, hopeful for some redemption of their cross-country gamble.

Bill was impressed, especially by the Chopin. But he wanted to know how I'd sight-read. We played a four-hands piece together on the beautiful instrument, easily the best piano I'd ever played. This was my ace in the hole; I was a wicked sight-reader. After that, my father remembers Bill saying "I'm going to keep this one." An interesting way to put it—the sense of acquisition. He agreed to take me on as his first and only private student. My parents would say this all the time at parties: "Jeremy is his *only* private student." This wasn't just bragging. My parents needed to constantly reassure themselves of my talent, to make them less terrified that I was becoming a musician.

𝄐

The first lesson wasn't at Bill's house, but in his trapezoidal studio on campus—a former lecture room, cavernous and musty. Against one diagonal wall stood an organ, with its array of pipes and stops, which I was never allowed to touch, and along another a music-staff chalkboard, covered with theory lessons he'd given to his college students.

Bill was then in his mid-forties. He wore glasses with thick square frames and looked like a friendly visitor from a previous pedagogical era, maybe a narrator of a 1950s instructional film, something about combustion or the miracle of nuclear energy. (Nuclear was often on the mind in New Mexico.) He was tallish and fit—he jogged—but the skin hung loosely off his face, and had a slight grayish tint. He'd joined the New Mexico State faculty in 1969, which meant he'd already been there eleven years when I met him, and he constantly talked about how hard it was out there as a pianist, how lucky he was to have a job. He didn't realize how fantastical the idea of a job was for me then, and how irrelevant it seemed.

"Do you really want to be a pianist?" he asked at that first lesson. We were finally alone. What was I supposed to say? I'm not sure the word "want" figured in my plans. My philosophy of life so far was much more about avoiding the unwanted.

Bill said I had to get a black composition notebook, to keep a record of what happened in each lesson. Documentation was essential, the cornerstone of real and systematic study. The second assignment was to get some new music: Mozart's Viennese Sonatinas, Bartók's *Mikrokosmos,* and a little album of Romantic repertoire.

There was (and still is!) a music store in Las Cruces, called the Music Box. It had pleasures for all the males in our family. My brother looked longingly at trumpets and whacked on drums—anything to separate himself from me, and irritate Mom and Dad. I dreamily browsed through the stacks of music I hadn't even heard of. And Dad flirted with Joy, the French hornist who worked the register with a charming smile. He'd lost some key years to the monastery, and I don't think Mom was in the mood anymore.

My new *Six Viennese Sonatinas* had a red cover. I'm sad I can't locate that treasured score today. It looked like a new sound, and felt like a new life. The first sonatina began with some pomp, a fanfare in C major, but then without warning came its opposite: a shy little cluster of dissonances, which made me cherish the rub of two notes. I remember writing in fingerings in the den of the rental house, and playing that dissonant echo over and over, thinking how cool it sounded, the clashing C and D, how transparent, and so much less clunky than Clementi, while Mom lay a few feet away on the couch, trying to nap. Mom nagged me to practice nonstop, but she also—at unpredictable intervals—needed peace and quiet. "Just stop already," she'd say, while I pouted, stung by injustice.

"But Mom, you *told* me to practice!"

These arguments threatened to escalate, like in the old New Jersey days, but then petered out. Since arriving in New Mexico, Dad was a new and improved man, filling yellow legal pads with impressive to-do lists. Mom, stuck at home with us, seemed a mix of better and worse. Her energetic yelling was gone, but she seemed listless. Mom blamed this and some mysterious stomach ailments on the heat.

It had been coming on in New Jersey, but in that early New Mexico period I really began to think of my mother as an enemy. Perhaps that was typical rebelliousness for a boy my age (10.25 years old), or maybe it was a reaction to something deep and dark we had in common. Drinking had by that point become Mom's true discipline, demanding daily repetition and devotion—just like my piano playing. Both of us were getting more serious, digging in. I practiced for long stretches without thinking about what I was doing, and then Bill would get me back on the rails. Mom didn't have a teacher, of course, to correct the excesses.

In fact, I don't remember The Issue coming up in family conversation until it was too late. Josh and I still didn't understand alcohol or why people liked it. Maybe Dad hoped New Mexico would solve the problem through a combination of spirituality and sunshine, but our more laid-back life just gave Mom more time for addiction. The only moment of laying it all on the line happened one day when Dad was driving us along an irrigation ditch to school and asked, out of the blue, "What would you think if your mom and I got a divorce?" Josh and I stammered. How could we answer an adult question like that? We wondered why Mom wasn't part of this conversation, and reacted with enough panic that Dad rejected the plan, and it was never discussed again.

⟨

Bill and I got to work on the Music Box acquisitions: Mozart, a potpourri of Chopin, some bits of Bartók. From the outset, Bill told my parents that his highest priority was to not destroy my joy in music. He said that all the time, reminding himself, just before assigning me some new unpleasant task. I thought I'd escaped from scales when I left Lillian, but they appeared on the first notebook page:

watch thumb position in F minor! (no left thumb on G!)

Bill felt my scales were lumpy, and became obsessed with my thumbs, devising a symmetrical, synchronous exercise in which they reached under the other fingers, crablike, for ever more distant notes:

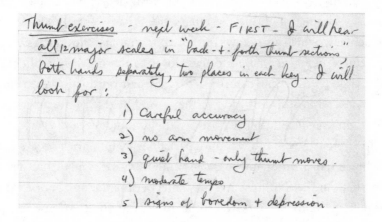

Number five is classic Bill. He'd already figured out that irony was the key to my heart. If I could laugh at my own failings, I might be able to address them.

After scales and thumbs, Bill's next priority was tempo. Bill loved benchmarks. One of his earliest instructions was to "go through repertoire list and *time* each piece." As if I were a runner timing sprints. Just a couple weeks later I'd sense his desperation, a growing awareness that rushing was woven into my personality, something he'd have to rip out of my playing like a weed. He wrote, "If you *have* to play something fast, play something *else.*" Then it got serious: "Don't play this without the metronome all week." The metronome was essential for Bill's cunning scheme to prevent me from playing everything as fast as I possibly could. But even that strategy hit a snag:

Mozart . . . You must check your metronome—bring it to me if you want.

}

I know exactly what happened—I'd told him mine was on the fritz. Yes, maybe it was shameful for me to lie, shifting blame to an innocent device. But the metronome didn't have feelings. So it was a victimless crime—and wasn't I scolded enough?

}

My parents were ready to commit to New Mexico, and decided to buy a house. They wanted us in a better school than Central, our current elementary, which was downtown, a bit scrappy, and half Spanish-speaking. They also wanted to live closer to the university. But their most urgent real estate priority—they harped on this—was to stash the piano off in a distant wing so they could be free of my practicing. This didn't seem fair. If I had to suffer, they should too.

The house they found was unremarkable: a white-brick square with a Spanish red-tile roof, low to the ground. But it sat in an extraordinary spot, high in the foothills, in a newish experimental neighborhood in the desert. We found ourselves in the middle of pointy sprouting yuccas, actual running roadrunners, dipping and curving arroyos—a playland of endless topography. We ran through the sand and leapt over cacti, and Mom pulled countless thorns and burrs out of us. Tarantulas often appeared on the screen doors, and my dad had to go after them with a shovel. Despite all this strangeness, the place felt calm, truly like a home—something that we hadn't felt since North Carolina.

My parents put the piano in the front bedroom, farthest from the kitchen and den. It had a big arched window, through which I could watch jackrabbits run by, or, after school, contemplate the sunset. It was my first private piano studio. The beat-up Behning took up two-thirds of its square footage. I have affection for that room in my memory, and dread. Sometimes it felt like a long forced march down the hall from my bedroom to the workspace, though it was barely ten feet. It wasn't as private as it seemed. Often, Mom would open the door without knocking to say, "That doesn't sound like practicing."

}

In place of the paste-on stars used by piano teachers everywhere, Bill drew stars in my notebook by hand, giving nuance to his praise: sometimes the stars were beaming with pride, sporting halos or crowns; sometimes they had sidelong glances, to reflect mitigated success; some stars were amputees, and limped on crutches; and sometimes things were so disappointing that he drew a slug, a caterpillar, a poisonous centipede.

One of his most ambitious stars appeared after our first milestone: the 1981 National Guild of Piano Teachers Auditions. Bill treated this as if it were my debut with the Berlin Philharmonic. He got me extra time on fancy pianos at the university. He made me play for his wife, Melba—a deeply unimpressible person who taught kids for a living. In the notebook, he wrote with more encouragement and urgency, like a coach psyching up a team. I was playing a Kabalevsky sonatina (which my mom hated, like she did all "modern stuff"), and he wrote: "Terrific job—you're getting patience! this is a lot cleaner and more detailed." As for my Mozart: "Excellent work on details—you did everything I asked for." Cleanliness was good; detailed was better. But where was the big picture?

After all that, my audition went pretty well:

The Guild divided the art of piano playing into thirty-five parameters (they were also detail-oriented). I received thirty-two A's; only three C's. I would have been horrified by this result in regular school, but at the piano it seemed like a victory.

After this success Bill let me forget Kabalevsky and start fresh, with a Mozart Sonata in G Major. For a week I was in hog heaven. This happiness was infectious. In the next notebook entry, Bill allowed himself a rare burst of enthusiasm:

Mozart: EXCELLENT WORK! Bravo! Main detail is less pedal. Play only where marked.

"Bravo!"—I read that over and over to myself in my piano room, smiling and bowing to imaginary applause. But while praising me, Bill realized that I couldn't or wouldn't use my ears to solve the Mozart pedal problem. He decided to eliminate all uncertainty:

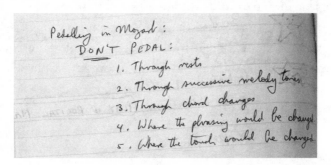

And also on that same day, the day of the Five Commandments of Pedaling, he told me to get a book of studies by the Hungarian composer Ernst von Dohnányi, called *Essential Finger Exercises*.

The Dohnányi had to be special-ordered. After it arrived, Bill stood over the piano and gave me his chum-now-listen look. He called me chum, or kiddo—never Jeremy. He opened the book, circled one passage in red pen, then gazed at me to see if I was paying attention. I wasn't. He added a few arrows around the circle, and the words "NIHIL OB-STAT." "Do you know what that means?" he asked. I gulped and said no. "Ask your father," he said, and then made me read the following aloud:

The less time spent on purely technical studies, the more important it is to practice with full concentrated thought. It is absolutely useless to practice exercises in a thoughtless, mechanical manner, especially when the eyes are riveted on the music. When playing, even the simplest of finger exercises, the full attention must be fixed on the finger-work, each note must be played consciously, in short: not to practice merely with the fingers, but through the fingers with the brain.

Dohnányi was a new horizon of boring. The cover was a faded blue, like an exam book, with mystifying strings of Hungarian (*a legfontosabb ujjgyakorlatok*). And every exercise was structured exactly the same: a series of four chords, modulating up a half step, and back to the beginning of the pattern. It was like one of those escalating organs at a baseball game, ramping up excitement. But there was no home run to look forward to—only rinse and repeat.

One day, after a few weeks of Dohnányi, of looking at my fingers and thinking about motions and quiet hands and non-musical bodily things, I was practicing a sixteenth-note passage in my Mozart sonata when I realized an obstacle had vanished. My fingers released after each attack, and their release brought them to the next note, as if they were playing themselves. Transference. Notes on the page seemed to sound before I could read them. It felt fast, faster than I could yet control, and so satisfying. My conscious mind was on the side looking on, admiring how I was doing it. I was a real pianist, maybe. I paced around the room, taking it in.

᠁

Our new school was Mesilla Park Elementary, surrounded by pecan groves and cotton farms. My first day I arrived late, and sat in an empty classroom waiting for everyone to come back from recess. As the other kids filed in, they saw only my blond hair as I sat hunched over a book on my desk, and thought I was a girl. The teacher explained that I was a boy, but the damage had been done. The name "Jeremy" didn't sit well either. It was rare in Las Cruces. I explained it was after Jeremiah from the Bible. My years in New Jersey with twelve other gifted kids didn't teach me what sorts of things not to say. My father observed in his memoir that I "shut down for a year." I mainly remember a general menace. A classmate hit me at the bus stop because I was a teacher's pet (was that bad?). I went into a whirlwind of countermoves, a strategy that worked in an unexpected way: all the other kids burst into laughter. I was too absurd to fight.

My parents began to agitate, consulting the principal, then a school superintendent. There was no alternative program in Mesilla Park Elementary, or in Las Cruces—what were "advanced" kids supposed to do? Eventually they were put in touch with the superintendent, J. Paul Taylor, who was a legend around town (and would later become a state representative). Josh and I were brought to him one afternoon for an interview. Paul was all gentility and charm. He wore a bolo tie, handsomely and without irony, and lived in a sprawling set of rooms off the historic Mesilla square. It was like *Alice in Wonderland* meets Santa Fe style, one curvy kiva fireplace after another, chambers giving way to chambers, tiles and windows dispersed with no system or symmetry.

After some discussion with our parents, Paul turned to me. He asked me to tell him something I liked, and I blurted out "x equals negative b plus or minus the square root of b squared minus four ac all over $2a$." He asked, "What's that" and I replied, "The quadratic equation," thinking he was a bit of an idiot. How could a state representative not know the quadratic equation?

Paul—who had saintly patience, it seemed—arranged a meeting with a woman named Kathy Easterling. She seemed fun and overcaffeinated, listening as if I were the most interesting person in the world. Her nodding and prodding questions reminded me of the therapist from New Jersey. I couldn't help noticing that I required a caseworker wherever I went. Dad and Mom had big arguments in front of Kathy about my schooling. Dad thought the most important thing was for me to avoid boredom. Mom thought there was value in a normal social life. Dad thought it was too late, that I wasn't normal and there was no use pretending. I should just make use of the time and hope for happiness in college.

Kathy sketched out a compromise plan to gradually bring me closer to the grades I should be in. This meant skipping sixth altogether and launching into junior high. Dad, having won the argument, immediately poisoned his victory with second thoughts. He said, "Junior high kids are the worst," and Mom agreed.

♩

Bill kept me on Dohnányi through the summer of 1981. Separate hands, patience, repetition. Every other week, he'd let me return briefly to regular music, to remind me of the goal, to make sure I didn't lose heart. But it was tough. Imagine that you are scrubbing the grout in your bathroom and are told that removing every last particle of mildew will somehow enable you to deliver the Gettysburg Address.

Technique felt like whack-a-mole. Bill would demand focused fingers. The next week I focused so hard that my shoulders hunched. When I got my shoulders loose, my wrists went rigid. Meanwhile we still had to fight recurring bugbears. I played a dippy little piece called "Forest Murmurs." Leland wrote, "Forest Murmurs, not Forest Fire!" And then a line or two later, in all caps:

A SMOOTH THUMB CONNECTION IS ONE OF THE MOST IMPORTANT TECHNICAL FEATS YOU CAN MASTER!

I wondered *Will I ever be done with the thumb?* The answer was *No, never.* The thumb is a transit system, helping to lubricate scales, arpeggios, passages of all kinds. It is at once an anchor and a springboard. It's the finger that often forgets it's a finger.

I guess we made progress, because at the end of the summer Bill told me to get the music for a concerto by Mozart in A Major, K. 488. We came back from the Music Box with a yellow Schirmer edition, decorated with laurel leaves. My first masterpiece. The opening measure had an accidental, a natural sign, and this note made the music feel different, darker, as if it folded in rather than out, as if deciding to reflect before it acted. After folding in, the music suddenly piped its way up— a mischievous and joyous scale. A bit later, in what Bill taught me was called "the second theme," certain chords seemed to live between other chords I'd previously played—chords with lush dissonances that resolved only into other dissonances.

For a short while Mom didn't have to pester me to practice. I worked hard on the first movement, motivated by discovery. Bill wrote the usual no-nonsense commentary:

> Slow, hard practice on 16th note passages. Careful phrasing. *Solid tone,* even on soft passages—never weak. Hear *every* note.

What did it mean to hear every note? I wasn't sure. It didn't seem helpful. A week later he told me to "go on to the cadenza." Toward the end of those two weeks of devouring Mozart, I have a clear memory of an epiphany: I was learning the same music I'd learned before, but in a different key. *What a drag,* I thought, but then realized this was convenient. In the dozens of sonatinas and sonatas I'd played, I'd never understood the symmetry at the heart of sonata form. I was supposed to be the kid who knew everything, and this often blinded me to the obvious.

"This is exciting, Dad," I said, deciding to give him an impromptu music theory lesson. "Look, it's all the same!" Dad had installed a little computer desk in the back corner of my piano room, and had begun to invade my space for his own studies and projects. Maybe he liked spying on me. But it's worth noting that this was also the geographically farthest point in the house from Mom.

Dad grunted. "Enough talking, get back to work."

}

I started the accelerated school plan: a mix of seventh and eighth grade classes, plus ninth grade math (algebra). Kathy thought my mom was right to worry about socialization, and asked me to keep a journal of my feelings. I had to submit this to her every so often. Kathy eventually created a literary magazine from these journals—mine and other "special" kids she'd recruited into her growing program. In the first issue, a poem I wrote was featured on the back page:

DEATH
> *What is death? Is it just a passage into another world, or is it the*
> *end forever, or a*
> > *trip into oblivion—*

My poem had lots of dashes, not because I admired Emily Dickinson, but because periods seemed like too much of a commitment.

Letting me loose on a journal was (as you can see) dangerous. I had no patience with small crisp details of life, only big mushy themes, and I felt ready to express the hell out of myself after all the reading I'd done. Math fell out of favor. English became my favorite class, with Ms. Dresp, a blond woman with shockingly pale skin who'd been through a recent divorce. Dad admired Ms. Dresp's deep red lipstick and contempt for marriage. Under her tutelage I composed a short story about the evils of marijuana and the ennui of middle age, entitled "The Twilight of Human Ambition," which began:

> The cool sensation rippled over him as a wave of consciousness came to his mind. Thirty years old, frustrated, unsatisfied, he now felt that his life was fulfilled . . .

After Ms. Dresp taught us about transcendentalism, I decided to write a manifesto for a utopian society, a perfect world called Garmac 12, predicated on the dual pillars of art and time management:

> Each citizen, once analyzed for talents, is delegated a certain amount of hours per day to do artistic work, government work, and enjoyable activities. The basic framework is:
>
> 4 hrs. -Artistic Work
> 4 hrs. -Governmental Work
> 4 hrs. -Enjoyment
> Rest of day -Sleep
>
> (All values here are alterable according to individual talents or strengths.)

NOTES

1. Artistic Work time may not be reduced below 1 hour and may not be increased over 7 hours.
2. Governmental Work Time may not be reduced below 2 hours and may not be increased over 6 hrs.
3. Enjoyment time may not change.

Note the distinction between "Artistic work" and "Enjoyment."

}

Bill and I kept at K. 488. We made a go at the tragic and halting second movement, with very little notebook commentary, then went on to the leaping joy of the third. At this point Bill sprang a surprise:

Mozart 3rd mvmt. practice the way we did together; listen for the mercurial changes of touch and phrasing (also dynamics!)

"Mercurial" was underlined with a squiggly line, for special emphasis. It is the first truly expressive word in the notebook. After all his systems and lists and rules, Bill wanted the unexpected? I don't remember this lesson, but reading about it gives me a warm feeling. I see us there in his studio, playing side by side, child and adult, blond and graying, looking at the same Mozart revelation from different angles of life. Nearly forty years later, that's one of the ideas I cherish and teach most: that Mozart's music is not one voice but a shifting array of voices; that you never know what the character of the next moment will be— serious or light or high or low or some shade in between. "Mercurial" is for me quite near the heart of Mozart's great gift to us; it is also one of the most common words people use nowadays to describe my playing. One teacher's comment, even one you've forgotten, may become the essence of you; it's just hard to know which one.

Then, just as we were ascending Mount Olympus, getting to the really good stuff, Bill hit the brakes. He told me to leave 488, for a while. He sensed a recurring pattern: progress, boredom, bad habits. My passagework was weak, so he dug out some Conus exercises, which were even more boring than the Dohnányi. Why would he do that to me? Dohnányi had been about strength, he said, but these exercises were about finger independence. The Conus started a month-long journey, with diagrams of my head being filled bit by bit:

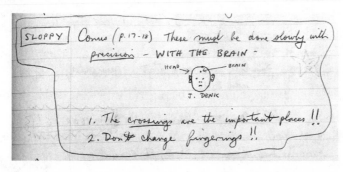

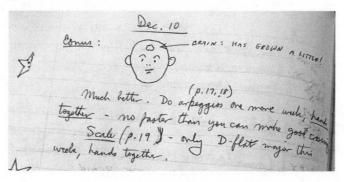

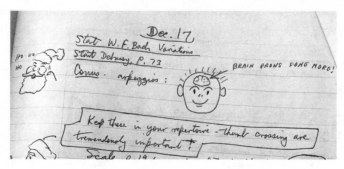

At school, everyone complained that I was too brainy—couldn't I give it a rest?—but Bill always wanted *more* brain. This was confusing.

On the bus to junior high, I heard a lot of music—much more than in elementary school—and hated all of it. *How can people listen to this garbage? If only they knew there were options; if only someone could show them a better way.* I came up with a plan. My parents had at last bought me a portable tape player, after much pouting. I loaded up a favorite cassette of Strauss's lush Romantic tone poems and forced the player into my backpack. I took my solitary seat on the bus like any other day, waited a few moments, and then pressed play. The reaction wasn't quite what I expected. First came general confusion, as if everyone had just noticed a disgusting smell. Then the tone of the conversation changed. Someone yelled, "Where is that #*$! coming from?" as I tried to maintain a look of innocence. Eventually a group of kids were clawing at my backpack, ripping it open, pulling the tape out. It's a wonder I'm still alive.

Despite this and other attempts at self-sabotage, I began to assemble a group of friends. Our whole family did. Dad had been right about New Mexico—it was much easier to meet people. Most of our connections were made at church. We got close to the Birnbaums, for instance, whose kids, David and Eva, were part of the growing "gifted and talented" program. Also the Willems, who had a quite different vibe. Ray was a soft-spoken idealistic engineer; Dad talked to him about science. Ray's wife, Adelina, was Dominican, insanely gentle, empathetic. She became my mom's greatest resource and support. Ray and Adelina had two beautiful daughters with diametric characters, tender and tomboy, demure and wild, and at some point I had crushes on them both. Last but not least, my dad and a man named Bruce Streett always ended up complaining about Catholic school. Bruce was director of development at New Mexico State. He'd been to Oxford, which he mentioned quite a bit. He had a formidable and cheery wife, Mary, and four attractive children—a big, healthy, wealthy clan. Bruce agreed with Dad that there should be room for doubt in Catholic education.

Bruce and my father came up with a bold and heretical solution: to create our own Catholic educational collective. We four families got together on Sundays after mass, ate Adelina's incredible cooking, and then sat around for an hour's discussion of Christianity mixed with literature, ethics, politics. Bruce tried to re-create Oxford in New Mexico.

He and my father loved learning through argument—or just argument, it was hard to tell. Bruce posed earnest dilemmas. My dad ironized back at him, quoting theologians and skeptics by turns. Ray offered sincere, caring perspectives. Ana Willem would always ask, "What's the point? Who cares?" David and I would try to impress and one-up the adults.

The collective had a crucial consequence for my future. Bruce took an interest in me. Every so often he would ask me to lunch. Mom would instruct me to put on something nice—a bitter struggle ensued, until I looked presentable. She'd drop me at Bruce's office, and he'd take me to the area's fanciest power-business restaurant, in a historic square. The Double Eagle resembled a brothel, or the palace of a villainous town tycoon. I would sit as straight as I could and make conversation with Bruce, a charmer, a big alpha talker with a deep voice and lots of connections in town. On our third or fourth lunch, he explained his master plan. He wanted me to be a Rhodes scholar, like he had been. He felt I was the perfect candidate. I had the academic and musical strength. There was supposed to be an athletic component, he said, "but"—eyeing me wryly—"I suppose we could finagle that."

≀

By the fall of 1982, I was twelve years old and half in high school, doing geometry, which was a bit harder than earlier math, and trying to elude the Plog brothers, who, ever since my classical music stunt on the bus, chased me every afternoon from the bus stop to my door, threatening to kill me. Bill began pushing me to practice more. "An hour and a half is nothing," he said with a scoff, "just enough time to warm up." He demanded three hours. Where would the time come from? It was necessary, he said, so I could play my debut recital.

This had been on his mind for a while. He'd relented a bit on Dohnányi over the last months, and let me learn a bunch of new pieces, like the Debussy Arabesques. At first Debussy created a minor crisis: triplets in one hand, and duplets in the other. How could I ever play that? But Bill showed me that the second duplet snuck in, perfectly, halfway through the second triplet. And so yet another insuperable hurdle was crossed. Bill seemed taken aback by how naturally this music came to me, how light and danceable and expressive it was. Maybe my mom's hounding about dancing had done some good, or maybe it was the new Murray Perahia album of Mozart concertos, a gift from my parents.

Along with the Debussy, I'd learned new Bach and Chopin. Enough for an evening's program. Bill outlined a three-concert, low-budget tour—"at my house, then at Good Samaritan Retirement Home, then at the university"—but the idea was quashed. Later that fall, he decided I was at last ready. We couldn't book the university, and ended up downtown in the Branigan Cultural Center, a museum of sorts in a mostly abandoned walking mall, next to the community theater and a dollar cinema where I would see *Home Alone* on my twenty-first birthday (perhaps the saddest detail of this memoir).

I was nervous, but it is a happy memory: the raised stage, an old creaky white room with dark wooden hand-hewn beams running through the ceiling. There were paintings along the walls, a local exhibit. The program ended with my big achievement: the first movement of the Mozart Concerto in A Major, K. 488. Bill played the orchestra part on the second piano. Before that were other light, elegant things: Debussy Arabesques, Beethoven's "Cuckoo" Sonata (op. 79), a Mozart Rondo. The audience was friends of my parents, probably wishing they could be anywhere else. There was a reception afterward, featuring the first of many celebratory finger foods, where I received lots of congratulations, and then my parents drove me home, like any other night. That last part was melancholy, as it often is, landing alone in my room with memories of nice words and missed notes, the rush fading.

My debut accomplished, it was time for another big milestone. The El Paso Symphony Guild was holding a competition for young artists. Bill said I'd have to learn to compete sometime. We prepared and drilled, especially Mozart K. 488.

El Paso was an hour away and seemed like a huge, forbidding city. As we got closer, the highway widened into four weaving lanes of traffic; my mom fretted at my dad like in the old New Jersey commutes. The hall, quite near the border with Mexico, looked like an adobe space-ship. My brother made blasé comments. Backstage, a swarm of officious guild members and kids warming up. I remember walking onstage, the piano far away, marooned in the vastness as if at the center of a tightrope, the darkness of all the empty seats, the judges scattered around, vaguely visible, and the harshness of the stage lights. I played my joyful Mozart, a scary Bach Prelude and Fugue, and a melancholy Chopin prelude, the "Raindrop."

What do you know? I won, beating many older kids. Bill was thrilled, and yet regretful that winning would encourage me in the world's most thankless profession. The judges said my Mozart was good, but the Chopin was what sold them. That was also what Bill said, at my first audition for him. Nowadays, I am reluctant to play Chopin, with all the traditions and expectations, but then I just played it with a child's heart. I loved to play those repeated notes in the middle section—actually, not play so much as pound them out, and in the process drown out the world. All the judges talked about how musical I was. That puzzled me. Yes, Bill and I talked about phrasing, but a lot of that was just me, experimenting like a mad scientist. I'd place a certain note, play it a little louder or softer or gentler or with more surprise, and then the music would mold time or escape from time, and I knew I'd found it. Was that musicianship? It was strange to think of that private act as my best chance of success in life.

≀

The big prize of the El Paso competition was a scholarship to the summer music festival of my choice. I chose the Eastern Music Festival in Greensboro, North Carolina, but I'm sure my parents really chose. They had friends there from the old days, spies who could keep a watchful eye.

I took my first solo airplane journey, connecting in Dallas. My parents' friends picked me up, then dropped me on the brick-and-ivy Guilford College campus, telling me to call them whenever. I called them once. A summer of freedom! Freedom, at that time, meant I could get a Slurpee whenever I wanted. It also included the idea of not taking any showers, even in Greensboro in July. Much of my time, though, was splurged on nerdy conversation with other young musicians. I ran into one of them, Tim Lovelace, many years later at the Ravinia Festival. He apologized for being cruel that summer, but I'm not sure what he meant. I remember him being my best friend. Tim was willing to talk to me, despite the fact that all I did was provoke arguments about whether the Brahms B-flat Concerto was better than Rachmaninoff's Third. Since my Mozart, I'd decided to explore the world of piano concertos, and had made some moral decisions. Some pieces were just for show, all virtuosity and posturing. Others had meaning and truth and beauty. The Brahms B-flat was pure, I told everyone, while the Rachmaninoff was cheap. For good measure, I plagiarized my dad's favorite insult: I said Rachmaninoff's torrents of arpeggios were "fountains of toilet water." Tim laughed, sometimes, but other kids got upset. How could anyone not like Rachmaninoff?

My parents wrote me letters throughout the summer, hoping to hear about all the exciting musical things I was learning. I sent back one letter, explaining that I had seen *Jaws 3-D*, which was awesome, and that Tim had made a joke that was so funny that I spit up my can of strawberry soda all over his white bedspread.

As far as practicing went, the summer was almost a total loss. At the beginning of the festival you were assigned a teacher, based on your audition tape. I didn't get any of the teachers I'd hoped for, from reading their blurb-ographies—for instance, Victor Rosenbaum, who had performed in many places and taught at a famous music school, the New England Conservatory. Instead, I got a woman named Bernice Maskin. I have googled her to atone for my sins. She was, it seems, a wonderful and capable teacher, and a boon to her community: She founded a youth orchestra and a chamber orchestra; she ran a chamber music series. She made it possible for people in Gainesville, Florida, to love and study classical music. Her son became a Nobel Laureate in economics.

To me she was a nightmare that croaked like a frog. The sound, the word "Maskin," still gives me a deep, Pavlovian cringe. Why would you practice if it was just to have all your joy squashed by her? She was short, with a gravelly voice, and had some unpleasant spots on her arms. She was matter-of-fact. I mean, I thought Bill was matter-of-fact, but he was a gushing Romantic poet by comparison. I complained about this to Tim. He told me that Bernice specialized in kids. I didn't come to my first grown-up festival to be a kid. Didn't she know I was reading the complete Shakespeare in my free time?

Maskin wanted me to practice Beethoven's First Concerto. I thought the piece was juvenile. Also, I had a complaint about concertos: all that waiting around. I felt discombobulated when the piano stopped and the orchestra started up. The discontinuity was upsetting, like switching off a TV show, as my mother often did, just when things were getting interesting. So I'd play the orchestra parts too, just to hear what happened, and because it made sense musically, and cruel Bernice told me not to "waste time practicing the *tutti*s." Yet another sign of her lack of enlightenment. We got in an argument about the Beethoven, whether it was any good, and I said it certainly wasn't the Brahms B-flat and she said, "You know, I've had students who've had great competition success with this piece, especially the last movement." I remember thinking I liked the sound of the word "success," if only I could get rid of that word "competition."

After a couple weeks, a fellow student and gifted pianist named Rose Shlyam took me into a listening booth at the library and said she had something important to tell me. I waited. *You're the greatest pianist I've ever heard,* I hoped she'd say. "You shtink," she said, after some preamble. She had a faint Russian accent. "I'm not trying to be cruel, but you need to go take a shower right away." Mortified, I ran off to take a long shower in the dorm and in those steamy minutes missed my piano lesson, which I had forgotten about. I threw on some clothes and ran over to the music building. "Mrs. Maskin, I'm sorry I forgot our lesson, I was showering," I told her, and she just smiled at me like I was a hopeless case, with a look that implied *It's OK, you'll never be a pianist anyway.*

Despite and against all of this, the summer was having a secret benefit. I was amazed by the college library's stacks and stacks of records, like my parents' collection times a million, more than I could ever listen to. I got to work. No one interrupted me there, maybe for the very reason Rose explained. I discovered Berlioz's *Symphonie Fantastique,* and read the story, and marched around the tiny room as the brass took us to the scaffold, whatever that was. Then came Bartók's Concerto for Orchestra, with its array of colors and joy so removed from my Mozart joy, and then I remember one day being in the dorm lobby when Tim said something about *The Rite of Spring.* "The right of what?" I asked and he said, "Come on." I sat on Tim's bed and listened and—what was this? The opening was hard to take, but then came the second number, which felt like rhythm freed from everything, from teachers and metronomes and boredom, lashing out from time to time in sheer wildness. And the harmony was so gritty, so fantastic, so "punk" (as the other kids said, making a reference I didn't understand). Several days later, in that same lobby, I ran across another kid and we started screaming to each other—

chunk chunk chunk chunk chunk CHUNK chunk CHUNK chunk chunk chunk chunk

—rocking out on Stravinsky together as we descended the stairs of the ivied dormitory. At last, I knew what mattered. A different, maybe even better truth than Brahms. A sad follow-up came twenty years later, when I saw the score of this passage: it was a bunch of 2/4 measures with syncopations. How prosaic. It seemed like pure revolution when I sang it with this other boy at music camp. This is an important lesson about the written musical score: In some ways, for all its virtues, it doesn't want to be seen. It "is" the piece, and yet its most important task is to disappear.

≀

The piano department knew I was unhappy with Bernice Maskin. If not a virtuoso pianist yet, I was a virtuoso complainer. They gave me a chance to play in a studio class for my desired teacher, Victor Rosenbaum, in front of all the other students. I should have asked Maskin what to play, but how could I ask her anything? She didn't get me, or music, or life. She was merely an obstacle. It didn't occur to me to call

Bill, either. I was free from home, and all that. Bill had assigned me the delightful Ravel *Sonatine* just before the summer. But God, that piece was so finicky: so many refined markings, so many *pianos* and *pianissimos*.

So when Rosenbaum asked me what I wanted to perform, I announced: *"Pictures at an Exhibition."* Rosenbaum laughed outright; all the other kids did too. I could barely reach octaves. "Great Gate of Kiev" would have landed me in the hospital. I played a bit for him in my sight-reading fashion—hoping inspiration would carry me through, since everyone told me I was so musical!—and he sighed and said, "If you're going to play a big piece like this, you have to at least start with a concept of sound," meaning the sound of the trumpet, from the orchestra. But I didn't have my technique set up, yet, to do that. The lesson was over in a few minutes, a total loss.

The department also gave me the chance to play in one public master class: Mozart's A Major Concerto, first movement. Since the El Paso competition, I felt I was the king of that piece, and didn't need to practice it. I got lost in a couple passages, and in my embarrassment rushed through others. The teacher, Randall Hodgkinson, had my number. "The problem for you," he said, "and one you'll have to deal with all your life, is that you can probably sight-read everything, and you don't see the need of working hard to get things to the next level. You should be ashamed. This is not the level you should be playing at."

I heard only the negatives, and not his desire to help. After he stopped talking, and some pitying applause, I tried to sneak out of the hall and flee to my room. But there was Rose again, running after me on the sidewalk yelling "Yeremy! Yeremy!" and saying that there were good things, and that I played some beautiful phrases—but really, I should have practiced. While Rose was slowing down my escape with her Slavic kindness, a group of other pianists arrived, including my roommate, whom I thought I hated, a fourteen-year-old boy who was tan because he came from Florida. I had some secret feelings about this boy, and we'd played strip poker one night in our room with interesting results, and he made fun of me for getting lost in my Mozart, which (he added) was for babies anyway. I told him he was a jerk. He came at me.

We sort of fought. I went down in a heap, getting mud on my concert clothes, then ran off and started to do the first real practicing I'd done all summer. I tried to make up for a summer of scattered dreaming with two days of furious diligence. In a dark, stuffy practice room in an unfamiliar corner of campus, a room I should have been haunting for weeks, I tried to cram all kinds of new notes into my fingers, and realized that piano playing was lonely—so lonely—and meanwhile it was time to return home.

4. *Harmony* LESSON TWO

PLAYLIST

GOUNOD: "Ave Maria" (sung by Barbra Streisand)

BACH: Prelude in C Major from *The Well-Tempered Clavier*, Book I

NINA SIMONE: "Just in Time," from the Tomato Collection

I was on the phone with a wonderful pianist and teacher friend, complaining that I had to write another chapter about harmony, because I only got so far with the last one. After the usual making fun—*Couldn't you choose a broader topic*, etc.—he asked me what more I thought I had to say.

"Well, the problem is," I started, "I'm not sure I can discuss harmony without talking about sex."

He laughed. "No," he said, "you can't do that."

Probably not, I agreed. What about innocent young musicians who might read the book? A moment of silence ensued. He was up in the mountains resting from a long day of cross-country skiing; I was in my city apartment after a long day of whittling sentences.

"It is, though," he said.

"What is?"

"Harmony is kind of like sex," he said. I felt encouraged and texted the idea to another friend, a violist. He messaged back immediately. "Harmony and sex are the same? Such a pianist."

𝄾

There are (at least) two senses of the word "harmony": one is a noun, and the other is an art. You can refer to a chord, like C major or C minor (both triads, meaning three stacked notes), or a seventh chord (which is four notes), and so forth. Really, any simultaneous sounding of three or more notes can be labeled a harmony. This is a valid—but limited—use of the word.

The art is what is interesting—how to take those chords and put them in sequence, deploying them over time into sentences that make sense and create waves, or lines, and complicated sensations of motion, eloquent tensions and releases. I can play you a chord—I often do this when I demonstrate onstage—and say "This is C minor." This sentence has some truth, but at the same time it's a bigger lie. The chord is only *really* harmony when it's in action or motion. A taxidermied squirrel is not a squirrel.

There are limitless things to say about the subtleties of putting chords in order, even if you limit yourself to Western classical style (György Sebők, whom you will meet eventually, used to say there were "larger and smaller infinities, infinities within infinities"), and those books are out there, waiting for you to delve into them—but be warned: jargon ahead. Or, as many classical composers have also felt (Beethoven, Mozart, Schumann, Chopin), I'd suggest you can find much of what you need in Bach's *Well-Tempered Clavier,* assembled and published in 1722, which doesn't just cover all the chords but what to do with them.

If we don't have time to cover all the possibilities, let's make sure we don't forget the obvious: at the heart of the art of harmony is desire. That is, the desire for one chord to go to another. In every sentence of chords this desire operates, to one degree or another, sometimes playfully, other times urgently. One of the most common motions between chords is from what we call the "dominant" to the "tonic." If you don't know what that means, sing "Happy Birthday" and then stop at the end, on the last two notes, "to . . . you." There's a wonderful scene in the show *The Office* where bumbling Michael Scott reappears in the middle of a birthday party and sings a preposterous bit of harmony at the end of the song. Despite or because of his terrible singing, you can feel the urge. Michael even slides from "to" to "you," emphasizing the *need* to get from dominant to tonic, a need that doesn't mind getting a bit dirty.

We all tend to slow at the end of "Happy Birthday" and sing with more emphasis, for good reason. You hold the last couple notes in order to hear and feel the resolution of the chords—but also because once you've resolved, the song is over. This reminds me of one of the most musical short stories by Balzac, "Sarrasine," in which a man narrates a story to a woman, hoping she will sleep with him as a reward. But once the story is finished, she no longer feels amorous. The French literary critic Roland Barthes explains that this is because storytelling is a transaction, that it extracts a price from both the teller and the listener, whether we know it or not, and sometimes the cost changes everything. In music, the price of resolution—the very thing the chords seem to want!—is that the phrase (or piece) will be over. You'll have to start again—*what should my chords do next?* There is nothing sadder than listening to certain less gifted contemporaries of Mozart resolving their chords all the time, seeming to follow their natural inclinations and ending up always back at the same chords they started with, like someone in the snow trying to get their car going and sliding back into the drift, ever deeper.

The game of music plays between these two imperatives. First, you have to take seriously the needs of chords, especially their need to resolve. Second, you want the release not to happen too soon. (I hope I don't need to explain the intended entendres.) To put it another way, we all know we're going to die, a necessity and command of life, and yet in the meantime—why not have as much fun as possible?

}

In the opening Prelude of Bach's *Well-Tempered Clavier,* the famous one—which I got to know through Barbra Streisand's glitzy and gutsy rendition of a rendition by Charles Gounod ("Ave Maria")—you have the sense that Bach is laying down a gauntlet. There are no melodies (in the original). There are no changes of rhythm, just a continuous stream of notes. Nothing to pay attention to but the harmonies. It reminds me of when my mother would take everything off my plate, except for the broccoli. *You're going to listen to the goddamn harmony,* Bach seems to say, *whether you like it or not.*

The cast of characters in this story of harmony is basically split in two: triads and seventh chords. Triads are groups of three notes, as I said, a fairly simple sandwich; for instance, take a G, and then add a B above, and then a D:

D
B
G   = TRIAD

And if you have that chord (the G-major chord), it will very happily resolve to a C-major chord, *plop plop*—you will feel very good about it, and everything is as it should be. But if you add one more note to the sandwich, stacking it yet higher, you get a seventh chord:

F (one more!)
D
B
G   = SEVENTH

This chord also "wants" to go to C major—but even more. The extra note piles on desire and intensity.

Within the world of seventh chords too, Bach tells us in this seemingly simple piece, there are other worlds. Some seventh chords are like the one I just described (what we call a "dominant seventh"); they have the most straightforward direction. But others are stacked slightly differently—a flat note here, a bit of minor there—and they want to go forward too, but less urgently. They seem more content in their unresolved state, a bit like when you're lying on the couch, thinking you really want ice cream, but that means you'd have to go to the refrigerator and get it, so you decide for sure you are eventually going to get the ice cream, but meanwhile you'll spend a few minutes on the couch, imagining the taste of ice cream instead.

No, I can't quite believe I'm writing about Bach this way either.

The first two measures are a simple gesture, like the squeeze of an accordion in and out. We start with the pure C-major triad—no urges or unresolved notes, by definition. We are home. Then we have a minor (couch-wanting-ice-cream) seventh, which goes to a dominant seventh, and before we know it we are back. Four chords. The first and last are the same. The ones in the middle are beautiful trouble. I think of this like the flexing of a muscle, or a breath in and out—things you do to be ready, to prepare you for greater things. This progression tells us where we are, by defining the smallest possible journey, and hints at what the next journey will be.

In the next phase of the piece, Bach widens the field of possibility. We hear a minor triad, for the first time—the first hint of melancholy—and other seventh chords, a stream of them. We pass down a scale, exploring how you take a line of notes in a row and "harmonize" them. The lesson is about how you build these beautiful stacks, with their kaleidoscopic colors, while still accommodating the musical equivalent of a support beam.

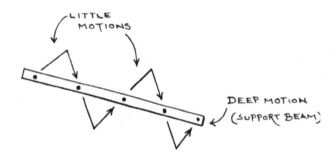

Halfway down, Bach stops harmonizing using sharps; he starts in with the flats. At first brighter chords, now darker; exterior, then interior; day then night. Not only can he do the tightrope act, he can change costumes while he's doing it. As we go through this process, you hear a lot of little miniature dominants-to-tonics, resolutions along the way—just like you solve problems in day-to-day life, and yet you know they aren't the real ones. It's all exploratory, this touching and grazing of various chords, a kind of (again, forgive me) foreplay.

At the bottom of this scale we find the true destination, which is in turn a desire. The bass twists toward G, the fundament of a G-major triad, which "wants" to go to C major; yet often the art of harmony is not what chords you choose, but how long you choose to prolong them. The bottom note—that G—becomes fixed. We call it a "pedal tone" because of the organ pedals, the act of putting your foot down and letting the bass command everything. From the point Bach lands there, you have the sense of one purpose. No more little purposes, no more chords shifting here and there.

So many wonderful harmonies happen within that G limitation. It is as if the piece is trying to deliver a moral, a life lesson: *Within even one purpose there is so much possibility.* It's hard to pick, but perhaps my favorite is in bar 29, a chord that seems to be a resolution, almost a triumph, but is actually still as unresolved as any of the others. This chord makes you feel, in other words, the incredible fulfillment of being unfulfilled. Streisand also loves that one—she really belts it out there. Pause for a moment to observe that I listened to her performance of this hundreds of times, without the slightest inkling that I was gay.

One reason this passage becomes so electrifying is that Bach makes you listen to each chord twice. You *know* the chord is desperate to resolve, but you still have to wait. Back in the earlier portions of the piece, this "everything twice" problem was not sensed as a problem; after all, we were just exploring and looking about. It was nice to hear beautiful new chords one more time, to appreciate them. But now impending desire and the cosmic patience of the pattern are on a collision course. So when at last our G finds C major, I feel it is one of the most earned resolutions of all time, one of the most released releases. The piece lasts just over two minutes, and yet you have the sense of a full, well-lived life.

I wouldn't argue that this piece is erotic (although, given Bach's twenty children, he was objectively virile). But that force is there, behind it, and if you consider the form and process, the way it harps upon a certain spot until a desired result is obtained—it is suggestive. Sex is not something we associate with classical music, not in popular culture anyway, where classical music is mostly used as a stuffy accompaniment at rich-people galas, or placed next to horrific acts of murder as a kind of hypercivilized foil (*The Silence of the Lambs, Apocalypse Now*).

In general, popular culture demonizes classical music in a way that popular culture is not quite willing to take responsibility for, because most people feel this music is too full of itself, and deserves bullying.

I'm going to make a slight, or maybe monstrous, generalization here, and say that much of the sexuality of what we call classical music is in the harmonies. It can be in the melodies, of course, especially in opera and song, and to a lesser extent in the rhythms (with obvious exceptions—*Bolero*); but I'd say, by and large, the deeper and darker urges make their home in the chords. Whereas if I listen to some jazz performances, for instance, I immediately feel sex in all different parts of the musical fabric: the timbre of the voice, the bending of notes of the melody, the sultry backbeats, even the process, the improvisatory feeling-around. And it's hyper-evident in a lot of pop, too—the human voice above the pounding beat, often-raunchy words, and harmonies that stay out of the way, to let the other parts do their work. When people who are used to other styles of music come to classical, I often sense they are looking for these visceral pleasures, but they're not there, not in that form. And when I listen to other styles of music, too, I often have to remind myself that I'm missing the point. I'm looking for pleasure where I'm not meant to find it.

}

One night, after some fifteen years in New York City, I came to realize that yet another of the guys I'd been in love with was never really interested in me, and so I went to the movies. A specific film, which I thought would be therapeutic: *Before Sunset*, with Ethan Hawke and Julie Delpy. I snuck in the back with a giant Coke, and settled in to meditate on my romantic misadventures while gazing at two beautiful people.

Ethan and Julie rehashed a night wandering Vienna some ten years earlier—the non-action of the previous film, *Before Sunrise*. For two more cinematic hours they dithered, and wondered why they didn't follow up. At the end, it seemed history might repeat itself, that they might again talk away another naked opportunity (so to speak). But then Julie invites Ethan up to her place, and puts on a record: Nina Simone, singing "Just in Time." The previous film also ended with music: a riveting account of a Bach slow movement, featuring Yo-Yo Ma and a wonderful harpsichordist, Kenneth Cooper, who improvised over the written notes at the end to give the sense of passing time, of moments re-seen. Whatever had been cheesy about *Before Sunrise* was forgiven, because that music seemed so radiant—in fact, the movie taught me something about Bach.

This time I was far less willing to forgive the film, but again it didn't matter, because Nina Simone's singing and playing had me in my seat, almost pinned against the sticky fabric, not daring to move for fear I'd miss something. She begins the tune, almost casually, with a sense of space between the phrases (declamation) . . . she runs through the gesture of the song, to the phrase "found my way," which is at the same time the harmonic arrival (clever composer!). She passes through the chords once as if it is nothing, just like Bach "warms up" at the beginning of the C Major Prelude. A member of the audience tries to take pictures, and she stops singing to scold them, saying "click click click click click," and everyone laughs, and meanwhile the band is still playing the song.

Then Simone begins to play the piano (her other voice). What happens then, over the course of those two minutes back in 1968, is an unbelievable escalation. Nina, a true musician's musician, hears beyond the tune to its structure, and to its purpose and meaning. She focuses her laser mind on an obvious aspect of the song, and reveals in the process intensities that the composer didn't or couldn't anticipate. (In a way, she teaches the composer about his own work.) The melody runs "Just in time, I found you just in time," and most of the notes are the same (*just, time, found, just, time* all on the same pitch). But underneath the harmonies change so that each same note feels differently directed, and never quite settled. In most other versions, this compositional idea presents as charming and fancy footwork (compare with Tony Bennett, four years earlier, for instance), but for Simone the contradiction is a force of nature, this tension between the single melody note and the roving chords. As her solo evolves, you hear her start to insist on certain notes on the piano, hammering out a G and an F, a dissonance, a seventh (remember Bach's sevenths), a source and unit of musical tension, something that cannot be forgotten; and then, as she begins to sing again, you hear her rapidly repeat the G in a tremolo, making sure you are still thinking about non-resolution, making it tangible in the rhythm, a kind of quiver. For a long while she's singing just one or two notes. When at last she begins to climb in the melody, she frequently leaves off, interrupting her own expression, and a half second later you hear the harmonies crash behind the voice like a wave. Harmony and melody are locked in a battle of sorts, each trying to supply what the other has left unfinished.

It's well known that Simone wanted to be a classical pianist, and was turned away from the prestigious Curtis Institute, and that she loved Bach, as you can hear quite obviously in some references—the fugue in the middle of her performance of "Love Me or Leave Me," for instance. But I think that kind of reference is a superficial homage; this performance shows a deeper connection. At the climax of "Just in Time," as I hear her sing "Change me! Change me!" over and over—ironically singing about change as she repeats the same notes, sliding through those notes with searing desire while the harmonies are still waiting and needing to find E-flat major—it's impossible for me not to think about that long, glorious, satisfying-frustrating pedal tone at the end of the C Major Prelude.

I have to say, I find something very moving about this, about her connection with a white guy from all those centuries ago who wouldn't have given Nina Simone the time of day. I see the two of them, in their distant rooms of history, both working with seemingly abstract chords, both connecting motions of chords to our humanity. Simone absorbed all those "classical" harmonic ideals—those sexual needs of chords that sometimes seem like rules or precepts or limits—and bent them to her will. She transformed the desire to resolve into what seems like its opposite: the desire to break free.

5. *Moments of Truth*

I returned from my first summer at camp the opposite of a conquering hero. My parents gathered me at the airport and peppered me with questions. I answered and deflected. Before I knew it, we were walking back through the front door of our house, into its sad, moldy-sulfur smell. The house felt too quiet. I couldn't sit still. Yes, I'd met all sorts of new people. But the main thing was that unlit corners of music history had come alive, pieces I'd feared and hated without knowing them, like those monsters in Sendak that live in your closet. I tried to explain this to my parents, in feverish snatches, but it didn't make an impression. I wanted them to know in their hearts that my summer and scholarship hadn't been a waste, even if I hadn't practiced or won anything.

My thirteenth-birthday $20 gift certificate to the record store lay unspent in my dresser drawer, a hidden treasure, and a few days later I convinced Mom to make a trip to the mall. The record store (long since vanished) boasted a large classical aisle (even longer since vanished). I hunted around until I found the perfect thing to educate my parents with: a tape of *The Rite of Spring*. The cover was designed like a postage stamp, as if History were sending you an urgent, life-changing letter. The next day I put the tape in the living room stereo, turned it on, and cranked it up. Yes, I thought with relief, it was just as unbelievable as I remembered. The lonely strained bassoon was joined by other wind instruments, one by one, in all combinations and permutations of rhythm: a mutant aviary, set loose and amplified. My body hummed with fantastic and jarring notes.

From the kitchen, my mom yelled: "Turn that noise off!"

"What *is* that crap? You're going to blow out the stereo," my dad warned.

So much for that. I had to let my parents fend for themselves, in their ignorance. Festival life had been a constant music roundtable, even if I was often effectively conversing with myself, but now I had to tolerate the family dinner table, the conversational equivalent of Clementi. Dad would scoop some casserole and talk about work, and Mom would reply in her fashion, either not enough for Dad or too much, eliciting a grunt or a lash-out or a weary sigh. Josh, across the table, was mostly silent, nursing understandable resentments after his summer stranded as an only child, listening to my parents bicker. He knew the rules of the house were rigged in my favor. He couldn't seek refuge at the piano— that was my thing. He took refuge in himself, I think, and comfort in knowing that he wasn't me. If possible, summer camp had made me even more insufferable.

}

A couple weeks later came the second consequence of my win in the El Paso competition, which my dad had been so proud of. (He'd moved on to "What have you done for me lately?") I was engaged to perform the last movement of my Mozart concerto with the El Paso Symphony, six times in three days, for their children's concerts.

My first-ever rehearsal with an orchestra was at 8:00 p.m., close to my usual bedtime. Bill drove me down in the dusk. The conductor was Abraham Chavez, a local legend and native son. He was kind, with deep brown skin and sad eyes, but I couldn't really find time to look at him. I was too busy trying to remember the correct number of measures before I came in—and of course trying not to rush, as Bill reminded me from the sidelines. I slept on the ride home.

Early the next morning I was back in the Arts Center, warming up on an upright piano. Bill had to teach a class, and Dad was at work, so it was just me. That first dressing room is vivid in my mind, with bright vanity lights but otherwise sepulchral, and a nervous energy played against a pedal tone of waiting—the first of countless times I've been in that same uncomfortable place. I paced around a small patch of gray tile floor in between playing through the tricky bits. Over the monitor blared the piece before mine—Britten's *Young Person's Guide to the Orchestra*. What a marvelous piece, I thought, eager for distraction. The piece had a narrator. I wished mine had a narrator.

The principal bassoonist of the El Paso Symphony was also the mayor of Las Cruces, a charming guy named Ruben Smith. My parents didn't love the idea of driving an hour each way for three days, and so they'd prevailed on Ruben to take me. I didn't exactly know what a mayor did. I liked him, but he tried too hard. He had an endless repertoire of cheesy jokes. Most of them fell on deaf ears, since I brought a book with me every day and read the whole trip. This was nothing against mayors; if I'd carpooled with the president, I would have done the same.

On the morning of the second day, Ruben looked at me with a mock frown.

"Maestro Denk," he said, "put down the book. I have an offer for you." He pulled out his wallet, extracted a five-dollar bill, and said, "I'll give you this if you agree to play a little bit slower in the Mozart." There is a tricky bassoon solo in that rondo, an exposed run of eighth notes. I agreed to moderate, and Ruben handed over the money.

But I didn't play slower. When I was nervous my fingers had a will of their own. Ruben was undaunted. He offered me cash again the next day, and I took it again, without shame. This was turning out to be quite a revenue stream. I wondered why Bill didn't try paying me to do the things he wanted me to do.

A few minutes before the third day's morning performance, I noticed a passage in the Mozart that could go one of two ways, like a Choose Your Own Adventure. You could emerge from it to find either the end of the first section or the end of the last, depending on whether you played a sharp or a natural. That seemed unkind and perverse of Mozart, honestly. So many hazards in this profession! I riffled through the music, turning pages back and forth, a little frantic. How had I not realized this before? A fateful knock; I made a snap decision, and walked out onto the stage.

A couple thousand kids sort of applauded. I looked back through the orchestra at Ruben, and gave him a smile to say I was going to honor our agreement. He waved back. Then I launched into the first theme—like a bat out of hell. On my second entrance I tried to take the reins, but it was too late. The mayor, startled by my tempo, had already muffed his big solo. The fact that I noticed was, I suppose, a small improvement. A little further in, I took the turn I had decided on backstage—but it was the wrong one, I realized in a few seconds, and there was no going back. I sailed forward in one key, the orchestra in another. It was the same feeling I had some years later on the way to a gig in rural Pennsylvania, taking a curve in the aftermath of a rainstorm and drifting into the other lane, helplessly, just watching myself sideswipe a minivan. (Luckily, no one was hurt.) The procedure following both accidents was the same: everyone stops, and you have an awkward conversation.

The orchestra ground to a scraping halt. Abraham Chavez lowered his baton. His forgiving smile helped me through the embarrassing ordeal of walking to the podium, where we had a whispered conversation over the score, which was lit dimly from above; it reminded me of the wan lamp over our family dinner table. After a fifteen-second powwow, I told Chavez I was ready, even though I wasn't. Clenched the whole time, thinking it could happen again, second-guessing everything I played, I labored on to the end.

When I got home, I made the mistake of telling my dad this story. His eyes went dark and he shook his head. He was more humiliated than I was. To console him, I explained that there was a spot in the music that could go one of two ways—how weird was that?—but Dad was already ranting that I had to practice a lot more, and that also it was all somehow his fault, for not knowing this would happen. Mom wondered (reasonably) if it was just that I was tired.

Both my parents were wrong. Practicing wouldn't have prevented that particular disaster. What had happened was going to happen at some point: my child's instinct ran into an oncoming adult's knowledge. I had been gliding through the piece, joyfully and guilelessly, following the thread of Mozart's inspiration, but at the fifth performance I looked down from the tightrope.

{

That fall, my mom's drinking got the best of her liver. I remember a scene at the breakfast table, sitting with my usual bowl of cereal. Dad walked in, took a look at Mom, and said, "You don't look good." She was gradually turning yellow, especially in her eyes, like she'd been invaded by an alien or was transforming into a reptile. She was also retaining water—fifty pounds' worth.

Mom went to the doctor, who sent her to the emergency room. At first she was too fragile for us kids to visit her in the hospital. For a week or two only Dad went, and came back with an unaccustomed nurturing face, saying it was very serious, and could go "either way"—like my last movement of the Mozart. I wonder now what my dad felt: freedom at the prospect of no longer having an alcoholic wife, or guilt for not having intervened earlier.

I remember a sense that the bottom was falling out of everything, even though Mom was my enemy and tormentor, and thinking *either way,* and running back to the piano room. Bill had just assigned me the "Pathetique" Sonata, my first real Beethoven. It began with a satisfying, dense C-minor thud, an easy catharsis, and so I started with that, and played for a while, until Beethoven got too difficult, and I had to think about stupid fingerings. Then I started improvising around in C minor and related dark harmonies. I remember a horrible moment. My feelings were real—I was sure of that. But unloading them at the piano felt fake. I was performing something that shouldn't be performed. I was sadder and emptier than before. What was the point of music if it didn't save you at a moment like this? In the middle of those thoughts, Dad threw the door open and told me to stop. "Either concentrate, or don't play," he said. "Also, dinner's ready." He never liked it when I improvised. He didn't want any part of my piano life to be casual or tossed off.

For a bit, my memories go blurry. All of our routines got rethought. Piano lessons were canceled indefinitely. We were excused from school for a week, and my father stayed home with us, but then he had to go to work. Someone had to care for us. Dad hired a nanny named June, maybe forty years old, with glasses and long brown hair. She cleaned and cooked and lived in what had been Josh's bedroom. Josh got to sleep in the living room and watch TV, the lucky bastard.

June was an interesting addition. She knitted in her room in her off time, and watched Spanish-language television, she said, in order not to let her Spanish get rusty and risk losing her heritage. She had a particular New Mexico accent, with a Spanish inflection hovering around the English sentences, coloring the vowels and softening the consonants, one of the most beautiful and musical hybrids I know. Under this lovely way of speaking, June's content was no-nonsense, even brutal. It started out OK. But as June cooked for us, she realized we were not good at cleaning. "Are you guys going to clear the dishes?" she'd say after dinner, and we'd look at her. "Isn't that your job?" we'd say. On TV, maids did everything, and in our trauma we thought we should be free of trivial responsibilities. After a little while, we fought with June worse than we ever fought with Mom. She said that we had no appreciation for how good our lives were, how privileged. She called us "spoiled brats," same as Mom. This was fair, but I wasn't ready to accept it, and this tension climaxed one day, while June was in the middle of vacuuming. I hurled a nasty insult at her about the "mariachi crap you listen to." June waited for a moment, looking off into space while the vacuum whirred, then switched it off and stared me down, like a cowboy in a western. It's heartbreaking to remember my instinctive racism, my desire to hurt the woman who helped us through a dark time.

After six weeks, my mother came back; June stayed on a bit, aiding with the transition, while Mom convalesced in her king bed. I remember only one conversation about Mom's recovery. Dad said that the doctor had taken one look at her and told her she had to stop drinking that very moment, and never touch another drop—otherwise she would die. Mom just listened while Dad explained. Many alcoholics hear this medical advice and choose to die anyway, but Mom had a strong, grim survival instinct. She began to make sun tea, setting jars outside on the blazing sidewalk, something to drink in the afternoons.

❧

In December, my piano lesson notebook resumed. Bill wrote: "now the famous and esteemed Jeremy Denk, Esq., will embark on some truly adult repertoire." On top of my stormy "Pathetique," he assigned me some late Brahms—a Capriccio, the A Major Intermezzo, the G Minor Ballade—and, in case that was too dour, the Mendelssohn Rondo Capriccioso. To my Mozart we added a new, frothy Romantic concerto: the Saint-Saëns G Minor.

Paging through the notebook thirty years later, it's sad to see one particular change: Bill stopped drawing hilarious stars next to each piece. He drew Santa Claus next to a perfunctory "HOHOHO" for Christmas, and a portrait of Beethoven lecturing me for being grumpy ("SIGH. man muss zufrieden sein!"), and from then on it's all business. The comments got sparer too. On one page he wrote only:

> Take one day of practice this week and do *only* left hand (not just brute technique, but musical detail: making conscious decisions). *Mark these decisions in the music.*

That was it—an hour's lesson, a week's work. No more stars, and no more coddling verbiage. *You're an adult,* he kept saying, *it's time to grow up.* This strategy was met with mixed success. Bill and I worked at my maturity in the scherzo of the Saint-Saëns concerto, which is odd, since that piece craves a childlike bounce. As the weeks went by, its wit and charm evaporated.

The lesson I remember most clearly from that period was on the slow movement of the "Pathetique." I played a bit, and Bill sighed. He grabbed my music from the music rack, returned to his listening chair, and started writing in my score. He used a pen (!), so this critique was for the ages, but it also seemed like he was making it up on the spot. He gazed around the room. A familiar and reticent white ball of fur purred by. Bill grinned to himself and went back to writing. It's such a cliché and power play to make your student wait in suspense while you write out your considered judgment, but I must admit, when I teach nowadays, I sometimes enjoy it myself.

At last—"Here you go, chum"—Bill put the music back on the rack. There was a new ribbon of words above the notes, lyrics for my Beethoven:

I see Fluffy,
and she needs another cat;
it would be so nice—
just you go and ask her.

I tolerated Fluffy, but she was no match for my new dog, Socratesia (aka Soc),* who howled with a mixture of glee and pain when I played in E-flat major. I looked at Bill, pleased and perplexed. "It's time to get serious about slurs," Bill said, one of the infinite times he began with "It's time to get serious about . . ." The point of the lyrics was that they would force me to observe the slurs written on the page, taking breaths with the words. Painstakingly, I played, while Bill made me sing along, serenading Fluffy's loneliness, and he yelled, "No—a breath after 'Fluffy'! Breathe after 'nice'!" We practiced until I could do all the slurs exactly as written, which seemed fussy and prissy—you might even say feline.

Many years later, when I was in the doctoral program at Juilliard, a visiting professor did an extended spiel on this same, all-too-famous

---

*As the reader might have already guessed, the dog was meant to be named Socrates, the result of an all-male conference in the car ride home from the pound; but when we returned, Mom pointed out that he was a she and so adjustments had to be made.

melody. He informed us that Beethoven was still feeling his way toward his mature notation, and that these slurs were just a sloppy shorthand. They were meaningless. Beethoven, he said, *really* meant one big connected legato, which was at the heart of his revolutionary rock-star persona: the emerging Big Sweep and Big Line, the doorway to Romanticism. I reminisced in the lecture room over poor dead Fluffy and all those weeks of practicing possibly bullshit slurs.

A lesson can be bullshit and essential at the same time—a key lesson in itself. It took some years, but eventually I took Bill's slur sermon to heart. These days, I find the slurs almost more beautiful than the notes. They tell you about the play of the music against the beat, the visible against the invisible. As I write this, one of a million examples pops into my head—the final movement of Mozart's G-minor Piano Quartet. In the second theme, Mozart's slurs mischievously tell you to syncopate, and send every offbeat to the next beat. This creates a forward, self-regenerating motion, like hopscotch, where notes seem to leap over each other in search of the next. Without the slurs, the theme would be stodgy; every other note would feel unnecessary. But with them, it dances.

Slurs look like an arc, and imply a journey:

At the beginning of the arc is an attack. At the end is a release. In between is connection. A simple marking, with lots of meaning-baggage. It tells you when to start, how long to continue, and when to let go. How often in life do you crave to know all those pieces of information? The continuity is important, maybe the essence of the slur. But the releases invoke all sorts of other verbs—laugh, skip, jump, kick—actions of escape, whose main purpose is to express the pure joy of being.

While Mom continued to recover from her near-death experience, I found another, less fraught musical outlet. Since the late New Jersey days, I'd been sort of playing the viola, an instrument my parents made me promise never to really practice. I haven't mentioned it up till now because it was such a side note of life. I was happy to have one thing I didn't have to excel at, and I'd been diligent in doing the bare minimum, slugging it out in junior high orchestra, playing hopeless arrangements from *Star Wars*.

All this changed when I began half days at high school. Every day, I'd arrive in a "gifted and talented" minivan mid–lunch hour, pick up pizza and tater tots and napkins to soak up the grease, find a seat on the concrete walkway next to the garbage with its bouquet of flies, and listen to the high school orchestra rehearse. The door was always propped open as the air-conditioning was not ideal, and inside was a vat of hormones and odors. One day they started up Pachelbel's Canon. I didn't know that piece yet, by some weird mischance. Those harmonies, that sweet string sound! I was eavesdropping on paradise. It became my dream to play in this ensemble, and the year after music camp, despite my age and incompetence, I got accepted. I didn't realize how desperate they were for strings. Normal kids with practical minds played in band and went to the football games, a chain of causality that led to getting laid.

Donna Herron, the orchestra teacher at Las Cruces High, should have a book of her own, instead of obscure mentions in archived issues of *The New Mexico Musician*, which is all I could find of her on Google. Donna came to my father's funeral in Las Cruces (thirty-some years after I played in her orchestra), and I was amazed to see her kicking along exactly as before, because it always seemed like she might die at the end of our rehearsals, or during, when her voice would rise and she wouldn't exactly shriek, but "shriek" is the closest word for what she did when we were playing carelessly or perpetrating the same stupid miscount from a previous day. Her voice rattled when she got angry, like the sounds some birds make at the end of their calls; but after that rattle, when she asked us to try it again, both her voice and body would deflate. This one-two punch was powerful. She kept us in line with the rage, and kept us rooting for her with the despair.

She also chose to give us real music, well beyond our abilities. I'll never forget rehearsing the Mendelssohn *String Sinfonias*. We knew this music was good; we experienced its goodness in real time as we massacred it. The joy was inseparable from the massacre. It was young persons' music, with intricate, rapid, ADD dialogue, and allowed all the string players to be involved, instead of (as often happened) the double basses and cellos getting bored and sullen and cracking jokes while the rest of us screwed up our solos. Once we'd rampaged through a couple Mendelssohns, she gave us Bach's Brandenburg Concerto no. 3. That was unwise. I can see her lifting her baton to get us started, like someone raising an arm to avert a blow from a blunt object, and then we would all come thumping in with our lazy rhythms, as if Bach had composed the piece for a parade of retired sumo wrestlers.

Things improved by the third movement of the Bach, especially for us violas. We had all kinds of loop-de-loops and featured counterpoint. Scales up and down; scales, in fact, never sounded so good. What had Bach done to make them so delicious? Pure motion, kinetic energy. God, it was great. Why hadn't Bill taught me this? I knew in a flash the joy of inner voices (an important lesson I was learning "by accident"), of passing an idea to the alto voice and hoping the second violins would take up our momentum, and glowering at them when they came in late. I remember the back stands of the seconds often staring back at me, droopy, bovine, partly from tater tot torpor but mainly confused about how enthusiastic I was, which, come to think of it, is the same way second violins often look at me now.

My stand partner was a guy named Reggie Oyler. I hated him, sort of. He had a big flouncy mop of pure black hair, green eyes, and pretty pale skin. I remember we had just finished some passage of the Bach, or, more precisely, Donna had brought us to a clattering halt and was trying to figure out which part of the ensemble sounded the worst— like those moments after the last dinner party guest has left and you survey your kitchen to see if any corner of the countertop seems like a reasonable place to start, or whether you should just sell your house instead—when Reggie looked at me and opined: "Dude, that bowing is fucked." Larry Stomberg, who sat principal cello and was becoming my best friend, overheard that remark and gave me a sly glance. Reggie wasn't a big fan of dependent clauses, and he favored the verb "is." An alarming percentage of his sentences took the form "*x* is *y*" where *y* was either "rad" or "awesome." Larry and I made endless fun of him, and yet I can see him now, playing that Brandenburg, heading up and down the scales, surrendering to them with all his heart, leaning with his viola to the left to express a sense of direction, and I feel ashamed of all those mean-girl remarks. I was jealous of Reggie because he had his own viola, while I was playing a terrible school instrument, and also because he practiced and took lessons, and therefore had a decent, vibrato-laden sound.

Donna sensed my sadness about this, a sadness she must have shared. Here was a student who cared about music as much as any student she'd ever had, with the caveat that he didn't care enough to practice his instrument more than five minutes a day, or even take a lesson. She squeezed in little mini-lessons in her office, before or after class. She taught me how to tune my instrument and rosin my bow. Her office was actually a former closet at the far end of the room—cinderblocked, windowless, thankless. It had a window, actually, but it just looked onto the rehearsal room, as if to say *There is no escape*. She smoked in there, often, which reminded me of my mom. All kinds of confessions happened in that small room. I told her about my mom's illness. Donna told me that I didn't get into the better all-state orchestra, but Reggie did, and she wanted to soften the blow. She told me how the school was threatening to cut funding, and how the orchestra was always being neglected in favor of the more useful band, and how they had to play certain terrible pieces because of deals with music publishers. "But for now I guess we're still playing," and she'd hold on to the cigarette, puffing at it until the last possible moment before the bell rang, looking at me conspiratorially—"OK, here we go"—implying *How will we survive this rehearsal?* As if I were an adult, of sorts, a fellow traveler. Like Bill, she wanted me to be aware of the hardship of musical life.

Back out in the rehearsal room, I'd joke with Larry. Donna would get up on the podium, offer a wry rehash of her current complaints, and begin to wave her arms; we'd look up, not often enough, at her baton and her frizzy dirty-blond hair, going out in every direction like a Chia Pet. On rare occasions, our playing would make her smile. This was against the grain; it strained her face and etched subtle lines, making her appear much older. After she smiled, she'd step down off the podium for a moment, in shock that she'd managed to make us care. The pleasure was an unexpected burden. With the possible exception of Señor Lujan, my Spanish teacher, who exuded an imperturbable and untranslatable resentment, Donna Herron was the saddest teacher of them all—and yet it was the happiest class.

}

My father also found a compelling outlet in that post-trauma period. The university had an active theater program, but it often lacked older character actors. He got recruited for a couple productions. He complained he was getting "sucked in"—what a waste of time, he'd never do it again, he said, hamming up his faux annoyance at our dinner table. We went to see him as lecherous Lazar Wolf in *Fiddler on the Roof,* and as a crusty, haggling London lowlife in *A Christmas Carol.* "I'm a specialist in grouchy old bastards," he said. "Typecasting."

"Yes, Joe," Mom murmured, with a razor's edge.

I'm sure Dad was fun to have in a cast. He was charming in transient social situations, and had a vivid stage persona. The community theater (Las Cruces's rival theatrical venture!) got wind of Dad's talents and started offering him more central roles. An old dream revived. He could be an artist at last—and this gave him an opportunity to address social lacks too. He was gone a lot of evenings for rehearsals. He began to learn back roads around town, through neighborhoods we'd never visited. When we went out to eat, people waved to him, said "Hey Joe! Loved you in *Fiddler!*" and so forth. He acquired some local celebrity to compare to my notoriety at school.

Mom complained that he was neglecting us kids, among other things. But just as my father realized that he wouldn't have many more chances to pursue a creative outlet, Mom realized that he wasn't going to stop. She was powerless to do anything about it, or even to buy her own clothes without him complaining. She got to work building an independent life. She took classes: accounting, computer science, writing. She started a journal and wrote about memories, things lost, how the construction in our neighborhood destroyed a nest of owls that she loved. (Dad made merciless fun of her for being an aspiring writer, "a profitable career choice if there ever was one.") And then she applied for jobs at the university—part time, so she could work without leaving us alone after school. Before long she got hired as a secretary in the art department, which gave her the thing she seemed proudest of: her own bank account.

Meanwhile, my brother's piano studies had been slowly degenerating. Why should he even try? To be compared to me was unbearable for him, I'm sure. My parents let him take up other instruments. He went for the oboe first, but after a squeaky year he settled on the double bass—a perfect fit. I'm sure he enjoyed the outlandishness, how inconvenient it was for our parents to have to squeeze it into the station wagon, how its gruff, rough tones added another frequency below the piano practice, making the two of us an acoustic triple threat, impossible to ignore and painful to hear. But it also was a friendly instrument, immune from ambition; you just laid down minimal licks and went home to relax. He was and is musical. He played a great and swinging bass line. Meanwhile he cultivated friends as far from my world as possible: laconic guy-guys, non-nerds. My parents didn't like them, which made him like them even more. And the ultimate distancing move: he started listening to rock music, loudly, in his room. This guaranteed I wouldn't knock. In between my scales, I'd hear his drumbeats going, trying to drown me out.

You would think that having nearly lost one of our number, the family might have clung together. Instead we ran away from one another in different directions, while leashed to the same house.

⸘

Toward the end of that spring, Bill thought my "Pathetique" was ready, and he entered me in my second piano competition, run by the National Guild of Piano Teachers. It took place in Hobbs, New Mexico, a big drive from Las Cruces, almost five hours, almost to hated Texas. That meant a lot of boring plains, and the expense of an overnight hotel stay. But Bill reminded my father that, as an amateur pilot, he needed to log hours to keep his certification. He suggested he fly us all over and save some time and kill two birds. My father was thrilled. I didn't get a chance to express my qualms.

A few days later, we drove out to the airstrip. After a few administrative details, we walked out onto the runway and got in a plane that looked not much larger than our car. I was buckled in the back, in my uncomfortable suit. Dad and Bill sat up front. The tiny space filled with a tremendous noise, a burrowing *rrrmmmmm*. When my panic subsided, I leaned over the front seats to look out the window. Bill said, "Isn't it amazing?" Between the mountains, scattered in ridges and occasional lone pimples on the desert, I saw a black nameless road, slicing through otherwise trackless space. I would have felt safer down there, alone on the asphalt, dying of thirst. My dad, on the other hand, laughed about the heat currents bouncing off the ridges far below, producing little gremlins of turbulence in a cloudless sky. "That was a good one!" he said, his eyes wrinkling in a smile.

We landed. I hated Dad and Bill. We took a smelly taxi over to the local high school, and some minutes later I remember walking in to audition. The room was gray, with off-white acoustical tiles, a clicking clock, and a beat-up Steinway. I thought, *If only I can just survive this first chromatic scale toward the end of the introduction,* and in my head I talked to my fingers, even counting them off, *one two three, one two three four,* to be sure I didn't accidentally land my thumb on a black key, with a crash and an impasse. The rest of the piece was a stormy blur—musical excitement merging with a sense of near-death from the plane—and the judges said "Thank you!" I remember gasping for breath as I stood up to take an unnecessary bow.

Somehow I won. My second triumph. Between Hobbs and El Paso,

I began to feel like the piano king of this sparsely populated quadrant of the Southwest. I was supposed to stay for an awards ceremony and perform at a dinner. But Bill had to return the plane. The competition organizer lady was furious. (Competition organizers and concert presenters are often furious.) We left nonetheless. On the way back, Bill and Dad laughed about how mad the woman had been, while I was quiet, suddenly exhausted. Bill offered me a reward: Would I like to fly the plane? "Planes drive themselves," he said. "They're not like pianos. They want to fly. Just don't interfere." And so I was lifted into the cockpit, and for the second time that day held my fate in my hands.

$$\}$$

That summer, there was no music camp. Mom's medical expenses had sucked up funds, and Bill was still bitter about how little I'd practiced. This year he'd keep me under his control, without school distractions, to get my technique in order "once and for all." I would have not one, but two lessons every week: one just on technique, another on repertoire. No cross-contamination between suffering and pleasure. Mixed in with the Dohnányi, Bill allowed me to play some Chopin Études, a big life step, but only ones that taxed the right and the left hands equally. He waggled his finger at me: "I don't want you to become a 'right-hand pianist.' "

That was my fourteen-year-old summer: baking sunny days, sullen distant family, solitary practice hours, fingering the tricky, tongue-twistery C-sharp minor Étude, playing it for Bill hands alone for two months until he finally let me play it all together. I found just one avenue of social and musical escape. The conductor of the Las Cruces Symphony, an extremely combative and Italian woman named Marianna Gabbi, started a string academy at the university. She asked me to play some chamber music, and matched me with my friend Larry, from high school orchestra, and a violinist I can't remember.

We wanted to play the Brahms B Major Trio. Marianna said, "Yes, if you feel you can, but I wouldn't." I don't know why she didn't force us to play a Mendelssohn trio, which we might have ruined less. The Brahms begins with a fabulous surging melody (which was why we were desperate to play it), but at some point Brahms starts developing his musical ideas. The emotion seems to think too much. Its waves keep cresting, and cresting again, until you realize you're kind of tired of cresting. There's a struggle, but you're not sure why. I can see the three of us in that classroom, jostling for space in every sense. Me on a tinny Yamaha grand, wedged into a corner by a blackboard, the strings sharing a nook between desks. They always thought I was too loud, and I'd say, "I promise to play a little less, but please, *please* let's all do more." This was my way of negotiating. We argued and argued, while looking for the magic curtain. We couldn't wait to have a coaching, where a teacher would tell us who was right.

But as it happened, the coaching was inconclusive as to the victor in the eternal war between piano and strings. Marianna had brought in the excellent Thouvenel String Quartet from Midland, Texas, who performed the Bartók Quartet no. 2. My mom and dad were nonplussed, but I sat spellbound through a *pianissimo prestissimo* passage. What a miracle—how did they play so fast and yet not loud? I explained to my parents, again, how stupid they were, a task that was as tiresome as it was necessary.

The following afternoon, we played our Brahms for Eugene Purdue, the Thouvenel's first violinist. If he was amused by us, by the way we were sowing our Romantic oats, his smile didn't show it. We wandered through the opening melody and he talked about "pacing ourselves," which, duh, was the key to the whole thing, though not a well-known skill of teenagers. We then came to the mysterious second theme and its twists and turns; Eugene stopped me. I was sure he was going to tell me I was too loud, and the string players would smirk.

But instead he said: "I know it's tempting to take time at the ends of phrases, and before the beginnings." I steeled myself—*no, not again*—for a mention of the metronome. "But in Brahms," he continued, "the real beauty is often in the middle, and *that's* where the phrase should expand." He made reference to Brahms's protruding stomach in the famous painting:

and to the hairpin indication in music—

—which Brahms used to sign his letters, in late life. A shape that grew to its center, found something, and released to its end.

I remember staring at Eugene while this information rewired my brain. He could see that I had just been blown away. I'm not sure I had thought of time except as a decorative element of that more generic idea, "phrasing," and I hadn't thought of different composers having different ways of using time, and for sure I didn't know about the joy of taking time when something needed to expand into itself, in life or in music. Eugene looked happy that he had connected with me, and in that magical and deceptive beginner's-luck way I nailed it the very first try, and he said, "Yes! Yes! Exactly." He put a hand on my shoulder. And that is all I remember. I forgot about my colleagues, and it no longer mattered whether I was right.

Eugene's advice was part of no system; it was anti-precision, anti-metronome. It was not (sorry, Bill) a detail to observe in the score, but something beautiful that couldn't be written in any score. A world of love and possibility occurred to me, one where you lingered anywhere, not at the commas or periods, not after Fluffy, but when ravishing notes seemed to force you to stop or slow, like when you're in front of some skyline, sunset, or field. I took Eugene's gospel to heart and began, like a child with a new toy, to drop these mid-phrase timings in everywhere. I reveled. Bill had no choice but to be the bad cop, and stop me from ruining every phrase I touched.

⁊

At the end of that long working summer, Dad knew we needed a break. He had a ready-made pretext: a computing conference in Snowmass, Colorado. The bonus was that I could go to concerts at the nearby Aspen Music Festival. Mom couldn't handle the altitude, so it was just us guys, driving twelve hours north, first along the Rio Grande to Santa Fe, and then up through wilder country, far from public radio stations. Dad decided we should entertain ourselves productively. He was engaged to appear as Willy Loman in *Death of a Salesman* that fall—his meatiest role yet—and he pressed me and my brother into service to help memorize his lines.

After Santa Fe came a long stretch of foothills, a complex topography of sage and scrub, with mountains hanging in the distance to the left and right. It seemed like these sandy hills should have eroded long ago, or washed away in the first good rainstorm, but there they were, always more or less the same. It was around there, at the uncanniest part of the journey, that we got to the crux of the drama.

"I'm so lonely," Dad whined in an oddly Jewish Willy voice.

Josh piped up from the back seat in a pretty good imitation of June Cleaver: "You know you ruined me, Willy?"

"What a nice thing to say," Dad said in a sarcastic voice that felt a bit too familiar.

"No, Dad, he says 'THAT'S a nice thing to say,'" Josh corrected, slipping back into his usual voice, low and lazy with an undertone of irony.

"Goddammit," Dad said, and then tried again. He was practicing, just like me, iterating and obsessing over errors. But it felt different when the raw materials were people and not musical notes.

I had the role of Biff, despite being the most un-Biff person imaginable. Trying to sound like I'd just burst into the room, I explained to Willy, my dad in the play, my dad in reality, that I'd not gotten the points I needed on my math test. That I wouldn't graduate, that I was a failure. (All my fears of failure!)

Together, my father and I made fun of the math teacher with the lisp—"The thquare root of thixthy twee . . ." But then I discovered him with another woman, and was disillusioned.

"Exactly what is it that you want from me?" I asked him, as Biff and also not as Biff.

Dad delivered his big line. "I want you to know, on the train, in the mountains, in the valleys, wherever you go, that you cut down your life for spite!" Josh yelled "No!," I yelled "Pop!," and then all that was left to do was read the stage directions, where Dad died, a casualty of his dreams. We passed the conical mountain at the border, my favorite mountain, Antonito, which seemed to say something gentle about death, and entered the great, wide San Luis Valley, thunderstorms in the distance.

A few hours later we arrived in Aspen. Josh did normal vacation things, skulking around the condo, hiking with Dad, lounging in the hot tub. I went off to every event at the music festival I could squeeze in. I heard dozens of concerts, feeling virtuous and dedicated, and forgot them all. But one morning I went to a master class by Edith Oppens. I'd heard a couple students say that she was famously mean. It would be good therapy to see someone else get reamed out, I thought, and maybe good fun.

A young woman played Beethoven's op. 7 Sonata, a piece I'd never heard. It seemed like a lot of passages. After the woman finished, Edith Oppens sat back in her chair and intoned: "Really, people should take these early sonatas more seriously." The student blinked. And then Edith harangued her, measure by measure, showing her that it wasn't supposed to be easy, this music, or tossed off. Eventually they got to the most difficult part, a place where the right hand is whipping around a series of fiendishly fast notes, while the left hand does almost nothing—just a series of long B-flats, up and down the keyboard.

This passage was amazing, the more I heard them work on it. You'd think Edith would have focused on the hard part—the right hand—but she spent ten agonizing minutes on the B-flats, trying to get the student to play them with authority and meaning. (Maybe authority *was* the meaning.) At last Edith took a regal pose and channeled the composer: "Do you know what Beethoven is saying here? He's saying *This is my territory, I am here, do not ignore me, this space*"—she paused on "space"—"*is all mine.*" She surveyed the room of sleepy pianists for a moment, who'd been fighting over practice room cubicles since dawn. What is it to own something, something as universal as an octave, the idea of a space?

I couldn't stop thinking about that section over the next weeks. It resonated with my life—one hand maximal and maniacal, trying to fit in as much as possible, almost more than was possible, the other obsessive and single-minded, unwilling to leave one note. Edith's lesson seemed to be that the single-minded hand should control the other one.

⸘

The new school year started with a decision. I'd been racing through grades. I could hustle for one more, work like crazy, and graduate from high school at fifteen. Or I could take a few extra classes for self-enrichment, and postpone college until the ripe old age of sixteen. Dad was all for the sprint, and Mom, who knew anxiety's effects, still preferred patience. Mom won by subterfuge. She got a class schedule approval form in the mail and sent it back without telling Dad. She'd put me in the slower track "for your own good." This brought about a huge fight.

Even in the slow lane, school life was odd. I was fourteen, but taking junior- and senior-year high school classes. I cultivated intimate, desperate connections with teachers, to protect me from hostile classmates. My English teacher (Mrs. Woodward, I think?) was for a while my closest friend. She taught me about the Thesis. She insisted that sentences should have a point and a well-chosen verb, both of which rocked my world. I also had a warm spot in my heart for my chemistry teacher, Mr. Bardwell, who joked with me until I was able to forget my incompetence in the lab. With math chops and a fervor for memorizing, I was an ideal chemistry student, in some ways. One day Bardwell did a little prancing maneuver, and a gesture with his wrist. An effeminate guidance counselor had just left the room. "I'm from San Francisco, I have AIDS," he said in a falsetto to the whole class. Then he chuckled and turned away, back to his office.

Mom initiated a new ritual to help us recover from intense school days. When we came back from the bus, she'd be sitting in the kitchen, calmly spreading peanut butter on crackers. She told us we all needed time to wind down before Dad got home, with his demands and energy. We'd sit in the kitchen, a little munching trio—it was true, this snack half hour was far more restful and communal than dinner. Mom had become exponentially kinder since her drinking days. She started to talk about her life like a normal person, instead of the yelling, blameful caricature. All three of us needed this human connection—we just weren't used to it. It felt good but weird, as if Mom were trying to befriend us, a bit too late. After the crackers, strangest of all, she didn't even hound us to work: she'd let Josh play video games, while I went to the living room to listen to music.

One of these afternoons, I was listening to the Brahms B-flat Concerto, my new favorite piece, and I was in the throes of the passionate second theme, conducting wildly, when—a rare occurrence—the front doorbell rang. Mom was still in the kitchen. I plucked the needle off the record and went to answer, but there was no one there—only a box sitting on the doormat, the sound of a car driving off, and some laughter. I pulled the lid off to find an assortment of porn and a lollipop that revealed a naked woman as you licked it. My classmates thought it was pretty funny that I was only now going through the whole hormonal deal. Heart racing, humiliated, I ran out into the desert and tried to bury the box with my bare hands. Wounded by a remnant of cactus, I had to return and hide it in a corner of the garage, where my father must have eventually discovered it, though I never heard a word.

⁊

That year, Bill let me graduate from the "Pathetique" to the "Waldstein" Sonata, from early to middle Beethoven. Bill wrote his most evocative passage in the entire notebook about it:

> ... think more musically than technically now. Begin with establishment of a mysterious mood—melody floats over quietest background—no break in the hypnotic character (just the tiniest rise in the r.h. interlude)—then a real outburst at the trills. First episode needs more excitement—sense of direction and arrival at sf's. Lots of drama. Second episode very stormy, even though triplets have to be very well controlled. Third episode—keep "sempre pp's" very strict. Also, begin to make better distinction between p & pp, and f & ff. On page 396 and 397 (triplets)—experiment with ways to handle the long crescendo: one hand cresc. without the other, save pedal for later, accent bass, etc. Plan dynamic changes.

It is interesting to watch him start out with mystery and character, but then revert to his comfort zones: system, planning, control.

What I remember about practicing the "Waldstein" was finding limits, and then bashing my head against them. The beginning notes, full of energy and drive, were no problem. I mean it was hard to play them soft enough, but I got there. After the first fermata, though, came a tremolo version of the same thing, in notes twice as fast. How could I make my hands go that speed? My right hand would, sort of, but my left refused. I remember faking it, and knowing I was faking, but Bill didn't seem troubled. He said, "It sounds fine to me," which was unusual. It worried me that Bill didn't realize this was a crisis.

I encountered another impasse in the middle section, in an endless series of arpeggios. I wanted it all in one big gesture, louder and louder, intensifying—but this was a non-solution. Maximal effort, minimal result. My mom, sensing my struggle from her listening post on the other side of the house, decided that the "Waldstein" was a terrible piece, and heavy, and it didn't dance for sure, and that I had a problem with

Beethoven. Mom's doubt stuck with me, and for many years—until one lesson in Oberlin, and another in Indiana—I thought Beethoven was my fatal weakness, unavoidable kryptonite, and maybe also not worth it.

Those impossibilities of the "Waldstein" merged with the general crunch of expectation. My academic teachers were eager for my future, with college looming. Bardwell thought I should be a scientist and encouraged me to enter the Chemistry Olympics. My math teacher said I was a born mathematician. My English teacher felt I should do a creative writing workshop. My gym teachers, however, never wanted to see me again.

But Bill put his foot down. He reminded my parents that I had auditions the next year, and that this was the time for piano focus—now or never. He convened a tense meeting of all the Jeremy-invested parties, including my parents and a school counselor. He insisted that we had to find a way for me to practice three good hours each and every day. The adults hatched a plan: I would get up super early and work two hours before the bus came—from 5:30 to 7:30 a.m. They said I would be fresher then, before school wore me down.

So began a strange era, where I was first up in the house. I remember the alarm ringing, attacking my deep teenage sleep; making my way in a fog to the kitchen, tripping over well-known end tables, seeing nightlights reflected in dark windows, turning on the hated overhead, scarfing down cereal in the glare, and padding back to my back room to play. I remember all the prep, but none of the playing. Imagine how Josh must have felt, hearing me start up my scales in his sleep, like he could never escape from my career either. My dad got up a bit later to do some calisthenics before his morning jog—we grunted at each other.

This era of productivity lasted two weeks. I promptly got the flu and couldn't go to school or even practice for a while. Our doctor said I was exhausted. It was decided that I was not a morning person and other solutions would have to be found. Hard choices had to be made, even at a time of life when all my options were supposed to be open.

ξ

A month or so after that, still recuperating, I had a terrible and memorable lesson on Mendelssohn's *Variations Sérieuses*. Bill would not let me leave the house until I managed to play all three lines of this one variation in different articulations. There was a legato line in the tenor. Then there was a plucked bass. This meant the left hand had to be schizophrenic, one side long and one side short. The third and final layer was a rapid, tricky, wandering staccato passage in the right hand. I tried once.

"You held that note too long," Bill said, pointing to one of the plucked bass notes.

I tried again.

"Don't fake it with the pedal!" he said. "That ruins everything!"

And that went on for fifteen minutes or so, and I felt as I had many years ago with Lillian, after the "Moonlight" Sonata: that the point of piano teaching was to drain the pleasure out of pleasure. Sometimes my two hands just did their things, without me having to concentrate. But other times required mind-bending effort; it seemed impossible, and unreasonable, to make your brain sing three voices at once, even if it was only a simple practical thing: putting one finger down while lifting another.

Dad drove me home from that lesson, asking "Are you OK?" I didn't say much. At home, I found my mother and Josh sitting at the kitchen table, in the usual spots, taking their respite. I joined them. Dad changed clothes in his room and went back out the door. We heard the garage open and close, and his new Honda Accord speed off. Mom gave a look around, waited a moment, and then said she had something to tell us.

She said, "I think you kids should know . . ." and trailed off, and then, after a moment: "Your father is gone a lot these days." Then she let it out: he was having an affair. That's why he was away; it wasn't just theater rehearsals. She even told us the woman's name.

I remember nodding and pretending to be a good listener, the kind of empathetic listener you'd see on TV, while my brain was still going over Mendelssohn failings. All my emotional reactions were scripts or plots. I felt a burst of chivalry, like I needed to defend my mom's honor. And I felt scandalized by my dad's behavior, even though I didn't know the first thing about sex except that some urges were causing me distractions from my studies. Did this mean that Dad was having sex? Even that fact seemed cloudy. No one had talked to me about birds or bees. My encounter with my summer camp roommate had been suppressed. Meanwhile, Mom continued listing grievances. That she was now physically unable to take care of herself, alone; that she needed my father for financial reasons also, and was therefore bound to him; and how unfair all of it was.

Josh and I listened. Mom trailed off. The afternoon ritual ended, not as calmly as usual, and we dispersed to our rooms. I said to Josh, "So what about Dad?" and he said, "Yeah," and that was the extent of our fraternal support. In my room I started recalculating. Normally my father was far more fun, more childlike, more willing to go on adventures and so forth. But as time passed he had become more sarcastic, or I had gotten more sensitive to it. Mom would worry you to death, but at least she wouldn't mock you. And she was fragile, even hobbled. She now relied on a cane. How could you not feel sorry for her? So now Dad, I guess, was the enemy.

}

At the end of that year, I entered my third piano competition. It was held in Albuquerque, and I was included in the proper high school age bracket—no more kiddie pool. The first round was midmorning, and the drive was at least three hours, so we got up at five and piled into the car. As the last door slammed, puncturing the arid calm, my mother asked if my father had remembered to turn off the coffee pot, to which he non-replied, as always, "Jackie!"

A couple hours north of Las Cruces, we entered the Jornada del Muerto, the Journey of Death, where Spanish explorers dropped like flies on their way up to Santa Fe. A checkpoint stands in the middle of its most desolate stretch. Border control officers peered through the window at me and my brother—the cargo—and waved us along.

I had to perform the first movement of the "Waldstein" Sonata. I passed through the first round, which seemed good news until I realized I had to perform it again in the next. Back to the warm-up room for an hour. Another cycle of adrenaline. I walked onstage again and did my thing, and then found out that the results of the second round were not going to be revealed until the end of an 8:00 p.m. awards concert. Oh, and also: I had to perform my piece there, yet again. This began to feel like manipulation—was I a puppet, a dancing bear? We tromped off to a dinner, a hunk of beef, mashed potatoes, languid green beans. I "made conversation" with piano teachers of New Mexico and my parents, not exactly smiling back at their questions, obsessing over only one thing: Did I win or not?

The finalists' concert was a true event, in front of a crowd in a real concert hall, but in my mind it was pointless: my ranking had already been decided. I played terribly, even by my own standards. Applause. I sat down to listen to the other finalists, shaking with three rounds of nerves. At last, after many thank-yous to donors and helpers, they announced I hadn't won, and I had to smile onstage while receiving honorable mention.

My brother was pleased by this outcome, since I tended to win a lot, and it was enough already; he sat smug and silent on the drive back to the hotel. My father, however, was full of remarks. I didn't have as big a sound as the winner, he said. Bill, perhaps, was not teaching me what I needed to learn. Mom disagreed while wondering if Dad was right. The winner had played Gershwin's *Rhapsody in Blue*. What a crowd-pleaser! Why hadn't I played something like that, instead of difficult Beethoven? They fanned the flames of each other's doubts. Apparently I didn't have a big sound. That seemed like a central issue. Maybe years ago—my parents continued deconstructing my past—they should have switched me to Audrey Brown, the real piano teacher for kids.

In the middle of all this, we decided to have a late "celebration" meal in the Big Boy diner next to the hotel. I ordered a special favorite, banana cream pie, terrifically fluffy in the display case. We were all huddled in a booth, and I remember taking a couple bites of my pie, and gazing out at the parking lot, and knowing I was going to throw up. I held it in, but my body's gears were seizing. After some minutes, my parents realized my feelings might assume projectile form.

My father took me back to the hotel, dragged a wastebasket from the bathroom, and set it next to the bed. He sat with me and, on top of all the other regrets, began to criticize his own handling of the day, and his parenting more generally, which had left me so vulnerable and fragile. He pushed me either too much or not enough, or both. I lay back on the bed and tuned him out and focused on not throwing up, in the same way that when you play the piano sometimes you focus on not missing any notes. I hovered in that unpleasant limbo until I trusted something and began to breathe slowly, in and out. Many years later György Sebők, my great Hungarian piano teacher, gave an unforgettable lesson about all the different kinds of breaths, different composers' breaths, the ways in which you feel them, and—especially—the dangers of forgetting them.

{

After Albuquerque, my first competition loss, my parents' faith in my piano life was shaken. Before, they lectured me about "focus." Now they began to invoke "options." An elderly neighbor invited us over for tea and cookies to tell me that music was not something you really did, not a profession per se, and I hated her from then on. There was a gathering sense of a deadline, a momentous life decision, and—as I'd seen countless times at the grocery store or Kmart—my parents had a hard time choosing what they wanted, even when they knew what it was. They had little faith in wants, for good reason. In the summer leading up to my final school year, Dad decided to ignore Bill's warnings about practice time. On top of my last high school requirements, he made me take three college classes—ten credits, almost a full slate—American history and calculus for my brain, swimming so I wouldn't be such a wimp and wreck.

Bill and I spent the summer preparing repertoire for college auditions. The dynamic had shifted. Before, my parents were roughly allied with Bill, but now it felt like my piano teacher and I were conspiring against my parents; the two of us had to find a way to overcome their doubts. Bill spent a lot of time choosing my repertoire. He wasn't looking for pieces to expand me. Now he was trying to find pieces that *were* me, that revealed me for who I was.

He suggested the Schumann Concerto in A Minor. I loved it so much more than the Saint-Saëns, or the treacherous "Emperor." I poured my frustrations into it, all my difficulties with the "Waldstein," all my annoyance in principle that I hadn't been kissed. Unlike the "Waldstein," the Schumann rewarded my uncertainties. We also revisited an old piece, the Mozart Sonata in A Minor, which I'd started on May 17, 1982, the day after my twelfth birthday. It was composed after Mozart's mother suddenly died in Paris. (My mother had only almost died.) This piece shook me. It had something to say about edges and boundaries, about shocks to the system, and realizations that come with them.

By the fall, this repertoire was getting solid. I knew and felt the stakes. Leland worked on recording my audition tape for weeks—an act of love if there ever was one, trying to find me a future in his profession. We created a microphone setup in his studio. We did a few takes, listened back, then did many more. In a way, this was Bill's dream scenario: he could control me and the environment; he could be the constant voice of reason on my shoulder, an angel of discipline.

I still have that recording of us together playing the Schumann. The cadenza is probably as good as I've ever played it, or ever will. A series of chords builds to a colossal climax, chords like horn calls, roaming over the fields of harmony. Bill got obsessed with how crisp these chords could be. He devised an exercise specifically for it (of course!). One last system for making me concentrate, just this one last essential time. And in the recording, it all works. It's also obvious that it was too late for options. Deep inside, I'd decided on music.

~

My résumé: straight A's, probable valedictorian, fifteen years old, a year's worth of college already under my belt, and no chance of my ruining all this by knocking up anyone. I'd won the Chemistry Olympics, with a super-precise titration. I had gushing recommendations from my English teachers and my calculus professor. Bruce Streett arranged for me to meet with Ivy League alumni around town. He accepted that

I wasn't going to go to Oxford, or become a Rhodes scholar, because I needed to focus on piano, and yet he still wanted to help.

At this point, with all my achievements on the table, my parents and I began to negotiate. They insisted on backups, and I kept saying the piano, and we all argued around the dinner table about whether to choose with our heads or our hearts. We developed a compromise: a double degree. I still wanted to do it all, even though the last couple years of trying that hadn't been a marvel of calm and easy achievement. But double degree it was—and with that in mind, I sent off a slew of applications: modest music schools closer to home, as well as storied Eastern institutions, Harvard, Yale, Oberlin. I remember lots of typing in my room, bottles of Wite-Out, Xeroxes, and vast emotional energy spent on essays.

After some weeks of anxious waiting, all my teacher's-petting and manic overachievement paid off: I was accepted everywhere. I wanted to choose Oberlin, which had a real double degree, an equal and divided course of study. But it wasn't cheap.

My dad suggested the University of Kansas: "big fish, small pond." Or possibly Trinity, in San Antonio, Texas. "They called me and said your Mozart was amazing," he said. I craved flattery, but felt I shouldn't go to San Antonio. Did my dad really think I would get better teaching in San Antonio or Lawrence? I began to realize how much money was factoring into my father's decisions. I had gotten more distrustful of him since my mom's revelations. Also, since I was a little kid my parents had said, *You have to get straight A's, to get the money to go to college.* I took this as a promise: if I worked as hard as possible, the money for college would appear.

But the money, after all the documents were submitted, didn't appear. We had screaming fights. I told them they lied to me, that I'd worked like a dog for a decade and had no fun and didn't kiss any girls and now the money wasn't there. Why hadn't they planned better?

A few days later, my dad said I had to call my grandfather. You may notice his name hasn't come up much so far, and for good reason: Dad never mentioned him. I remember being perched next to the microwave in the kitchen, on a landline, the cord constantly getting stuck in the microwave door, a place reserved for awkward family conversations, for dutiful Christmas greetings and thank-yous. Dad said hello, talked to his dad for a minute or two, the absolute bare minimum, and then got me on the line. I squirmed. I didn't like interviews. I said I got into Yale, Harvard, and Oberlin and I wanted to go to Oberlin. My grandfather wasn't too pleased.

"Why don't you want to go to Harvard?" he asked. I tried to explain: music, the double degree. He listened, skeptically. Dad got back on the line, and after he hung up said we had to make a visit to my grandfather; he wanted to meet me, at last.

So the whole family flew to Chicago. I remember sitting out on his deck, saying hello, shaking his hand as if at a business meeting. Before long the topic strayed to politics, and Jesse Jackson, and my grandfather called him the N-word. He just spit it out. Mom and Dad looked away; they'd heard all this before. They'd tried to keep me from all that. But now we had no choice. He had a fair amount of money, but had married a much younger woman who was taking care of him in his decrepitude, and who would inherit it all. This was their last chance to extract funds for my future, and Josh's, a couple years down the road.

On the flight home, my parents said it was a success: my grandfather promised $5,000 a year for four years. But this still wasn't enough. So back in Las Cruces, my dad talked to Bruce Streett—maybe this was difficult, even humiliating. Bruce was a saint. He assembled a consortium of businessmen in Las Cruces, contacts from fundraising, including Glenn Cutter, owner of a jewelry store, and a car dealer named Sisbarro—they each threw in a small amount, altogether another $5,000 a year. A third from my racist grandfather, a third from these generous businesspeople who thought a gifted local boy should have a chance in life, and a third from my family—and now I was finally able to go do whatever it was I was going to do in Oberlin. It was quite a contract. My parents said I had to live up to all the faith these people had in me. The decision was made, and then reconsidered, in agonizing detail.

"You should have gone to Trinity," my dad said after the acceptance letter had been returned. "You would have gotten so much attention." Of all the things he said to me over the years, this was the hardest to forgive, with all its lack of ambition for my musical future, after all the pushing and standards and sarcasm.

I went to my last lesson with Bill. He was happy with all the work we'd done, and thrilled that I was going on to the next step, but he also had regrets:

"You should have been born fifty years ago."

I couldn't do anything about that now, it seemed to me.

"There were fewer pianists then," he continued. "Someone like you could really make a mark. Now there's a million pianists who can play the notes, and it's almost impossible to make a living. The winner of the Cliburn Competition wrote me just the other day, to see if I knew of any jobs."

Jesus, you too? I thought. But off I went.

6. *Harmony* LESSON THREE

*L*et me set the scene. We're in the sweep of Bach's epic and encyclo-pedic *Well-Tempered Clavier,* a piece that visits every key. We started with an idyllic study in harmony—C major—and now (two hours later) we've wandered through every imaginable nuance of joy and sorrow and dance and wit and determination and rumination to find ourselves at the far end, in B minor. If we started driving at the Atlantic Ocean, now we face the Pacific—a colder ocean, with tremendous sunsets but also bewildering fog.

What confronts us is not so much a musical idea as a puzzle. Bach begins with three separate notes: F-sharp, D, B. The specific notes don't matter so much as the fact that when you stack them up you have a chord, in fact the right chord: B minor. These three notes are a clear declaration of place, telling us: *This is the key we're in.* Toward the end of the theme, you have again three separate notes: a C-sharp, an A, an F-sharp. Stack these up and you get an F-sharp-minor chord. This is also the right place, the right destination: *This is where we're going.* From B minor to F-sharp minor is the fundamental, required, expected chord progression of a Bach fugue subject.

But in between these two landmarks we have a series of curious events that appear to have nothing to do with the bookends, that defy them or (you could even say) mock them. Bach writes notes in groups of two. These pairs are always right next to each other on the keyboard. If you don't know what I'm talking about, go to any keyboard, play a note, then play the note immediately to the left of it, a bit quieter and shorter, and pull your hand away. You've done it! You are now a master of Baroque style! (This joke is by no means to be interpreted as a slam on Early Music, or Early Music musicians.) These pairs of notes have a long history as a primal musical gesture, a piece of mimicry: they act and sound like sighs.

What makes these sighs a puzzle is that we don't know which note of each pair is the "right" one. By the rules of Bach's musical language, two adjacent notes on the keyboard can never be part of the same consonant chord (I promise this is as wonky as we're going to get). One is always a problem. But there is no pattern to this right/wrong, and no way to know, because, at this early moment, there are no chords underneath to tell us. Imagine a policeman with two conflicting witnesses and no security camera footage.

What's more, Bach takes these groups of two, these sighs, and makes them leap about in an odd pattern:

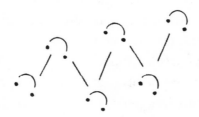

I would say he's combining pattern with elements of (what seems like) randomness. A deliberate circuitousness. Between the pairs we find various chasms, distances of a couple notes on the scale or many more. Our mind tries to interpret these distances, to "cross over" them, but it's not the easiest thing in the world, and just when we feel we've begun to absorb one disorienting event, the next arrives.

So, if I had to diagram this theme for you, not in a get-the-answer-right-in-class way, but to reflect how it feels, I would draw this:

In other words, a journey from known to known, via unfathomable mystery. Bach has written a musical shorthand for a common question we ask ourselves, especially as we grow older: *How the hell did I get here?*

{

My parents were not fans of road trips. We did the one multiday move from New Jersey to New Mexico, and after that, reluctantly, once a year or so, we'd roam the Southwest: Aspen for the music festival, the Grand Canyon, Santa Fe for the opera. These road trips gave Mom the opportunity to fuss Dad to death, her worries for once entirely justified. At some point, Dad would begin to drive down a road that looked lonelier and lonelier, and then we'd pull up in front of an abandoned service station, or at the juncture of two meandering dirt tracks leading off into unsurvivable wastelands. The sound of the idling car. Silence among the four passengers. At last, Dad would break the tension: "Well, Jackie, I guess I'm on my way to Cincinnati."

This made my mom laugh, though she was dying to say "I told you so." This was a recurring family joke, Dad's theory for why he was so often lost: deep inside, he claimed, he had a homing beacon, an animal instinct or profound spiritual need, that drew him inexorably toward Cincinnati. Why Cincinnati? It could have been Cleveland, except Cleveland had the famed orchestra. He chose it for randomness and lack of glamour: a place in the middle, but in no way central.

Once Dad invoked Cincinnati, he'd conceded defeat. That meant it was time to consult the map, which was buried in the glove compartment and had been refolded and misfolded over many years, such that you couldn't consult it without a storm of rustling and wrinkling in the car, punctuated by cussing and ripping sounds. I always think of those sounds when I hear on TV some gobbledygook about "a tear in the space-time continuum." At last, New Mexico would lie unfurled in front of us, and it did seem comical that we'd managed to get lost in a state with so few roads. Our car would be just on the edge of one of the state's many vast blank spaces, and we'd have to retrace the dotted line we'd ended up on—a provisional or seasonal route—back to the highway.

Classical music has plenty of Cincinnatis, and dotted-line roads, and Patagonias (places I've always wanted to go that are impractically far), and Antarcticas (impossibly far and deeply undesirable and yet alluring—just to face something so bleak and so cold, to see if you can survive it); and harmony is the well-folded, all-too-used, constantly ripping map that tells us where we are, and how to get where we want to go.

I hate to use an example from the Approved Archive of Classical Music Theory Examples, but it's a good one: "Auf dem flusse" from Schubert's song cycle *Winterreise*. It begins in C minor, and the singer (as is sadly typical for song cycles) is talking to the body of water in front of him, saying

You that so flowed so happily, you, wild and shining river.

The music appears to be a folk tune with the most rudimentary of accompaniments, bass-chord-bass-chord, like something you'd assign for a first lesson in How to Play Harmonies. But then the singer says,

How still you've become.

And as we imagine the river icing over, the bass shifts down one note and we are now in B minor, just a tiny half step away. This chord change is not what we in the music biz would call a modulation: where you travel from one chord to another, from place to place. Modulation implies good faith, some sense that we have "earned" the motion from one zone to another, some step-by-step attainment of a goal. No: this is a slippage, or if you like, a tear. We blink and find ourselves in Antarctica. Its tremendous effect has everything to do with a surrounding set of harmonic expectations and conventions that it ignores. Like many of Schubert's most vivid moments, it implies that you are just one step or misstep or wrong turn from absolute disaster.

You don't have to toss harmonic norms to get uncanny journeys. The first section of the Joplin/Chauvin ragtime "Heliotrope Bouquet" (not an Approved Music Theory Example) is a kind of puzzle too, after its innocuous intro. That is why I can't resist playing it. It starts with a complicated yearning chord, which leads to a more normal chord, and then to an even more normal one, which dumps us where we want to go: G major. A sequence I might label like this:

?——→ oh, wait——→ I totally get it now———→ arrival (G major)

But we only land on G for a moment—as if you drove all five hours up to Santa Fe and didn't stop for even one green chile stew or massage (something as a self-respecting New Mexican I would never do)— before off we go, back on the road, back to the complicated yearning chord, and then again, *oh, wait, I get it,* and again we arrive. But then— this is the real kicker—off we go, *one more time.* If you're driving around a traffic circle, it's perfectly normal to miss your turnoff, and almost socially desirable in circle-hating America, but if you come around the second time and miss it again: now *that* is something, a real incompetence, or the sign of a scattered mind, that your thoughts are elsewhere, on a journey of their own.

If the Schubert mystery chord was Antarctica (going with the obvious ice imagery), the Joplin/Chauvin question-chord is also distant, but less forbidding, with more than a hint of sensuality: let's say Buenos Aires, or Rio.

As long as we're playing this fun geographical game, let's label a third destination, a famous place in Chopin's Fourth Ballade where we come to a halt on what seems like the most beautiful chord ever invented. All pianists know the spot I'm talking about. I'd label this moment a sun-kissed Greek isle, something tubercular Chopin must have dreamed of often. A place where the earlier F minor, brooding, tossing back and forth from melancholy to storm, is impossible to imagine. The pianist plays an improvised arpeggio up and around this A-major chord (that's all it is, more or less)—as if taking it all in, the blue Mediterranean, the lack of urgency, the absolute calm.

But then comes the best part. You start playing fragments of an earlier, melancholy melody—but starting from where you are, in the Mediterranean harmony. You can imagine Chopin, riffling through the glove compartment and unfolding the map, searching the land of harmony one chord at a time, one bit of melody at a time, quadrant by quadrant, accepting that Greek paradise is not his place, that he has to get back to rainy, moldy Paris. And as he changes chords, the old sad waltz sway takes over, without you knowing it. We have returned. This great passage carries a truth: You do not decide where to go, and then begin going there. In real life, while you are deciding where to go, you are already traveling.

In "Auf dem flusse," the change of chords is from the main key of C down one half step—just one note to the left on your piano keyboard, be it black or white—to B minor. *Aha,* the attentive or nerdy reader says, *there's a connection to the Bach fugue,* and indeed there is.

If you play a C-major scale, and climb from C and keep going, *do-re-mi,* one note at a time, eventually you get to B, the seventh and last note, the one before the next C, where the scale begins to repeat itself. B is called the "leading tone" because it rather desperately implies that you are going to play another C. On its own, that note has an irrepressible urge, like a rock pushed to the top of an incline and sitting at the edge of a cliff, waiting to fall into the C below. Or it's like a sign on the outskirts of town, saying *Welcome to C-major-ville, Home of No Sharps or Flats.* It's so obviously going where it's going that in some ways it almost *is* where it's going.

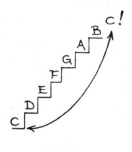

But if you stack a chord on top of your B, you have a different animal, a chord that in the land of classical music harmony—which interacts with the freer land of melody but has its own rules and ways—is quite far away. You can play a single note C and then a single note B, easy-peasy. But you cannot just step from a C-minor chord to a B-minor chord, as Schubert does, without a sense of violation (exactly what Schubert wants). There are many, many steps to go through.

Bach being Bach, he's not content in his *Well-Tempered Clavier* just to write a lovely piece "in" B minor. No, at the end of the road, he wants a bigger statement. He writes a piece that is somehow "about" B minor—that is, about the nature of the leading tone, about the two lives that the one note lives, one in melody, the other in harmony, about the intersection of the intimately near with the impossibly far.

This explains the fugue's curious subject—two "normal" chords, separated by chromatic madness. Because of its complications, you feel that you travel through this fugue theme, more than you hear it. When the second voice comes in, you hope that it might help to make the journey clearer. But the journey gets worse before it gets better— a kind of trip we all know about ("I need a vacation from my vacation"). Bach takes special pains to make the entrance of the second voice sound even more torturous, with undigestible, abrasive dissonances, as if the keyboardist got lost, or the divine muse went silent.

When the third voice comes in, however, the journey appears less strange. Not normal, for sure. But the errors are now comprehensible, part of a plan, decorations of harmonies we know and love. The third voice is the tipping point—because with three notes at once, we have triads, meaning harmonies. Chords explain the mystery of the melody, to the extent it could ever be explained. And so you could say this fugue explains the consolation of harmony, all bound up with another of life's key comforts: a sense of place, the presence of a map.

{

After the fourth and final voice comes in, Bach does something so ridiculously great that all the other accomplishments of *The Well-Tempered Clavier* recede in the rearview mirror. The fugue theme vanishes. We come to what's called "an episode." Usually, episodes rove with the aid of cut-and-paste—taking a group of notes and grafting it onto the last, shifting up or down step-by-step. We call this movement a sequence. The main question is: When will the journey stop?

This first episode in the B Minor Fugue has none of the theme's complications. It sails smoothly and soothingly along, without difficulty, as if to say *Life doesn't have to be this hard.* You could fall asleep to it, and if you woke up hours later, the same sequence might well be going on, with no task other than repeating itself, and hearing the beauty of one chord drifting on to another.

But then a middle voice enters. It offers just one comment on all this drifting beauty: three separate notes, F-sharp, D, B. The B-minor triad—how the fugue (and this chapter) began. These three notes call out, then vanish. The sequence restarts, and we go back to being lulled, to sweetly passing through harmonies, but that simple triad, orphaned from its original melody, haunts the memory. I feel Bach's voice in those three notes, like a message in a bottle, trying to cross the ocean of harmony he himself has created. What's the message? Those notes don't say *We're in a place*—how could they? We're still en route—but they remember being in a place. They remember having a home, while the chords (time, life) keep shifting on.

PART TWO: *Melody*

7. The Real World

PLAYLIST

‖ BEETHOVEN: Sonata in F Minor, op. 57 ("Appassionata")
‖ BEETHOVEN: Symphony no. 7 in A Major, first movement
‖ CHOPIN: *Berceuse*, op. 57
‖ SCHUMANN: Toccata in C Major, op. 7

When I arrived at Oberlin, in August of 1986, I'd been sixteen for all of three months. After a spree of cross-country plane-travel bickering, my parents dropped me at my dorm, stocked my mini-fridge, and left me free at last. My roommate was named Sasha. He had dark stubble and slicked-back black hair, all of which felt way too adult for me to handle.

My dorm was Dascomb, known as "Scum." I needed the hall monitors as parental proxies for a while, and for help with basic life skills. But I didn't like them—too earnest. I preferred unhelpful reprobates: two tall roommates, Hugo and Pete, who played video games all day and turned their room into a general clubhouse, and a tousled, creaky-voiced guy across the hall named Dave. They all gave off a mysterious vegetal scent, which I assumed was incense or body odor, and laughed about anything and nothing—a medicine I'd been needing for years.

I remember a welcome-to-Scum picnic. Calm and inclusive things were said out on the corner lawn. A golden late afternoon, warmed-over dining hall burgers. After the eating died down, noticing I didn't have particular companionship, the dean of dorm life took me aside for a private chat. He told me he appreciated the challenges of coming to college at my age, and said *Just call me, whatever I can do.* He was kind, but I recognized this situation from high school—the separation, the kid gloves, the official sympathy. This sort of protection no longer seemed useful, or relevant.

There was one other sixteen-year-old in Scum, named Polly. She lived at the far end of the women's hall. I had to walk past thirty open girls' doors to get to hers. Female beds were an unknown and menacing world. Polly's straight black hair had a cultivated asymmetry; she was forced to brush or blow bangs from her eyes every few minutes, a ritual that didn't seem to trouble her. She seemed like an alien, not a cuddly E.T. or a ravenous monster, but a wacky alien from a sitcom, full of quirks. I've always had a thing for wacky, which is part of why I ended up in Oberlin in the first place, a teacher's pet craving a certificate of cool.

Polly and I had an escalating series of conversations in her room— her on the bed, me safely on the floor. She felt I needed a new education. She refused to treat me with kid gloves. Her big thesis was that I knew nothing about music, by which she meant life. I played her some Brahms, to demonstrate her error, and she asked, "What's the point of music without words?" I was speechless. At last I objected that she only talked about lyrics, and never musical notes. She gestured to a giant Elvis Costello poster on her wall, as if that were the final word in this and almost any argument.

Her room was a frenzy of strewn clothes, a lair. This sloppiness, infinitely more ambitious than I'd ever achieved in battle with my parents, seemed like distilled rebellion. There was the smell of her, and the occasional moment when she would not quite accidentally brush against me, while lecturing me with a scolding twinkle in her eye about music I'd always hated. I was in the enemy camp, and loving it.

}

Since I was pursuing two degrees, I had to make decisions earlier than most Oberlin students. If I didn't, there was the risk of an extra year, and more money. My grandfather said neither was an option. Chemistry had been a solid subject for me in high school, and my dad had been a chemist in his first unsatisfying life. So I decided to make chemistry my other major, though I didn't want to be like my father in any way. It seemed wiser to plan for unhappiness, or at least easier to explain to my parents.

My life soon split into two buildings, housing two worlds. Chemistry lived in a low quadrangle of dark blue brick, matching nothing else on campus. You entered a concrete hallway with a terrific echo but no chairs or sofas—no sense of arrival, certainly no welcome. It smelled of solvents. The only places to gather were classrooms or the library.

The Conservatory, on the other end of campus, was centered around a roomy windowed lounge, a human-sized fish tank with banks of vending machines, benches, tables, well-worn cushions. An array of students were gossiping and slouching in every possible unhealthy position when I first arrived, as if they had been there forever. A Japanese garden awaited contemplation outside, with a pond that was often empty and mournful in the freezing Oberlin weather. Hallways led off to different zones—practice, study, rehearsal—giving the feeling that the building was an organism or microcosm, a cocoon where everything and nothing would happen.

I hiked back and forth from one world to the other with my overloaded backpack, a relic of high school life that Polly made endless fun of, but that I wouldn't surrender.

ʔ

The chemistry department took my credits and AP scores at face value. But in the Conservatory, I had to be placed and ranked. I suppose this is what I'd always wanted—to know how I'd rate in musical reality.

My first exam was sight-singing. I was waiting in the second-floor corridor when I met another incoming freshman pianist. My earliest encounter with my own species. We exchanged peculiar, assessing greetings.

"Who are you studying with?" he asked, a harmless enough question.

"Joseph Schwartz," I replied. I didn't know anything about my teacher except for what was written in his bio in the catalog. It said that he'd won the Naumburg Competition—something I'd heard of, a badge of fame. It occurred to me that I'd made a dangerous gamble. *Why did my parents let me do this?*

"I'm studying with Ms. Walker," my fellow pianist announced, with an air of familiarity. He knew about her, he knew what she was going to offer. Then he launched into an anecdote, with a certain insider musical tone that I've always hated. "Ms. Walker told me that she just heard someone playing Schumann's *Carnaval*. That wasn't you, was it?" he said, sounding concerned.

"No," I said. I'd heard of *Carnaval*, and I'd even looked at the first page. But I'd thought, *No way will I play that piece, ever.*

"Oh good," he said. "Ms. Walker"—repeating her name gleefully—"said can you believe it, they rolled all the chords at the beginning! I mean, the student had no business playing that piece, because their hands weren't big enough."

My hands were certainly not big enough. No business.

This guy kept going, ignoring my looks of doubt, my anxious peering at the door where the exam would take place. "Also, Ms. Walker said," he said with a bit of a fanatical smile, as if her opinions deserved to be chiseled on tablets, "the central principle of piano playing is no wasted motion. And you know she's right, she's soooooo right."

I nodded. My brain was racing. It seemed impossible and silly to try to play the piano without wasting motion. Every motion was wasted, if you looked at it in a certain light. But there wasn't time to ponder these infinities and impossibilities. The door opened. "Jeremy Dink?" they called. My name being sort-of uttered in a famous music school! I went into my sight-singing exam. A friendly-looking nerdy panel sat at a long table. They gave me all kinds of music to sing, and I nailed it—until things got atonal. "Dum dum dum de dum de dum," I sang, notes flying everywhere, and they laughed. All right, you passed, they said, but have you ever considered (still laughing) the word "la"? I didn't do as well on my music theory placement exam the next day, and had to start with remedial classes, which for a valedictorian was pretty humiliating.

〜

It came time for my first lesson with Joseph Schwartz. As I said, I picked his name based on his bio; I hadn't visited campus—too expensive—and had no test lessons. This was a blind date, with the expectation of a four-year relationship. Music students do this en masse every year, like lemmings—they leave the cocoon of their teachers at home, their ways of doing things, and entrust themselves to someone they've met for an hour at most, to a name or a reputation. Being a musician often requires living on the border between faith and recklessness.

Schwartz's studio was on the top floor. I can still remember the unpleasant feeling of climbing up there, feeling I would be judged by unknowable standards (too much Kafka in high school) and might have to start over. I was tired from my rubbery mattress and Polly's social demands—the first time in my life I'd experienced social demands, per se. The fateful pre-lesson knock. Joe welcomed me at the door, at the same time shuffling a studio-mate out, who appeared timid but unharmed. Joe was then in his mid-fifties, with curly gray hair, thick round glasses, and lots of wrinkly forehead. He didn't radiate energy.

Walking to the window and dumping my backpack, I saw he had one of the best views in Oberlin: across Tappan Square, following a herringbone brick sidewalk through the trees to Fairchild Chapel's august stone entrance. It was especially beautiful in winter, when the plowed paths and snow transformed the design into a maze. The magic of this view didn't seem to permeate Joe's studio, though. It always seemed dark, and quiet, even when you were playing. There was almost no decor. I often felt that some part of me disappeared once I went in that third-floor door, to return only when I came back, often almost running, to the lounge, to reality—joking with other students about what I'd screwed up, and what Joe had said.

The first couple weeks, Joe took my measure. I would play a little, and he'd say it was good and we could talk more later. He asked me what pieces I liked, how my classes were. At first I acted around him just like I acted around all my other teachers: eager to please, with a side of bragging about my accomplishments. He raised his eyebrows about the chemistry, about me being sixteen and also being a math person, and loving literature. He was impressed, but also worried. "You're the ideal Oberlin student," he said, which didn't sound like a compliment. Like many phrases in Schubert, Joe's use of language was both comforting and unsettling. He typically wore a half smile—not a *Mona Lisa* smile; something less committal.

Based on what he learned, and on my audition tape, Joe suggested I take on two big virtuoso pieces: Beethoven's "Appassionata" Sonata, op. 57, and the Schumann Toccata in C Major, op. 7. Maybe Joe thought the "Appassionata" would be a way for me to let my fingers rip. That's what I wanted or needed, in his mind. I had never thought of myself as a jock pianist, or any other species of jock, but other students said I was already famous for playing crazy fast and loud in the practice rooms. Maybe I did revel in technique for the sake of it in those days. But Beethoven makes you earn your difficulties. You can't just go wild. The fireworks are always held in tension against some spine of meaning.

Every pianist knows and dreads that first "Appassionata" outburst: three notes, the piece's obsessive "knocking" motif, become a thorny arpeggio, first heading up, turning a corner, then hurtling down to the bottom of the keyboard. This terrifying release pretends to come out of nowhere—although at the same time it is a logical result of the opening tension, like a burst dam. The arpeggio features an awkward combination of black and white notes—thumb hazards—and a brain-teasing array of intervals, including the famous tritone, the "devil's interval." It requires strength, agility, fortitude, focus: lots of virtues I wasn't sure I had.

I practiced it, but every day I found new and creative ways to miss notes—not the kind of creativity I was hoping for. In my third week, I played it for Schwartz. The famous passage came out maybe 20 or 30 percent worse than in the practice room. It sounded like a tornado that slipped on a banana peel.

"Keep your hands close to the keys," Joe said.

I did that, but still missed it.

"OK, try focusing on your thumb," Joe said.

In some mysterious way, I made my brain arrange itself around a single finger, becoming more aware of its existence and its place. It worked. I nailed the passage. Triumph! I looked at Joe, happy as could be. But then I had to test it again, to see if the magic was real, and missed it even worse than the first time.

Joe was familiar with this process and its limits. But I thought college would be more definitive, that it would have less of childhood's circular frustrations. After Joe offered a third solution—"Why don't you lower your wrist?"—I was having trouble believing any of them. At bottom all I wanted was for him to heap praise, to tell me I was on the right track, that I'd made the right choices. But praise was not Joe's strong point. The best you could hope for was temporary contentment.

"Don't worry," he said with a smiling sigh, "keep at it. It's a tough passage for everyone." This seemed a cop-out. Joe's sympathy made me feel like just one of a suffering horde of pianists. I didn't want to be one of many; I wanted to be The One.

{

Joe and I then came to a peculiar transition, with a series of repeated notes. These notes are an obvious link to a beautiful theme in the near future, but Beethoven wants us to believe they are uncertain, unstable, haunted—even maybe a dead end. They pulse anxiously; dissonances and syncopations dance around them, above and below. To prepare me for passages like these, Bill had given me a special repeated-note exercise, one of the most hated pages of my Dohnányi book. But this exercise didn't tell you the first thing about how to get Beethoven's spine-tingle. It was like if you asked someone how to kiss a girl, and they gave you a diagram of the anatomy of the lip.

I had to stay in rhythm but add unease, and also remain quiet, with no bumps. Why did composers have to be such a pain? Some of the repeated notes wouldn't sound at all. My hand got tight and then tired. I didn't yet understand how to stay within the sweet spot of the key, not letting it rise back all the way. What I needed was a delicate control, a calibrated motion between things—a motion, in a way, mirroring the passage itself.

But Joe didn't like to wander into the technical weeds. He didn't want to mess with my natural abilities. He wrote this on my music:

LH too loud

Yes, a problem, which I knew all too well. Then he added:

Keep in tempo

But why did my fingers go down quicker than I wanted them to? At last he added:

Don't rush!

—which I now tended to ignore, it was such a frequent refrain. Joe was big on the diagnostic What, stingy with the prescriptive How, and mostly avoided the animating Why. He figured I didn't need much Why. But I craved Why—and I needed a hell of a lot of How.

After we labored through the repeated notes, we reached another storm, where Beethoven rages away with fast notes in both hands. Suddenly, I played as if possessed. My hands felt so much more confident when they didn't have to play alone. Joe sat back and laughed. "Yes, that's pretty amazing, Jeremy. I'm not even sure how you're doing that."

There it was, a glimmer of hope.

Then Joe said, "So how do we transfer that into the rest of the piece?" How do you convert accidental skills into a general and purposeful good? Excellent question.

⅋

Over on the other side of campus, I'd skipped the first year of general undergraduate chemistry, and was into organic, taught by Professor Nee. Organic did not require imagination, only memorization. I hoarded its patterns, its combinations and permutations of molecules. It filled a deep need, because you applied yourself to it and then (unlike music) it was done. I sat in the science library for hours. If Polly wanted to find me, she'd try there first, make a lot of noise, and provoke a round of shushing, which made her smile, as if it were applause. I'd get rid of her even though I was happy to see her, and then return to savoring the unmusical silence, memorizing building blocks of life . . .

In the lab it was a different story. Everyone else seemed able to clean their glassware in a few minutes, but I'd lose half an hour. My beakers were always crusty, my towels waterlogged. When I was finally ready to start the experiment, I was in a panic, and the professor had to come over and make me think one step at a time. Mr. Nee didn't expect to be a babysitter, I imagine. I didn't like when my mind had to bridge over to the practical and physical—which is (come to think of it) what piano playing is all about.

The other focus of my first semester was "Guest Writer"—a whole class on one living author, the essayist Annie Dillard. My parents rolled their eyes at spending tuition money on this indulgence, but gave in. The class was in a huge, raked lecture hall, with a hundred or so students. Dillard didn't arrive until the last week of the semester—a disappointing discovery. In the meantime, the professor made us read everything she wrote, a slew of Emersonian, radiant thoughts on nature. I remember one where an eagle grips its prey in its talons, taking off, and how it was a metaphor for grabbing moments of life, moments of experience, and how loss and violence and destruction were part of the way you held on to time.

The professor lectured on these essays, and opened the floor for milquetoast discussion—always the same vocal students, speaking a language I didn't quite get. The only assignments were to keep a journal of our reading and, at the end of the semester, produce an original creative piece. Dillard's prose was a complicated influence. It was ecstatic. I racked my brain for something to be ecstatic about. I mean, I guess there was music—but couldn't I think of something else? At last I fell back on one of my favorite, perennial, comforting themes: death. A girl had committed suicide in my high school the previous year; I'd cried at her funeral; I would "meditate on" that, somehow.

The class was too large for workshopping; there was no one to stop me or question my choices. I assembled a few momentous epigraphs to sit at the beginning of my eight pages, as if I were writing a vast novel, then hurled every cliché I could find at mortality:

The normal social life of the high school stagnated; moral barriers, once fallen into dust, re-arrayed themselves in all their glory. Gossip, once free-flowing, ran dry. The coffin which we had all piled our personal dirt upon seemed to be lying, uncovered, in the middle of the main hall . . .

But I was just getting started:

Death did not seem that close; it seemed far away, like the mountains on the horizon.

A devastatingly original simile! Followed by the big wrap-up:

When our poor English teacher took out the binoculars and said "Here, look" we ripped out our eyes like Oedipus so as not to see.

Next to which my professor wrote: ". . . a bit much?" At the end of my piece he wrote some kind words and an A minus. I'd poured all my emotions into this thing, and that was all I got? Maybe I wasn't a writer. A relief, in a way: I could cross off one possible life path.

⸲

After a few weeks of hitting the "Appassionata" first movement hard, Joe asked me to start the second. I opened the music in my practice room. On the page, it looked innocent: a hymn, one basic chord after another. I felt this was a scam. You often encounter a boundary in Beethoven, when he prunes music to the fundamentals: you think he's gone too far, but then you realize he hasn't. I hadn't evolved to that second stage. I was more than willing to call out Beethoven for being a hack.

My lesson rolled around. After I played the theme and one variation, Joe said, "What's going on? What happened to you?"

A bad comment—maybe one of the worst. I decided to confess. I told Joe I thought the piece was boring, even a bit cheesy. Joe didn't order me out of the studio, or lecture me on how this is one of

Beethoven's holiest visions, inhabiting a space between childlike wonder and deep reverence. He gave me the look that Jerry Seinfeld gives
George Costanza when George proposes some new morally vacant
scheme, and then shook it off with a sigh, and decided there was nothing else to do but approach the problem practically. God, what I
wouldn't have given for something impractical, I was so tired of sighs
and rolled-up sleeves.

"OK, Jeremy, let's start with the tempo," he said. "It sounds glib."

He made me start again, a little slower, with the idea that I would
listen to the chords and receive their reverence. I tried, but I always
hated the feeling of a leash. As the tempo got slower, the piece con-
gealed into tedium, partly because I wanted to show Joe he was wrong
to hold me back.

"OK, OK, now it's too slow," Joe said, trying to calibrate, his patience
beginning to fray, "give it a little direction." *Which is it?* I wondered. As
I got faster I began to glimpse something in the distance that might be
a phrase. But Joe interrupted me just when I was getting going. *Wouldn't
someone just let me play?* I thought, forgetting the whole point of piano
lessons.

"Follow the bass line," he said, "and make sure the dotted rhythms
are right." I was familiar with this critique—but why were these weird,
jerky rhythms infecting this simple procession of chords in the first
place? That was perverse; it didn't fit. Was it a march or a hymn? Little
did I realize how close I was to Beethoven's secret, to the curious genius
of this movement—the way serenity and solemnity combined with
play.

Finally Joe said, "Maybe you should listen to some recordings." Joe
rarely demonstrated: sometimes a chord or two, maybe a phrase. This
seems like a missing piece of the puzzle, in retrospect. Joe was a great
pianist, with a gorgeous, Romantic, pillowy sound—what made him
not want to touch the keys? Maybe he thought demonstrating was a
cop-out, or maybe it was fear—but I suspect, for dark reasons I'll never
quite know, that at that juncture in his life playing the piano didn't
bring him pleasure.

Off I went to the listening carrel, one of my favorite places in Oberlin. I picked out Daniel Barenboim, who seemed like an authoritative person to consult, someone who would know how to play very serious Beethoven slow movements very seriously. I marked up my music in detail: every dynamic nuance from the record, every timing. I would nail down the feeling using the scientific method.

At the next lesson, Joe asked again, same as the week before, "What happened to you?"

"I'm playing it like Barenboim!" I replied.

He grabbed the music, saw my obsessive markings, and looked at me with new, sad eyes. What I'd done was diligent but hopeless, like taking dictation when you don't know the meaning of any of the words. "Let's leave it for now," he said.

}

The first semester climaxed with a battery of tests and late-night dorm snacks. I aced organic chemistry, and you'd have to commit a felony to get below an A in piano. I had survived. A brief break with the parents, an interlude of profound annoyance and nonstop sunshine, two rounds of McDonald's in DFW Airport, a pensive late-night shuttle through Cleveland's snowy suburbs, and I was back again in my dorm, my own, rapidly morphing person.

The second semester had a different spirit. A lot of this was because of Romantic to Modern Poetry, my English elective, with a gentle professor named David Walker. Only fifteen students were enrolled. We sat in a tiny circle and discussed. Lack of preparation was obvious. David's gentleness was just an outer layer; behind it was strength and taste. He was in his mid-thirties, with fine reddish-brown hair, fair skin, thin-rimmed urbane glasses, and a voice that often stood at the boundary of the inaudible, which he never raised to grab attention or steal the mic. His questions felt like X-rays, trying to see if ideas had good bones. He'd ask you what you thought about a word, a word that seemed innocent, and then he'd inquire (gently) about how it interacted with the next word. Was there a conflict? Yes, maybe there was. I began to suspect all the more complex words, if he found ambiguity in the simplest ones.

David assigned short papers, due every other Monday. I lived those assignments. The world and the piano went away, while I did battle with ideas. I concocted thesis statements using my high school English teacher's recipe—three prongs—creating three paragraphs of content like a factory puts out ready-to-assemble parts. But what if there was nothing to say? My first paper began:

Much of Wordsworth's work concerns his relationship with nature . . .

In the margin, David wrote:

Great start Jeremy! This is really more a paraphrase of the poem's central idea than a very original or provocative argument about it . . .

His verdict was always handwritten in a neat, long paragraph, where he told you what you'd achieved while at the same time explaining—sympathetically—that in the real world, it was pretty much meaningless.

I got a mediocre grade on that Wordsworth paper. I wasn't sure if I got Wordsworth, any more than I got Beethoven's hymn—it seemed like a lot of "nature is beautiful," and did that really need to be said? I went to David's office to talk this crisis through. The English hallway had an unfamiliar hush. His office had bookshelves everywhere, a desk crammed in, one porthole window: real estate was stingier in the humanities.

I told him about how I was used to writing papers. And how my high school teachers had always said my writing was so excellent. I needed him to tell me the new rules, what was required to make him happy. He could tell I was upset. He thought for a minute, then said, "Jeremy, I think you are capable of being far more creative. Don't settle for your first thoughts. Or the obvious ones."

Two weeks later, racing through the nineteenth century, we came to Emily Dickinson. I kept reading over the poems in the anthology, and either they didn't move me or I didn't understand them. At last I chose one that seemed ripe with symbolism, and concocted an allegorical interpretation. I loved analyses where all the meaning got wrapped in a neat bow. This time, David's comments were even worse: "Do you really think this is the way the poem feels? Or is it more like . . ." I don't recall David's alternative, but I do remember how the word "really" struck me, an innocuous thunderbolt.

I sat in my desk chair, thinking *Really*. He was right: my allegory wasn't it. And a paper didn't have to be a game for a grade, or for David's praise. It had a higher purpose: to search after poetic reality. And what was that? For days, I walked around frigid Oberlin trying to get my head around that question, feeling a puzzle element and a freer other thing, which seemed like a gateway opening between my solitary scholastic side and the wider, more normal and feeling world. That was the first time I encountered the idea of honesty in relation to a work of art. A truth that was difficult to find, a hard-won reward, the real goal of study and practice. I didn't know it yet, but in English class I got my most important music lesson.

I cornered David after the next session.

"David, I just want to say I totally get it," I said. "That comment changed my life. I can't believe I was so stupid. Thank you."

David seemed at first pleased, then taken aback by my conversion, which had some residual teacher's pet kiss-ass floating around it. "Jeremy," he said, "it wasn't that bad. You're a good writer. And a smart young man. Just make sure you're always checking back in with the specific words, and with the author's intent." *Yes, yes*, I thought, already impatient, since I now knew everything that David had shown me, and his wisdom had made me invincible.

❧

Spring semester, my social life began showing signs of improvement. Around the beginning of February, during a typical aimless hangout, tall and funny Pete (who'd been through three girlfriends in five months) turned to me and said: "You were a real pain at first, but now you're pretty cool." The rest of the room chimed in, a chorus of agreement. I thought back with shame at how horrible I must have been, but on the other hand I was thrilled to be tolerable at last.

Polly and I were still close. She also thought I'd improved, but not much. My scrupulous chemistry devotion mystified her. She said I had to think about my priorities. Did I really want to live this way? She continued her musical lectures, now in the form of occasional mixtapes, while I tried not to surrender to her other charms.

We weren't dating, officially. But I'm not sure I would have survived that year without her. We went to see Woody Allen's *Love and Death* in the campus movie series, which was held in my chemistry lecture room, and I cried from laughter; she held my hand. Another night we went to the chapel to hear the Cleveland Orchestra play Beethoven's Seventh Symphony, and sat up in the balcony with all the other Conservatory students. Polly, like many students at the College, had a dim view of us "Connies." She thought we were mostly airheads or nerds, or both—never mind that this was impossible. The opening of the Beethoven destroyed me. Polly didn't think much of it, but she liked the look on my face. The oboe solo, of course—the legendary Cleveland Orchestra wind section—and behind it the timbre of the orchestra, the sound, the fullness and sense of polish all the way to its corners. Luminous in a mostly dark room. A source, a spring. How was it possible for a sound to be so beautiful and therefore, in itself, so meaningful? The Connies stomped thunderously when the piece was over, creating a fantastic din and sense of communal love in old Finney Chapel. A bunch of us musicians huddled backstage, trying to catch a glimpse of our professional idols, talking in elevated tones, and Polly got shunted to the side and felt excluded, and I felt bad for her, and torn, but not enough to do anything about it.

}

To Joe's great annoyance, we were still slogging our way through Beethoven's "Appassionata." Too many distractions, he said. But at last I managed to learn the final movement. I had a native ability to surge through its arpeggios, and shape the restless waves. There was just one major stumbling block: a place in the middle where the two hands had an intricate, tangled dialogue.

Joe asked: "What's the problem?"

No, you tell me, I thought. *You're the teacher.* I played it again, thinking I'd magically make it better, and yet un-magically it was the same.

"Well, Jeremy," he said, blinking behind his glasses, "why don't you just play the hands at the same time?"

I wasn't sure how to apply such obvious advice.

He explained: "Make sure every note in the right hand is together with one in the left." And that idea of matching thing with thing unlocked the problem. It placed my brain somehow between the hands. Maybe Joe was on to something! He had a funny look on his face, not quite interpretable.

The coda also gave me some trouble: I got going, ramping up my excitement, until there was nothing left of the tempo but a smoking ruin. It was impossible to continue for long if you were always catching up with the snowballing terror of the last few notes you played. Joe laughed and said I would get it someday. That seemed to be that, all appeared to be fine, we were laughing together—but then, a minute later, he seemed annoyed that I wouldn't even try to restrain the onrush. He said "Don't be ridiculous," with an edge in his voice. I often wished Joe would give more vivid opinions, but then—like at this moment— some boundary was crossed. He became unaccountably mean. The goodness in him couldn't hold out, and my fear of when the darkness would unpredictably arrive reminded me of long-ago afternoons in New Jersey, when nothing you did could be right.

Our other ongoing project was Schumann's Toccata. Schumann declared with pride that it was the "hardest piece ever written." I knew it was difficult, yes, but because of all my horrible summers of technique with Bill, I could do octaves at a good speed, and much of the rest of the piece almost played itself. Joe felt if it wasn't broken, he wouldn't fix it. He kept saying "Yes, that sounds all right" and tweaking things, but there was none of the intractable quicksand from our work with Beethoven.

In fact, my most vivid memory of working on that piece was in the practice room, one peevish early-spring day. I was trying to deal with a place where the hands had to move from one task to another, staring out the window through the parking lot at Lorenzo's Pizza, when my dad knocked on the door behind my back, giving me quite a shock. This was typical of my vagueness. I knew that he was planning to visit, but I didn't really have a solid notion of when or where we would meet, or what we would do.

I think Mom had finally persuaded him to worry about my emotional survival among all the older kids. My father came in, said "Hello, stranger," and smiled. "Hi," I said, "oh you're here." He confessed to me that he'd been watching me for a while, and for a few seconds his expression was tender, nostalgic, even doting. I felt this collision of worlds was unwelcome. I felt his love, more than ever, but I no longer wanted it. It threatened something I had just begun to build. In any case, the bubble of tenderness evaporated. Dad switched to more familiar sarcastic greetings, making fun of my hair, which was admittedly pretty bad.

}

I never had spring fever in high school, though seniors were always talking about it (and something called "senioritis"), maybe because New Mexico didn't have winters. But that first year in Oberlin, it hit me hard. I was preparing for exams in a Scum study lounge with a guy named Bryan, an unusual Oberlin creature who looked like any old frat boy—with tight-fitting T-shirts and arm muscles and baseball caps—but spoke gently, with a vague twang, and loved to tease out several sides to any argument. He was one of the few people who took the time to be nice to me, and listened while I explained my geeky concerns.

Bryan's face was absorbed in his work, reading and unaware of being observed, a sight I still love; but meanwhile the windows were open and tons of students were sprawled out on the lawn with their shoes kicked off. I can still smell the breeze and hear it. Just a rustle, then a page turning. A moment with no musical notes. My organic chemistry book lay in front of me, and I was memorizing reactions out of habit, but it seemed to me that everywhere in Oberlin was an excitement, a sense of possibility mixed with fear, and an expectation of growth. The pieces I was working on didn't fit into any of it. The grand struggles of the "Appassionata" had nothing to do with me. Schumann's hormones were buried under finger-work. And when I looked down at my innocent page of chemistry, I knew that I hated it too.

The next day, I was passing through the music library carrels when a flutist I knew waved hello through an open door. He was listening to the Chopin *Berceuse*. I hooked up headphones, and had another moment. The calmness of the rocking motion—that alone. There were rich repeated D-flats in the bass, telling you where the measures were without heaviness, telling time without hurry, as the melody began to unfold in gorgeous spirals. If Beethoven was always questing forward, looking to resolve or solve or whatever, Chopin was content to lie in the sun and be. Yes, I thought, that was something essential in piano playing, that intimacy, that simplicity—the sensual sound as much as anything else—and at the same time I connected it to some of what I realized were my happiest moments at Oberlin, moments of new vulnerability, when David explained I was wrong about a poem, or when Polly tested my limits, or when I was sitting with Bryan in that study room.

Without consulting Joe, I started work on the *Berceuse*. I felt it was going fantastically, because I was loving playing it. Those practice days still stick in my mind. The joy of letting my hand wind through whorls and loops. The iterative process: fingerings first, then stumbles, then your first taste of ease. It felt good enough that I thought I'd bring it in for a lesson. I bounded the stairs up to his studio, hoping to show Joe that I wasn't the person he thought I was.

After I played, he just laughed, and then his voice changed and he said it was "unbelievably terrible." How was it possible that I was able to play so many other things, and then fail to feel a lullaby? I was devastated. In my mind it was so beautiful. Joe didn't even try to fix it. He thought I should abandon the piece since it didn't suit me, like a piece of clothing. And at that moment I began to feel we weren't on the same side.

෫

I played the Schumann Toccata in my freshman jury, and got lucky. My muscles flowed without panic. For seven minutes I was the master of myself. Then they asked me to play the "Appassionata"; it went just OK, I think, but at that point I didn't care. Then I joined the rest of the freshmen in the lounge, waiting for word from our teachers. Joe came out of the mysterious conference and said I played well; he smiled and left. But then other information arrived: another faculty member said it was funny watching the jury listen to me, because none of them could play the Schumann as well as I could.

I was just digesting this information (which made me insufferable for such a long time) when the official comment sheets came out. Frances Walker—the teacher of the first pianist I'd met at Oberlin—wrote, "Perhaps you should pay a little attention to what the composer is trying to say." I shrugged it off as sour grapes. I mean, I was better than the faculty, and she dared to think I wasn't paying attention to the composer? It was impossible for me to receive compliments and criticism at the same time.

After this little burst of not-quite-self-awareness, I remember two essential concluding events of my first year of college. The first was with the flutist who played me the *Berceuse*. We were rehearsing something for his jury, he said "Jeremy, you're amazing," and somehow that was the deciding vote of confidence, the moment I decided in my heart that I would make my living as a musician.

The second was that Polly came by on the last afternoon. She hadn't lost hope. She said, "I can help you pack . . ." I stuffed my belongings in boxes while she described various dreams for her summer. Then her gaze fell on my organic chemistry visualization set, a bunch of spheres and polygons with little connector pegs.

She grabbed a few atoms from the box, and set about trying to assemble some sort of artistic molecule. Not every combination assembled; that was the lesson of the set. But she wouldn't accept those limitations. I remember watching her bend a peg, to force it into a forbidden hole, when *snap*, it broke. She started laughing hysterically. But I lost it. God, the storm of metaphors and anxieties that unleashed, my sense that she would break me, all her mockery of my studies, her belief that I needed to abandon some or all of that to become the person I needed to be, the sense that we were playing with life, with each other's lives.

We had a huge spat. She just got up and walked out. I thought I would not see her until the fall. But later in the day she came back to not really apologize. I'd acquired what in my mind passed for perspective. It was just a chemistry set, after all. We talked, then lay down on the bed, and stopped talking. We just lay there, a molecule minus a bond, hoping one or the other would make a move, and neither of us did; and then the next day, still remembering and regretting and wondering, realizing I'd wasted the most obvious of opportunities, I flew back to what no longer felt like home.

{

When I landed in El Paso, my parents took me for nachos in a pub by the airport, a block from the highway on-ramp—a long-standing and convenient tradition. While I was happily ingesting a heart attack's worth of trans fats, they let slip that the money for the fall semester wasn't certain. I might not be able to return to where I'd just left. New Mexico was a sprung trap.

Everything was still being decided and figured, they said. In the meantime I needed to learn responsibility. They had set up a summer job for me—with my benefactor Bruce Streett. What would I be doing? I asked. Data entry, they said. I didn't know what that was. I was to report to Bruce at the New Mexico State University Development Office. I had a few days' reprieve, which I lazed away.

Summers in Las Cruces are hypnotically hot. The sun-baked days keep coming with almost no variation, just strings of white clouds here and there, traveling from one arid mountain range to another, sometimes getting stuck and rattling around a peak for a while, and turning darker. There are strange dangers: returning to your parked car, you burn the crap out of yourself on your seatbelt buckle, the shiny metal leaving a bright red welt. "Jesus!" I'd say every time it happened—not the fastest learner.

Every morning, I drove over to the university with my father at eight, when the day still seemed livable, entered a maze of cubicles, and wound down a dark flight of stairs to the basement. My desk was a temporary add-on in a corner of what appeared to be a closet. My task was simple and numbing: to enter decades of old donations into a database. I was a pretty fast typist. I'd enter a month's worth of receipts at top speed and wait while the accountant double-checked my figures. I brought along a book for these waiting periods, to demonstrate I couldn't be bothered to waste time: *War and Peace*. I thought it was surprisingly good. I snacked on sugar cubes and vending machine Coke.

At 3:00 p.m., my so-called work done, I'd walk to the music building and enter one of its space-age practice pods. The music building was abandoned in summer. Silence reigned, made deeper and sadder by soundproofing. You had to practice with your back to a glass door, which made a tiny sucking sound as it closed you in. I kept imagining people sneaking up on me, as in a horror movie. Those hours were excruciating, and yet—I had to tell myself—it was the only time of the day when I was doing what I wanted to be doing.

I'd do lackluster work on those upright pianos—data entry left my brain fried, like a video game minus all the excitement and sense of accomplishment—then head back home for dinner with my parents. Dishes, TV, bed, rinse, repeat. Chores were required, "as long as you're living under our roof"; childhood had me back in its grasp, and not in a Proustian way.

I began to fall apart. First, an odd pause while eating. I would try to take a bite, and feel like my throat was closing of its own accord. A little nausea, a tickle. This caused me to pay attention to the act of swallowing, which—now that I thought about it—maybe I had never properly mastered. This small curiosity grew into a tremendous worry. Was it possible I had escaped my parents and gone off to college, only to die of starvation?

The eating problem escalated into a sleeping problem. I'd read Tolstoy till 3:00 a.m., checking in with my oversized alarm clock, then wander out to the kitchen to sit at the empty table, where I'd invent conversations with imaginary parents where I told them all my concerns and resentments, and they attentively listened. Sometimes I'd encounter my actual dad just getting up for his morning jog, doing his huffing, puffing warm-ups. I'd head back to my bedroom, snatch a couple hours' sleep, then be awakened by my father (now back from his run) just in time for a bowl of Froot Loops and a drive to work.

By late July, I couldn't eat much except sugar cubes. I was hyper-emotional but unwilling to talk to anyone. Instead, I had internal negotiations with Fate. I kept thinking I would give anything, anything in the world to return to Oberlin and do things with Polly. I began to skip practicing, because the silence was too concentrated. What was the point, if my life was over? Instead, in the late afternoons, I'd walk over to the library, where silence was at least communal.

One night, I sat down to dinner with my parents, stared at an unwanted plate of food, and had a flashback to a moment after my big competition loss in Albuquerque. The memory suggested a solution. I took a deep slow breath, then let it all out. I did it once more. Amazingly, the nausea retreated. *Good God.* I snorted a small laugh that my parents ignored. What an idiot. All summer, without noticing, I had been holding my breath, a bit more each day—holding out against uncertainty and solitude. As I reminded myself to breathe, my body remembered how to live. I overslept. I overate. I was groggy, bloated, and relieved. A week or so later, life exhaled too. The money was found; I would return to Oberlin in the fall.

8. *Melody* LESSON ONE

PLAYLIST

‖ BRAHMS: Trio in B Major, op. 8, first movement
‖ BEETHOVEN: Quartet in C-sharp Minor, op. 131, first movement

When I decided to write a chapter (or two or three) about melody, I had doubts. The topic was both obvious and slippery, like, say, a well-oiled dog that you try to grab but which slides through your hands and runs off barking with delight, causing everyone around you to laugh. It would be extra-humiliating to fail to say something interesting about melodies—the part of music that everyone knows and loves, and (maybe most important) remembers.

I consulted musical friends, who not only failed to allay my concerns, but even amplified them. For instance, the following response:

> Melody is so simple. It just flows. It can be dissected but doesn't need to be, right? Humming a tune is something most people can do. But rhythm, harmony, structure, pitch etc., those need to be studied for sure. My one thought!

This felt like wisdom. Melody is music's most pure, innocent gift. Why cloud it with thought? And yet it seemed to me that, because of all these good reasons, important things about melodies rarely get said.

⅜

If you forced me at gunpoint to pick a favorite tune, I would choose the beginning of Brahms's first Piano Trio, op. 8, in B Major. I first heard and played it at age fourteen, and in my mind it still lives there, thinking fourteen-year-old thoughts. Brahms begins this tune in the piano, in its richest, most chocolaty register—what's called the tenor. The melody launches from a low preamble note, then climbs, one note at a time. For the first few notes, it's just a major scale, nothing memorable. But then Brahms decides to skip one note. This act is crucial and defining: the melody acquires identity and purpose.

One skipped note—no big deal. You might say I'm making a mountain out of a molehill: a cutting and fitting indictment, if it weren't for the fact that melody is the greatest device ever invented for converting molehills into mountains. It's a stage where details are destined to become momentous. You understand this skipped note is important because Brahms immediately returns to the note he left behind. The gap he's created must be addressed. I'm trying to describe this in analytical language, so that musicologists won't roll their eyes at me, but meanwhile it tugs at my heart. I feel the need created by the act of skipping over—the sense of a loss in the line, the pleasure of filling it in and completing the past. It mirrors so many moments and patterns of so-called real life.

What's more, Brahms's act of skipping and returning creates a group of three notes, which I'd call a musical "love triangle" . . .

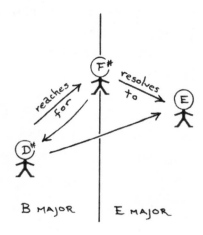

B MAJOR   E MAJOR

You often find this star-crossed trio in music. The first note belongs to one chord; the third note belongs to another chord. But the middle note belongs in a way to neither: it looks back to the first harmony, like Orpheus to Eurydice, but is desperate to resolve to the second. It is torn. Its purpose is to be torn. This is the center of Brahms's melody, its motivating idea—even, if you're feeling poetic, its soul.

One could easily rewrite this passage so that the melody would neither skip nor return. It would ascend straight to the E. In that case the magical high note would never appear:

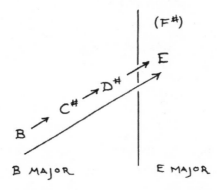

This is efficient: if we don't lose the line, we don't need to return to it. But the melody becomes pointless, all of its yearning gone. Melody, among its many virtues, affirms the necessity of the unnecessary.

ʒ

Around the same time that I learned Brahms's B Major Trio, I had another vivid first encounter. I was at my desk studying, in my tiny rectangular bedroom. The radio was on. I'd procrastinated away the afternoon. My mountain-postcard window revealed only a featureless desert night. In the middle of puzzling out a geometry proof, I heard the announcer say "And now we will hear the great late Beethoven Quartet in C-sharp Minor, op. 131, which begins with a famous fugue that Hector Berlioz described as 'the most terrifying beginning in all of music.'" I was up from my desk in a flash, stuffing one of many blank cassette tapes in my boom box—just fast enough to catch the opening measures, which did indeed kick ass, I thought. The next day I lent the tape to my cellist friend Larry. Soon, it was our mutual favorite piece. For his birthday I had custom sweatshirts made, so we could wear matching socially damaging outfits, and on the fronts I had printed the terrifying opening of op. 131: one of the geekiest things I've ever done, and maybe also one of the sweetest.

Opus 131 begins with the violin alone. The violin plays one note and then immediately skips up two notes. (An odd way to set out on a journey: your first act is to leave something behind.) For one more note, the violin continues rising:

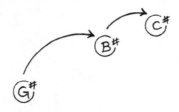

But then something happens—an awareness?—and the violin returns to the note we skipped, to hear the thing we didn't hear. (By this point, of course, Beethoven is mostly hearing things he can no longer hear.)

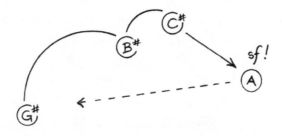

Beethoven puts a *sforzando* on this returned-to note: his most important form of emphasis, an accent that is more than an accent, with a vast range of meanings. In the Brahms you feel the return to the skipped note is a kind of release, a breathing-out. But in the Beethoven it feels like it has weight—what you might call the weight of sorrow, mixed with some shock. The note rearranges the previous notes around it, in the same way that when you confront a grief or a loss it changes your valuation of the ordinary things in life. At fourteen, I hadn't had much grief or loss, I didn't think, and yet this note, this A, played heavily, almost violently, rang me like a bell. Like a bell, I suppose, it created the sense that some part of me (or of life more generally) was hollow. It reminded me of any number of empty moments, either sitting alone in my room, or in a desk at school feeling no connection to my classmates, or staring across the dinner table feeling at once way too much and too little connection to my parents. And yet that Beethoven-induced sensation was so intense and distilled that I found it cool, excellent, bracing, with the result that I felt better about emptiness, and more willing to face it.

The message of the late, lost Beethoven fugue subject couldn't be more different than that of the youthful Brahms Trio. But both rely on the same elemental melodic power—a few connected notes, and one absent note. The sense of a void, and the desperate need to fill it.

}

I was recently picnicking in New York's Riverside Park with a couple of gifted musician friends—cellist Mike, violinist Stefan. Stefan was playing the Brahms B Major Trio for the first time. "It's so great," he said, not knowing or caring that in current musicological circles the word "great" is now suspect.

I mentioned that I was writing about that same piece, in a sort-of-essay on melody.

Stefan said, "Oh yeah? So what are you saying?"

I was preparing to pretend that I already knew what the point of my essay was, when—stroke of luck!—Mike interrupted to ask, "Is it a piano melody or a cello melody?" (Just the sort of a thing a cellist would ask.) Relieved, I exclaimed, "Exactly!" One of the most important events in this melody is that the cello interrupts the piano. You could say the cello "joins in," but it then sails up to a note so ravishing—an A-sharp, to be precise—that it makes you wonder if it ever was a piano melody at all.

But here's the catch: this new note is not new. In fact, we've already heard the entire cello melody; we just didn't know it. While the piano was playing its tune, down in the middle voices there was a hidden twin-tune, shadowing the top voice, following it up and down:

This is one of melody's superpowers: to run in parallel with itself, like train tracks. The composer can shift from one track to another, from one voice to another "equivalent" voice. This sounds mathematical, but can be ecstatic. In the Brahms, you can't just say that the cello continues the tune. It does something far better—it discovers what was hidden. It waves a magic wand, and inner becomes outer. While Beethoven's fugue burrows back into its losses, this melody opens itself up, to reveal beauties within.

What's more, these two parallel melody lines don't just talk between themselves. They recall thousands of pieces you've already heard: Viennese tunes, waltzes, sentimental love duets, in fact anything with two singers crooning together, "singing harmony." This specific melody plays on the wider world of Melody like an instrument; it manages to be original while footnoting like mad. All this calls to mind a wonderful quote of Robert Schumann's: "In order to compose, all you need to do is remember a tune no one has thought of."

Since that picnic with Mike and Stefan, I keep returning to this nexus between melody and memory. Yes, we love to remember melodies— they're often the only thing we retain from an hour-long symphony. But melodies also love to remember themselves. For instance, in the first ten seconds of the Brahms, we already have several layers of recollection:

1) the cello recalls the inner voice of the piano
2) both instruments recall all kinds of other music
3) the melody keeps remembering notes it left behind

This is far more seamless than the "flashbacks" that novelists or screenwriters use. I recall a party in L.A. some years ago, where I was staring out a big pane of glass onto a pool and recovering from the sense of having played a concert that was less good than the audience seemed to think it was, when a tan writer came over to congratulate me. To stop his relentless questions about music I asked, "What did you do today?" And he said, with handsome weariness, "Oh, just backpiping." When I confessed I didn't know what that was, he explained that he'd gone through a script to put in all the stuff the audience should already have known. These moments in scripts are awkward and thankless. You have to create ham-fisted pretexts to fill in backstory. But for the most part, melody glides effortlessly over these narrative problems, because it has backpiping built in. Melody rewinds the clock without wasting time.

In the Brahms Trio, the opening bit of melody ends with a beautiful falling pair of notes:

The second bit lands on another falling pair: this pair's a bit lower, and wider.

A pair of pairs, a dialogue of descents. The second fall calls back to the first, both similar and different. Melodies are packed to the gills with such hyperlinks: a stream of connections, of compare-and-contrasts.

After just a bit of diva-cellist intervention, we've visited *four* pairs of falling notes:

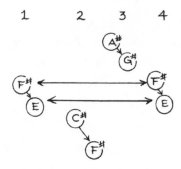

As you listen, this quartet of gestures—how can I put this?—dance against each other in the mind. Like a family, or a group of friends, talking back and forth. Each pair can be contemplated alone, but their meanings depend on interconnection.

I used the term "hyperlink"—but I think I prefer the old-fashioned word "rhyme" for what these bits of music do to each other. Instead of a coincidence of sound—as often in poetry—musical rhymes have more to do with meaning, like events and coincidences that rhyme in the course of your life. They make you remember the last event that happened, while at the same time they act on it. It seems to me that one of melody's (and by association music's) most central virtues is this merging of memory and action in a single gesture.

Look once more at the diagram above: the last pair of notes is the same as the first. This is no coincidence. As they rhyme and graze over notes they visited before, melodies cultivate an affection for notes within them. You get attached to these notes in the way you get attached to ideas, places, or people, except that you wouldn't want to pin it down: those notes are pure affection, love divorced from the necessity of a specific object. An affection we crave, or we need to be reminded of, that somewhere and somehow we hope to reattach to reality.

9. *Motivations, Pure and Otherwise*

PLAYLIST

SCHUMANN: *Symphonic Études,* op. 13
MICHAEL DAUGHERTY: *Snap!*
SHOSTAKOVICH: Cello Sonata in D Minor, op. 40
BRAHMS: Cello Sonata in F Major, op. 99, first movement

In late August, Oberlin looked the same, but I'd nearly died, or so I felt, and I was determined to live. I had two big acquisitions from the desperate summer: Schumann's *Symphonic Études,* and a plan to obtain my first kiss.

There are many passages in music where it's clear that the harmony must resolve, and yet in the meantime the perverse composer writes every other note than the one you need. Sophomore existence had lots of new notes. My suite-mates were all heavy pot smokers from Scum—this felt less charming, close up. Inorganic chemistry was far more finicky and precise. I had to take Music History 101, which began with dozens of hours of listening to medieval music and learning to recognize the difference between 1250 and 1350. A guy named Peter was also in the survey. After an hour or two of Machaut, he insisted I come to his room—he had something important to discuss. He pulled up a chair very close to mine and told me he might be gay and asked if I'd like to experiment. He was friendly but urgent. I was horrified. He said, "I'm here if you change your mind," while I tried to politely flee the room—it took me a few days to calm down. And then when I played the Schumann in my lesson, Joe said, "Oh wow." Fear of death and the lack of anything else to do had, it turned out, been great for my piano playing. He wanted to leap into this exciting project—a lot to do, details to refine.

So it took far longer than I'd hoped to address the emergency of my virginal lips. A few weeks went by. When I finally came by Polly's room she wondered why I was so eager, after a year of dawdling. She insisted on discussions of what our feelings "meant," what we each wanted. We re-narrated our lives. I explained my dad's sarcasm, and my mom's alcoholism—all of this seemed a natural and reasonable part of Oberlin courtship. At last, when she got tired of hearing me form circular sentences, we made out. The thing I'd craved was darker than I thought it would be. So many layers of defense scratched away, so much opening of things I preferred closed. I stared at the clock on her dresser just like I'd stared at my childhood clock in New Mexico, and wondered what I was supposed to do. After a couple sleepless hours I snuck out and crossed campus, back to my smoky room.

The very next day, a thunderbolt. I got a B on my inorganic chemistry test:

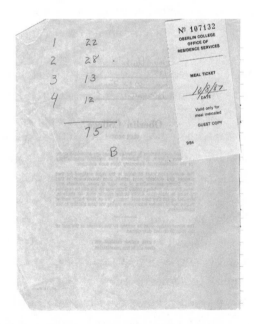

Which had almost never happened before. It was fine to get an A minus in creative writing, a class for fun, but the sciences were my strong suit and my backup life. I hadn't received a B since elementary school. I was losing my overachiever cred quickly, and not on my own terms. That afternoon, a witty but reproachful letter arrived from my father:

October 2, 1987

Dear Jeremy and Broad:

While I should not be the one to complain, given my writing habits of the past month or so, nevertheless I am the one to suggest the fact that there must be a broad in your life - what else could cause long hiatus'es in communication? I don't mean Lisa Pierce, the Jenny Lind of Ohio. I mean some regular cafeteria-swilling broad who entraps young, budding musicians and forces them into a life of holding hands in a quad somewhere on earth. Practicing so much, my deriere (spell-checker has no French, scusa!)!

It is amazing to see all Dad's rampant sexism (a broth I grew up drinking, without knowing), but he was trying to be charming, I think, or he was desperate for proof that I wasn't gay. Anyway, the timing freaked me out. I read the letter in the mailroom, and there was something about his preternatural way of knowing, exactly on the day that I'd lost it all. My dad was right, I was going to ruin my life for a girl, a fear piled on top of the unbelievable horribleness of parents being right about anything.

I made a mature decision to vanish into work. If Polly came by my room, I wouldn't be there. I'd be in the chemistry library, or if she was too persistent I'd flee to dark recesses of the main library, to research an English paper, or to a different dining hall. She knew something had spooked me—maybe just normal male emotional stunting. She was patient; she left me notes, letters, amusing gifts, but I ignored them all.

At last Polly tracked me down one night, in one of the coveted double piano rooms. Her face appeared at the door. She didn't bother to knock, and punched my shoulder hard on her way to the window alcove, where she sat on top of the heater vent. I remained on the piano chair, facing the piano. Occasionally I'd be brave enough to turn and look at her—behind her head, through the window, I could see all these other students working away, doing the things they needed to do, their bows sliding back and forth, making invisible sounds. Finally I managed to confess to her about the B, and all that was expected of me. "Oh Lord, a B," she said. She was amused and hurt and withering. She told me I would be unhappy. Then she realized I wasn't really paying attention anymore, and she left me alone with Schumann.

⁂

Joe nominated me to play the *Symphonic Études* in an Honors Recital, an important prize for younger Conservatory students. A vote of confidence! Then, for a few weeks, he hounded me. He seemed younger, and I felt older. We worked on the notorious chordal variation, how to use my wrist and arm for ease and relaxation. Technique for survival. Elegance of motion as a way to avoid exhaustion. Joe was a master of elegant motion, and in that period I had enough patience to listen to his advice.

The theme of the piece is somber—his beloved Clara's nobility and poise. But the first variation has Robert's mercurial, mischievous spirit, which Joe encouraged—"Yes, that's perfect." But when I got to the big finale, a joyous march that keeps going on and on in Schumann's manic way, pouring itself out, Joe obsessed about making the rhythms crisper, so that the structure of the whole piece, and all our work together, wouldn't collapse from last-minute laziness.

Just before the finale is the most shattering variation, the one that feels like "real Schumann," after all the fantastical visions at last showing us his heart. The melody is haunted by a quintuplet pulling against the four beats of the measure, refusing to let its notes be confined. Joe

kept saying "Sing!" which helped to a point, but only to a point. The feeling was so intense that I pressed with my pinky until its last tiny knuckle was sore, my fingertip numb. Then—danger out of nowhere—I'd miss a bass note, and my suspension of disbelief shattered, and my left hand could move only in fits and jerks. I was a dreaming poet one moment, and the next it was all I could do to survive.

I remember the performance night, the mood-lit hall with a smattering of listeners. I won over the fear, for that half hour. It went as it was supposed to go, including the impossible variations, the ones requiring every ounce of daring. Joe talked with me backstage for a while. He was as close as he got to beaming, the proud father, the sense that our time had not been wasted. Maybe I was a virtuoso. We both wanted our relationship to continue just like that. But I never saw him quite that happy with me again.

⁊

I've neglected to mention one more stress early that fall. The conductor Larry Rachleff came and found me in the lounge, while I was chatting with some other students. "Can we walk and talk for a minute?" My friends looked at me—*whoa*. As we paced down the corridor, Larry started selling me hard on his Contemporary Music Ensemble. "I'm assembling an elite squad," Larry said, as if it were *Mission: Impossible*. "I really need you to be a part of it." I asked Joe—he hated the idea. He warned me it would be too much work. Do you really like that music? he asked. I didn't know, but I accepted.

My first assignment for Larry was a monster, called *From the Dying Earth*, by a composer named Nicholas Thorne. The music was a rental, worn and wrinkled, even though the piece was supposedly new. It had a chaos of markings, signs other pianists had been there—like cave paintings, or cries for help—hash marks and lines and triangles and instructions to watch the conductor. Under all this graffiti, the page was covered with swirls of notes in unfathomable rhythms. At one place I saw the ratio 11:5, at another 17:13. How could one hand play thirteen while the other played seventeen? It seemed impossible that anyone could tell the difference, or that anyone needed to care, but Larry cared, and knew when I wasn't with his beat, in a way that seemed superhuman.

Nothing else about Larry felt superhuman. His posture drooped, his voice almost wheedled, and there was that odd red mustache. He had none of the from-a-distance charisma of a Great Conductor, or much close-up charisma either. But he sniffed out any discrepancy between what was written and what we were doing—he was a relentless musical bullshit detector. This was his power. Contemporary Music Ensemble was (I learned) a fear-based club. The main goal of rehearsal was surviving the hour and fifteen minutes without getting reamed. Larry wasn't about feelings, and especially wasn't about feeling good; there wasn't time for it. He cracked jokes constantly, not to cheer us up, but to prevent lapses of attention. His jokes always had an edge; they weren't the kind you'd tell at a wedding or on holiday; they were more like jokes you'd tell in the gulag, as winter approached.

He'd make people play alone, and critique and tease them in front of everyone, and despite all that we liked or maybe even loved him. We Conservatory students were awash in garbage ideas and judgments like young people everywhere, but we had an underlying imperative that the students at the College didn't. We wanted to sound good and play well. When we did, life was good, and when we didn't, life was terrible. It was as simple as that. And Larry knew how to make us sound better; he had the key to the one thing in life we all wanted the most.

After a week or two Larry said, "Jeremy, why don't we have a sectional in my office, just the two of us?" His face looked kind and casual but his voice had a nervous undertone. I went to his office, wondering what a "sectional" was, thinking of a scary visit long ago to the principal. Larry asked if I'd played much contemporary music, and I said, well, the stuff my teacher made me play. None of it was as good as *The Rite of Spring*. My "new music" for piano all felt dorky—Kabalevsky, Ginastera. Dissonant, but not too dissonant—like a person who adopts a few hip mannerisms that don't convince anyone.

"OK, lesson one," Larry said. "Let's do cross-rhythms." I already knew two against three from the Debussy Arabesques. So he started with three against four. Larry said to me, in a clipped monotone:

pass the god-damn butter

I said it back at him, slightly scandalized, and he said no—

PASS the GOD-damn BUTter

It was a delight to yell "goddamn" in a teacher's room. It was so rhythmic, whichever way you accented it. We yelled back and forth for a while, then moved on to the next logical fraction—5 against 3. Rhythm was just bodily math, I realized, and my inner geek started to ooh and aah with pleasure.

After forty-five minutes or so, Larry felt we were ready to look at actual music. He beat out a few of my Thorne rhythms with a pencil on the piano. I hated the sense of being rapped at. I'd never been to Catholic school, but it still reminded me of nuns and rulers and wrists. I played back at him with no enthusiasm.

Larry had great empathy, but he used it only to get us to play better—he didn't think it was wise to care too much about us otherwise. Sensing how much I hated the pencil, he got up from his chair and started to sing the written rhythms at me, with wild inflections, like an Ella Fitzgerald scat: "ska BA da pow ZA!!!" and then he waited a moment and did the next measure, "Be bop a DOO fa DOO." He seemed so white and persnickety that this eruption of jazz felt like a possession, a pastor speaking in tongues. I looked at him, hesitating to let loose and wanting to. Rhythm wasn't about letting loose, I'd thought; it was a matter of playing at the correct time. What was happening? For some reason, I thought of Polly, and her Elvis Costello poster.

Larry's rhythms were unlike any I'd heard from my piano teachers. His syncopations sounded like syncopations, and his beats like beats; they had an implicit character. Notes were either "with" or "against," before or after, anticipating or delaying, sly or emphatic—far more eloquent than a metronome. Metronomes knew a good deal about time, I realized, but nothing about rhythm. All my teachers had told me not to rush, and to play with the beat, but not one of them had given me an incentive—an urgent reason not to rush. None of them had shown me the alternative, the joys of strictness.

I saw Larry's idea. I felt and knew he was a great teacher. You traveled through the metronome. It wasn't a destination. Then came the quite different problem of making my fingers do it. I tried re-creating Larry's *ska BA da pow ZA*, but when I sent in my thumb for the first accent it waddled into the key—late and soft, but also somehow startled, like a sloth woken from a nap. If my thumb was a sloth, my fourth finger was a slug or maybe an amoeba, an organism without volition. As rhythm and expression folded into one thing, my body split in two: a brain that was willing and hands like the postal service, subject to inexplicable delays in delivery.

≀

A few weeks of rehearsing Thorne went by. Larry gave me fewer quizzical Spock eyebrows, and occasional praise. One day, after rehearsal ended, the cellist of the group padded over to my piano bench on bare feet—he walked around school like that until the first frost. He introduced himself as Darrett Adkins.

"Sounding good, Jeremy," he said. "I guess you learned how to count."

He'd just arrived in Oberlin from Tacoma, a year after me, but he was a year older, and decades more comfortable in his own skin. He was gifted, and all too aware of it. He was also alarmingly handsome: brown hair, blue eyes, cheekbones. A slight irregularity—a thinner-than-normal face—saved him from being the Boy Next Door.

Darrett was not popular with the other Contemporary Music Ensemble players. He constantly suggested things in rehearsal, interrupting Larry to say, "Hey, why don't we try another bowing" and at times even arguing with him—a dangerous, one would have thought even life-ending, maneuver. But Larry seemed to welcome a break from his endless day of telling people how to play better. One day, Darrett came to rehearsal in a kilt. Larry raised his baton, took a look around the room. "Darrett, my man," he said, "I sure hope you have underwear." It felt unfair, that freshman Darrett got away with all of it, and that Larry liked him.

A tradition began. Darrett and I had little discussions before and after Larry's rehearsals. We'd talk over a difficult passage, or something wry Larry had said, or whether the piece we were playing was worth it. At some point he shaved half his hair and dyed the rest purple, which reminded me of dangerous kids I'd avoided in high school. But even purple-haired he was as much of a music nerd as I was, maybe even nerdier. A discomfort, but also a fellow traveler. Part of Darrett was disaffected—an influence of the rainy Pacific Northwest, the wisdom of someone who grew up too fast. But this cynicism gave way without warning to a fierce idealism, where he affirmed that nothing mattered as much as whatever mattered to him at that moment. Most of all, he felt a continuous need to say what he thought, to declare what was good and what was bad. Many students feel that need, and teachers have to find a way not to kill them.

One afternoon I was half-heartedly practicing. Joe had assigned me a bunch of music to follow up on my Schumann success: the Barber sonata, some Rachmaninoff *Études-Tableaux*. Romantic and useful repertoire, maybe, but in my new incarnation it felt a little middle-of-the-road. I was thinking that these rhythms and harmonies were tame, after the Thorne. Too audience-pleasing. Darrett's grinning face appeared in my window. It was annoying how one misaligned tooth only seemed to improve his smile. He held up a little pile of music he'd gotten out of the library, for cello and piano. Would I like to do some reading?

If you're in a conservatory, I'd advise you not to get involved musically with people you have even the remotest sense you might be in love with, which can be filed under Advice No One Will Ever Take. We read through Brahms, Rachmaninoff, Grieg, Beethoven, whatever. Our sessions started out joyous and fun, with an edge of mutual showing-off, like the mating rituals of certain birds. They quickly devolved. Darrett was laser-sharp and had a fantastic ear and in no time figured out my pianistic weaknesses. He didn't bother to sugarcoat. Actually, he bitter-coated. He complained when I rushed, or played too loud, or used poor voicing. "Jeremy," he said, "whenever you get to a climax, you get too excited and the last few notes before the top get lost." *Yes, but why?* I wondered. Why did my fingers give out when I was giving them all I had?

I threw accusations back at him, while licking my wounds. I was especially delighted when he played out of tune, or ran out of bow. Once we'd exhausted reproaches, we would manage to play for a bit without saying a word, and almost against our will the pleasure of the music would come back, along with the reason we were friends.

Every so often, Darrett got tired of this frenemy dynamic, and would start talking about his teacher, Norman Fischer. "Norman," he'd say, his voice softening with adulation, "Norman could really help you with all your issues, Jeremy, I don't know how . . ." He seemed surprised to find himself referring to a higher authority. Darrett respected Larry, but felt I needed to learn something bigger. In a sense, it was nice that Darrett thought about what I needed, but also, who the hell did he think he was?

{

Joe Schwartz had been right to worry. Contemporary Music Ensemble became a massive obligation, leaving far less time for solo practice. Larry had us working toward a recording session in January—a step on the path to fame and fortune, I imagined. The disc was to feature new pieces by Oberlin faculty composers, including a young and promising recent arrival: Michael Daugherty. Daugherty's pieces all had poppy names like *Snap!* and *Blue Like an Orange,* which reminded me of cereals. He was famous for coming into our practice rooms, unannounced, to make us try some lick that he just wrote, to see if it sounded good. We all thought this was sketchy. Shouldn't a composer know what notes sounded like?

I'm not sure now if *Snap!* is the worst piece ever written, though it seemed a contender at the time. It was supposed to be zany and light, it seemed, a rebuke to dissonant, serious, rigorous new music. But despite its silliness it had an impossible beginning, a syncopated fugue, with "pass the god-damn butter" percolating through the ensemble. It sounded like a nightmare zoo, in which every instrument/animal was heard in its worst light: the oboe strained, the clarinet hooted, and (especially) the poor trumpet belched.

Because we were all trying to play against inaudible beats, no one could settle in. Against all this doubt, Larry kept preaching the religion of subdivision. He told us to concentrate and divide each beat into equal parts, and in the process find the perfect, preordained place for each of our discombobulated notes. (Later, in Bloomington, I heard the most passionate rebuttal gospel, an attack on subdivision as the end of spontaneity, from the mad-genius pianist Michel Block.) Everyone subdivided, frenetically, but it didn't sound much better. All this mass effort, this placing of notes on abstract points, felt pointless—*bleep-blurp-bleep*, like a nihilistic joke at the expense of our entire musical education.

Larry looked pained. His baton got jerkier, like his arms weren't lubricated, as if he were a malfunctioning robot. Exaggerating the click of the beats, he lost the sweeping motions in between. At last he stopped altogether, shook his head in disappointment, and yelled at himself: "Larry that's exactly what they tell you NEVER to do in conducting school, that's only going to make it worse, what kind of amateur hour are you running here . . ."

I looked over at Darrett, who smiled an evil smile. I didn't feel like smiling. After all the confidence Larry had given me, this felt like a betrayal.

≀

A few weeks later I was unlocking my bike to go cram for a musicology exam, when Darrett appeared, as he did mysteriously often, saying "Dude, you of all people don't need to study anymore." He then turned his mocking attention to my orange bike, a new purchase with NO-BODY'S FAULT painted in purple on the frame. "You're just jealous," I said. Was I mistaken or did this hit a nerve? In any case Darrett abandoned his mockery, as if it were nothing at all, and asked, "Hey, why don't we go for a ride?" It was that rare thing in Oberlin, a sunny day in February, with the deceitful promise of spring, and he felt I should really see some of the country around the town. He said I needed to escape the cocoon; it hadn't occurred to me it was a cocoon.

We left the four-block confines of campus and entered blank Midwestern roads, which didn't lead to places but just to other roads. Only Darrett knew where we were going. Time without a goal. We came to an unavoidable, broad, four-lane highway. I was insecure starting across, and Darrett coached me, without any hint of rehearsal critique, oddly patient, even parental. He laughed and told me to stop braking so much, and to let myself go down the hills.

That afternoon of speed and wind and sun changed things between us. I hadn't been sure if I hated him—but now it was clear that I didn't. I'd found someone who didn't mind my combination of insecurity and arrogance. So I agreed to play for him in his lessons, and to meet the legendary Norman.

We decided to start with the Shostakovich Cello Sonata. Or Darrett decided, probably. A cool piece, but the music often seemed too pretty. It posed trick questions. An idea would emerge like an actor in a spotlight, clothed in ravishing Hollywood harmonies, but then a dissonance appeared and you knew it was all a facade.

At the appointed hour we approached Norman's door. In the string side of the faculty hall, for some reason, students came and went, chattering about recent events. Just forty feet away—was this an illusion?—Joe's side of the hall looked dark and abandoned. Darrett knocked aggressively, a few big raps in a prearranged rhythm. The door swung open.

"Welcome!" Norman said.

"Nice to meet you, Professor Fischer," I said. Both Norman and the room exhaled halitosis and cologne. These smells seemed to amplify each other.

"Call me Norman," he said. "I've heard a lot about you. No kilt today?" he added, turning to Darrett, who had shed most of his clothing affectations.

"In the laundry," Darrett said. "Why aren't you wearing yours?"

Darrett and Norman seemed easy and familiar and able to mock each other without offense, like two guys at a watering hole.

Norman was tall, with a big bushy black-and-gray mustache and a head of tightly curled blackish hair. He might have been imposing except that he wore JCPenney khakis, colorful plaid shirts, and (worst of all) suspenders. In the first minutes, as we settled in, he told a couple dad jokes, and yukked them up. I imagined my father frowning at this rank amateur in the art of comedy. The phrase *used car salesman* went through my head. I looked over at Darrett, my new icon of cool; how could he possibly be seduced by this?

It was too late to back out.

We started in on the Shostakovich. At first, I could focus only on Norman's fidgeting mustache. We began playing the theme of the last movement, a march in staccato notes. Norman stopped Darrett after a few measures to say it had to be more staccato. Darrett played shorter. No, not just shorter, Norman said. He grabbed his cello, lifted it over a pair of music stands, and placed it right across from Darrett's, as if it were a duel, and played the march—not for him, but at him. His bow bounced off the string after each short note, way off, feet into the air. It was a mixture of dangerous and ridiculous, a totally unnecessary physical excess. He almost hit Darrett in the eye with one rebound. Darrett winced. I wanted to look away. It seemed like Norman was performing for a stadium rather than a twelve-by-twelve room. But I had to admit that the short notes were more malevolent when Norman played—not a charming or hopping kind of short, but like a voice on the phone cut off, or a thread severed by a knife. Norman stopped and said to Darrett: "Got it? Got it?" I could see that Darrett wanted to argue, but didn't. Norman required and then demanded a more striking character. If need be, he would extort it out of you. It was always about character— not moral character, but acting character, being "in character"—and there was never enough.

Later in that same movement, I had one big solo passage, a rampage of scales that came out of nowhere. I had put in some fingerings, like a good boy, and was just trying to read them and cross my thumb and not miss too many notes (but I missed reams anyway). Norman lumbered over, stood next to the piano bench, and stared me right in the face. He didn't say a word, but put on a deranged expression, like in Munch's *The Scream,* and pointed at the beginning of the passage. Oh God, his breath again. I couldn't help but play the scales in a wild, manic, satiric rush, thinking of his face, fearless because I was desperate for it to be over, and for Norman to go farther away.

"That's it!" he said, returning to his cello and to Darrett. Yes, I sounded much better, confident and unleashed, but I felt violated. The effect was cultish. I'd surrendered my right to privacy, my precious personal space, which was all the piano had been about, maybe, in some deep way. At all my Bill and Joe and Mona and Lillian lessons, no matter how scolded and seared, I still felt I was playing the piano in my bubble, doing my thing, and there was a dignity to that, even in failure. But Norman wouldn't let me have my bubble. His teaching required me to give up my dignity, as the price of something better.

As we walked down the hall after the lesson, Darrett asked me what I thought. I saw an unusual look in his eyes: a need for approval. I mumbled something middling. It was all I could manage. Who knows—maybe I wanted to hurt him, for reasons I wouldn't find time to examine.

{

Toward the end of the spring semester, Leon Fleisher—a deity of the piano if there ever was one—came to visit Oberlin. I'd known his recordings since I was ten, more or less, the Beethoven concertos with Szell and the Cleveland Orchestra. Everyone did. And we also all knew the tragic follow-up, how his right hand seized up and he lost his musical voice in his prime.

Since the faculty still remembered my *Symphonic Études*, I was selected to play them for Fleisher's class. Anyway, my Barber wasn't ready yet, nor my Rachmaninoff. While attempting to learn and form opinions about the entire Western Canon of classical music, I also had chemistry labs to finish for a grade, and other labs to teach for my tuition. I'd decided I couldn't lose another year of life before reading James Joyce, and so I'd enrolled in a Classics course—*The Ulysses Myth*. As the weather warmed I spent idyllic hours in the quad, following Leopold Bloom around Dublin, delving into every allusion to every other book I hadn't read. I tried to date Polly once more, not quite overcoming her skepticism. So despite the honor of being asked to play for a god, I didn't spend much time preparing. I assumed I still knew the piece from back in October, when I'd played it to a great deal of praise.

You never "still know" a piece, really. You have to force yourself to know it again, even rebuild its foundations. I played at it, sketching it over. But when the night came and I was waiting backstage, about to walk out, I realized that it wasn't clear in my mind. Certain places could go one way or another, like my Mozart when I was twelve. As I sat at the piano to play (in front of all the faculty and my fellow students), I had a terrible case of nerves, the kind that feeds on itself. My fingers hesitated, and then tried to make up for lost time.

I don't remember what Fleisher said first, but it was clear that he wasn't impressed, and maybe even not that interested. He invoked the word "cosmos," while he looked up at the ceiling, and he had a fantastic metaphor for one variation: "Imagine the gods, bowling with the planets." He played these gods with his viable hand: scurrying notes, swinging majestically into new harmonies and beats. This was incredible playing, I could sense in one part of my mind, while the other was in shock. We all went to a reception to meet the great man and he didn't talk to me. Joe came over to say, "Well, you didn't play well, but at least you got a great lesson out of it."

I walked back across campus in my ill-fitting suit; it had just turned dark. A few passing College students made fun of my tie, which was way out of place in North Campus, far from the Conservatory's rituals. I got to my room at last, and was peeling off my detested dress shoes, when my roommate Dave came home.

"What's up, how ya doin'?" he said.

Without waiting for my reply—who knows what it would have been?—he proceeded to tell me that I should really wear socks with my sneakers because they were stinking up the room. I thought about Rose at the Eastern Music Festival, saying more or less the same thing seven years earlier. Maybe nothing had changed.

⁊

I told Darrett about the Fleisher debacle (but not about the socks). His diagnosis was straightforward and cutting: "You didn't practice, did you?" Fair enough. I was able to laugh about it with him, and shed the anger and regret of self-sabotage. Darrett apparently forgave me for not loving Norman at first sight. We got closer. We took more walks around town, and had long, late talks in the lounge.

Darrett declared that our next project after Shostakovich should be the last cello sonata of Beethoven, in D major.

"I thought you didn't like Beethoven," I said, ready to catch him in hypocrisy.

"I don't like middle Beethoven," he said wearily, as if this should have been obvious. "The D Major is totally different."

We brought in the first movement to Norman. The piano opening had a leap that I was terrified of missing, and Norman just let fly an oversized guffaw—no big deal, he said. The idea was the strain, the sense of leaping into the unknown, it was OK to miss it—part of life, part of being a musician. What came after was more important. Darrett had to play one beautiful note in his first solo, and Norman played it at him, again and again, like he did in the Shostakovich, like a dog with a bone, until that one note felt heard. (I often say that to students these days: "I hear the note, but I don't hear you hearing it.") Then Norman moved through the score, unpacking character shifts: an angry bass that turned mischievous, a declaration of love that dissolved into a dance. I realized the dynamic of the lesson had shifted: he was spending far more time on me than on Darrett. I realized I was his project.

Larry Rachleff kept hounding me for precision, ensemble, exactitude of observation—an almost inhuman level of perfection. But Norman was the opposite: he wanted me to humanize everything first. He wanted every musical idea to have motivations, backstories, urges. Most of what Larry wanted was printed on the page; but most of Norman's desires weren't.

We eventually got to the second movement, a dark and profound Adagio, where Beethoven writes a hymn, but slows it to a crawl. The hymn has become, by some genetic malfunction, a funeral march. Its first practical problem is obvious and humiliating: How do you play together? If you want to hear one of the Epic Fails of Legendary Masters, listen to the great, long-lived Pablo Casals and equally great but short-lived Julius Katchen try to play this opening. Not one note is together. It's like a slapstick comedy, photoshopped on top of the deepest tragedy.

Darrett and I weren't any better (we realized) than Casals and Katchen. And we argued worse than ever, because we felt the stakes were higher. Darrett said, "Your hands aren't even together." This was true. Just like in the old Bill days, if I thought about strengthening and focusing my fingers, my wrist got tight; when I relaxed my wrist, my fingers became wet, impotent noodles. So I would lash out: "Well, if your bow change was smoother I might be able to tell where to play." And then we got into long discussions about where each phrase was going, not knowing that "going" is one of the vaguest words in the musical universe.

Norman had played for years in a professional quartet—the Concord—and, like any quartet player, knew all the unproductive interpersonal baggage that can undermine rehearsal. We played this movement for him in studio class, in a small concert hall, for an audience of thirty young cellists. He did a quick diagnosis.

"Jeremy," he asked, "what's the saddest thing you can think of?" That was not the question I expected in front of all these people. But a memory leapt to mind: when my parents threatened me, at nine years old, with the end of piano lessons. "Don't say it," Norman added before I could open my mouth, "just think it. And keep thinking it." Then he asked me to try playing my chords at a speed that would not break the spell of that sadness, like a baby you don't want to wake. I will never forget that image, and holding on to that secret onstage. It occurred to me that Joe or Bill never told me to play with more sadness, or encouraged me to draw on my own emotional life as a resource. (Why not?) I tried it, and it worked—my chords were deeper, and my tempo was steady, as if held within an invisible force field.

Norman warned me with a mustache wiggle not to forget—"That's good, hold that thought." Then he turned to Darrett. He told Darrett to imagine that each note was a three-dimensional object, and that you wanted to follow its surface to the end, all the way to its corner—no shortcuts. The fullness of each terrible note, he said, is like a drop of sorrow that gathers, and falls only when ready. Darrett said OK. What can you say to that? He had a few moments of not being able to control his bow. But then he found a new sound, the notes slowly—more than slowly, almost imperceptibly—changing color and tendency through their full duration, instead of seeming bored midway through.

Norman hadn't notified us of his strategy, or raised our alarm bells.

He knew we were so busy trying to prove each other wrong that we'd never looked within. But then came the last, most treacherous step. He told us to look right at each other and trust in the time it took to say what we each had to say. *Good Lord*, I thought, *New Age nonsense*, but it was too late to back out. We met each other's gaze and played the hymn. I didn't know which was more unbearable: staring into Darrett's blue eyes in front of everyone, or the way that Beethoven's chords wanted to move forward, but couldn't. We played, at last, more or less together. The sorrow and the sound also felt like one simultaneous thing. Norman did the impossible, now that I think about it. He fed our young angst to generate an old man's wisdom.

}

As the cool spring weeks slipped by on their journey to May, Norman's tics faded into the background—jokes, jeans, smells, cartoonish expressions. These were just incidental costs, I realized. Darrett was almost incidental as well. I began to follow Norman's arc, mainly; a way of thinking I wanted to see to the end. Darrett and I no longer said hello on our way through Norman's door. We grunted and got down to business.

Our next project was the Brahms F Major Cello Sonata, a Romantic epic with lots of tricks and pitfalls. I threw down my massive backpack (now filled more with music than anything else), sat on the bench, and played Brahms's opening, which was "just" an F-major chord, with a roll written on it, and Norman stopped me immediately. He got after me for ten minutes about that one chord. Could I get more snap? he asked. Not quite. He went further: Could I get my fingers to crackle, as if the latent energy of life were summoned in that one moment? Darrett snickered while I struggled.

While I was yelling at myself—thinking *Yes, of course, I should have known that's what Norman would say*, and wondering *How will I know in the future*, and a little bit of *Why is it so important to me now what Norman thinks?*—Norman had a wild duet with Darrett, trying to get him to play his first gestures with sufficient joy. "Daaaa DUUUUUUUMMMM," he screamed, with crescendos at the ends of the notes, as if off into infinity. Darrett's opening explosion subsided into odd rumbles. Norman said: "Imagine that the music is thinking about itself, trying to understand itself." I could really associate with this idea—I thought about myself constantly.

A new heroic theme emerged from the rumbles, with the following too-basic rhythm:

da da dum

I played "da da DUM" and Norman said no, "da DA dum." He did this until I almost hated him again. But at last I got the emphasis right, and the music acquired a regal strength. "Yes," Norman said, "don't forget that . . . otherwise the piece just stumbles on." And so we worked, trying to grab every moment of the piece like the eagle in the Annie Dillard essay, with its prey in its talons—as if the piece were life.

The climax of my relationship to Norman and Darrett happened on our third pass through the Brahms, on a normal-seeming afternoon. By then, our sessions didn't feel like playing and then commentary, but like a fight to the death, between us and Norman and maybe Brahms too, to get somewhere, and find rarer expressions and meanings. Norman roamed and stormed around the room. We complained about our technical problems, and he told us to shut up and play. *Use what you have. Stop stalling. No, I know you have more.* Measure by measure, we slogged through, and when it was done, the most unsettling thing happened.

The room was hot and (comparatively) quiet. All three of us were exhausted and sweaty. Darrett was packing up his cello. I was still half-practicing a difficult phrase with leaps in both hands, reaching for the ends of the keyboard. Norman was sitting at his desk, typing at his computer. He mumbled, "Jeremy, let it go." I ignored him and kept practicing for a few more pointless tries, but when I stood up from the piano I realized Norman had also got up and crossed the room—he was only a few inches away—and before I could think he enveloped me in a bear hug, cologne and all. He murmured, "That was really good." I stood there in his arms for a while, long enough to be repulsed, mortified, to breathe into it, to wonder why it was happening, and to realize that my father had never hugged me like that after a concert, or really ever, or spoken to me so sincerely, without irony or second thoughts. Finally, Norman let go. He looked at me; his expression seemed to say *I know*. I pushed around him and managed to find my way to the studio door. Darrett called down the hall, "Are you OK?" but I was far away— from him, from everyone.

10. *Melody* LESSON TWO

11 BEETHOVEN: Sonata for Piano and Cello in A Major, op. 69, first movement

*A*t the beginning of Beethoven's A Major Cello Sonata, op. 69, you hear a melody played by the cello, which for once doesn't have to worry about being heard over the giant black piano. Unfortunately for cellists, the melody happens to visit a "wolf," a note that makes many cellos vibrate with a hideous rasp, so this delicious moment of freedom is marred by the chance of a humiliating screwup.

The lack of accompaniment creates a puzzle: you have to deduce the implied chords from a line of unfolding notes, much in the same way you piece together half-heard bits of conversation into complete sentences, supplying what your ear missed. Your brain (without you knowing) tries to group the notes, to comprehend and find sense in them.

This is not to say that the melody would be "better" with chords underneath. In fact, the opposite is true: this emptiness creates a fullness of meaning. Beethoven is drawing on a power shared by any number of musical experiences, experiences we know or can imagine: singing a tune to ourselves in the shower; a mother humming a lullaby; a farmer singing a working tune in the field; a monk or cantor singing a chant; and so many others. You could call this the power of *monophony*, meaning "one voice." One voice does not create a more individualistic music. In fact, tunes sung by one person or played by one instrument seem especially at home in communal experiences—"Amazing Grace" at a memorial, for instance. Monophony feels open. It requires us, as listeners, to come in and fill in the musical blanks, and empathize with the performer all on their own.

Beethoven understood all this. This opening cello melody creates something outside the usual musical experience—like an invocation, and an invitation. It reminds me of a clever bit of literary detective work by Roland Barthes (yes, him again). In the middle of analyzing a short story by Balzac, Barthes finds a peculiar sentence. He inquires: Who is speaking? Who is the source of this sentence? It's not the narrator, or the author, or any of the characters, he realizes. It's an un-locatable voice, a hidden and elusive authority. Beethoven is especially good at this kind of voice, and at melodies that live in a mythical space, between the mass and the individual, between everything and one thing.

{

This famous melody has three parts. The first, and most important, is just three notes, what I like to call the Motto:

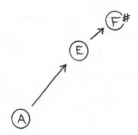

The first two notes are structural, like cornerstones. But the third is a mystery. The notes go up, like the inflection of a spoken question, and pose a musical question: How will the last note be resolved with the others? The answer is—it will and it won't.

The second part of the melody, which I like to call the Response, descends back through the notes of the first, until we return to the note we started on:

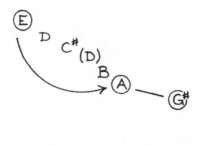

But when we arrive back—as often happens in life—home has changed. It is now a dissonance, and has to resolve away to another note. This is a useful, fundamental tool of melody—it takes a single unvarying note and understands it differently, which is to say, it rethinks the recent past.

Part One (the Motto) is all about the newness of its last note. Part Two's Response reinterprets the first note. One looks to the future; the other back. Different messages, one after the other, linked in a thread. The catchiness of melody disguises its powerful flow of causality. Melody creates a feeling, even an urge, that a first idea requires a second, and that the second is the only possible consequence of the first. It creates a river, a flow of thought to thought—even from one thought to its opposite.

⟨

In the third part of the melody, a little paradox: the notes descend, but the harmony remains up in the air. At this point the pianist is (at last!) allowed to come in. This is a wonderful moment, and I'm not just saying that because I'm a pianist.

As the piano rises in reply, you feel the melody keep extending itself, by stream of association, from instrument to instrument, building expectation. It's an unfolding thread in which each answer only partly solves the last question, and creates another. At last, there is a pause. Like any shameless singer, the pianist plays a cadenza covering all the space we have heard so far. And still we are waiting: What's behind the curtain? Where is this melody taking us?

Then we hear the same, mysterious Motto:

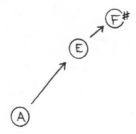

The answer to the question is the question itself! Many melodies have bits that wind up and bits that release, like a tennis player arching back to hit a serve, and following through. But here it's all wind-up and no release. The theme searches for a way to round itself off—but all the while, it doesn't really want to be rounded off. (Do you know anyone like that?)

For some minutes, the piece goes about its mostly merry way, and the opening melody takes a behind-the-scenes role. It doesn't reappear (as such), but is often hinted at. As we cross over into the middle of the piece, however, we realize the melody has been biding its time. It returns to life, or gets a second life, never to be heard the same way.

Beethoven begins this process by refashioning the first three notes, the Motto. He creates an overlap, allowing the third note (the one that "wouldn't fit") to sound at the same time as the first. The theme used to unfold its mystery one note after another; now it is stacked upon itself, creating an internal echo, an uncanny effect.

Then Beethoven turns to the Response. He puts plush arpeggios in the left hand, and—once the support is established—he lets the second part of the melody sing its heart out, up in the treble. It's virtually Romantic at this point, a stone's throw from a Chopin nocturne. Isn't this why you took piano lessons in the first place—to play ravishing tunes over rippling arpeggios?

The second part of the theme, as you may recall, is all about moving to a dissonance:

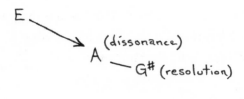

With all that harmony underneath, this proposition morphs into an intense expression of sorrow. The cello imitates the piano, and they lament together and accumulate, moving to one dissonance after another, trying different sorrows on for size. The Classical reply is now a Romantic catharsis.

In his Norton Lectures, Leonard Bernstein talks about "transformational linguistics" and makes connections between grammatical transformations of sentences and musical variations. But it seems to me we're much more emotionally attached to melodies than we are to sentences (mostly). Grammatical transformations are not as vivid as the ones we see in front of us all the time—the seasons, our moods, aging, loss, growth, deaths, births—or even the ones we encounter in literature, in Ovid, or Kafka, where people are transformed into animals as a just or unjust punishment, a life mishap, or a revelation of some inner truth. People change because of who they are, or some element they can't avoid, or because change is everywhere.

Beethoven's melodies aspire to act more like people or ideas than sentences. They crave agency and philosophy. Beethoven tries not to vary a theme just because he can, or on a whim; he aims for transformation to be purposeful. In his world, those transformations are almost the only reason for having melodies at all.

}

As the development continues, Romantic sorrow unleashes a storm. The cello saws away like a maniac. The pianist pounds out the second part of the melody, struggling, now dissonant with itself. It is violent well beyond anything else in the piece, and it makes sense only because of the sorrowful version we just heard. Beethoven describes an emotional logic: rage emerging from despair.

All of these variations, with their wildly different emotions, are (deep in the background) outlining a bigger story. We had a mysterious Motto, then a sorrowful Response, then a storm:

Motto, mystery
    Response, lament
        Response, storm

At this point, Beethoven—through a magnificent transition—returns to sorrowful part 2:

Motto, mystery
    Response, lament
        Response, storm
    Response, lament

And at last, continuing this backward time travel, we return to the initial mystery. Look at the overall scheme:

Motto, mystery
    Response, lament
        Response, storm
    Response, lament
Motto, mystery

Amazing: a vast symmetry, with the mystery of the first three notes framing the arch, and a violent outburst at the center.

In the act of development, Beethoven has managed to give his melody a new life, far beyond its original duration, dwarfing its original emotional implications. At the same time, he has rounded the arch that the melody itself could never seem to complete. Only by feeling its way through, and accumulating the wisdom of all its versions, does the melody feel fulfilled. It acquires longevity through depth. And I think that's why, after all the vicissitudes, when you hear the original theme again, it's not just the usual ooh and aah, and "We're back." At this juncture,

Beethoven puts us in touch with one of melody's central contradictions. On the one hand, melody's desire to be memorable, repeatable, like a keepsake or beloved photo. On the other, a native ability, and a desperate need, to transform. Melody (Beethoven reminds us) keeps switching between noun and verb, being and becoming.

11. *Self-Destruction and Self-Salvation*

PLAYLIST

> SCHUMANN: *Dichterliebe*
> BRAHMS: Sonata no. 3 for Violin and Piano in D Minor, op. 108, first movement
> SCHUBERT: Sonata in B-flat Major, D. 960, first movement
> MESSIAEN: *Oiseaux Exotiques*
> BRAHMS: Concerto no. 2 in B-flat Major, op. 83
> BACH: Partita no. 1 in B-flat Major, Gigue

*M*y memory-pictures of the first half of Oberlin are colored by a sense of discovery. But the final half all looks anxious, even in the rearview mirror. If I had to pinpoint the moment of origin, it was a poor choice at the end of sophomore year.

In 1988, I had a huge mop of blond hair and two promising summer options. The first was a small but selective chamber music seminar in Taos—work, rumination, nature. The second was to be the pianist— the only pianist!—of the brand-new American-Soviet Youth Orchestra, with a politically charged and glamorous tour: Zubin Mehta, the Kennedy Center, Avery Fisher Hall, Moscow, Leningrad. I picked the orchestra. I wanted to launch myself into the world, and see my name on posters.

It began well enough. The orchestra gathered in Oberlin to rehearse. We were given a few Russian lessons, with cameras and reporters everywhere. The Soviets realized we were pawns, but we Americans didn't. We each imagined we were converting the other. In the interest of cultural exchange, we played chamber music, and I got assigned to perform the Brahms D Minor Violin Sonata with the concertmaster, a gaunt and odiferous brown-haired Russian guy of maybe twenty-four. He stopped me in every measure to say "Here, pedal," or "Must be strict," or "Where is bass?" He felt it was only natural and right for him to tell me everything to do, and make me his puppet-accompanist. He had to teach me what he had been taught. I resented him, but not enough to risk an international incident.

I was also assigned the Shostakovich Quintet. This was easier, with some nice young Russian women, but still shocking. In Oberlin the professors were always telling me to play less, so the strings could be heard. But the Russians played three times louder than Oberlin students, even when the music was written *pianissimo*. I'd point this out to them, timidly: "Isn't it supposed to be soft?" They'd respond with a riot of explanations, about how they knew Russian music and how it was supposed to be played. I went silent. They had belief in a tradition, and I realized I didn't. They made me play my solos as loud as possible, as if each finger were a hammer. I was wiped out by the time I finished my first scale, six seconds in. Did they really want that? It certainly didn't sound beautiful to me, but maybe I needed to revise my concept of the beautiful. One of the Oberlin faculty came up after the concert and said, with a wicked smile, "Let me guess, they made you play that way?" and then added: "It sounded good."

I was absorbing all that interesting musical information, and convinced more than ever of the importance of deodorant. But once we left Oberlin for the tour, music faded into the background. It became a job, almost like data entry. Rehearsals were cursory. There was no time or place to practice or think. I sightsaw. Only glimpses of the world's wonders, then hustling to buses and trains and airports. Young oboists and percussionists came out to me late at night in New York and Moscow hotel rooms. I complained miserably about having no air-conditioning in Berkeley, and got such a withering look from the administration that I never felt I could complain again, not even when I got devoured by an army of bedbugs in Leningrad, and contracted bronchitis in Riga, and ate tongue at a musician's house in Moscow,

which gave me ferocious dysentery followed by dehydration in Sherem-
etyevo Airport, where I passed out. This wasn't fair. I'd made the opposite choices from my previous summer, but ended up in the same
place, on the brink of death.

}

Junior year, I had a new dorm—a quaint old redbrick building on the
north quad—and a clean and funny gay roommate named Will. The
first day, he taught me not to come in when I saw a rubber band on
the doorknob. In my mind I can see a desk in a corner, stacked with
chemistry textbooks, and a nice view of the expansive lawn. The quieter space gave me refuge. Conversation with Will was light, and
brought calm.

Even though I was still coughing and exhausted and covered with
fading pink welts, I took no moral or warning from my summer, and
plowed ahead in all directions. I tried one more time to reconcile the
irreconcilable: chemistry and piano. I took Thermodynamics (last requirement), History of Science (science through a humanities lens),
Schenkerian Analysis (trying to make music scientific by graphing it),
The Modern Novel (in some corner of myself all I wanted to do was
curl up and read), and Mahler, whose music was suddenly one of my
great passions, and the opposite of science, a visceral howl. I was a lab
assistant six hours a week, paying off an insignificant percentage of my
tuition; and a staff accompanist, paying off even less. Somewhere in
there I lost my virginity. And the last, biggest problem was that word
got around that I would agree to play almost anything. I loved music
but also the feeling of being in demand, which I confused with being
loved.

I especially couldn't get enough vocal music; even singers couldn't
keep me away. This fatal attraction had been building stealthily, ever
since my former roommate Sasha made me aware of a cycle of songs by
Schumann called *Dichterliebe*. "*Dichterliebe*" was German for "the love
of a poet." Sasha used *Dichterliebe* as a kind of Bible. While staring at a
girl in the lounge, he'd murmur the ravishing opening: "In the wonderful month of May." If she wasn't interested, he'd switch to a later song,

with a pounding heavy-metal accompaniment and the famous line where the poet unleashes on the "serpent gnawing at your heart."

It occurred to me: *Dichterliebe* was perfect for Polly. I could prove to her, once and for all, that classical music was relevant. The piece had love songs and breakup songs: everything you needed in college life. It was the structural equivalent of a mixtape but it had a narrative, not to mention excellent chord progressions, which made it so much better than the moronic harmonies she listened to. This explanation went over as well with Polly as you might imagine. After a delicious diatribe on the annoying timbre of classical singing, her voice laced with the sense of yet another clueless Jeremy event, she asked: How could anyone take the story seriously?

It is embarrassing to summarize the plots of Romantic song cycles. A sensitive young man falls in love with someone he barely knows, then loses this love (to a brawny hunter, or someone rich, or some other symbolic representative of male insecurity), and finds no other option but to kill himself. You had to ignore this story in order to hear the story the music is telling. As the singer/poet/narrator falls in love, you encounter a series of musical moments. One feels pure—almost religious. Another is a breathless rush; the next is languorous. As each of these visions appears, you recognize, *yes, that's part of what I feel is love,* and you add it to the pile like a dragon adds to its hoard. At the peak, you worry that this pile is too full, almost bursting. But fear not. The composer begins to take those joys away, one by one, song by song, in a series of negative revelations. He shows you menace in the same musical ideas where you once found delight. The only compensation is that the losses are often more beautiful than the gains.

{

I took on two of the most important cycles—*Dichterliebe* and Schubert's *Die Schöne Müllerin*—with a baritone named Chris. He required a lot of rehearsal. I felt as though I were in Chris's head, tasting his words. We built to clusters of threatening German consonants (*schlang, schlecht*), then dissolved into yearning vowels (*liebe, sehnsucht*). It was incredible to map thoughts onto notes, with an empathy I lacked in reality. I could ham it up, and it was just fine—more than fine, it was part of the style.

Chris's teacher was an Oberlin legend, Richard Miller, who'd written a famous pedagogical book: *The Structure of Singing*. His studio occupied a prime location just off the grand main entrance, an entrance no normal person used. The room had trappings of luxury: a Persian carpet, a fern, an antique music cabinet. When Richard opened the door, he had a Gothic vibe. I wouldn't say he resembled a vampire, but he might have been the butler in a vampire's castle, telling you to make yourself at home.

Our first lesson: I dodged a frond, and seated myself at the piano. After a couple of phrases, Richard stopped Chris to address a problem with his sound—it was strangled, he said. He hadn't yet found the right headspace. (Voice teachers were always trying to find cavities within their students, in the head or throat or diaphragm, as if the human body were a gourd waiting to be hollowed out for the purpose of sound.)

Before long, Richard was demonstrating: he began on one note, "Aaah," oozed up to a somewhat higher one, then let it slide down randomly to some lower note. The actual notes didn't seem to matter, only the release of the vocal apparatus. "Now you try," he said.

"Aaaaaahhhhhhhh," Chris tried.

"No," he said. "Like this," and he did an even more slithery version, oozing higher, sliding lower.

"Aaaahhhh," again replied Chris's vocal cords, not as free as they could be.

"Feel the height of your head, like a dome. Aaaahh Eeeeee Iiiiii Uuuuu," Richard said, going after most of the vowels.

All of Schubert's emotional subtleties had become irrelevant. Richard and Chris honked at each other for ten minutes, like geese. I was the blinking, mild-mannered naturalist in the corner, trying not to interfere.

At last we returned to the page of music, which showed a series of six equal notes. But not one of Chris's notes was the same length as any of the others. I didn't have a clue when to play. My index finger hovered and quivered over the keyboard, like a hummingbird having a panic attack. Singers have no idea how much anxiety this rhythmic anarchy causes us non-singer musicians—or they do, and don't care. I glared at Richard, the professor, who I hoped would intervene. But he looked sublimely unconcerned. The unthinkable had happened: I missed the metronome.

Because these lessons rarely ventured far into musicianship, we had to supplement them with advice from another teacher, recently arrived in Oberlin, a vocal accompanying specialist named Philip Highfill. Philip and I were an odd couple. I liked music best when it veered off the rails; Philip preferred to polish and admire the rails. He offered a constant stream of calibration and control: "Yes, Jeremy, I think you're right that the feeling is unsettled; but do you think the vein of intensity is pulsing quite so actively as you're playing it? And does the tempo have to be so deeply, shall we say, involved in the feeling of *agitato*, which you could see as a character and not an indication of time?"

I'd sit back down at the piano, not knowing how to find a compromise between anxious and terrified in my college closet of emotions. I'd play in a confused manner, and Philip would say that it was better. Philip had a mustache, like Norman—an upsetting coincidence.

I met many other singers in Philip's studio, who brought me like a captive or trophy to their own lessons. Their teachers would look at me with surprise. I was rumored to be a hotshot pianist, but here I was doing freshman singer duty, something even they didn't really want to do.

I spent a lot of time that I didn't have accompanying a young soprano named Rebecca. I admired Rebecca's sarcasm, which gave her an aura of invulnerability. Her teacher was Carol Webber, a soprano with an active concert career. Carol had a different sort of invulnerability, and I had to constantly resist the urge to tell her the story of my life. She was ample—just the right amount for a singer—with curly-to-permed dark hair. She always wore flowing shiny garments, usually white. In other words, she had a look: gossamer angel, with a hint of cherub. All the voice professors, by the way, had a look. String players and pianists were encouraged, almost required, to be schlubs or geeks. But even here, in the middle of the decaying Rust Belt, singers felt they had to put on a show.

One day, we were working on some ditty from the classic book of *Twenty-four Italian Songs and Arias,* which every vocal student has to suffer through, just like I'd had to suffer through Clementi. (Vocal students are about twelve years behind pianists, in general.) There was nothing for me to think about in this music. Thinking would have made me far less useful. I mostly looked at Rebecca and wondered what it would be like to lie next to her in bed.

A phrase or two in, Carol said, "Rebecca, you're not here today."

"I know . . ." she said.

"Why aren't you here?"

"I don't know, I'm sorry," Rebecca said, looking upset with herself and also like a child caught out in a lie.

"Rebecca, go to the mirror."

She walked over to a large floor-length mirror, and faced her reflection.

"Rebecca," Carol asked, "is that you?"

"Yes, that's me."

"Really?"

"Yes. That is me."

"Good. Now, I know there must be other things going on," Carol said. "Your mind is full. You have to forget about your father, and home, and all of it. You have to let it all go."

I felt only part-shielded by the piano.

"Yes, Ms. Webber."

"You have to be present for the work. You have to respect the work."

"I'm present, I'm ready."

"Good. Now, sing."

Rebecca sang a little bit of a phrase, but at the top note her voice got strained—nothing was coming or going. A sob emerged out of the flat high note, like a song of its own in an alien dialect. All the invulnerability I'd crushed on melted, revealing something I didn't want to know.

Carol got up from her chair and flowed over to Rebecca and the mirror. Her way of walking reminded me of opera, of a moment in a video of *La Traviata* I'd loved as a child, when Alfredo approaches Violetta to tell her she's doing the right thing by abandoning the love of her life. Suddenly Carol turned back to me, with a different operatic flourish, as if just realizing that the villain was lurking nearby. She said, "We don't need you anymore." I fled as fast as I could.

{

When I got tired of emotions and well-coordinated outfits, I had the perfect antidote—a violin professor named Greg Fulkerson. Greg was short and gnomish, with a bit of a tummy, acres of forehead, a prominent mole, and a Cheshire cat smile. He could play the hell out of the violin. He wore the most boring possible heterosexual clothes, always topped with a baseball cap—he said classical musicians *had* to love baseball, because it was so forgiving of failure. I'd lucked into Greg's studio because another pianist canceled. After a few minutes of his vicious abuse, I was hooked.

We students grouped Greg with Larry Rachleff. We often saw them in the hallway together, chatting, colluding (we assumed) on some new way to make us all feel terrible about ourselves. Greg had, like Larry, a sense of unfinished business with me. He said I sometimes played almost as well as anyone he'd ever heard, but then: Where did that "great pianist" go? The air quotes were his. A question I often posed to myself, but it seemed more urgent when he asked it.

I studied all kinds of violin repertoire with Greg—Ives, Beethoven, Grieg, Mozart—but the lesson that sticks in my mind was on the Brahms D Minor Sonata. I'd adored this piece ever since my teacher Bill played it in New Mexico seven or so years before. It was a dream to play it for myself.

My dream did not last long. "Umm . . ." Greg said, barging into the middle of the first sublime and hovering phrase. "The sign of an actually good pianist is that they can make connections with their fingers and don't need the pedal as a crutch." During the opening of the

Brahms, the pianist's right and left hands play the same notes, but time-lagged, one slightly behind the other. If you pedal through it, you get an easy effect—a blur—but what you want is something better: clear unease. It was much more complicated to play this passage without pedal, or with a subtle fluttering of pedal to reflect the fluttering feeling.

"Yes, playing the piano is soooooooooo hard," Greg said, "poor Jeremy! Just be thankful you don't have to deal with vibrato."

Then we came to the second theme—one of Brahms's best themes, which seems to want to be sung out for all it's worth. I was emoting along, pleased with myself, delighted that I didn't have to flutter and tiptoe anymore. Greg stopped me again. He said, "Jeremy, I hate to ask," though he didn't hate to ask, "but have you really *looked* at the score?"

This theme is built around a simple idea. A note surges to the note above it—it seems to long for it, to desperately want to become the upper note. But almost as soon as it gets there, it returns to the first note. Therefore the most desired and beautiful note is also the briefest—a moral and a meaning, hiding in an "innocent" tune.

Greg pointed to an emphasis on the short note, a *sforzando:*

Fine—I played it again, with the emphasis. It seemed beside the point. It was emphasized by definition, just by being that great note, I thought.

"Good," he continued, "but there's also a staccato."

I stared at him.

"No, that's ridiculous," I said, not realizing that when the composer's marking seems most insane is when you need to pay the closest attention. But there the stupid staccato was, on the music:

Fine. I played it short, to show him how ugly and absurd it was. Greg had gone to the window, setting his trap. He turned back to face me, an evil smile mixed with evil delight. "Yes, you're right. That does sound terrible. But you forgot one more thing... [in a lower voice]: the pedal."

Argh! Yes, there it was, down at the bottom of the music, where my eyes didn't often roam: a pedal marking on the short note. This, too, made no sense. Why would Brahms write staccato on the note, telling you to let it go, but at the same time put down the pedal, which meant the note would hold on?

"Just try it," he said. After a few false starts, I did all three markings: the accent, the staccato, the pedal. What the hell! The perverse trio was quintessentially Romantic. It made the upper note speak with more urgency—and then linger through the lower one, like when you still feel the touch of someone you love, after they've left. It was no longer just a note but an unsettling reminder, a second layer of experience.

I looked at Greg with gratitude. What he'd shown me was logical and emotional and, if you looked at the printed music, obvious.

"Not so ridiculous, is it?" Greg said smugly. Even while opening your eyes to great wonders, he wanted you to resent him. "Why should I have to tell you this stuff?" he continued. "Aren't you supposed to be, like, a prodigy? You should at least know how to read." And then he softened his tone to deliver the moral of the day: "When I hear you play, I should be able to take dictation of the score. I want to hear every marking."

This image—taking dictation—didn't appeal to me. Dictation and reproduction weren't an end in themselves, were they? But Greg's careful observation of detail had created an intensity that made all the emotional voice lessons feel tame.

{

By this point at Oberlin, I had more mentors than combined fingers and toes. I didn't think, or care, that all these teachers might be pulling me apart: the rational Greg-Larry axis, the miscellaneously irrational singers, and many other interlopers between brain and heart—like the wonderful violinist Marilyn McDonald, who'd spent years reinventing Baroque music, and her soon-to-be ex-husband, another Larry, a recovering hippie clarinetist. I recall one Larry lesson where he said, "It sounds beaty, doesn't it?" The clarinetist and I nodded, realizing we were gallumphing through what should have been a waltz. "If you want it to be less beaty," he continued, escalating into a mild scream, "PLAY LESS BEATS!" Excellent advice, then and now.

But I don't recall the details of even one lesson on solo piano repertoire from that entire junior year. I also didn't learn any new solo music. I was treading water on Barber, Rachmaninoff études, and a Bach Prelude and Fugue—which I played more Romantically than either the Barber or Rachmaninoff. This laziness must have annoyed poor Joe—I don't remember that, either.

I do remember two piano studio classes, though, because of music I heard for the first time. These classes had the misfortune of occurring on Thursdays at five thirty, when lunch had long worn off. The godforsaken hour was only part of the problem. When we pianists got together, it felt like fundamentally antisocial animals being forced into a herd. We assembled in Warner Hall, a cold modern space with stone walls and high, thin stained-glass windows. Sounds and words vanished into the reverberation.

The first class I remember was when a skinny, well-groomed senior played Beethoven's Sonata, op. 109. Joe said, by way of preamble, "This is one of the most important and profound pieces ever written," in the same tone of voice that you'd say "Oh you know Annie who works at the DMV." He loved music, but hated fanfare. To me it didn't seem like a piece as much as an acid trip (not that I knew what that was).

In the other class, a few weeks later, a rosy-cheeked classmate I'd spoken to here and there got up to play Schubert's last piano sonata, D. 960. I've forgotten her name. She had a farm girl vibe: Oberlin's granola, without the grit.

The B-flat Major Sonata was written in Schubert's last months, in 1828, at the end of a long syphilitic decline. It has a bitter logic: the more beautiful it gets, the less hopeful it is. This girl was nineteen years old, sweet, unspoiled, on the cusp. That day, she was wearing a paisley skirt. What about Schubert's diseased worldview did she feel the need to experience? And how could she express it in a paisley skirt? As she began, her sound was round and gorgeous. It cast a spell on all of us trying to survive another bleak, lake-effect winter afternoon.

The opening melody was consoling, but didn't do much. It kept close to itself, rehearing a few basic notes. Only one moment seemed like a real action—a sudden rise up four notes from B-flat to E-flat, a foothold, a desire. I wanted to follow it, but it seemed like Schubert didn't want me to see where it led. Meanwhile she played on and on, shifting from light to dark to light, but then she had a memory slip, and had to stop, spoiling the tragic climax. I fell asleep. I was always exhausted my junior year, and often ill. Tepid applause woke me.

"It's coming along," Joe said, walking halfway up the long aisle. "Look, you've got to work on the memory," he added. But he didn't explain how. She smiled back at him, humbler than any of us: "Yes, I'm so sorry about that, Professor Schwartz, I don't know what happened." I wanted to like her, but her endless kindness seemed suspicious.

"That triplet section," Joe said, "it didn't feel settled." As he spoke, he squished his face into itself, a common Joe maneuver that evoked Kermit the Frog. The girl tried the triplets again; they were still unstable. So Joe delivered another trademark move: a verbal emission ("eeehhh-hhmmmmmm") while moving his hand back and forth like an airplane banking left and right, meaning: *yes, no, sort of, someday?*

She tried it yet again. Her fingers tangled. It seemed she might cry, and to my great surprise Joe immediately relented. "You know, what you're doing is good, it's beautiful, don't worry. Just keep working." He was so much kinder to her than to me. *What is this?* I thought. *Why aren't you nice to me? Do I have to cry more?*

Then Joe turned to all of us, asking "What do you guys think?" When a teacher opens the floor, and asks you to teach yourselves, it's not innocent. This is the occasion where bullshit has its greatest opening in college life. I felt a desperate need to mansplain, even though the word hadn't been invented yet. "I loved it," I said, "but I thought maybe you overpedaled when the sixteenth notes got going."

She thanked me kindly for my pointless comment. After twenty more seconds of silent squirming, a dubious pianist who mostly considered himself a composer blurted out, "I just don't get it."

"What do you mean?" Joe asked.

"I just want to know . . . why is this piece supposed to be so great?"

Joe tried to laugh it off: "You'll know in time."

"No," my classmate said, in that admirable, irritating Oberlin way— equal parts idealism and the desire to destroy. "Those triplets, they're just arpeggios," he continued. "I mean, anybody could write that."

I saw Joe's face stiffen. Did he regret the signing of a contract some decades earlier, when he decided to take a job in a small Midwestern town and wait for each new year's worth of self-obsessed teenagers to come and flail away at the Western Canon? You spend your life passing on a tradition to a younger generation, and sometimes they can't help themselves—they have to spit on it.

"You should listen to Schnabel play it," Joe said, with less space between words than he usually allowed. "It's about hearing over long distances, about patience, inevitability, the sad and beautiful unfolding of time, OK?" This was by leaps and bounds the most poetic utterance he'd ever made in my presence.

Joe scanned the room for sympathy. I looked down; I didn't want him to look at me. I understood the student composer's point. The triplet passage resembled arpeggio exercises I learned when I was twelve. It looped around one chord, then another, and came back to the first. A few moments later, the left hand did the same. It all seems calculated to provoke some jerk to ask, "Is that it?" The same problem crops up at the piece's next big juncture. We encounter a melody, stranded in the treble: one naked unaccompanied note, trying to bring a massive section of music to a close, like a mouse trying to draw curtains across a grand stage. The triplets were "just harmony," and this stranded note is "just melody": another act that is not quite enough.

Later in life, I realized that these flaws weren't flaws. Schubert wants you to feel insufficiency. In a way, that is the sensation he's after, more than any of the more popular marquee emotions (sorrow, joy, nostalgia). It's as if he is saying *Yes, that's it*—and, now that you ask, it's the only thing possible, the only thing left to do, after all the hopes and losses. This kind of moment in Schubert, simple to the point of breaking, like a fabric stretched thin, represents one of his most important truths—when he connects to the actual experience of life rather than some composed ideal. Life's narratives are not full; often there is no story, or an inadequate story, not covering the gaps.

Even Beethoven, who has plenty of truths to offer, doesn't supply this one. Ludwig's up in his Platonic ideals most of the time, creating dramatic, incisive, revolutionary works. If he seems lost, he's pretending: deep down, he knows exactly where he is and when he will return. But Schubert sometimes finds himself down here with us, slumped on a threadbare couch, staring at a stain on the floor, unable to leave an unproductive or tedious circular thought, not quite sure how to go on, or why.

}

I played almost a hundred recitals that year: four or more years' worth of masterpieces half-learned, stuffed into my brain as fast as I could. I kept my concert clothes in my locker for convenience, and because—this happened a few times—I'd forget a recital and someone would run to find me in a practice room, yelling "Dude, you're supposed to be onstage right now!"

In February I agreed to add another piece to my hoard: Bartók's Sonata for Two Pianos and Percussion. I'd learned in Music History that Bartók was one of the true "good guys." He refused to kowtow to the Nazis; he collected folk songs from the people; he stood up for music as music. (And therefore he died in semi-poverty, unlike pompous Richard Strauss.) How could I resist? As I started to work, I noticed it had long passages in parallel sixths. Bill had avoided sixths in my Dohnányi studies, I recalled, worrying I would strain myself.

One afternoon, after a couple hours of Bartók, I sat in music theory class and watched my fourth finger. It tingled. But the eeriest part was how it would lift itself, every so often, without my willing it, as if trying to play a note that I forgot. The fourth is the weakest finger, I remembered hearing, and then I also remembered that Schumann tried to strengthen it with a machine, and crippled himself for life. I was mentally spiraling, after only two hours of bodily injury. The teacher rhapsodized about Schenker's distillation of the contrapuntal genius of music. The finger kept grabbing my attention, like a child tugging at my leg. I wondered whether music's genius would be possible for me anymore. If I couldn't play, did I even care about music?

The next day, I decided it had all been a bad dream. I went back to the practice room to play Bartók, as before. Soon I had a dull ache in my tendons, radiating up to my shoulder. Injuries have a way of branching out over the body like a toxin, partly because of your fear of them, but also because the whole body is involved in piano playing, a fact pianists often forget.

I went up to Joe's studio, and interrupted a lesson to tell him my bad news. He said, "Well, you should take breaks. Every fifteen minutes." This was excellent advice. Short breaks relieve the muscles and mind. But it seemed like a cop-out. I forced my way into the studio and played some Bartók passages for him, hoping he could find the problem quickly and prescribe a magic pill.

"Ehmmm, it looks OK, doesn't look like you're doing anything wrong."

This was annoying. I was obviously doing something wrong. Why couldn't he see it? Teachers are reluctant to make medical diagnoses, for good reason. Many of a pianist's strengths and weaknesses are invisible. The motions are small-scale. Tensions hide behind the scenes.

I went back to the practice room. In the following days, I didn't know whether I should play or rest, and when I sat at the piano it was hard enough listening to the music without having to constantly listen to my body. When my fourth finger was still acting up a week later, Joe was a little more worried. He advised me to talk with Robert Shannon, a colleague on the piano faculty, who taught the Taubman Technique. We all knew about Shannon—he was for when injuries became serious. This topic came up frequently in the lounge, because a few of us were always being picked off by tendinitis, and quitting for a semester, or leaving school—some were never heard from again.

Shannon had an amazing origin story. He'd been unable to play and then brought himself back from injury, guided by the methods of a woman named Dorothy Taubman. He wouldn't even touch pieces from the pre-Taubman days—too many old habits would come back. With him you had to throw your past away, and rebuild your technique from scratch, reevaluating all your patterns of motion.

The idea of starting over was terrifying to me, almost more terrifying than the injury. Nonetheless, I cornered Shannon backstage after a student orchestra concert. Everyone was milling about, congratulating. I told him what was happening, and he was kind—he listened patiently.

"It doesn't sound irreparable," he said. My brain got lost in that word "irreparable" and then I realized through the din of conversation that Shannon was asking me another question: "Where's the pain mostly?"

I showed him.

"On the top of the arm, that's not so bad. The bottom is more dangerous." I felt a shade better.

"If you really want help, you should come in and play for me . . ." he offered, but this was too much, the idea of becoming a patient. If it wasn't irreparable, I'd design my own method. I was smart, right? So, starting the next day, I kept at the Bartók but stopped when I felt the slightest strain. I practiced one of the world's most visceral and wild pieces while walking on eggshells. I released all tension from my fourth finger—but I didn't have a good alternative. I just created a void, an ellipsis between my third and fifth fingers. I still feel it now, from time to time, the memory of the loss, the sense of danger and a desire to flinch as I pass through the right half of my right hand. In the middle of the most passionate phrase, my mind will murmur, *Don't hurt yourself.*

}

In the middle of this crisis (which I still wasn't sure was a crisis), all the juniors began to contemplate a momentous question of Oberlin Conservatory life: what to play for the concerto competition. You could enter only once. You lost or won, and that was the verdict on your Oberlin time. We had no idea how little this competition would matter in the scheme of life, and discussed our options ad infinitum.

I set aside the question of whether I'd still be able to play the piano at all. I thought long and hard about Beethoven, my nemesis since the "Waldstein" and "Appassionata," since the moment my mom planted in my mind the idea that I was bad at Beethoven. And yet he seemed like an integrity move. Mozart was a charming choice, but we agreed as a group that he never wins. Too easy! (One of the many evils of competitions.) There was Liszt—shallow, lots of octaves. I suppose you could pick Rachmaninoff, if you were feeling whorish (can't wait for the hate mail on this one). You could dare Prokofiev, but Martha Argerich had sort of been there and done that, for all time. The Schumann was beautiful, but not a competition piece, everyone said—not enough raw display.

As we went through the canon, it began to seem like there weren't that many piano concertos, and it started to seem limiting to choose your identity from this folio of greatest hits (welcome to the life of a classical musician). Then a ridiculous idea occurred to me, a piece I hadn't thought about much in my Oberlin years: Brahms's Second Concerto, the first piece I ever decided that I loved, when I was twelve, a ghost from my parents' record collection.

Brahms B-flat! A comical choice for an injured pianist, like deciding to ascend Everest with a broken leg. It is one of the most difficult pieces in the piano repertoire, more difficult in many ways than Rachmaninoff no. 3. But I kept going over it in my head. I couldn't stop obsessing about the opening, a horn call, a rising scale with a little curlicue creating a subtle upward energy, the sense of a question. And after the horn ascended, how the piano came from the unsuspected other side, from the deepest bass, creating a cushion of sound around the horn, a foundation beneath a foundation. The timbre of the horn, the sense of space, the call in the mountains resounding over the valley ("He wrote it in Italy!" one conductor reminded me; another cellist friend said, "Here is the universe"), and then the pianist/protagonist finds nothing better to do, nothing more important than just to echo back the horn, to re-hear the beauty we've already heard: egoless, listening.

That was it, I decided. I would conquer the greatest, purest piece ever written, and conquer fear and my injury at the same time. Joe didn't object to this plan. He saw a light in my eyes when I talked about it, a light he hadn't seen for a while.

≀

To put this plan in motion, I became a control freak, for once in my life. I couldn't do my great work at home. I had to go to a summer festival, preferably a long one. I made a tape for the Aspen Music Festival and School and got in. Many other Obies were going. I contacted real estate agents and found six of us a three-bedroom apartment, which we could all split. Then I just had to wait out the early summer in New Mexico.

I hitched the long ride up to Aspen from Las Cruces in a tiny blue Toyota hatchback, with a cellist visiting instructor at New Mexico State. She looked at my suitcases with alarm. Some items got bungee-corded to the top; others dangled out the back. We played Bach cello suites on her tape deck, mostly Casals—old-school playing, lots of groans and scratches. I complained that it was *so* out of tune and she told me I'd understand, eventually.

All was fine until some miles out of Alamosa, when we started to climb the Rockies. The Toyota gave out. She said it would be OK, if we'd just let it rest a few minutes. She had a gigger's calm, an orchestra musician's resignation, a sense of oh-well-that's-what-happens-when-the-conductor-does-that. From the foothills, we watched clouds slowly cross the vast valley. My arm ached. Her car started up again. We skirted the chasms of Independence Pass as I gazed out the window in terror. I had to survive and get to Aspen to save myself, just like two summers ago I'd had to return to Oberlin to kiss Polly.

We descended into the old mining town, which would be surprised to see what it has become. I greeted all my roommates. I tried to establish a strict regimen of chores and meals, to exert control over my rebellious body by tyrannizing everyone else. Then I went to register for practice space. The lady at the table told me the only times left were from 6:00 to 9:00 a.m., and late at night, 9:00 to 11:00 p.m. I couldn't believe this. I grabbed every undesirable hour I could—five or six a day. Are you sure you need all those slots? she asked sourly.

That night, I set my alarm for 5:15 a.m. When I woke up, I said to myself, *Fuck you, Aspen,* then bashed around the kitchen. It's never been easy for me to eat or wake quietly. In a fog, with my precious Brahms score in my backpack, I walked down Durant to the bus station—clusters of vacationers waited in the dawn for whitewater adventures, hikes, balloon trips—and caught the first shuttle to the practice building. The music school lies in a valley, along a rocky creek. The morning was dry and winter-cold; my hands were freezing by the time the bus dumped me off, with one or two other students. I was practical that summer, but not quite practical enough to buy gloves. I wandered over the bridge. All was quiet except for the rush of the creek, a sound less soothing than violent, like a continuous crumpling and ripping of paper.

That was my daily routine, for nine weeks. Several mornings I fell asleep and ended up back in town, right where I started, covered in drool. Someone—a Robert Shannon student—had told me not to start with scales, that they were a dangerous warm-up: too many small muscles. So I started with chords, defining a safe space, trying to observe my tendons, though they were concealed in my arms. At first it was half-dark and the main light was an overhead bare bulb. Gradually the window glowed, then beamed. Outside the creek kept rushing, while I tried to be patient.

}

I'd requested and received one of the most desirable teachers at Aspen: John Perry. Joe Schwartz loved the idea of me studying with John, as did everyone, more or less. Perry was so desirable that you got few lessons—I got two that summer—and they took place in a big room, in front of all the other pianists.

His lessons were inspiring, and they made you feel music was the most important thing in the world. But there were complications. Imagine a series of lectures by Danny DeVito on the sublime. Short and bald, with his straight mustache and prominent belly, John constantly insisted on beauty, to the point of yelling about it. Music was difficult, and a problem. You didn't play it, you grappled with it.

One of the first lessons I watched was on a late Beethoven Sonata: the A Major, op. 101. This is a tough piece, for everyone. The first movement is proto-Romantic, part gentle country dance and part inchoate yearning—a weird mix, and despite all its little eloquent gestures, often the movement doesn't really add up. I was just as unsatisfied as John seemed to be. No, I thought, *this phrase needs to stretch more,* and then a moment later, the opposite problem, *Now I need to know where I am.* How do you know when to give and take, and if you don't know now, will you ever know? I couldn't help it—my body got involved while I listened. After the class John called me over and said, "I can tell you're a musician just the way you move. You get that music." I felt selected and understood. We shared the same frustrations.

John's kindness was tempting, and he revealed it often, but his patience would suddenly drain out, like water before a tsunami. He would say innocent phrases like "all right" in a cold fury. The same granola girl from Oberlin had come to Aspen and was playing (again) the Schubert B-flat. She still wasn't ready to perform. Perry wouldn't teach her; he said a few words about responsibility, then told her to sit down and let someone else play. A pianist with tremendous fingers and no apparent desire to phrase played a Tchaikovsky concerto. Perry made fun of one transition ("What a genius!" he said, plunking out notes sarcastically, which I loved), and then, while the guy played, looked at us all with an expression that said *How do I even start?*—which I loved less. There was a legend—apocryphal?—that Perry left the room after one performance and returned with a roll of toilet paper, which he placed on the piano in lieu of commentary.

꛱

In the practice room, I decided to attack a famous passage in the Brahms's last movement: a scale in thirds at wicked speed. At age twelve, when I first got the score to this piece, I thought it was the most unplayable of all unplayable things. Simple enough: I would conquer my twelve-year-old fear, then move on to new fears. I started by putting in a fingering, 2-3-4, 2-3-4-5. What else was I going to do? Seven notes made of two trips through the hand. And what do you know, after four or five days, I was making my way through the scale pretty quick, with lumps.

As I tried to smooth the lumps (as if piano playing were making mashed potatoes), I had to ping-pong between mind and muscle. I'd think first—cross the thumb. Then I'd play. Quickly back from body to mind, evaluating how my arm felt. (Did I press with my fourth finger? Any tingles or aches?) I wished life wasn't that way, but too bad, now it was. *Grow up, Jeremy.* I wished music was just thought and desire, and muscles had nothing to do with it. At some point every morning a twinge would race up my arm, and I would run out of the room and freak out, staring at the grass, letting my arms dangle from my sides. Then I'd talk myself back in: *OK, you can still play, try again.*

Maybe only now, surrounded by precipitous slopes, did I feel how much of the piece was about leaps, and how they were both scary and a show of strength—the pianist appearing to hit every register at once, the heavens and the depths, fearless. A piece about the majesty of space. I whittled up my batting average, day by day. It seemed cruel to be able to find the note one day, and not the next. I must have spent fifty or sixty of my precious practice hours on one light, transitional passage where both hands sailed off in either direction. It was supposed to be balletic. I kept throwing myself into two unknowns.

꛱

Between John's infrequent sessions, his wife taught makeup lessons. I brought my Barber sonata to her—still not my favorite piece. I played three minutes and she stopped me.

"No, you have a serious problem," she said.

I knew that. I started telling her about my fourth finger.

"Yes," she said, "clearly you will continue to injure yourself, if you don't strengthen the frame of your hand."

This somehow seemed the opposite of what I'd been trying (that is, to loosen my hand so I could play with more relaxation).

She said, "Yes, you don't have these muscles built," and she brought her hand over for me to feel, the webbing around the fingers, the muscles within the hands that would support the force you were bringing to bear. Then she went to the cheaply paneled condo wall and leaned on it with her hands, using her outstretched fingers for support, like Spiderman. The thought of doing this, of putting a body's worth of weight on my recovering fingers, filled me with terrible anxiety. Who was this quack?

To humor her I tried it, and had a few seconds of panic and revulsion. Then I removed my hands from the wall and said it was too scary. She looked at me with a mix of sympathy and annoyance and said, "OK, you have to try when you get home, a little bit each day."

Because she was "only" John's wife, I ignored her, and even mocked her advice to my roommates and friends. But she was the only one telling me key muscular truths. I couldn't solve everything, long-term, by becoming a floppy mess, like a puppet without a hand. In my midtwenties, a colleague and dear friend at Indiana University explained this same concept to me, working not on the wall but on the surface of a table, and it made a huge impact. Ignoring Perry's wife therefore cost me about six years.

{

Eventually I had to face the Brahms's most famously crazy lick: a run of fast, quiet octaves in the middle of the second movement. It's supposed to sound not just mysterious but supernatural, like a scurrying of ghosts. You can feel Brahms channeling his mentor Schumann here, doing something outlandish, something that threatens to collapse the piece, but turns out to work by sheer force of imagination.

This passage was a nightmare for me, because you would normally play it with alternating fourth and fifth fingers—ground zero of my injury. How stupid was this? I was the guy in the horror movie who can't resist going into the basement. I decided to do the whole passage sliding about on my pinky. I thought about this cop-out for hours. I consulted other pianists (a thing I generally avoided). Some of them asked, "Can't you reach it?" Others were nicer and said sure, use the pinky, that's the safe solution.

While mulling this existential pinky debate, I had a revelation: I could now distinguish between my finger sitting on the key, like you'd sit comfortably in a chair, and pressing down pointlessly, after the fact. (You can find a spilled-milk life lesson there too.) This seemed so central. I was furious at all my teachers for not explaining this to me, for beating all kinds of other details in, but not this one master key. I did three notes without pressing, then four. And, after a week, the ghostly impossible octaves began to play themselves.

This brought on another, paired revelation—that this whole quest to un-injure myself, which seemed like a terrible loss of innocence, was the best thing that could have happened, because when you played with a more efficient and healthy technique, somehow the music sounded better too. I explained this to some other pianists at lunch and they were like, duh.

}

At last I played the first movement of the Brahms for Perry. I was reluctant to share my private journey of redemption, but eventually I would have to be judged. John offered some lovely compliments and then said: "The second theme seemed underpowered, like you didn't quite know what to do with it." That was my favorite part! Before he could say any more I started playing it again, now fully relaxed, with no stakes, and it was fantastic. I sang through all the chords and leapt about the keyboard with gypsy abandon.

John looked at once delighted and annoyed. I'd done what he wanted, even more than he dreamed was possible, but he hadn't said much to produce it.

He asked, "Why didn't you do that the first time?"

Good question! I thought. Because he liked me and loved the piece, Perry gave me extra time to play some of the slow movement. "I want to hear what you do with it," he said. It starts with a patient soliloquy, like a slow waterfall of notes, with the hands in different rhythms, exposing beauty after beauty on their undulating way down. But we didn't get that far. John got caught up on the first few entrances, where the piano starts in the bass and reaches up to the high treble. He wanted me to feel the reaching, the difficulty of attaining the stratosphere.

I felt this was right, musically. But when I started to think about musical difficulty, my dull arm ache returned. I didn't know which muscles to tense and which to release. Part of me had to be plugged in, another part distanced. I felt torn between these two selves in front of everyone. Perry, attuned to the music, in love with Brahms, didn't seem to notice that I was at a loss.

⸘

The second movement of the Brahms is a massive scherzo, far from the charming minuets of Mozart and Haydn some sixty years earlier. The dances have been given steroids. The act of play gets heavy. It starts with the piano and cellos having an argument, the piano up in the treble, the cellos deep in the bass. They trade ideas that can never seem to settle or coincide. Then, all at once, dissent vanishes. The violins reveal a new quiet melody, with a haunting oscillation between two adjacent notes. After all the unbearable tension of distance comes the even more unbearable tension of nearness.

This quiet violin theme was another of my favorite moments in the piece—but difficult. The piano takes up the violin notes and drapes them with ever more amazing harmonies, which means you have to leap down in a series of rapid-fire gestures to grab new bass notes, and summon an expanding world. The first measures could be played by a child;

but eight measures later you were an adult,

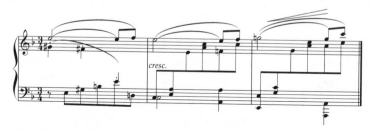

and after that it was the limit of human possibility.

I played this passage thousands of times. One late night, I was out in the grass courtyard between the practice rooms taking a break, and spied a fellow pianist named Alex Goor. He was always talking with a sarcastic and gifted pianist named Lisa, whom I fantasized about— sarcasm was still my most active erogenous zone. In a fit of bravery, I knocked on his door. He was happy to be distracted, and jumped off his piano bench to come listen.

And so I started to play the second movement for him, while he sang the dissenting cello and bass lines back at me, goading me. Great fun and exactly what I needed. But when I came to the quiet theme, he just said "No." And again, "No, no, no, no." I stopped, crestfallen. He grabbed me by the arm (I felt a tingle, not the injury ache or numbness) and pulled me out through the practice room door, and we walked a little distance until the lights of the practice room cubicles could no longer dim our view of the sky. He had a goofy smile, shiny brown hair, a manic charisma.

Alex threw his head and arms up at the sky and said, "That's it."

I threw my head back, like his. We both stood there for some minutes, listening to the creek and watching the incredible glittering array of stars. Although my neck was getting sore, I didn't want to look down. I breathed the cool night air, and for the first time in my hyperproductive summer truly took in my surroundings. He said, "The stars, all those stars, look at them, that's how you should play that passage; if it's not like that, don't even fucking bother." A good lesson, which I didn't ignore.

}

When I packed up the condo and hitched the same dubious Toyota down to New Mexico, I had the Brahms learned, and my fourth finger felt weak, but much better. My parents asked me how I was, and I said I was good, and it was true; I felt solid now, in a way I hadn't for months.

Back at Oberlin I moved into a cheap form of adulthood: a rental apartment with singer Chris and former roommate Sasha, on the "outskirts." This apartment had seen better days. The bathtub fell into the kitchen sink at one point, which didn't upset me. I was always at the Conservatory practicing, or listening to recordings of the Brahms.

For September I was a man of only one goal: the concerto competition. Joe Schwartz was thrilled, again, after such a long abandonment; we worked as hard as we ever had. He accompanied me in his studio. Like me, he loved the piece. It was rare for an Oberlin student to attempt it. He brought in a former colleague, a likable man named Jack Radunsky, to hear me—he thought I might listen better to another voice. Jack told me my second movement was too fast, which it almost certainly was, but I dismissed his advice. I wanted the second movement to be unleashed. There were two recordings of Brahms B-flat by Gilels: an official one that I thought very boring, and an earlier bootleg one that I thought was the best thing ever, and that was what I wanted to play like. The piece needed a mature sense of architecture and nobility, yes, yes, but it also needed young audacity, a force in tension.

I almost forgot to sign up for the competition. Joe warned me just before the deadline. I had to scribble myself in at the bottom of the form—"Jeremy Denk, Brahms Concerto No. 2"—and everyone thought that was my strategy. My classmates all hated me for trying to secure an advantage by going last. I told them the truth, that I was just desperately disorganized, but they didn't believe me.

So I ended up playing in the first round quite late—around 10:00 p.m. I don't remember it, my usual pattern for unhappy performances. All the others had played and were gathered in the lounge to sigh with relief or misery. After some nervous waiting, I made it through to the finals with three other pianists. Joe said, "Ehmmm, it was OK," but it was clear that I'd squeaked by. He told me to come in the next day to talk. He had to remind me to listen and breathe, to give me a list of things to do when everything is going wrong, ways to react when it seems like there is no time left.

The finals took place in a much friendlier room: Finney Chapel. No stone or cinderblock or windowless efficiency—only creaky wood. Finney was the concert venue, if I won. I remember playing that round, every moment. It was a mild fall morning, and someone backstage gave me a smile, and I especially remember sending my arm up confidently for that first ecstatic moment of the cadenza. For much of the cadenza the pianist storms and leaps about. But then an unstable G-flat slips down just one note to a low F, and this one change seems to "solve" all the previous leaps, to encompass them, to embrace and reverse them. At that moment, you feel, everything melts. Harmony becomes a liquid—not fragments and questions and shards, but complete. I remember playing that chord, and settling into it, and hearing it, with sunny rays crossing the stage, and a few judges far out in the creaky pews.

I won! Amazing news, and redemption of all my devotion and fear. Sasha's father, who was on the faculty, warned me not to get cocky. He said I "happened to play well" at the finals, and not so well in the semifinals, and that's what did it. He knew the truth: I had no dependable system, and my excellences were random. But I heard through the grapevine that Maurice Abravanel, the guest judge and a legendary conductor, loved me, and talked about me. It was great to get confirmation outside the Oberlin cocoon. When I'd entered Oberlin, it was the wider world, and now it wasn't.

❧

No question, I basked in this victory, and reveled in the sense that I had rescued myself through hard work and willpower. But normal life had to resume. I still ran about Oberlin, playing reams of music. Darrett had a girlfriend, which altered the duo dynamic, but we learned more iconic sonatas. In our lessons, I ignored Darrett and sucked out all the inspiration I could from Norman. Norman no longer hugged me. He was still great but less vivid. After the first wash of information, and the shock of his musical ideal, now our work was incremental, hacking away at the harder stuff—not ideas, but ways of executing them.

Larry remained a key presence. He harangued and convinced me to learn a piece by Olivier Messiaen, a small concerto for piano and winds called *Oiseaux Exotiques*. Larry said we were going to take it on tour: my first concerto tour! It was only one gig, in Austin, Texas, but never mind. I decided to play it from memory, an unnecessary over-achievement. I remember sitting at a corner of a dining table, ignoring my friends, shoveling shepherd's pie into my mouth and memorizing numbers of rests, 5 then 3 then 2½—rote, lonely cramming, like in my old organic chemistry days.

The Messiaen concert arrived. I played decently—at least, I never came in wrong. Occasionally I felt my right hand couldn't quite spit out the rhythms and articulations (if only I'd listened to Perry's wife!). But it was close. Larry seemed happy. I was basking and lounging onstage afterward, talking to my small group of friends, when Greg Fulkerson came down to the front of the hall.

"Congratulations," he said noncommittally. "It's really impressive that you memorized it," he added, as if he had my number, as if he knew perfectly well that I did that stunt to impress, and not to serve the music.

"Thanks, Greg," I said.

"However, you missed the whole point," he continued, smiling, without any sense of crossing a boundary, as if telling me the weather. "Messiaen isn't just about rhythm, it's also about color. It's mostly about color." (*Color, yes,* I thought, *dammit, color.*) "Did you read any of the descriptions of the birds, how he's trying to depict each plumage with a different collection of notes?" (No, I didn't.) "Try to keep in mind that it's French music. You have to let the piano ring, let it resound—don't just pound the rhythms out." Greg leapt up to the stage, surprisingly spry. The piano hadn't been rolled offstage yet. He demonstrated how you might do those things: how you'd touch the key in order to allow the piano to ring back, like a vocalist trying to get their voice to spin, and free their vibrato (something Richard Miller might have taught me?). They were subtle, the differences between Greg's attacks, like the sorts of things you saw percussionists getting obsessed about: the exact way to bring down a mallet, how much follow-through, whether to accelerate or slow into the target, how much arm and wrist to use, an awareness that the sound lived after the attack, and that the whole point of playing was to create ideal conditions for this ongoing reverberation, this fragile afterlife.

I ran back to the practice building to work until it closed. I'd focused on one virtue with Larry, and almost nailed it, but forgot about all the others. I tried to make my sounds more different, but they kept coming out the same. I tried to imagine colors in my head, but that had limited results, because—I often had to remind myself of this—you actually play the piano with your fingers. I didn't yet know about key speed, maybe the single most important and infuriatingly subtle variable of piano playing. But I was beginning to get a glimmer.

⟨

In December, the idea that I was going to leave Oberlin began to manifest in my mind. My parents' old doubts—how will you live as a musician?—began to seem relevant, almost as if they had foreseen things that I, at sixteen, had not. I told them I was done with chemistry and in fact anything other than music. No more indecision. They replied that I would have to pay my own way from graduation on out.

I knew John Perry wanted me to come to USC to study with him, based on things he'd said at Aspen. A good, solid option, a well-known teacher—why look elsewhere? And so I didn't spend much time preparing audition repertoire, unlike most seniors that year.

In January, though, I realized I could aim a bit higher and audition for the famous Curtis Institute, in Philadelphia. Brilliant idea! Unfortunately, they required Chopin Études. I couldn't bear to practice them, or I didn't know how. I didn't give them time to marinate. I brought them to Joe only once. None of our Brahms dialogue or wrestling, just a first draft, and then I flew off, an early shuttle flight from Cleveland, a grungy taxi into a scary city, two minutes of my insanely romantic Bach, and two more minutes of hesitant Chopin. I had little experience with live auditions. Gary Graffman told me I had a nice tie. But I didn't get in, not even past the first round. I pulled off my wrinkled suit and cried on the floor of my fancy hotel room on Rittenhouse Square, which even at a day rate seemed like an unbelievable wasted expense. When I returned, Darrett said, "Let me guess? You didn't practice?" again, rubbing it in. It would be John Perry at USC, then, I decided: a great choice.

Only a few weeks later, in March, in the middle of trying to understand my new girlfriend, Kate, and not knowing what the point of my classwork was anymore, I went to hear the Hungarian pianist György Sebők, visiting from Indiana University, where he taught. Oberlin had very few visiting artists, for whatever financial or faculty-ego reason.

It was odd, the way he walked onto the stage of Warner Hall, my most dreaded room, as if the stage floor were not wood but some sort of sliding and supporting carpet. He looked exotic and also much calmer than most people did around school. Sebők was then in his late sixties, short and squat, almost triangular, and epically bald down the middle of his head. He played a serious, hefty program, scaling heights and plumbing depths—Mozart C Minor Sonata, Schubert *Wanderer Fantasy*, Liszt sonata—and then offered an evanescent encore, the gigue (or jig) from Bach's first Partita.

The witty premise of the gigue is hand-crossings: the right hand burbles away in the middle of the keyboard, filling in the harmony, while the left darts over and under it, picking out scraps of melody and bass line. Toward the end, Bach arrives emphatically on the bass note F. He is, in music-theory terms, just one step away from the home key—the imminent end of the piece is implied—but instead of wrapping things up, he doubles the pace of hand-crossing and tightens the frame, so that the hands seem to whirl around each other. A clever paradox: though the piece is frozen in place, it seems to be moving faster than ever. As the hands whirl, the notes descend, and Bach visits every daring harmony he can, while sitting in the driveway mere moments from harmonic home. At last, in a flash, the piece resolves, and the left hand leaps up several octaves, like a slingshot or a skipping stone.

While performing this devilish sleight of hand, Sebők appeared angelic and unperturbed. The words "musical" and "unmusical" did not apply. It was as if the concepts behind the notes, playful and profound, had come alive. As he revealed each audacious but logical chord change, I experienced both shock and comprehension—surprise at something that made perfect sense. I can still see the last notes, his left arm gracefully crossing over his right, describing an arc to the final B-flat, his face conceding a small shadow of a smile. That moment felt like music escaping from the boring necessity of sound.

The next day, Sebők gave a master class at which I was scheduled to play. He was elegantly dressed, and smoked, in flagrant contravention of college rules, from a long cigarette holder. He rested his smoking elbow in the palm of his other hand, while I played through the first movement of my Brahms concerto. After the big orchestral passage, the pianist must somehow respond, and Brahms has you enter grandly, with low bass notes leaping up to treble chords. I played with nervous caution, missing a few notes. In front of everyone, Sebők told me to close my eyes for a full minute. There was silence, and I could smell the smoke from his cigarette. Then he told me that I knew the piano better than I imagined. (This rang some bell in me.) He had me visualize the whole area of the keyboard around and including that low F that I had to start with; he enumerated notes to think about, the dangerous E-natural next door, the F-sharp just above; and then—he was rational as he led me, step by step, through this mystical procedure—he had me play the treacherous passage with my eyes still closed, throwing my left hand confidently into darkness. Whether it was chance, or whether Sebők had managed to unlock a subconscious knowledge of the keyboard accumulated through years of practice, I nailed the passage. The sound was deeper and richer, even thunderous. A lifetime of difficulty had been replaced with a moment of ease.

}

I made my decision before I knew that I'd made it. I sat in the spell of Sebők's Bach for days; Joe noticed it too. We talked about it at my next lesson. And I kept thinking about the way that Sebők aimed to make the Brahms easier, whereas John Perry seemed to want it to be more difficult. Did I want my future to be easy or hard? I asked Robert Spano, a visiting conductor that year, and he said, "You should study with Sebők before he is gone. There aren't many people left like that." I asked another piano faculty member, Robert McDonald. Bob had attended my master class, and seen Sebők unlock something. "A rare connection," he said, as if finding a piano teacher were like falling in love. Even Greg, who I was sure would find Sebők too flowery and philosophical, told me he had no doubt; I had to go work with him.

But it was already March. I faced a flurry of tasks: applying to Indiana University, begging for a last-minute audition, borrowing a car, driving six hours down in the morning, waiting for a late-afternoon time slot where I played Brahms B-flat and some Bach-Busoni Chaconne and then they told me after ten minutes they didn't need to hear any more, then the six hours' drive back up, through the dark, thumping over the railroad tracks of Ohio's state highways and small towns, blurry-eyed and exhausted.

Indiana was happy to have me. My parents were surprised by my sudden change of plan. To them, Indiana University didn't appear prestigious. I explained to them things I had just learned about all the famous teachers there, all the great European masters, Gingold, Starker, Sebők, Pressler, Gulli, and all the imports from the golden era of the Cleveland Orchestra, Lifschey, Bloom, and on and on. They said, "Well, you know better than us, I guess."

I had to do something terrible: call John Perry at USC and explain to him that I wasn't coming to study with him. Inexplicably, I chose the pay phone in the Conservatory lounge, surrounded by people using vending machines. I hoped he wouldn't answer but there he was, and when I told him my news he said "What do you mean?" and then something else about missed opportunities, and "I can't believe this" and then at last "All right," the same thing he would say to pianists when he was getting ready to wallop them in front of everyone. He said "Good luck," but the tone in his voice reminded me of when I broke up with Polly the third time.

That wasn't the end of it. Larry Rachleff, who was also planning to teach at USC for a while, came to me explaining the importance of being in a big city like Los Angeles, all the connections and opportunities, and how much John wanted to teach me, and what an honor it was to be selected by him. That there would be money for me to live and study. All of this was true, and Sebők would never bother to do a full-court press like this. Nonetheless, for the first time in my life I was sure; I'd made a decision based on what seemed to me to be musical truth. I wouldn't drift to a teacher by accident; I would choose.

⸘

May blossomed (just like the first song of *Dichterliebe*). I paid hundreds of library fines. I went to Norman's studio to thank him for everything. He was sure I'd have a wonderful future. I went to Greg to say goodbye. He'd lined up a summer job for me—we would see each other all too soon, he said with his wicked smile. Joe told me to try to concentrate, and that I had a huge talent. Carol Webber hugged me in a big cloud of perfume. David Walker, my English prof, took me for a walk and urged me to keep writing. Philip Highfill told me it had been an honor to work with me. Kate, however, decided she was done: she didn't want to date anymore. She wanted no part of "long distance." Standing next to me, she felt it was already long distance.

My parents arrived for commencement. I sold all my chemistry books back to the bookstore, while they looked on uncomfortably. That was that. The school convulsed with protests about apartheid, a series of candlelight vigils, beautiful and unsettling. Dad said it was sure different from Notre Dame.

The night before graduation, a panic set in. I abandoned my parents and got drunk on a couple White Russians and felt shooting stomach pains. I craved my year-end packing ritual with Polly—why had I been such a jerk to Polly?—but she was elsewhere. Home alone, I couldn't sleep; a few hours later I woke up, shocked at how I looked in the mirror. What had I learned in four years? I cut myself shaving. I toilet papered over a few wounds, donned a cap and gown, and headed over to the quad alone. The sun was warm—too warm. I won a slew of prizes, both piano and chemistry. An embarrassing number. The president of the college took me aside after I got my diploma and said, "Keep in touch." This should have made me feel amazing. But everyone and every idea I'd ever cared about was vanishing in one ceremonial day.

My parents, never lingerers, had booked us to fly out of Cleveland airport that evening. After a few dozen harried goodbyes, they drove me over to my apartment to fetch my things. My father came upstairs to help, and so we both saw it at once: I hadn't even begun to pack. The room was a wreck. The rental car idled below on the curb. How could I not have noticed? I began to sob. There were hours, maybe days, of sorting and cleaning to do. The only answer was to grab what I could and move on. My dad asked helpful questions—Do you want to take this? Do you want to leave that?—but I had no voice to reply.

{

You may have noticed that I left out one part of the story: my performance of the Brahms concerto, theoretically the great prize at the end of a long process. I often feel performances are afterthoughts, even now. It happened on a Tuesday in early April. The conductor was a new arrival named David Pollitt. I really wished it had been Larry. Pollitt was a cipher, and he might have been annoyed to negotiate this adult work with a child.

None of Sebők's fresh advice adhered to my performance. How could it? I don't remember any highlights. Just the lighting of the stage—too bright—and a few moments of holding on for dear life. My parents organized a little post-reception in my slum apartment: I have pictures of me in a tux, with long and tousled hair, and my girlfriend in the closest thing she had to a dress. My parents loved Joe, which made me feel weird. A day or so later a review appeared in the *Akron Beacon Journal*—why were they at a student orchestra concert?—saying that at first "Denk's interpretation was apparently unclear even to himself," but that as the movements progressed, it got better, and I deserved my hearty ovation by the end. As it happened, I felt most strongly about the first movement and much less passionately about the last. I wasn't too upset about it, but with this mixed review—my first real review—the whole love affair, the Brahms story, ended; I have not, to this date, performed it in public again. It is still my favorite piece.

I haven't spoken much about the third movement, the slow movement, the most powerful of the piece's achievements. It's not easy to pinpoint how the opening cello solo works. There are hardly any sharps or flats—no fancy harmonic footwork, and not much striking melodic motion either. It distills unbearable loss out of the common and familiar. It declares that you don't need to leave the good old B-flat-major scale, saying *It's all there, still; the old chords and ways aren't played out yet.*

Eventually, the movement turns into the minor. Sorrow, formerly restrained, beats its chest. We approach Romantic cliché: a worn-down protagonist in tragic collapse. But with one move, Brahms rescues us from both tragedy and cliché. He re-spells a note: B-flat becomes A-sharp. It's the same note but not the same. This creates a doorway from one key to a remote other key, and another world—like the wardrobe I used to love, leading to Narnia.

Once we've stepped into this alternate dimension, Brahms keeps the pianist occupied with a humble task: leaping toward, and landing on, high notes. Something about these gestures, their naïve and obvious aspiration, is heartbreaking. The piano can easily play these upward leaps, but because of the decay built into the instrument, the high notes can't sustain. You get direction and desire, but not continuation. In his genius, Brahms summons a second soloist. A clarinet begins to play, and hold, the high notes that the piano has reached. This doesn't solve the problem of the piano so much as call emotional attention to it. There is an uncanny transference from the *ping* of the keyboard to the stream of the wind timbre: the clarinet becomes the sustain, the breath, that which the piano (or pianist) can never be. You might say it consoles the piano for being a piano.

The Oberlin Orchestra clarinetist offered me money (déjà vu of Ruben, the bassoonist mayor, at my very first concerto gig) not to play this passage too slowly. He was running out of breath. I told him I'd do my best, but I always wanted it slower. In this passage, Brahms is after the illusion that we have left this piece of music, or any piece; that we've abandoned the very idea of composition to find ourselves in a suspended moment of experience. By some allowance of the gods, time has agreed to stop. This temporary paradise comes at a price. The music feels endless, but also—already, long since—over.

12. *Melody* LESSON THREE

‖ E. T. A. HOFFMANN: "The Fermata"
‖ VERDI: *Falstaff*, Act I, Scene 2

J recommend that everyone who loves music make just a little time in their lives to read stories by E. T. A. Hoffmann, who pried open a fantastical door to deep musical knowledge, and is also extremely funny. In one of my favorite of his stories, "The Fermata," we meet a young, idealistic German musician in a provincial town. This young man's main influence has been the local organist: "a dry arithmetician, he plagued me to death with obscure, unmelodious toccatas and fugues." Only one singer lives in the area, a Miss Meibel, with a "horrible squeaky voice" and a penchant for "ludicrous flourishes and roulades." Our protagonist mocks this poor lady while his organist-mentor eggs him on: "The more decidedly I came to share with my master his contempt for singing, the higher did he rate my musical genius."

But when two slender, mysterious Italian singers arrive in town, he throws all his old music on the fire, and devotes himself to melody with absolute zeal. It's unclear whether he is more attracted to the ladies or their irresistible Italian tunes. He begins to tour with them, conducting their orchestral accompaniments. Hoffmann writes hilarious scenes about these rehearsals, how the ladies berate the young man, mock him, praise him, shower him with affection. Melody is capricious, but our love-blind hero doesn't care.

One day it all comes to an end. He's conducting the wilder of the two singers, and she decides to take a fermata on her high note—hence the title of the story. For those who don't know, a fermata is an attractive musical symbol, a kind of period with a halo, that instructs you to hold on to a note (or a silence) for an unspecified length of time.

On a whim, she extends this high note beyond all reason, and for some reason today of all days he loses patience with her, and with melody itself. He brings in the orchestra before she's ready to move on, trampling her great moment. She goes into a fury. This interruption is a mortal sin. What he's done is unforgivable, and even worse, German.

Beneath the comedy lies a moral. Hoffmann shows how a common musical marking has tremendous resonance: the fermata is a symbol of melody's prime directive. A melody "wants" to sustain, to hold on, to keep spinning out. The more you examine melodies, the more you see this survival instinct at work: the way tunes keep threading through a few notes, trying to find new ways forward. Sometimes this holding-on can seem desperate, at other times egocentric, indulgent, or tedious; but at its best it is an act of attachment, a preservation, a tenderness.

In the Brahms B Major Trio (from the first Melody chapter), there's a quintessential tender moment of that last sort. As we descend from the cellist's first ravishing A-sharp, Brahms slowly inches down the scale, one pair of notes at a time, aiming for repose. But at each step he climbs back up to hear the last pair again. He (or the music, or both) can't quite let go. As this melody moves into the future, it keeps clinging to the past: not a bad summary of human existence.

When I worked as an opera coach in grad school, I'd walk down the hall and hear dozens of singers in their separate rooms, practicing run-ups to famous high notes. There'd be a few unrecognizable words of Italian or French, a sentiment of love or woe or duty (it didn't matter—they could deal with meanings later in life when they were professionals), and up they'd go, a young unknown voice making an assault on the fort of the old and famous Held Note, which would be tight, or wobbly, or (rarely) perfect. Anyway, all three options gave the same practice room result: if good, they'd try to reproduce it; if bad, they'd try to fix it. So almost every high note was cut off too soon (the moment they realized what had happened), in mid-soar, like the cry of a chicken as the blade comes down. It was pretty funny to hear all that ecstasy, mass-produced then thrown away: all those holds, unheld.

In the pianists' practice area, it was a different story. Young pianists almost never practice melodies. They practice passages: fast ones, like the gnarly one near the beginning of Beethoven's "Les Adieux"; or the coda of Chopin's Fourth Ballade; or the famous skips at the end of Liszt's Mephisto Waltz. There's no ego or triumph at the piano in holding a long note. It's the easiest, least satisfying thing in the piano universe. It shines a spotlight on the piano's weakest point. So pianists tend to practice fast passages, disjunct leaps, forests and thickets of notes, while singers labor and labor to find the right approach to just one beautiful note, and eventually hold the hell out of it, as a summary and culmination, a gateway to fame.

{

In Verdi's last opera, the comedy *Falstaff,* he wrote any number of ravishing tunes, some of the most lovely of his long life—he was eighty-four years old—but they don't tend to stick around. I've always loved Randall Jarrell's description in his novel *Pictures from an Institution:* "little themes that come in, flicker their wings once, and are gone forever."

A perfect example flickers its wings in the second scene, when Falstaff's identical love letters have reached their destinations. Alice and Meg, the recipients, read them aloud to Nanetta and Dame Quickly. All four mock the craven, bumbling fool, copying and pasting his booty calls. But then the comedy seamlessly gradates into an ecstatic Italian aria (how does Verdi manage that?). The voice leaps up twice, with a tiny curlicue in the middle:

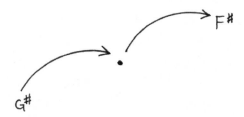

The first leap is four notes; then there's another leap of five—the details aren't important, except that there are two leaps and two gaps. Verdi then makes the singer leap both in one go, like a horse over two obstacles. This helps us to hear the distance. And once we're on the F-sharp, while the words of the letter sizzle away, he begins to retrace the notes he has left behind (here we are again, with melody filling our voids):

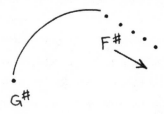

Verdi lets the voice slide down from the high notes chromatically—with close-spaced notes. This has an immediate, desperate effect, a sense of burrowing within the space we've leapt over, intimately touching each skipped step. The tune splits in two: one half a vaulting gymnast, jumping over spaces; the other crawling and sliding along like a rock climber, one handhold at a time. The tension is key—the conversion of ease into difficulty, the pull of one motion against the other, as if the voice were a balloon that wanted to drift up and up but some conflicting desire slowly pulls it back down. Melody draws endless metaphorical connections between motion and emotion.

After some commentary in the orchestra, the voice summons itself for one more leap. It sails from C-sharp, up five steps to G-sharp. But forget the individual notes—the crucial thing is that this new peak is one step higher than the previous F-sharp. Just one note: almost nothing on the piano keyboard, a rounding error; but a world of difference for the human voice. I cannot shake images of snakes in YouTube videos where they open their mouths quite wide to swallow a hamster, and then realize, mid-swallow, they have to open yet wider. The sense of something greater to fill, of a stretching muscle, of effort merged with desire. This high G-sharp is human achievement, without any of achievement's sad side effects. It combines the feeling of achieving with the not-yet-achieved.

At this rapturous apex, Verdi writes out a fermata. He allows the singer, and us, to hold on. I feel as though the previous elements of the melody—forces of ascent and descent—are surging and welling behind this great hold. In these sorts of climaxes you are made aware of melody's connection to breath, the body, to life itself. This melody's life is about to be over, but before it gives up it will do something spectacular and unforgettable.

In the normal and proper course of opera, such a fermata would be followed by riotous applause, flowers, and cries of "Brava!" But instead comes Verdi's unexpected masterstroke: the singer abandons the ecstasy, executes a few clichéd wrap-up gestures, and all four ladies laugh. I find this laughter shocking, like crumpling a Rembrandt and tossing it over your shoulder into the trash can. It makes sense within the drama, of course—they're laughing at Falstaff—but I get the sense that Verdi is mocking me, and you, in fact all of us listeners, and in some ways himself: *Did you fall for that?* he asks. *Did you buy into my bag of tricks?* This melody, you realize, was a lesson and a warning. An old wise man whispering that melody's innocence is not that innocent, and that its seductive gifts can be used for good or evil.

PART THREE: *Rhythm*

13. *"Nothing Is Done, Everything Is Done"*

CHARLES IVES: Trio, S. 86
MOZART: Sonata no. 14 in C Minor, K. 457, first movement
BARTÓK: Piano Sonata (1922), first movement
CHOPIN: Fantaisie in F Minor, op. 49
BRAHMS: Sonata no. 1 for Violin and Piano in G Major, op. 78

For a few weeks after Oberlin, I moped in New Mexico. Kate had broken up with me. My friends were scattered to the four winds. Only my parents were unaltered, and unalterable. One day my mom came to my room with a letter—"For you, bub"—from Polly. I closed the door and ripped the envelope open. Polly started with a mini-essay on life choices, and a flow chart, and then came a kind of James Joyce stream-of-consciousness description of everything that had passed through her mind, good and bad, while she'd seen me standing up in protest about apartheid on graduation day. It was the greatest love letter I'd ever received. But I couldn't figure out how to respond, so I filed it away in the bottom drawer of my childhood desk.

I was permitted to mooch and pout around the house for those weeks because, starting in mid-June, I had my first paying musical job. I'd been hired as staff accompanist at a string camp called Musicorda in western Massachusetts. Six weeks of labor, six days a week, twelve hundred bucks. I didn't think about whether an accompanying position served my larger career goals. My father worried about this, while practical Mom found me a cheap plane ticket to New England. They drove me to the airport, said a more emotional goodbye than usual, and ten hours later I was back in a dorm room with high ceilings and stark white walls.

Musicorda was housed in Mount Holyoke College, a gorgeous campus, all grass and stone and ponds and hidden gardens. My duties were to learn whatever the string students wanted to play. The days took on a purpose and a recurring rhythm. I accompanied lessons in the morning, slogging through decadent music like the Chausson *Poème,* or the Richard Strauss Violin Sonata, which had fun climaxes stacked upon climaxes. Then I practiced for long, humid afternoons. No worries other than trying to play well. In the evenings, some staff and students would head out to the Hu Ke Lau, a Polynesian cocktail joint with waterfalls, or skinny-dip off a sandbar in the Connecticut River with a cooler full of beer we'd hauled through the muck. This was a true summer. Though fully employed, it was one of the first times I felt free.

Good old Greg Fulkerson was on the violin faculty of Musicorda. He had gotten me the gig, and also asked if I'd play a trio by Charles Ives with him in a public concert. I said yes, of course. I'd heard about Ives in music history class, and half-played a couple of his pieces. Professors said he was Historically Important, but you couldn't shake the feeling that they talked about him because they had to. Ives was (as far as I could tell) the crazy uncle of American music, weaving familiar tunes—hymns, ragtime, marches—into unsettling quilts.

I remember walking in for our first rehearsal, trying not to look like a student. It was a mildewy room with windows onto a spreading oak and the usual clutter of music faculty offices: dusty scores on metal shelves, a desk covered with obsolete memos. Greg gave me the same impish smile I remembered from Oberlin, and seemed pleased to see me, despite all the doubts he'd expressed over the years about my musicianship. But by the time the cellist arrived, Greg's mood had already darkened. I'd bought a new, highly edited version of the Ives by John Kirkpatrick, who'd known the composer for much of his life.

"Composers' friends are the worst," Greg said.

The cellist and I glanced at each other. We were nervous enough to learn the piece. We couldn't deal, yet, with questions of textual authenticity. But for Greg, the truth of Ives was a big question, maybe the only question. OK, he said at last with a sigh, we'll cross out all the Kirkpatrick bullshit as we go.

We started. In the second measure, I brought my left hand up to help my right hand reach a few big chords.

"What do you think you're doing?" Greg asked.

"My hand isn't big enough for all those notes," I told him.

"Yes, well, deal," he said, in the same withering tone he'd used for Kirkpatrick. I gave him a helpless look. He sighed and began to explain Ives's premise: right hand for the first bit, left for the next, and only in the last section could I put my hands together. The halves came together in a glorious, hideous, dissonant crunch, a classic Charles Ives screw-you to the audience. This was obvious now that I looked at it, like a lot of Greg's advice. Why did I still need him to show me the obvious?

We played on. I noticed Greg often shifted his short, ungainly body to get ergonomic advantage. He had to find his center. Once it was found, and only then, he would venture a yearning crescendo, or a relinquishing slide. Everything beautiful he did required support. I looked in the convenient studio mirror and noticed I was a morass of floppy joints, still; a puppet without a hand, a house without a frame. This floppiness made me tense, I realized. (If only I'd listened to Perry's wife!)

Greg's playing gradually distracted me from these insecurities. I'd never played with anyone so good, or so clear about what he was after. For one moment he marched, erect and proud, but a few seconds later he slid across some naughty blue notes, and after that he was all ecstatic innocence—as if running offstage to switch costumes and roles between a bandmaster, a drunk town crank, and an untutored woman singing a hymn because that was her only avenue to transcendence in our wicked world. Each voice rang true, but none was the main voice. It was an entire vanished New England village, reanimated, re-created, arguing at revival meetings and hailing each other on the street. Ives's mistakes started to feel right. In fact, right and wrong inverted, exchanging meanings, like major and minor in Schubert.

We had to work slowly through the second movement, a joyful, deafening representation of a frat party. Lots of laughter and rolled eyes as the cellist came in wrong hundreds of times. But then, in the last movement, Greg began to play in an elevated style. I'd heard him demonstrate emotional passages before—bits of Brahms, saying archly, "This is how we played it in the Cleveland Orchestra"—but I hadn't heard this. It was like digging down through all his mocking layers of analysis and intelligence to a secret place where even he could find nothing to mock. The hymn was a reference point, but laid on top were chords and ornaments from the world of Wagner and Schumann. Incompatible styles that should hate each other. Greg's playing projected faith that it all belonged. I couldn't help thinking of Polly's letter, and her faith in incompatible me, after all my stupidity. Maybe I should have written back to her.

In the middle of the third movement, I had my big transcendental moment. I had to interrupt the strings to offer what can only be described as a sour blur. It's not clear where this blur comes from, or where it's going: it simply appears and exists for a while. I'd been taught that phrases were supposed to go somewhere, but this moment seemed serenely determined to wander nowhere.

"What should I do?" I asked Greg.

He offered some advice about pedaling, which didn't work, and rehearsal ended. But a day or two later, we were driving off campus for a proper meal and happened to cross a bridge, high over the Connecticut River. Greg said, out of nowhere: "You should play it like that." (Just like Alex Goor, the summer previous, in Aspen.) From the bridge the river seemed impossibly wide. It was bathed in late-afternoon light, oranges, pinks, and golds. Instead of a single current you saw a million intersecting currents—urgent and lazy rivers within the river, magical pockets of no motion at all.

Now I knew how to play the passage, and I saw rivers differently. Centuries of classical music had prettified them, ignoring their reality to turn them into musical objects. Schubert used tuneful flowing brooks to murmur comfort to suicidal lovers; Wagner placed maidens and fateful rings at the bottom of a heroically surging Rhine. But Ives gives you crosscurrents, dirt, haze—the disorder of a zillion particles crawling downstream. His rivers aren't constrained by human desires and stories; they possess the beauty of their own randomness and drift.

The cellist had been a good sport the whole time, dealing with me and Greg, two man-children from different generations, not to mention Ives himself. At last she got her reward. At the end of his Trio, good old Charles saves his best trick, which—like the opening movement—is a simple matter of addition. The blur (the river) returns. But this time, layered on top of it, the cello plays the hymn "Rock of Ages." In the piano, murk and mystery. In the cello, one of the most known and loved tunes of all time. The known and unknown reach out and find each other, with a shiver of epiphany. "I get it now," the cellist said, smiling and surrendering. She saw what Ives was about, and so did I. Like many music teachers, Ives did everything possible to piss you off and mess with your head, then begged you (despite it all) for belief.

The night of the concert arrived. We performed for a hundred or so people. A famous violin teacher named James Buswell came back afterward, yelling "That was fantastic!" Greg hugged me, a true shock. I'd found a new compositional hero. As I walked out into the New England night and the sound of crickets I thought, *Yes, it was fantastic,* and for once I wasn't thinking about myself.

{

Summer's idyll came to an end. I collected my twelve hundred dollars and headed to Bloomington for the next phase of life. I rented an apartment out by the mall and bought a tin-can car. Sasha had also decided to study in Indiana, so we were roommates yet again. We had a kindly, emaciated landlord, Leonard, who always smelled of bacon and eggs. Putt-Putt sat across the sad courtyard lawn. We taped up Klimt posters, got a VCR, filled a cupboard with Kraft Mac & Cheese, and voilà: ready to become State University Students.

On my first visit to campus, I walked the gray hallways of the music school reading names of legendary faculty: the Italian violinist Franco Gulli; the Hungarian cellist János Starker; the Russian-born violinist Josef Gingold. I was surrounded by Europe and at the same time marooned in cornfields, with a frat house across the street.

I'm afraid to say that I turned up for my first lesson in a T-shirt, shorts, and sneakers. Sebők came down the corridor in a three-piece suit and appraised me silently in the few moments it took to unlock his door. It was clear that we had no business meeting for any purpose other than music.

I played the Mozart C Minor Sonata—a bold move, since it had been the opening piece for his recital, back in Oberlin in April. When I finished the first movement, Sebők got up and went over to a Michelangelo drawing he had on the wall. He pointed to various lines in the drawing, ranging from quite dark to almost invisible, and began to flesh out a metaphor: Mozart is made up of two-, three-, four-, and eight-bar phrases, all in a row, and punctuated by cadences of various kinds. If you're not careful, the row can resemble a string of sausages. The solution was to find more varied and more sensual ways of ending phrases—like drawing charcoal over paper, creating a curved or straight line. Not every boundary was the same; in Mozart, even the punctuation was supposed to sing.

I nodded and listened, but Sebők saw the meaning was drifting over my head. We continued on to the second movement, and he neither praised nor criticized it. Instead he told me it was a Don Juan serenade, and began to demonstrate, drawing a connection between Mozart's florid ornamentation and the art of flirtation. The presence of sex behind Mozart's ruffles had been mostly unknown to me.

The aim of that first lesson, I later realized, was to ennoble the art of practicing. You were not practicing "phrasing," that generic and soporific word that so many teachers use; you were drawing like Michelangelo, or seducing like Don Juan. Sebők said many times that you don't teach piano playing at lessons; you teach how to practice—the daily rite of discovery where learning really happens.

At that first lesson he did one of his most sublime parlor tricks. He played a stretch of melody that culminated in a long held note, and warned me with a raised eyebrow to listen. As he shifted the underlying harmony I heard the melody note crescendo and blossom, by some confluence of overtones—defying the piano's innate decay. I looked at him with wonder and a smile, and tried to reproduce that incredible effect. It is typical of pianists not to remember to listen to the note after it is played—we are always, for all kinds of practical reasons, preparing the next. That's why Sebők sounded so different, I thought: because he listened and molded the sound, with gentle but firm hands, like someone forming clay at a wheel.

}

This kind of nuance was the reason I'd come to Bloomington, but the price seemed high. Bloomington was no Oberlin, I kept telling everyone, and myself. All that gray limestone. Too many normal people, too few philosophical discussions. Life was now much more a dance of logistics: parking, cooking, scheduling. The apartment abutted train tracks, and every night at 3:00 a.m. the hoots would wake you: some sort of commodity, hogs maybe, or wheat, something basic traveling across the country to be sold or slaughtered.

I was paying for grad school with an opera coaching assistantship. They gave me a small office in the innermost oval of the not-quite-round building (known as the "toilet bowl"), several radiation-proof layers away from natural light, with fluorescent bulbs and particleboard walls, and just enough room to stand. In private appointments with the singers, I taught them notes and rhythms. They didn't want to hear about phrasing. That was dangerous. They'd look at me like startled sheep, like I was trying to overload their heads.

These one-on-one sessions gradually gave way to blocks of rehearsal, when my life was no longer my own. My first assignment was Verdi's *La Traviata*—an opera central to the soundtrack of my childhood. But my hands couldn't live up to the recording I remembered. My *oom-pah-pah*s seemed so pedestrian, so un-Italian. Much of rehearsal had to do with maneuvering characters onstage so that the person singing would always be facing out. This was comical, then just boring. Still no discussion of phrasing. I'd start at random locations, in the heat of love or anxiety, while the singers tried not to aggravate the director, who loved the nasal sound of his own voice, and had a well-honed tyrannical shtick.

The singers came to cherish me after a while, as if I were an over-achieving pet. The conductor warned me I was playing too sensitively, and that I mustn't follow the singers, because then they would get used to it and would be in shock when the lumbering orchestra arrived. I told him I'd try my best to play like an orchestra, but then I'd get carried away again. The conductor would give me a wink of surrender and stop conducting (anyway, the singers weren't watching), and his eyes would say, *OK, do what you want,* and I'd let myself have some private ecstasy on that clanky piano.

One of the cast came over to chat a lot—his name was Lucas, I think. He always stepped on my coat, which I always put in a heap on the floor, next to the piano. Smart but odd, he did a perfect imitation of the director: "Honey, I've been doing this longer than you've been toilet-trained. Park yourself and sing out, OK? What kind of walk is that, are you in a Parisian garret or a shopping mall?" I snorted. It was true— you felt a disconnect between Verdi's abundant empathy and the bitchiness of the opera rehearsal process. Lucas and I exchanged brief life stories. He complained about his crazy roommate. I told him that I was really getting into cooking, now that I was an adult, that I'd just discovered it, and so he invited himself over for dinner.

A few nights later, I prepared a box of mac and cheese with special care. I added bits of chicken and—the master touch!—some oregano. Sasha shared the meal with us, at our folding table. After some conversation and a bit of hesitation, I told Lucas that it was lots of fun, and showed him the door. Sasha came into my room a few minutes later. "You know he didn't come over for mac and cheese, right?" he said. "What do you mean?" I said.

{

Sebők didn't exactly "walk" down the curvy hall of the toilet bowl building. He had an unusual gait—he explained at one lesson that he'd suffered a crushed disc in a labor camp (!) and therefore was angled forward, "which is convenient for piano playing." With his elegant suits, and his expression so far above the mediocrity of the architecture, and that sense of sliding along the hall guided by his middle, it felt like he didn't just enter your field of vision but manifested, a minor miracle.

For my second lesson, I'd taken Sebők's suggestion and learned the Bartók sonata. I got it in my fingers in a week—amazing to me now, and stupid then. The piece abounded with octaves and fourth fingers, in alternation—the same motion that produced my injury, which was fresh in my mind, and would even reappear sometimes for a day or two. Sebők was pleased I had learned it (he hadn't heard it yet). But first he said, "People tell me that you are coaching opera. Is this an interest of yours?"

"Yes," I said.

"Why?" he asked.

"That's how I'm paying for school," I said, and Sebők's face darkened.

"When I was a student," he said, "we had no money at all and we were often hungry, knocking on each other's doors, begging each other for glasses of milk."

"I also just love opera, the music is so satisfying," I replied, stumbling into it, trying to be truthful, feeling insecure that I couldn't express what it was, that the word "satisfying" wasn't satisfying enough to capture the visceral pleasure of an operatic climax.

This was a better answer. Sebők smiled. "Yes," he said. "When I was coaching *The Magic Flute* with Furtwängler" (and now we were back in a dazzling world, a European history that I knew only by reading, association, study, and in which I was always an outsider), "I remember how he conducted the entrance of the Queen of the Night . . ." Sebők trailed off, then sat to play a bit of it from memory, a deep memory, unlit cigarette in his mouth, head turned ninety degrees toward me at first, until he seemed to forget I was there.

"There is a lot to learn from opera," he said, "and a lot not to learn."

Then it was time to work. I played through Bartók's first movement, not too well, with a few stops and starts. Sebők paused to maneuver something cigarette-related on his desk, said "OK, thank you" (a formality), and then: "Every composer speaks a certain language. There is a grammar, and the music doesn't make sense until you learn to speak it, until you learn what are verbs and what are nouns." After all these words about words, he began to sing, sort of—it was more like a whisper with a pulse. There weren't notes, just hints of contour. The most important feature was the kick of each offbeat, which he produced with a slightly more emphatic breath. As he did this he looked off and up, diagonally, a pose I came to know well—finding the invisible music.

I'll never forget this moment, but it took years to figure out why he sang so quietly: to separate energy from violence. It didn't matter if you played these notes loud, soft, medium: the essence was the same. The offbeats created a continuous vector away and up. This was so different from other composers, from Classical and Romantic beats. In Brahms, you often find notes and beats in passionate friction. Beethoven's music is littered with *sforzandi,* which (as Sebők often said) represent "alternative downbeats," acts of will, as in *No, we are here, whether you like it or not.* But these Bartók accents weren't acts of will, or alternatives—they were frictionless. They were energy directed toward the future, a buoyancy.

Sebők reminded me of the many little slurs and articulations in Mozart that we'd paid attention to the week before. There were a million of those in the Bartók, too. "It's not the same if you play two separate notes or two slurred ones," he said, "the *meaning* changes." We worked on that for a while, and the second theme began to dance. Did I have to travel all the way to my great guru just to hear my mother's old advice? But then the dance collapsed into a big dissonant chord, and he stopped me.

"When the Notre Dame was built," he said, "the Magyars were still living in huts." Then he played the chord I'd come to, and some we were about to pass through, and sat on them to savor the grit. I had to taste those intervals. Even within all this fierce dissonance, he found degrees and layers.

A little farther on, we came to a C-sharp that gets played again and again. He stopped me, came over to adjust my arm, then returned to the piano.

"Idée fixe," he said, looking me straight in the eyes; it was a term I'd learned in music history class, from Berlioz's *Symphonie Fantastique*—a recurring theme symbolizing a romantic obsession. And then he demonstrated. His repeated C-sharp wasn't repetitive. It was an object for thought, both same and different. You wanted to hear what happened to it. How was that possible? Afterward, I went straight to my practice prison to explore hypotheticals: a series of repeated C-sharps played as if giving up on the note, thinking about the note, tired of the note, delighted with the note. Giving the smallest detail a backstory.

Still, this lesson was going on. It would be years before I could process all the information he gave me that one morning. In the middle of the first movement comes the most difficult, most changeable section, where I'd lost my place. The right hand slides up to an accented note, which becomes an "extra beat," after which the left hand starts up again. Sebők demonstrated. His right hand slithered up, landed on the accent, and then he lifted his left arm the slightest bit, giving it a tiny bubble of time and space to react. "This note should come a bit . . . too late," he said, and it was impossible not to smile at the tiny delay. His hands acted like people—discombobulated, reacting to the unexpected.

Notes that come too late or too soon were a big Sebők theme. I miss this so much now in adult life, in rehearsals with orchestras or colleagues. If you say "This note should come a bit too soon," most musicians will look at you with skepticism. Classical training has a bias toward notes having a place, arriving at the moment they're supposed to. But Sebők, like a jazz musician, loved the front and back sides of beats.

After a half hour of this teaching, I didn't have the desires of previous lessons: I didn't need to be praised. I just needed more of what he was giving me, and wished it would never end. He probably saw some danger in my adoring puppy-dog eyes, and decided—enough. He went on a tirade about the totalitarianism of the IU parking system, until another student arrived.

}

In those first weeks of the semester, I got back together with Kate. She was still in Oberlin, and still fascinating and complicated. Our connection was intense, but mutually destructive. Energy that could have been used to focus on my lessons got dispersed in six-hour drives, and sleepless nights with deep discussions and pointless fights. Some imaginary young-person problems, and some working through the issues of our parents.

I drove back from Oberlin late one Sunday night, and brought in the Mozart last movement the next morning. Bartók was undergoing renovations. The Mozart was quite brief, and I hoped Sebők wouldn't be mad. He didn't appear either pleased or displeased. But when I tried to play the theme—a series of syncopations that never seem to land—he stopped me short, to lay down one of his most fundamental rules.

"Some notes are up, and some notes are down," he said. "Don't play against gravity."

Sebők started with the left hand, making distinctions between notes that were anchors and those that led on. Then he took my right hand, which was flailing about, trying to keep up with a series of sighs, and manipulated my wrist.

"This is up," he said, and then I played, and he said, "No. Up." And I realized that I had no idea what up and down actually were, in relation to my piano playing. Everything was whatever direction I could manage.

"Now down," he said, and he grabbed my wrist and made it abandon its usual post, hunched above the rest of my hand like a vulture waiting to strike. *Oh yes, that's nice,* I thought. But it also felt unnatural at first, this simple concession to gravity, as if I were surrendering my will and absolving myself of responsibility. Outsourcing the act of music-making.

"It might feel," Sebők said, "as if you aren't doing anything."

Yes, and my wrist isn't used to being such a flexible and adaptable hinge, I thought.

"There is a Zen expression," he continued. "When nothing is done, everything is done." I admit that through all the wonder, sometimes the Zen stuff felt a bit much. What did that expression even mean? Wasn't piano playing an action, by definition? I thought back to beloved Norman Fischer, who always started by looking for much more, like Dagwood making a submarine sandwich, while Sebők also wanted to find more, but by way of much less.

My next lesson took place after yet another round trip to Oberlin, fraught with sex and doubt. I'd been still hammering at the rest of the Bartók, but it wasn't ready, and so I decided to cram the Chopin Fantaisie. I remember driving over to campus, and trying to parallel park my Volkswagen. My arms ached, not from piano playing. I could barely move the wheel. I cursed my lack of power steering as I walked several tree-lined blocks over to the music building, in a fog.

Sebők came down the hall looking pleased with himself. His wife was indisposed, a curious cause for joy. But because she was in bed: "I vacuumed this morning," he said. "I feel that I've done something." He looked utterly adorable as he declared that all his piano philosophizing was useless in solving the world's practical problems. I hated to get rid of his happy smile—but I had to play my Chopin. The keyboard seemed like a minefield. My fingers slipped off the black keys; I felt I had to hold on, with a tenacious grip that only made me more tired. In a panic about that, and to cover it up, I tried some wild musical gestures. The structure of the piece disintegrated.

Sebők let me play through half—about up to the first bombastic march—and then just said, "Stop, please." I was relieved to halt this ongoing dumpster fire. "Let us not waste time," he said in a monotone I'd not yet heard. This was the tone of his greatest moments of anger—when he felt he was being disrespected. He continued: "When I go to Japan to teach, every student is prepared, the music is memorized, they take care of everything." I was using sheet music for the Chopin. It had taken all my effort to try to fail to learn the rest of the Bartók sonata, and meanwhile I had opera rehearsals, and classes, and Kate.

Reminding me of Greg's rants, but sadder and less smug, Sebők went on a quiet tear about my lack of attention to the written page: Chopin's phrasings, dynamics, and meticulously marked pedalings. He was most incensed about the last. These days I know how careful and meaningful those markings are, but back then I assumed they could be ignored. "Oh," I said, "I thought those were just helpful suggestions."

"You are a full-grown musician," he replied, even more disappointed than before, "it's too late for 'reading comprehension.'"

I'd never had the urge to cry in Schwartz's lessons, despite all their

226 · *Every Good Boy Does Fine*

sorrows, but now I felt it coming on. I fled the studio. A couple of days later, I found out that I had mononucleosis, and called Sebők to tell him. "Ah," he said, "that explains a good deal." All seemed forgiven. But the honeymoon period had been brought to a premature end, and the possibility of mutual frustration entered the relationship.

}

The health office was great. They palpated my liver—sore and swollen—and told me to be serious about resting. I got out of opera coachings and trips to Oberlin. I lay on the couch and watched reruns of *Spenser: For Hire,* and realized that teriyaki mac and cheese was not a success. I recuperated in time for just one more lesson before Sebők left town, and, for whatever insane twenty-year-old reason, decided to bring in the first third of the "Goldberg Variations."

I'd played just one work of Bach my entire Oberlin time: that B-flat Minor Prelude and Fugue, which I thought was excellent, but everyone said my style was awful. Schwartz and my classmates assumed that I didn't care about Bach. I certainly didn't make any effort to learn about historical performance practice. The harpsichord seemed masochistic or sadistic, depending. But over the last couple years I'd heard certain recordings—a super-fast Ivo Pogorelich version of the English Suite in A Minor, which claimed to be all about motoric movement, and of course—who could avoid or resist the juggernaut?—Glenn Gould's two "Goldbergs." I thought the second Gould recording was silly, be-cause of how serious it tried to be. But the first—such lightness, crisp-ness, a vision of clarity. Finger-work made sublime. The way you were captured in the wistful theme—then out of it erupted raw energy.

At times, my fingers had clarity and energy—I couldn't count on either, yet, but they were there somewhere. I had this idea to "do" Glenn Gould, but with no perversity; which is like saying you want a roast beef sandwich without the roast beef.

Sebők smiled faintly when I told him I'd play the "Goldbergs" and then again when I finished. I'd had many comical collisions between my hands. At first it appeared I wouldn't get much of a lesson, again. He played a bit of the first variation and said, "Here's a polonaise." In the third variation he said, "Here's a duet," and later, "A gigue must dance." At last he offered one memorable, universal suggestion. In the middle of streams of notes, he said I had to settle myself. He'd make just one note last an iota longer, and slightly sing it. Those notes poked out of the stream, like friends waving from a passing train.

I tried it. "No, that's too much," he said. "There is a Hungarian saying: Don't put whipped cream on goulash."

Sebők added a second suggestion. He told me to bring my wrist down, to imagine, and reach for, the space below the keyboard. This impossible idea of traveling through solid wood seemed to help.

At the time, I feared this was another non-lesson. But his few words expressed one of the most essential tricks to playing Bach. Bach hates stopping, and loves to elide. His ongoingness is essential to his revelation—God's eternal plan, the spinning cosmos. But you must find repose, you must breathe while in motion, like the pilot of a plane turning in order to stay in place.

≀

That was it, for the first extended encounter with my guru—five weeks of lessons on different composers and their languages—the reason I'd reshaped my life. But when Sebők would leave for his residencies in Paris and Amsterdam and Tokyo, there were long months without his inspiration when I wondered what I was doing in Indiana. The chill demands of grad school would take over, a life of minimal deadlines. Its purpose (like certain organisms, and passages of music) seemed to be to prolong itself. A dozen or so Oberlin people had also made the move deeper into the Midwest. We frequented Bloomington's many bars: a rambling Irish pub, a pair of dive joints near the music school. Thursdays were sacrosanct—*The Simpsons,* then Long Islands. I often wonder about that *Simpsons* irony I was drinking in every week. How could I love both cynical Homer Simpson and my idealistic Hungarian Yoda?

I had a pair of decent musicology classes, from radically different perspectives. One was on *The Ring Cycle* with an old-school professor; his lectures were about harmonies and the greatness of great men, and he seemed to long for the moment when he could play the recording.

He'd put Solti conducting the Chicago Symphony on the lecture room's sound system, and we were off and away in orchestral and vocal splendor. We didn't talk much about anti-Semitism or all of that.

The other class was Nineteenth-Century Russian Music, taught by a wacky middle-aged woman named Leslie Kearney, with fantastical frizzy hair. Her lectures were much more about ideas, and problems of the Russian identity and soul. She gave an amazing talk on language, on tendencies built into Russian grammar, in particular a certain tense, the imperfective, which was "the only possibility for a present tense in Russian":

> The Russian present is intimately bound up with and inextricable from the concept of incomplete, ongoing, or repetitive action.

I thought of Sebők and all his belief in grammar, and how grammar had seemed so boring until recently, but now it was everywhere, and alive. Kearney took us through *Oblomov*, Ivan Goncharov's novel about a man who never got out of bed—what a joy, to be back with books!— and moved from there to apathy, the difficulties of effecting social change, the sense of hopelessness. She played a passage from Tchaikovsky, hammering in the same obvious idea a million times in a row. "When I tell my friends my specialty is Russian music," she murmured with a sly glance, "they say, 'Oh, I'm so sorry.'"

ξ

Sebők came back in December for two weeks, a rushed epilogue to the semester, and that's when I first experienced his studio classes. These were the spiritual and practical opposite of studio classes at Oberlin.

They took place at night in his tiny studio, and were always uncomfortably packed. You could be turned away, or you might have to stand for two hours in the crook between pianos. The students who came were mostly European imports, and stared earnestly at Sebők. I fidgeted. The only light came from a small desk lamp next to where he sat, which made him seem to glow. He did not refrain from smoking.

In one of the very first classes I attended, a talented Japanese student played the Bartók Suite, op. 14. Throughout the third movement, she was having trouble negotiating wild skips around the keyboard, and Sebők stopped her. "Motion is not that important," he said, "but mobility is."

Whoa. I was still absorbing that one while she set off on the darkly lilting last movement. Sebők listened to her play as if he were tired of teaching and hoped to experience the music for its own sake. At last he couldn't take it anymore, and demonstrated a few measures. In his hands, the music was not just morose but poisonous. There was a stunning distance between his eloquent hesitations and the student's aimless aimlessness. He stopped playing in the middle of a phrase, and we all knew that something special was about to happen.

Then he said, "To show love for someone, but not to *feel* that love"— long pause—"that is the work of Mephistopheles."

Hanging with the smoke in the dimly lit room, that fantastic remark verged on camp. It nailed the moment of the piece, while connecting it to a moral of life. Ever since, when I've played the piece, I've thought of Baudelaire's "beauties of sickness," of dishonest harmonies that at once seduce and repel. But Sebők made no further explanation. "That is enough for tonight," he said. I spoke to some of the German and French students out in the hallway, stupid with excitement. "Can you believe that?" I asked. Then I couldn't help myself—just like in music—and went too far. I tried out a Hungarian accent and said, "That is the work of Mephistopheles." And they looked at me like, *You Philistine, how dare you imitate him.*

‹

At the beginning of the spring semester I broke up with Kate or she broke up with me. I subsequently regretted it, and convinced myself I couldn't live without her, and we left passionate notes on each other's cars, and I made maudlin mixtapes, and my friends yelled at me, saying you're terrible for each other, get over it. All of this allowed me, at last, to focus.

Almost without knowing it, I embarked on a project of learning most of the solo music I know and love now. I began for some reason with Rachmaninoff's Second Concerto, because it seemed gratifying and good for competitions. Then, to feed my soul, I picked up a piece I'd heard in Oberlin, the elusive *Davidsbündlertänze* by Schumann. I also started in on the Liszt sonata. Sebők said he wasn't going to let me be like all the other stupid pianists, manhandling the score however I wanted for self-gratification. That was a tough Liszt lesson, trying to suppress my urges. I went after the Schubert B-flat Sonata (a memory of the paisley skirt), the E Minor Partita of Bach (now that I was loving Bach, I wanted to go further in), and Beethoven op. 109—all kinds of late music, all kinds of monuments. Maybe I would have been wiser to stick with earlier, lower-stakes things. I often tell students these days to do that, and they don't listen any better than I did.

Many masterpieces later, April came along. Bloomington got humid. We all said goodbye, with none of the drama and sense of loss that marked Oberlin springs. More of a routine, less attachment. There was no need to pack. Sasha and I sublet our apartment to a tall douchebag who taught golf at the local country club, who we (nonfatally and accidentally) poisoned for reasons I won't go into here. I went to New Mexico for a week or two and my father asked me what the result was. I said huge progress had been made. I had met my greatest musical inspiration and I was learning everything possible. But he noted that, on paper and in reality, I was returning to the same poorly paid summer job.

{

Musicorda was just as calm and hazy and simple, with two big exceptions. First, I became close with another staff accompanist named Michael. One night, he heard me perform Berlioz's *Harold in Italy*, which is called a viola concerto, because violists need all the help they can get, but if you're being honest it's an orchestral tone poem. Franz Liszt arranged the orchestra part, and so the piano writing is full of fireworks. I practiced it with unceasing, almost masturbatory pleasure.

After the concert, Michael said, "You know, when you play like that you make me wonder why anyone else is onstage." I was delighted. This was the ego-stroking comment of my wildest dreams. After one drink, his tone coarsened. "What the fuck are you doing here anyway?" *Being happy?* I thought. *Making money?* Michael said I seemed tight after all those octaves, and somewhat later, while we lounged on one of the campus's many secluded benches, he asked if I'd like a massage. I said why not, and it was like hazy New England decided to reveal one more of its secrets. But I wasn't that comfortable yet with sex in general, much less with a guy—and also, it was 1991, and HIV was still a death sentence. Just as things were getting interesting, I freaked out and went off to my room.

I threw all that energy into the summer's second big complication: Brahms's First Violin Sonata. If you're going to have a summer fling, you could do far worse. I'd massacred this sonata on a few previous occasions, but now it was time to solve it, once and for all. It appeared to have a secret story. The first movement is mostly sunny, with a side of Viennese bittersweetness. But some unknown misfortune happens before the second movement. The music turns darker and less certain. For long stretches, it even becomes a funeral march.

I was playing it with a wonderful young violinist named Baird Dodge—who has since joined the Chicago Symphony. We went in for a lesson with Greg. I needed to show him that I'd learned something, so I started explaining my new discovery—that the piece had an overall trick. The first thing you hear is a dotted rhythm. (If you don't know what that is, it's *long-short-long,* or the opening rhythm of *happy birth . . .* from the "Happy Birthday" song, or the most prevalent rhythm in Wagner's famous Wedding March—marches love dotted rhythms, and vice versa.) In the first movement, this rhythm *begins* phrases—it creates a natural waltz upbeat, a lift, a lilt. But the phrases of the second movement (I went on, lecturing Greg on something he surely already knew) always *end* with the dotted rhythm, making it a landing. The vector bends backward. Instigator becomes instigated. Cause becomes effect.

"Nice observation, Jeremy," Greg said, while Baird tuned and tried to stay out of the way. "But can you tell me why the piece is called 'Rain Sonata'?"

"Because of the raindrops in the last movement!" I said, confidently, referring to a pitter-patter of running notes under the violin's melancholy tune.

"Yes and no," Greg said. He took a moment to enjoy my deflated expression. "It's actually based on a song." A song! I didn't need to hear more. After the lesson, I scurried off to the Mount Holyoke music library—the perfect place to avoid Michael. There I found Brahms's song, and the voice of an old man musing in the rain:

Fall, rain, fall down,
Wake those dreams again,
Dreams from childhood,
When water foamed on the sand!

At the next rehearsal I played and sang the *Regenlied* to Baird, saying don't you see, this changes everything. He put up with my extra-credit passion and terrible singing.

I guess we played well for Greg, since he nominated us to perform in a public concert. Baird and I rehearsed for weeks, far more than was necessary—we took the time to do what later in life we might not ever be able to do. Baird asked me, "How can you be so sarcastic in reality and such a Romantic in music?" Eventually we came to the last dress rehearsal, in the old, creaky concert hall. It started at 7:00 p.m. but there was no official ending time. The director said, "Just shut the doors behind you."

By 9:00 p.m., we were discussing the last movement's raindrops. This music had an unusual tempo problem: it should be static, but not die. The musing old man isn't dead, obviously—only his hopes are. It was a rondo, according to the textbooks, but most rondos rollick and dance. Baird and I argued about this for a while—no, this felt too slow; no, now it was kind of flippant—and then something in my mind clicked: *The structure is the message.* A rondo's most basic idea is to alternate. It has a recurring theme and episodes, with a schematic like:

ABACABA

And in this piece, I knew and saw and felt it: the main theme (A) was the melancholy gray present, and the episodes (B, C, whatever) were the radiant past. That was the secret story. And it was also an unbelievable lesson in how you convert a form, a template, into an expression of the human condition, like a skeleton that comes alive. Once you figured this out, you could chuck all the usual rondo stuff—boppy, singsong endings, joyful returns. Actually, I told Baird, each return was a gate crashing shut on happiness.

After I delivered this line, my eyes crazed, Baird looked like he was processing and then quietly said: "Jeremy, you're on fire." This moment of communication made me maybe as happy as I'd ever been. I realized that Sebők had opened this door in me to metaphor. He'd given me permission to use a tool I'd always had.

We got to the end of the piece, when Brahms shifts from minor to major. Not a triumphant major, but a wistful major, full of memory and the irrecoverable. At this crucial moment, the dotted rhythm is reenvisioned. Often dotted rhythms sit on their last notes, like a dancer lands on a foot—

long short LONG

But now Brahms grafts them together—

long short long short long

—an endless chain, a continuous upbeat, leading forward and away without a goal. This new continuity reaches back to embrace the waltzes of the first movement, the funeral marches of the second, and now melts the seemingly frozen sorrows of the last.

No, no, I said—and kept saying to Baird while we played—we were distorting our rhythms, and cutting up the story that Brahms had crafted. We didn't have to do anything. We just had to ride along with time, keep on the trail, from short to long, or long to short, and follow it off to the end. Don't let it stop, I said. Was I talking to myself about life and Oberlin, or to Baird about Brahms, or Sebők, or what? Rhythmic integrity was so important, suddenly. I hardly recognized myself, far from the waywardness of my teen and undergrad years, from my hatred of dotted notes, from the constant fear of being clicked at with metronomes and pencils. Rhythm was not playing in time. It was playing about time. It was now a beat with a soul—and the missing clue that allowed the story to make sense.

14. *Rhythm* LESSON ONE

*C*he study of rhythm begins with counting. "COUNT" is scrawled in all caps all over my earliest piano sheet music, in every color of ink, then desperately circled, and re-circled, and surrounded by exclamation points. Mona and Lillian were both mystified by my resistance to this seemingly innocent word. But they didn't have all the facts. They didn't know how often my mother would say, "I'll count to ten and you'd better be brushing your teeth" or "I'll count down from three and if you're not clearing the table there will be hell to pay." "Hell" was code for spankings. Those were also counted, and added and subtracted depending on whether you were a brat or well behaved.

The antidote to my mother was my hero, the Count from *Sesame Street*. He knew how to count with panache, letting numbers explode from his mouth in his shameless Transylvanian accent, as if each digit were a miracle, until he reached the number of the day. Then seven chickens would appear, or seven chocolate brownies with eyes, surrounded by balloons and confetti. Numbers became living and dancing things, instead of listing tasks, or punishments, or vanishing into elapsed time.

By the time you are a professional musician, you imagine counting should be far behind you, like reading the notes. But every so often, you come upon a piece where the composer tries to trip you up, and bring you back to childhood. For example: the Sextet by Aaron Copland, with its fiendish combinations of twos and threes, a tongue twister of durations. In rehearsal, someone always plays a two instead of a three, and the piece comes to a clattering halt. Everybody looks around for someone to blame. This is the ideal moment to say to your colleagues, "I realize counting to three may be a bit difficult for you . . ." They respond with a justified finger.

These days, when I force myself to count, I feel remnants of the old, boyish resistance. I have to train my conscious mind on something that wants to remain in the gut. I have to consult an inner calculator, and remove a fraction of my attention from the hungry feeling of the music, to be sure that I play at the right time. This can feel like a disservice— a remedial and heartless act.

But counting is neither remedial nor heartless. For evidence, we can turn to one of the most loving pieces of music ever written: Mozart's *Marriage of Figaro*. The curtain opens on two young lovers, excited about their upcoming marriage. What are they doing in this joyous and expectant moment? Figaro is measuring the space for their wedding bed. Susanna is also measuring, looking in the mirror to see if her cap fits—she wants Figaro to look at her, to pay attention. Both in their own worlds, counting off their desires, while Mozart lurks behind the scenes, making their numbers charming.

An even better counting scene is in the last, magical act of Verdi's *Falstaff*. Falstaff is hiding in the dark, in the forest, behind an old, majestic oak. He's awaiting a delusional rendezvous at midnight—he's old and fat, she's young and beautiful and (anyway) married. He's counting down toward this exciting event, but there's a catch: a legend of dangerous spirits who haunt the oak at midnight, snatching souls. Therefore, Falstaff's counting leads to two quite different destinations—pleasure and terror.

The town clock begins to strike. Verdi weaves together three elements. There is the bell, ringing each new hour with the same note, F, F, F—just literal time. After each bell we hear Falstaff, sounding off the hours, *"uno . . . due . . . tre . . ."* and here you have to appreciate Verdi's dramatic cunning and empathy, his awareness that Falstaff needs to hear his own voice in the darkness—counting as a form of reassurance, as a protective spell. The third and last element is the most extraordinary: a series of chords, all including the bell's recurring F. Verdi uses that unvarying note as a hinge to reveal the wildest possibilities. Dissonances emerge from nowhere, interpreting the monotone of time. A sharp makes one hour feel shocking; a flat makes the next one feel painful or shaded with regret.

At the twelfth hour, we and Verdi arrive at F major—but what an F major! Because of the progression into it, this normal chord has been transformed into something uncanny—grand and regal, like Father Time, but also impassive and even a bit threatening. You get both the fullness of the hour and a sense of remove from human concerns. It certainly gives no comfort to Falstaff, who waits there, quivering with fear in the dark. But Verdi isn't quivering with fear: at eighty-four, the master stares down death, and counts gloriously down to midnight.

{

These overt, literal examples just scratch the surface. We haven't even begun to discuss all the amazing places where music only *feels* like it's counting, where it depends upon the sensation of measured time for its emotional effect. Near the opening of Mozart's *Don Giovanni*, after the title character stabs the Commendatore, there is a notorious moment where everyone stands around commenting in that peculiar way that opera characters do. Mozart starts up a series of triplets, notes in groups of three . . .

one two three one two three one two three one two three

. . . which begin marking time from the moment the Commendatore is mortally wounded. Time is counted, though the drama is frozen in place. All the characters sing around and about these triplets, their conflicting messages of fright and sorrow and nonchalance in personal rhythms, but the triplets are in charge—inevitable, unstoppable. As the ensemble comes to a close the music creates a devastating marriage of metaphors: the *drip-drip-drip* of blood out of the old man's body, which is also a clock *tick-tick-tick*ing down the last seconds of a life.

This scene made such an impression on Beethoven that he shamelessly stole it for the first movement of the "Moonlight" Sonata, a piece that represented my best chance of getting kissed in junior high school, since every girl in orchestra would ooh and aah when I started it up. You find Mozart's triplets there, and the other voices, and the same inevitability and gloom.

If you bring in the "Moonlight" for a lesson, your piano teacher probably won't mention *Don Giovanni* or the shadow of death, but they will almost certainly lecture you in an irritating way about the rhythm. The melody exists in a different time dimension from the accompaniment. Mozart's triplets divide the beats in three below, but the melody divides the beat in four:

one two three four
one   two   three

which means that the melody and accompaniment notes are the slightest bit not together. Almost together, but not—a tiny irritant, a pebble in time's shoe. You can obey your teacher and turn on the metronome and count like mad, but what you're after is that sense of the irreconcilable, a desire that it might all add up, and a fear that it won't.

♪

If fingerings (the first thing you learn at the piano) are a rich topic, a never-ending study, at least you can write them down. You put "5" over a note and you know your pinky is supposed to play that note, and you train your brain, and learn to do that forever—at least until you change your mind. But rhythm is different. Rhythms in classical music appear to be notated precisely. But there is an important distinction between rhythms written on the page and the rhythms that you actually play. No matter what your piano teacher has to tell you when you're little, these are not the same. A computer program can play back for you what's mathematically written—it sounds horrible. The rhythms on the page of music, interpreted literally, are lifeless, or worse than lifeless, like a zombie. If you play metronomically "right," it is musically wrong.

Once a real person plays, though, a million small "errors" creep in. Certain notes come a bit sooner, others a bit later—microscopic deviations, handfuls of nanoseconds—and suddenly we have what is called, for lack of a better word, phrasing. The performed rhythm is like a dance around the written rhythm, or a shading around it. This gap between written and performed is not a failing; it is the classical musician's only hope of success.

To call this "interpretation" is slightly off the mark. These little rhythmic non-error errors are more primal. They include some conscious decision and learned style, a helping of habit, and some added drops of emotion and instinct—ourselves reacting, developing feelings about what harmonies need. In our love for some notes and chords over others, we can't help leaving a rhythmic trace, a fingerprint at the scene of the crime. You cannot write down this rhythmic wobble, precisely because it's a riff on the written, a rebuke of notation; its very existence is an evanescent commentary on something else. I know because I've tried to write it all out, and ended up with a score covered in decimal points, irrational and infinitesimal fractions, and—Catch-22—all the freshness vanished; my sense of purpose was lost.

𝄽

For decades, I have obsessed over Artur Schnabel's recording of the Schubert A-flat Impromptu, D. 935, no. 2. This famous piece has minimal musical material. The framework is three beats per measure. The melody is built on a basic dance rhythm, which you can write out as:

one two———

The *two* is longer than the *one*. Imagine your left foot is a bit heavier than your right, or vice versa. Then we have a little upbeat, and the pattern repeats:

one two—— (and) one two——

Finally, on the third try, we get something that passes through to the next downbeat:

one two—— (and) one two————(and) one two three one

Now, there are lots of ways to play *one two*——. You can make the second note roll off the impulse of the first, like a bouncing ball:

ONE two . . .

Or you can emphasize the syncopation, giving the *two* a little kick:

one TWO!

But Schnabel chooses neither. He plays two equivalent impulses:

one two

When I first heard this recording it struck me, the way that this most sensitive of all musicians decided to do nothing. I couldn't get over the simplicity, the incredible refinement he gets from this lack of nuance. In his *one two one two*, I heard "that's all, that's all": as if the message of the piece were as simple as counting.

One two, (and) one two: these are the piece's units of perception. Whatever it is that this Schubert Impromptu has to say about life, loss, and heartbreak, it will get parceled out in these pairs. When the music flows through to the next downbeat (*one two three one*), Schnabel moves right along, arriving at the final *one* somewhat sooner than the metronome would. And because Schnabel "rushes," this last *one* has no sense of arrival. Your foot doesn't quite have time to land. Schnabel makes sure your ear and mind aren't focused on the flow, but back on those stubborn *one-twos*. He's telling you: this is not a dance about flow and sweep; it is no whirling waltz. His rhythmic choices tell us what is meaningful, and what isn't.

}

People often complain about Schubert's length, and for good reason. He loves to let his ideas spread out, like pets that hog the bed. But in many instances Schubert's repeats are there for the best reason: to accumulate meaning. As this Impromptu proceeds, and its pattern gets fixed in our minds, it becomes an object for meditation, a mantra:

one two. and one two. and one two three one.

Which means that a larger rhythm takes over, a rhythm of rhythms. Schubert is foreshadowing the techniques of minimalist composers a century and a half in the future: 1) set up a simple pattern; 2) repeat it; 3) introduce small changes. So that music becomes less about things themselves, but processes operating, like tectonic plates—in this case, the dance is caught and crushed in forces larger than it knows.

Schnabel walks Schubert through these minimalist steps. He comes to a place where Schubert instructs you to play louder. The dance is now oddly insistent. The idea seems less to be dancing than pounding out a rhythm for rhythm's sake. Schnabel plays the mantra, strongly and simply:

and one two. and one two. and one two three one.

Not too much feeling, mostly pulse. Then again Schnabel plays:

and one two. and one two. and one two three one.

And now, a third time, he plays:

and one

. . . but this time, there is no *two*. Nothing at all.

Even though this is the most tragic chord in the piece, the most shattered moment, at this point in the recording I get up from the couch and skip around the room for joy. I say to myself: *This is what music is for!* This is when Schnabel's way of telling the story pays off. Schnabel has set up his whole plain way of playing to allow this one moment's cathartic emptiness to speak. Sound, drained of the possibility of pulse. He plays that chord like a mountain or monument—it lands, and remains.

On the page, that chord is supposed to last for three beats, and I suppose you could count them: *one, two, three.* Schnabel doesn't bother; he knows there's no point. His playing was all about counting; but now, we have reached the uncountable. This is why being a pianist is so much better than being in an orchestra (I'm going to get in such trouble for saying that!). When an orchestra has a long note like this, everybody worries about being together again after the pause—so they count and subdivide the emptiness, to be ready for what comes after. But this chord isn't about *What about after?* It's way too late for that. You should have thought about after before you decided to play Schubert, whose music is mostly about things beyond repair.

15. More Europeans!

PLAYLIST

MOZART: Concerto in C Major, K. 415
BEETHOVEN: Sonata in F Minor, op. 57 ("Appassionata"), second movement
BEETHOVEN: Sonata no. 3 in A Major, op. 69, for Piano and Cello, third and fourth movements
MENDELSSOHN: Sonata for Cello and Piano in D Major, op. 58, third movement, recorded by János Starker and György Sebők

*M*y second Sebők year I went mad for Mozart, along with the rest of the classical world. It was the 200th anniversary of Mozart's death. The Indiana University Piano Department celebrated by performing his complete Piano Concertos, a group of stories that creates a far bigger, more complicated story. First: precocious youth feeling its oats, experimenting, flourishing, and with time achieving a rare confluence of understanding. There is barely time to appreciate this confluence before mortality appears and hovers—the D Minor, the C Minor, the ambivalent C Major, K. 503. But in the last B-flat Concerto, we are surprised to find again, with only a few scars, the child of the beginning.

Sebők had nominated me to perform an early-middle one—K. 415, in C major. It was full of joy and audacious tinkering. This was an honor and, I hoped, a vote of confidence. I couldn't let my idol down. I'd been practicing much of the summer at Musicorda, and on into the final days of August back in New Mexico. I sat in my parents' brown backyard, on a crumbling retaining wall, my favorite cramming spot for high school exams, staring into the sun, worrying that even with all the prep time in the world, it wasn't enough. I was still too young to realize that it is never enough.

So I took it in for a lesson with my old teacher Bill. He seemed to enjoy this session. "Sounds pretty good, kiddo," he said. "Try listening better to the decays of your melody notes." So I played one long note, and slipped the next one in where it belonged in time, but also in the previous sound's diminuendo. Right in the pocket like a billiard ball, appropriately enough for billiards-loving Mozart. This idea felt familiar, and when I got home from the lesson I pushed through all my mom's billowing clothes in the piano room closet to find my old notebook. There it was. When I was thirteen, Bill had given me the same advice. While adding new lessons, you have to keep listening to the old ones—as it happens, just like the unfolding notes of a melody.

}

Back in Bloomington, Sasha and I had new lodgings, a dilapidated white firetrap three blocks from the music school. We set up a Ping-Pong table and bought a blender. Those items did the trick. We became a party house. Oberlin nostalgia faded. Bloomington's routine had virtues—our little band of musicians practicing, cooking, drinking, living improbable and unsustainable lives. It could have been utopia.

When I played my concerto for Sebők, it was an interesting milestone: the first time he looked pleased and surprised. He expressed his pleasure through a lifted eyebrow and an almost imperceptible nod. What he said at last was a sandwich of criticism and compliment:

"You play slow things better than you play fast things."

I didn't know how to respond.

"This is not cause for alarm. But it is interesting to think about. What does it say about you?"

Sebők didn't like to give prescriptions before he probed causes. It was useless to put out fires if you didn't know where they started.

The first entrance of the piano was a good place to start, he said. Often these moments in the Concertos have a renegade quality. Mozart, cunning and theatrical, knows that when a new character comes onstage, they have to grab the audience, to deserve the spotlight and define themselves. In K. 415, the pianist enters with a C—the opposite of a surprise, the key of the piece—but then begins twittering back and forth between the C and the D right above it. You get a sense of indecision, like a roulette ball bouncing between two numbers.

Sebők called my attention to this, saying, "It's time . . . for play." This reminded me of a moment in a recent master class on the Schumann Concerto, when he'd said, "Now . . . it's time to dance." A recurring theme of Sebők's teaching was that acts had seasons and occasions. A section of music would have a purpose, a reason for being, and then you would turn to another purpose, when the time was right.

In this game, it seems like we might well settle on good old boring C—until the last moment, where Mozart twists back up to D. But before that D comes a naughty C-sharp—the note in between!—as if to say, *We don't have to decide; we can also land in the cracks.* Sebők played this C-sharp with a different key speed—saucy and cheeky, like sticking out your tongue at the end of a sentence. He intentionally sent himself off balance, and used this as a pretext to leave the bench and reunite with his cigarette, smoldering on the desk.

I sat there, thinking about the sound of that C-sharp. Schwartz had never talked about games or play. At times he'd say that piano music could be "charming," or he'd invoke the music-Italian word *grazioso*, meaning (sort of) graceful. But I realized I'd had to find a Hungarian to explain humor to me. A humor without meanness, target, or ridicule.

Sebők puffed for a moment, as I tried to re-create the magic. "No," he said. "You can't do it after the fact. You must know before. There are two Ds, and another at the end, altogether three. You need to know how many, and where each one goes."

I tried it again, wondering—how do you *know* in that sense?

"When I was on a jury with Rubinstein," Sebők said, vectoring off into the past as he described the importance of being present, "he told me there were only three performances in his life where he felt that he was with every moment of the music, as it happened. And that was Rubinstein! It is one of the great difficulties and puzzles of performing. You know what the mood is, and the . . . general character . . . but you are not keeping up with events. That is why your fast playing is less

246 · *Every Good Boy Does Fine*

satisfying." It was true. Sebők looked pleased with himself for enunciating it. His performance was done. My job lay before me: to be puckish and lithe, ready and awake.

Next, a different hurdle—a bunch of arpeggios and scales. In the middle, my right hand had to leap up to grab chords, and I was doing that classic student thing of focusing on the difficulty to the exclusion of all else. Sebők smiled while I made mountains of my molehills, then invoked another famous artist. "The secret to Heifetz was that he never imagined he could miss a note."

Sounds good, I thought.

"No. That sounds ridiculous to say, perhaps. But the thing is, he probably never practiced with fear. If he missed a note, he said, well, I have to shift a little higher or move this way or that way, but he didn't let himself learn the fear of the missed note. You, on the other hand," he continued, "are running for that chord as if it was running from you."

He made a little arc with his hand in the air. This arc had a message: that the motion from one note to another should know exactly how long it has to travel, and not arrive too late or, worse, too soon. The chord was there, waiting calmly for you to play it.

I did it! A small eager smile from me, and his best smile back from him. We worked on a number of other little isolated passages, like jewelers setting gems. "See you at rehearsal," he said at last, as we were both starting work with the orchestra that afternoon.

≀

The rehearsal room was in a basement, down some concrete stairs and through heavy metal doors, walled with acoustical tile, and lit with dangling fluorescents. It didn't seem right that Sebők would have to enter a space like that. All five of IU's student orchestras were put to service for this big project, and this was not one of the best. I can still hear them trying to play the D Minor Concerto's opening section, a famous unease, with syncopations that feel like anticipations, or palpitations. In school, students are taught syncopations in a certain Stravinsky-meets-metronome way—the opposite of what Mozart needs here.

The kind conductor stopped after one disastrous play-through and asked Sebők if he had anything to say. Sebők launched into excerpts from Mozart operas: characters, unsettled moments of plots. These references went over a roomful of heads. He explained that the notes in the bass were drumrolls, but now they were living in a foreign environment—the opposite of a march. I could see the bass section murmuring. Metaphor was too much. *Louder or softer? Faster or slower?* they wondered, like orchestral musicians everywhere. So Sebők tried to get specific and teach them a subtle shaping, where they wouldn't crescendo to their last notes but fall away, making the gesture resemble a shudder. But he might as well have been speaking Hungarian. And when everyone played together, Sebők made no effort to project—he wouldn't exit his empyrean plane.

I sat there, nervous for my own upcoming rehearsal and also in a rage, looking at the clueless second violins and thinking, *No, you cannot be doing this right now: all you have to do is pay attention.* But (as often happens in rehearsal) the conductor began to panic about getting to the end of the piece, and higher thoughts had to be pushed aside.

ꙮ

That evening, a great relief. We were back in a safe space, Sebők's mood-lit studio, and he let me play through the last movement of my concerto. I'll admit I was feeling dissatisfied with the main theme.

Sebők said: "You seem to apologize for the melody, like you wish Mozart had written something else." Everyone laughed, except him and me. "Let's take a closer look," he said. He moved to the second piano, and changed his tone.

"The first bar is in two," he declared. To prove it he played just that bit, with the dance feeling of one foot and then another.

Fine, I thought.

Then he said, "But in the second bar, something happens. The melody stops short, the left hand interrupts."

And he was right—another detail too simple for me to notice, or I'd been too arrogant to look. The right hand played two staccato notes, as if the melody got snipped. The left hand stepped into the breach with pairs of syncopated chords like stamping feet. This detail was discombobulating, fun, rustic. The plot thickened.

"Now, in the third bar," he continued in a tone that said he meant business, "we go on . . . how do you say that in English . . . a loop-de-loop." This was a pose. He knew perfectly well what he was going to say in English; his command of metaphor in his non-native language was eight million times better than any of ours. And indeed the right hand did just that, a loop—

—while the stamping left hand was now silent. Mozart wrote two drastic change-ups in three measures. Rapid-fire conflict, concealed by apparent simplicity.

"And last, in the fourth bar," Sebők said, returning to a tried-and-true formula, "it is time to laugh."

Indeed: there was a little wiggle of notes at the end. It seemed to be just a tag, a way to fill the time. But if you played it a certain way, it wasn't filler. Sebők played "wiggle wiggle," and everyone laughed and smiled. When I played it back, however, the room went dead silent. I was the tragic comedian whose joke just bombed.

Everyone in the room saw the theme's possibilities at that moment, and also Sebők's greatest qualities: wit balanced by elegance, refined attention to the smallest distinctions. The result was not a theme but a little machine for the production of happiness, with intricate, interlocking parts. There were no mysteries, in a way, since he'd explained everything; and yet mystery remained.

꒰

A few days later, the big Mozart marathon happened—five or six concerts in one weekend. I played close to my best. I remember a few bars of pure pleasure during the second theme, as the little whistling, innocent tune turned into the minor. And in the slow movement, I remember the strings laying down long, held chords, and thinking there is nothing in the world so delicious as playing tunes over Mozart's heavenly backup band.

Afterward, Sasha told me I'd rushed: like my brother, he didn't want me feeling too good about myself. My mom was a bit nicer. She'd come all the way out from New Mexico—a huge effort for her, with her hip and liver and pins in bones. She met Sebők in the front lobby of the music school after the concert, when everyone in our insular world was milling about.

I wanted my mom to see Sebők, and to know what a god he was, but I didn't exactly want them to meet. I feared she'd find a practical, Swedish way to make my guru disappear. I felt I'd narrowly escaped from one to the other. They didn't seem to know they were enemies in my mind. Sebők gave my mom a lesson in old-world charm. He shook and clasped her hand and told her she had a gifted son. "And what is more important," he said, "cultured." For a moment—this was unbelievable—Mom acted innocent and giggly, as if being asked out by a boy at a dance. But seconds after Sebők left, she told me she needed to sit down.

As we negotiated a spot for her on a bench, a new member of the faculty came to say hello. Her name was Evelyne Brancart—although she spoke with a thick accent, so I couldn't quite tell. Her husband was Atar Arad, former violist of the Cleveland Quartet, who had also just joined the faculty. (The Cleveland Quartet, yet another legend here in unlikely Bloomington.) She told me my concerto was "very good," and I replied that her K. 467 sounded amazing. It did. Her passagework was even and noble, and the sound glorious—pearly and yet singing. She said, "I am so excited to hear more of your playing, you have a voice."

I still remember this tableaux. My mom on the bench looking tired, Sebők ten feet away looking bored by the post-concert schmooze, me desperate for validation. Sebők would never have said what Evelyne said to me; it would have been too much. My mom would never want to spoil me, her cardinal sin of parenting. But here was someone willing to look me right in the eye and say that I had something to offer the world. I was always going back and forth from confidence to doubt, and Evelyne's look felt like a hand laid on my mind, telling it to stop vacillating.

≀

After the Mozart deep dive, after all the musical distinctions and elements of style, Sebők and I settled into a year of practical, physical work. He went after my technique, to figure out why certain things were difficult for me while others were so easy. He kept alternating between spirit guide and physics teacher, trying to bridge the gap between boring technical detail and the mysteries of the universe. He made me reexamine the hinges of my arm and wrist. When I was playing octaves in Liszt he wanted my arm to resemble a sewing machine, with up-and-down linear simplicity. But other times he wanted curves, circles, spirals. He always said that each solution was only one solution; that it was a matter of adding to my repertoire of motions, a question of options and possibilities. He never said "You must move . . ." or "You must do . . ." Sometimes you wished he would.

I decided I needed to learn the other Brahms concerto, the D Minor. Sebők thought this was a good project. When I tried to start the tragic opening monologue, he plunked a heavy ashtray on top of the piano.

"If I want to move this ashtray, I don't come at it with a lot of speed"—he showed how it would tip over if you hit it hard—"but slowly, at the speed I want to move it." He approached the ashtray with his outstretched hand, and made it glide across the piano lid. Something inside you calculated how much it would weigh and how to judge your intensity, without you knowing. At that moment I dimly remembered something Leon Fleisher had said about Schnabel—in my ill-fated master class, a few years past—that his secret was to envision the sound. Imagine, and then calibrate.

We kept working on the Brahms much of the year, on and off, and in March I won the concerto competition with it. Though Sebők and I had spent plenty of thought and effort, when the performance came around I felt unguided. He was less useful under pressure, when I had to get ready for an audition or a concert. He seemed almost peeved by these events, interrupting the flow.

Evelyne Brancart came to the concert, and took me out afterward for a postmortem. "You can't do that to the poor conductor," she said. What do you mean? I asked, and she laughed. "First you have to look at him, sometimes. You have to think about the practicality of all those people trying to play together." Sebők was a great, great musician, she assured me, but while all this was going on maybe, just maybe, keep an eye on reality.

⸗

The appointed period for my master's degree was drawing to a close, but despite Evelyne's warning I felt I couldn't leave Sebők, not yet. We were just starting. (Also, what was real life going to be?) So as the spring approached—Bloomington's second-best season—I applied for the doctoral program. I was accepted, but people warned me I had now stepped over the boundary into becoming a permanent fixture of the music school.

Around that point, my past phoned up, with an interest in my future. It was Darrett Adkins, from Oberlin days. He asked, "What are you doing with yourself?" and I said, well, I'm studying with this Hungarian genius, and he said, "That's great," though I could tell he didn't trust me to find the right gurus. Darrett was at Rice University, still with his guru, Norman Fischer.

"Listen," he said, "the Munich competition is going to be cello-piano duo this year, and I wonder if you want to try for it."

It would be amazing to go to Europe and bring back a prize and some paying concerts. Darrett had a ready-made plan. "We have to do this right," he said, meaning we'd rehearse all summer. Three weeks in Houston; five weeks at the newly hatched Steans Music Institute, at Ravinia, then three more Houston weeks—a final push with Norman. Imagine what we could accomplish if we really focused, he said.

So I turned down my beloved Musicorda job, and its lazy simplicity, and suffered through three weeks sleeping on Darrett's couch and getting drenched in Houston monsoons. We drove each other insane, like in the old Oberlin days, maybe even more, because he was now engaged to his girlfriend, Ingrid, and they were insufferable. On the couch, hearing them baby-talk and smooch and blow each other's noses (!) in the other room, I meditated on how single and unloved I was. At last we headed off to Ravinia, in the heart of Chicago's North Shore.

The Steans Institute was pronounced "stains," which was annoying to have to explain. It was a new venture. If you'd been traumatized by music lessons in the past, the Steans Institute would either cure or destroy you. The idea was an immersive number of coachings—three or four a week—from musicians who played your instrument and those who didn't. They'd built an anonymous half-polygon of a building, and we bounced around in there—thirty or so students and seven or eight revolving faculty—rushing past one another in the hall from lesson to practice cubicle to lesson and at last, with relief, to lunch. Amorous encounters took place on the floors beneath pianos because there was no other space or time—a fact I just happen to know.

The head of Ravinia was a famous teacher named Walter Levin. I'd never heard of him, but many other young musicians had, and spoke of him with fear. He'd survived the Holocaust, which seemed like kind of an honor to me. On the second day, we all packed into the concert hall for a convocation. Walter walked slowly to the podium. He had pedagogical glasses, like Bill's, and he was rigorously thin and slightly stooped, like a misshapen pencil.

"The art of musical interpretation," he said, pausing for what could have been effect, "is the translation of a musical text into its acoustical correlative."

I looked around the room. The assembled musicians and donors all appeared calm. But I was seething, wondering what Sebők might say, or Beethoven. As if everything could be written down, as if the music wasn't about creative inferences you drew. The word "correlative" was bad enough, but with his German accent and guttural *r*... Jesus.

A few days later, Darrett and I had a lesson with Walter on one of the most essential cello sonatas: the A Major Beethoven. It was a cornerstone of our Munich repertoire. I warmed up nervously at the piano. Walter stewed at his desk. Darrett arrived ten minutes late, in Oberlin-esque bare feet.

"Where are your shoes?" Walter demanded.

"In a practice room."

"Go get them right now," he said.

"Yes sir, boss, master, right away," Darrett replied, with more than a hint of sarcasm.

"What did you say?" Walter asked, primed to explode, but Darrett was already bounding out the door.

When Darrett returned, we had not so much a lesson as a character assassination. Everything we did was an indulgence. If we didn't slur, if we slowed down at a cadence, if we let ourselves Romantically rubato, Walter said, "Why would you do *that*?" Every nuance needed justification. No place for instincts or whims. He brandished his metronome like a scepter of holy objectivity. I couldn't believe this device was making such a comeback. Sebők had no metronome, it occurred to me—he'd never even alluded to its existence.

Walter believed Beethoven's tempos fell into classifiable types. This struck me as wrong, and evil—didn't each piece have to find its own speed through a process of understanding? But Walter would say, see, these are all of the Allegros Beethoven wrote in cut time, and here are the metronome markings, "which proves that it must be between 72 and 80 to the half note." His ideas were historically informed in a way I only dreamed of. But I couldn't help thinking that all of Beethoven's inspirations were being pinned down and laid out in a display case like butterflies.

Darrett tried to stick to these Walter-approved tempos. This was even harder for him than for me. Walter stopped him between almost every note. I saw Darrett cringe, then compose himself, then smile to seem eager and willing, and in that moment of vulnerability Walter pounced, and did his best to wipe even that conciliatory smile away. My grievances with Darrett were endless, not least that I didn't know I was still in love with him, but he didn't deserve what Walter did. I'd never seen a teacher-student relationship so defined by hate.

{

Walter's vision for his Institute centered around the Forum: a group master class with no master teacher. Everyone was encouraged to contribute, and to explore ideas together. It was, in principle, a democracy.

One of the earliest Forums was on Brahms's G Major Violin Sonata, a piece I felt I knew better than any other. As usual, I needed everyone to know that I knew everything already. A pair of students had just performed the opening, a violin melody over pillowy piano chords. Walter started micro-analyzing the violin's possibilities: strokes of the bow, vibrato, dynamics. Various faculty gave their two cents. At a certain point I raised my hand, was called on, and burst out: "You're all wrong. Nobody's paying attention to the piano." In an injured tone, as if the piano and pianists were oppressed. Running up to the stage, I demonstrated: "The phrase goes to *this* measure, obviously."

Everyone took an opportunity to point out how preposterous my idea was. Walter said, icily, "Do you really think the phrase goes to the lowest point of the melody?" A fair point. To be honest, the violin wasn't even playing at the moment I proposed was the climax. But nonetheless I fought on. I felt caged in that building and with those teachers. My voice quavered. I needed music to be more than it was, here.

Afterward, another student felt sorry for me and said, "I liked what you said, it was *interesting*." In retrospect, everyone in the Forum was wrong, including me. The absolute essence of this opening is that the piano and violin peak at different times. The violin falls, and in the rest, the piano plays one gorgeous, meaningful chord. The violin then aspires while the piano retreats. Its beauty depends on subtle, thoughtful disagreement, without rancor: what Walter's Forum could have been, in a better world.

One of the classic Forum topics was Dots vs. Wedges. Sometimes Mozart would mark this, meaning staccato:

•

And other times he would mark this pointier symbol:

▼

For forty-five minutes, we debated this difference. What did Mozart mean? Was one shorter than the other? Was one more accented? I was sure, again, that everyone had lost their mind. Music had to be more than a code.

𝄞

Darrett and I played our Beethoven for a well-known French cello teacher named Philippe Muller. He was short and unimpressed, his face stuck somewhere between a sad smile and a frown. Every comment he made was a negative. "No, don't make an agogic accent there," he said, meaning one note was slightly too long. OK, we evened out the notes for him. A few bars later, "Please, no *ritard*." We marched along, ignoring what we felt. "I don't like that hairpin, it is too much." For Muller, a system of taste and refinement was self-evident, but for us it was arbitrary prejudice.

The week after that, we played for a Swiss cellist with long, brown curly hair and shrewd green eyes. He smoked outside between lessons and gazed at Ravinia's vast lawn, with its rows upon rows of garbage cans and speakers, to all appearances an abandoned theme park. He muttered, "Music is not an occasion for a picnic . . ." He was our most helpful and practical coach, though he also despised us. We tried to make nice one day, sidling up to him while he smoked. Darrett gave him his best, handsomest smile and said, "I guess we're being too indulgent," to make him believe that we understood our shortcomings. But the Swiss cellist lectured us even on the meaning of "indulgence"; he explained that an indulgence was a fee paid to redeem yourself from a sin—not a pleasure, and not the sin itself—and from there it was a short step to how Americans had no sense of the past, and misconstrued the most important words.

Darrett imitated him later, with a pretentious Euro-accent. He was right: that lecture on indulgence was almost as bad as "acoustical cor-relative." The condescension was the thing. The Swiss cellist implied we would never belong or understand, no matter how hard we tried. And yet we tried.

{

When Darrett and I emerged from our summer at Ravinia, and re-turned to Houston for a final prep session, Norman said our playing sounded like an outline, rather than a novel. They'd beaten fear into us. He put us in full reverse. He tried to undo everything, to fill it all back up and flesh it out. This was tiring, trying to accommodate these radi-cally different visions, while still trying to play the right notes.

We performed much of our competition repertoire in a pair of recit-als at Rice, in their new-smelling concert hall. The Brahms F Major, Barber Cello Sonata, Beethoven op. 69, a few other things. At one in-termission I went to the restroom, and while I was standing at the uri-nal an older man started yelling at me. "Why do you have to play so goddamned loud?" he said. My heart beat wildly. "I'm so sorry," I stam-mered, zipping up. What else could I say? I wasn't doing it on purpose. I was trying to play as best I could, with involvement. The old man left but I still think of him. My whole summer had been old men yelling at me. Why are people so cruel? Why is the act of listening so judgmen-tal? I came into the second half of the concert with a sense of his angry face, and Norman said I sounded panicky.

We got cheap student tickets to Munich (a lot of money had been expended on this summer project now) and put ourselves up in a cross between a hotel and a hostel, near the train station. Prostitutes hovered around the front door. I devoured Nutella and dark rolls in the base-ment breakfast nook, and resented tiny cups of bitter coffee. Then we'd go off to play. I felt half asleep the whole trip. The maid would knock on my door, furiously, anxious to clean my closet of a room, while I slum-bered on Houston time.

We got through the first round—whew; otherwise a complete hu-miliation. But for the second round, when the jet lag kicked in, we had to play the difficult Brahms F Major Sonata. I can see the stage in my mind. A small concert hall, a bright Hamburg Steinway, the sound pingy and exploding under my fingers. I probably played too loud, like Urinal Man said. And we didn't pass through to the finals. A bunch of young musicians crowded around a posted list. Darrett told me we weren't on it, and I told him I was going home. I called the travel agent, paid to change my flight, drank four or five beers, ate a sausage, and went to an art museum—a Blaue Reiter exhibit. The lingering taste of hops and a colorful painting by Gabriele Münter seemed more memorable than any performances I'd just played. Darrett and I flew home to separate lives. That was our last project.

\}

At my first lesson back on campus, I told Sebők about Walter Levin and the Forums, and how everyone discussed Brahms until you had no idea how to play it.

"Ah yes," he said. He knew Walter by reputation. "It is difficult to make music by committee. This is obvious in orchestras. In the wind section, sometimes, you hear the individual musician. A beautiful oboe solo. But most of the time you hear the music of many, the music of what everyone can agree about."

I told him that we didn't get further than the Munich semifinals.

"Anyway," he said, "you are one of the few who can hope for a career as a solo pianist, and you shouldn't aim to be a collaborative pianist." This compliment eased the sting of failure.

A few nights later, in the next master class, I felt the full relief of homecoming. A young woman thundered away at Liszt's Mephisto Waltz—thrashing, head shaking, hair thrown about. Sebők's response was bemused: "If I did what you just did, I would be exhausted. I'd need"—he paused—"a vacation."

He had her replay one of the biggest passages, smiling and savoring her inefficiency. Then he went to the piano and, cigarette holder dangling from his mouth, brought his arms slowly down, creating a focused sound ten times as large. The room gasped. His huge sound had no trace of ugliness, and there was no recoil; his body was unaltered, like a boulder with arms.

Then Sebők skipped to the other big moment in the Mephisto Waltz: the seductive tune. This required a different angle of attack. "Try again," he said. She played it—it swayed and waltzed back and forth. Sebők nodded. Then he played it back at her, and with the quality of his sound performed the act of listening to distances. Notes close together, then far apart. Up and down weren't equal. In his eyes and through a darkening of the sound you sensed that the descending interval in particular had a sinister intent. It struck me that Sebők's most divine moments occurred when he was explaining the devil.

"Remember," Sebők said, "the music is not the notes. It is between the notes." *Yes, yes, yes,* I thought. A lesson for life, and also, by the way, one more time for the record, and with all my heart: *Screw you, Walter.*

~

That year, my lessons were often interrupted by a celebrity cameo: János Starker. Starker was Sebők's more famous Hungarian cellist friend and duo partner. One of them had pursued the world's success; the other had remained at a chosen (?) remove. But together they'd recorded much of the central cello-piano repertoire: Chopin, Mendelssohn, Brahms. Starker was skinnier than Sebők, but even more flagrantly bald, and his body (like that of many cellists) bent differently. Starker tended to stare right at you, without fear or any visible emotion, but then you'd find a little laugh in his eyes, a mischief, a sense of a mind needing more entertainment than it was given.

My housemate Lizzy had become Starker's assistant that year, and as a result I became friends with many cellists, especially European ones, who clustered around the music school coffee shop in the morning, insulting the pastries. "Zis is not a croissant," one would say. The rest chimed in: "No, no, no. Croissant!?!?!?!?" Lizzy would look at me, rolling her eyes, whispering "It's a bear claw." The prospect of explaining Hoosier baking traditions to Parisian cellists was too much to take before coffee.

These Euro-cellists were happier to pay for accompanists than Americans were, and for this most mercenary of reasons I ended up spending many hours a week in János's studio. At first I thought I was

invisible. Starker focused all his attention on demolishing and rebuilding his students. Depending on the person, the demolishing might be
more successful than the rebuilding. He had a way of zeroing in on a
fundamental flaw, and trying to fix it with a humiliating suggestion.
One day, he was talking to an awkward young cellist with residual acne,
who never let his phrases blossom.

"I don't know if it's possible for you to . . . 'let loose,' " Starker said,
putting the Americanism in implied quotes.

"Here's what you should do," he said, after trying a million different
tricks. "You should practice . . . naked."

The student blushed. There were a few other cellists in the room, as
always. Starker's lessons were never private. The boy tried to laugh off
his red face. The other students, including a few beautiful French
women that I'm sure the boy was in love with, also laughed. Starker let
himself smile for a moment with everyone else—a temporary reprieve.
"I am serious," he said. "This is a life-and-death matter. Get a mirror and
practice in front of it and become aware that you have a body."

With time Starker's critical eye fell on me. I came in to play the
A Major Beethoven Sonata—which I'd spent the summer practicing,
and failing to dazzle the world with. The cellist played his tune, and I
responded with a long scale, looping up and then down. It was lumpy
and pretty sad, considering all the time I'd spent on it. My octaves were
even lumpier, almost a satire of legato. I was, as often in those days,
hungover.

Starker stared at me from the other side of a career. "You are better
than that," he said. A classic double-edged Starker-ism: on the one
hand, the great master had opinions about me; on the other, I was a
disappointment. I tried again—still clumsy. He sighed. It tired him out,
having to explain. He told me to stay close to the keys. What do you
know? This fixed what months of coaching had failed to fix, without
fuss or emotion or philosophy. He gave a little pout of his lips. "That is,
at least, pre . . . sent . . . a . . . ble," he said, like a scientist dissecting a
word.

We came to the last movement, where the cello has a solo tune.
Starker had heard thousands upon thousands of cellists ruin this, miss-

ing the leaps, making a thin, scratchy sound. Sebők always appeared to think about your problems, but Starker didn't need to think. He'd start listing prescriptions in clipped syllables, with consonants like the click of a typewriter: first do such and such with the bow, make sure the vibrato is already going, use one-third of the bow only, then shift down, anchoring with your thumb . . . It resembled directions that came with your IKEA furniture. Always something to do, something to consider, which left no time to be nervous (or inspired). This rationalism connected him with Walter. But Walter never liked to talk about "technique," while Starker loved it. In fact, he summed it up at that moment:

"What . . ." he said, "is the key to a good technique?"

Many of the Euro-cellists lurking around the sides of the room already knew the answer.

"An. Ti. Ci. Pa. Tion," he said—perhaps his favorite multisyllabic, and the ideal of his teaching. This was not, of course, the kind of anticipation where you are looking forward to seeing someone you haven't seen for a while. His anticipation was cold-blooded: knowing what task comes next, like a contractor knowing where the next board must go. You didn't want to get attached to the boards. He insisted that the aim of performing wasn't to be moved yourself, but to evoke emotions in the audience, a selfless act that required detachment.

So Starker took it upon himself to be our musical cold shower. One day, I was playing the aching second theme of the Rachmaninoff Cello Sonata, and having the closest thing I'd had for months to an orgasm in the presence of others, when I thought I heard a sound from the Starker corner of the room. It had the volume of a mumble, but the precision of a recording. I stopped.

"Sometimes, in order to make a theme go through," he said, repeating himself more loudly, "you have to cut it up." He over-enunciated the *t* of "it" and the *p* of "up," and pronounced "it" as *eat*. Then, by way of demonstration, he started singing "la la la la la." It is hard to express the timbre of his singing voice. Imagine you forced a duck to quack while you squeezed it in a vise. I bit my lip. If I laughed, that would be the end of me, of my relationship with Starker, with Sebők, all my idols. "La la la la," he quacked or sang, rising with a total absence of passion, the

Great János Starker, then threw his arms up like someone giving up on life to indicate the place in the phrase where you had to divide, in order to eloquently continue. He ruined that phrase for me forever.

That love for division—it was a shared Starker-Sebők thing, a Hungarian obsession. They wanted to know what belonged to what, and by process of classification arrive at emotional truth. But it took quite different forms. I'll never forget my friend Lizzy playing the last movement of Franz Schubert's "Arpeggione" in a master class. The piece begins with what appears to be a folk tune. Starker made her play each bar with a decay, separated from the next—imitating the shortcomings (and strengths) of a piano.

Lizzy sounded terrible. The tune limped. I'm sure she felt she was betraying the composer, or herself. Starker seemed for a moment to regret his beloved tactic of making students feel that they didn't know anything. So he stared at her with unusually soft eyes, and played to her like a father singing a lullaby to his child, as if murmuring: *This is how you put all that back together.* It was all divided, but was still a complete line, and—more than that—a sound from another time, without the compulsive *look at me!* so characteristic of modern playing, where string players sustain and pianists bang out the melodies, as if they're worried the audience will forget they're performing. It was what it was: a lilting, rocking song. I scanned the room; everyone else was looking around too. It was a lesson in the freedoms of restraint, the joys of style, and I felt I heard another secret message: that the intellect was not the heart's enemy, as many people seem to think.

⁊

One day, in the middle of lamenting that I was "accompanying like an accompanist," Starker declared that he'd convinced Sebők to resurrect his chamber music seminars. Fantastic! This meant two nights a week of Sebők, in addition to my lessons. A few weeks later, in one of the first chamber classes, a Starker student and a Sebők student were brave enough to offer the Mendelssohn D Major Sonata, one of the Hungarian duo's most famous recordings.

Sebők was subdued at first. He helped them to balance the energetic first movement, and didn't say too much about the charming second. But then we came to the beginning of the third movement, where the piano played a row of rolled chords, outlining a hymn. Mendelssohn is after an obvious image here: an angel strumming salvation on a heavenly harp. The pianist's problem is to play these strums without monotony, to create subtle direction—the "yearning" of the hymn.

"Yes," Sebők said, "that is a difficult solo," and he took a seat at the scratched-up, tinny instrument.

"What you don't seem to realize," he said, looking up at her and then at all of us, "is that a rolled chord can go at many speeds, and can change in the middle."

Then he played. The student's chords had rushed up to their top notes, as if trying to get the difficulty over with. But Sebők unrolled them like carpets: the point was to see the fabric. His patience started with the lowest note—he had a way of playing the bass so that it sustained, like an organ pedal. And the top notes had a slight bell tone, not too much, not poked, not so much that you said to yourself "there's the melody." When he came to a chord with a splash of minor, he slowed his fingers in the middle, as if the carpet hit an imperceptible snag, and the harmony pulled at your heart. He wasn't playing the rolls because the composer said so. He was using the rolls to listen to the harmonies, and, while listening, to choose what needed to be seen. Sometimes I wondered what I was still doing in Bloomington, and then something like this would happen, and I wondered how I could ever leave.

The cellist started to play—it was a tough act to follow. After the hymn, the cello part suggests a skeptic, a doubting Thomas. The lovely French girl played with a lot of rhythmic tics and nasal harmonics.

"Why are you doing that?" Sebők asked.

She looked at him silently, as if she didn't know or didn't want to say.

"Try this," Sebők said, playing her part at the piano. His playing sounded more like a stringed instrument than hers did.

"But," she interrupted, "Starker told me to . . ."

Sebők's face stiffened. I looked at my friends sitting nearby with excitement and fear, like we would at last get some insight into what the Hungarians really thought of each other.

Sebők said, at last: "Starker and I survived the Nazis together," a tough line to come back from. The French girl looked horrified—it was clear she worshipped both of them. "I have known Starker much longer than you have been alive, so don't explain my oldest friend to me, please." Then Sebők softened his tone, and explained his vision of Starker to her, to prove that their contradictions weren't contradictions.

If you put on their famous recording (and I recommend you do), you'll hear Sebők's unearthly rolls, especially toward the end, when the cellist is done being troubled. Sebők calms Starker's doubts with the purity and ease of his harp sound. He creates the illusion that the roll is not made of notes ("music is between the notes"). You can also hear that one minor chord take a little longer, too, heartbreakingly, just like I heard in the master class twenty-five years ago.

But even better—to my surprise, now—is when Sebők takes up the cello's material, when he returns from heaven to earthly sorrows. Sebők's sound acquires a core. It sounds like another piano, and another pianist. He plays a few pleading notes, deep into the key, then circles down toward a melancholy landing. Sebők spent so much of his life aspiring to simplicity and teaching ease, but these notes reveal a love for difficulty. The guru of release digs in, and won't let go.

}

Not so long after that, it was announced that Sebők and Starker would play a recital together in the Musical Arts Center. The MAC was an enormous and inexplicably purple hall used for operas, ballets, and spectacles. Its stage was wider, the administration bragged, than the Metropolitan Opera's. This conjured the early glory days of the IU opera department, the largest vocal school in the world, when people would come from around the state, and farther corners of the Midwest, to see their annual production of *Parsifal*. The MAC wasn't full that day for Sebők and Starker—it would have been a shock to fill its 1,500 seats—but it was a good, excited crowd.

They started with some Variations by Beethoven. It became clear they hadn't rehearsed. The first few notes felt empty, unexpressed, disheveled. I learned later from Sebők that at this point in their lives he and Starker found rehearsal limiting. Next came a twentieth-century piece, a Martinů sonata, also underrehearsed. I found myself evaluating my evaluator, even though I didn't want to. They could play conventionally boring performances, like any of us.

I almost left before the second half. They were scheduled to play the famous Sonata by César Franck, a piece I had misgivings about. It often feels like a potboiler, with oodles of lyrical outpouring and virtuoso passagework—an opportunity for players at the top of their game to shine, or show off. My Hungarians walked out, with a parade of sad logistics. Lots of preemptive coughing in the audience, and, like an echo to all that, quiet adjusting and creaking onstage. At last, Starker got his cello settled, glanced back, and Sebők lowered his arm to play the A for him to tune.

Whispers ran through the audience. My neighbor leaned over to ask, "You're a pianist, how did he do that . . . ?" I wished I knew. That A was the most seductive sound I'd ever heard—so much center, so little edge. This was the Sebők magic, a gift only he possessed. But it was just a utilitarian preamble; why did it need to be so beautiful?

Sebők's first four measures of the Franck took up the thread of the tuning A: clouds of sound, with the aim of endlessness. But when Starker entered, he divided like mad. His phrases were always dying and returning to life. He proposed syllogisms and produced occasional triumphant sums. It seemed as if Sebők had smoked a few joints, while Starker chugged eight espressos. Trying to make sense of all this, of these weird visions, one spiritual, the other analytical, I felt myself going into a trance.

In the second movement, as the piano roamed the keyboard, you felt that Sebők never crashed into his high or low notes. He always rounded them, like a car rounds a curve. His attention was on the richness of the harmonies, and he sketched distances that allowed Starker's details, etched like his speech, to emerge in the center. Their playing was like Henry James, constantly showing what shouldn't be done, and saying what couldn't be said. Starker never wanted a moment of schmaltz, and Sebők never wanted to show off. And so the hyper-

Romantic Franck Sonata sounded like a shrine, a place where emotions went to get purified.

After the concert, people in the lobby said all kinds of silly things, as they do in lobbies everywhere. A Russian pianist said, referring to Sebők, "Too much ease," a fair criticism. An Israeli violist said that was classic Starker, for better and for worse—also true. But these remarks hurt. I went out with friends afterward for beer and wings, the usual opiates. No one wanted to talk first. At last someone said, "That was surreal." We all agreed. They didn't seem to be playing for the audience. After most concerts, we'd be talking about how the artists had just played—but tonight we found ourselves talking about why.

We weren't in any of the dive bars floating around the music school, but in a new microbrewery that had popped up in a strip mall, next to a twenty-story brutalist dorm. The beer was a huge upgrade, and yet the overall experience felt like a loss. I started in on my third pint. I had always assumed that I was the one to be altered, the promising musician to be shaped and formed, the center of the universe, and that my teachers were unchanging influences: stars to be guided by. But it was clear (at that moment) that the stars moved too. The Franck's odd and beautiful reserve brought to life what I'd only known intellectually: all that Sebők and Starker had survived, wars, Fascists, Communists, labor camps, all the homes and homelands and ways of life they'd left for boring, calm Bloomington. Their musical ideals were what remained, the few items of value that the world had not yet managed to take away.

⅃

I had to grab a taxi the next day to retrieve my car. Then I went in for a lesson, and begged Sebők to show me how to make that sound from the Franck. He looked out the window. He didn't like preemptive questioning. He felt it was his privilege to choose what to teach. Ignoring my request, he told me about a woman who had phoned him a few days earlier, a former student. She had encouraged him to write a book about music, or a memoir, or some combination.

"People say I should write everything down, all my 'great thoughts,' " he said.

"You should definitely do that, Mr. Sebők!" I replied. It was so hard to say "mister" without sounding foolish.

Sebők looked at me like a cute but annoying puppy. He said, "It's tempting to try to preserve things . . ." and I thought of all the times in class he'd invoked temptations and seductions, Liszt's and Bartók's demons, hubris, Faust, *Don Giovanni*. His eyes pretended to consider this dream. Then, shaking it off: "But no. No. The most important things I have to say can't be written down. They won't survive a book."

16. *Rhythm* LESSON TWO

PLAYLIST

❙❙ CHOPIN: Étude, op. 25, no. 9 ("Butterfly"), recorded by Ignaz Friedman

*A*s you pursue a career in music, you discover rhythmic choices have an unexpected moral dimension. Classical music is riddled with Time Puritans. Disputing the metronome—a sin. A friend of mine, the great cellist Steven Isserlis, plays on the strict side, because he always has a higher-level rhythm in mind—how many bars are in one phrase, and then how many after that. He'll say something like "This section is three plus five plus three," referring to forty-five seconds or so of music. I admire this rhythm of structures, this architect's sense of time, which gives his playing great integrity, and yet occasionally I feel that the moment-as-moment deserves more love. So I linger on a beautiful note. Steven looks at me with a comically disapproving look, which only partly conceals the fact that he's genuinely annoyed. "You took time," he says, with the tone you'd use to scold an unruly child. Maybe I took a bit more time than I would have otherwise, just to bring on that face.

"That's one way to look at it," I say. "But you could also say that I gave time back to the universe." This, to my great joy, only increases his oh-so-British exasperation.

Conductors get miffed when you do these things. In rehearsal, you'll wait a little bit before a downbeat—it seemed to need more time. The conductor stops the orchestra. "You're going to take time there?" he asks. There's just a hint of annoyance, cloaked in deference. He appears to want to know what you are doing, but really he wants you to know that you're doing something suspect, like when your significant other says, "You're going to wear *those* jeans to the party?" I try to smile. Even the act of saying "take time" makes it an event, an indulgence, a fuss, and you're not sure you wanted to do anything in the first place. It just occurred to you in that moment; you don't want to forge a life plan out of it. The whole orchestra, arranged in a grand semicircle, is now peering at the two of you. I realize that's just how they sit, but I can't help but think of children, circling a fight. The orchestra players are kind of hoping we will yell at each other—a good story for the post-concert drinks.

Recently, I went to listen to a dear friend play through some excerpts she was preparing for an orchestra audition. She wanted to move up from the section to principal. A bunch of supportive musician friends were there, making it feel somewhere between a social gathering and a group therapy session. Afterward, people gave comments, and I told her some rhythms could be more strongly characterized. Normally, this friend is more than receptive to my musical suggestions. But she seemed chilly and annoyed as she said, "I don't know . . . Thanks, though."

This was for good reason. At her previous audition, someone told her that her rhythms were too individual—her short notes were too short—and she almost didn't get the job. Rhythmic individuality could cost her a great deal of money. I pointed out that certain of the passages she had played were solos, and didn't have to be coordinated with anyone else. It didn't matter: how you played anything implied a moral aptitude for orchestral work. You had to be able to get along, to assimilate, to be a part of what was considered rhythmically normal. Of course, what one orchestra considers rhythmically normal might be quite different from another, and most modern orchestras have quite different rhythmic values than an orchestra fifty or a hundred years ago. Rhythm, like smell, is an atmosphere you get used to, that you don't notice after a short time. Our idea of what is "proper" rhythm seems so natural that we don't consider our biases, all the decisions that go into it.

This reminded me of certain dire occasions when I've been convinced to go out clubbing. While everyone dances away, letting their bodies succumb to the rhythm, I sulk in the corner. I can't help it. Some nice friend will come over and yell in my ear, "Hey are you OK? What's the problem?" I exploit their sympathy to explain my problem with popular music.

"Always an accent on the two and the four," I grumble. They look bewildered.

I continue: "Always the same pattern, chunk CHUNK chunk CHUNK," using an irritating mocking tone, and eventually they realize what I'm talking about.

"Oh that," they say. "It's just the beat."

Just the beat?! I order another drink.

If my friend's audition committee was going to complain about her individuality, they wouldn't say that her melody was wayward, or her harmony (anyway, we aren't "allowed" to change the notes in classical music!): it would mostly and fundamentally be the rhythm. For my childhood teachers, freedom and laziness were connected. To be disciplined was to be strict. There was no such thing as disciplined departure. I was allowed to play without the metronome only if I promised to be good—a musical parole. All this negativity and policing reveals how powerful rhythm is, how central, and—here's the thing!—how connected it is to the concept of liberty. This is just as true for orchestra members as for my clubbing friends who, while dancing to the robotic, prefabricated beat, are telling me to "just let go." Harmonies wander; melodies develop or disintegrate; but only rhythms can truly be free.

⅄

One of my favorite moments in all recorded music is Ignaz Friedman playing Chopin's "Butterfly" Étude, a piece—if you look at the printed page—all in the same rhythm. It's just one fast note after another, and it could be played like a machine if you didn't know any better. Friedman goes along pretty evenly for most of the piece, behaving himself, dancing his way through. But toward the end a chord captures his attention, and the rhythm enters a warp. The pace slows and bends. One note takes the time of several "normal" notes. You have the sense that time goes up in the air like a ball, arcing and not returning until Friedman allows gravity to resume. Let me add: there is nothing in the printed music, not the slightest hint, to tell you to do that.

The rest of Friedman's Chopin Étude is charming, but this moment is dazzling—the musical equivalent of a spreading, disarming smile, a symbol of generosity. If you play this recording for your piano teacher, they will probably give you some side-eye and say, hmm, very nice, but remember: you can't have freedom without a strict foundation. This is reasonable and practical advice, and also self-serving. Friedman's freedom, where rhythm becomes ecstatically fluid, resists being taught, because it's partly about unlearning.

Let's compare this to another moment of freedom. You may recall, from the last rhythm chapter, Artur Schnabel's recording of the A-flat Schubert Impromptu. You may also recall Artur playing a tragic chord, an outburst, and then refusing to count it. After this savage moment, Schubert returns us to the original dance:

(and) one two (and) one two (and) one two three one.

Everything seems suspiciously the same, considering what we've been through. But it's not. Schubert changes one crucial note. A white key becomes a black key. This tiny slippage steeps the world in regret. When Schnabel plays this darker harmony—a new harmony that feels older than the one it replaces—you could say that he takes a little bit of time. But it's more accurate to say that he takes the freakishly perfect amount of time, only the time needed to hear the meaning of that change, for it to land softly in your mind. Schnabel injects the rhythm with a tiny dose of sadness and moves on, shifting back into tempo before the feeling can grow stale. Just as in Friedman's Chopin, the music gives no specific instructions, no *ritard* or *allargando*. How do you attain the judgment, the knowledge of how much time to take?

Two freedoms: one for joy, another for sorrow. Schnabel and Friedman share rhythmic wonder, but in radically different forms. Schnabel acts like a narrator, or a poet, inflecting words and explaining meanings. His rhythm is about the why. Friedman, on the other hand, is a chef who disdains recipes. He prefers not to explain. He throws rhythmic mishaps in the pot—a late bass note here, a rushing middle voice there—but behind the apparent chaos is a world of taste. When he discovers the unsuspected but perfect ingredient, everything swings.

Taking time and giving it back is one of the performer's great powers. It can be a subtle, etching and notating power, like Schnabel's inflections, or a wild re-imagination, like Friedman's. Another way to put it is that the performer has two tasks: one is to do what's written in the score—incredibly important; and the other, even more important, is to find everything that's not.

17. The End of the Line

In the middle of my third Bloomington year, I got an unexpected phone call. A familiar voice from Ravinia: Diane Dorn, administrator and den mother of the institute. Diane did her best to keep the festival from falling apart, fluffing faculty egos and assuaging donor demands. She secreted a thin layer of calm, which concealed a deep organizational mania. Most of the time she looked like she was about to prepare you a cup of Earl Grey tea, and read you a story by the fire; but once every ten days or so you suspected she was plotting to kill someone—with justification. I'm thinking of the time a bunch of us stole a case of wine from catering and crashed a golf cart into one of Ravinia's dozens of enormous, looming speakers.

Diane said she was calling on behalf of Walter Levin. "You know," she said, "Walter really likes you. He thinks you are so talented, such a beautiful musician."

Walter? I thought he was my nemesis. But if he said I was talented, well, that complicated his nemesis status.

"We'd like to offer you a job this summer, as a staff pianist." Diane kept massaging me with compliments. I needed a job. My stipend wasn't cutting it. I'd just discovered the payroll tax for freelance income, in the library at the IU music school. I remember looking around the musty room full of complete works of Renaissance composers and reference manuals, a favorite refuge, and wondering how it was possible that I was emerging from all the pleasant innocence of score study to a harsh reality where I had to surrender 15 percent of everything I made, before taxes were even calculated.

Diane offered me four times what I'd earned in Musicorda. I jumped at it. Sebők didn't love this idea; he thought I shouldn't be "accompanying." But he let me make my own practical decisions—he kept a strict boundary on certain parts of life, which is harder to do as a teacher these days.

⅃

That summer I showed up again in Ravinia, and got a dorm room like everyone else; unlike almost everyone else, I was being paid to be yelled at. Each day, all the students and staff would pile into a series of vans from Lake Forest College, haven for the offspring of plutocrats, and shuttle from stoplight to stoplight through obscenely affluent communities full of landscapers and contractors and housekeepers, until at last we reached the legendary park itself, and then we were stuck: enclosed in a habitat, animals in a zoo. There was nothing to do but practice, and talk about practicing, and rehash our lessons.

I played a couple lessons every morning, then learned new pieces and rehearsed in the afternoons. A colleague nicknamed me "The Savior," because I would learn anything. I was still so proud of my sight-reading ability, and still didn't see what a handicap it was: a lesson I should have learned ten years earlier, when my jock roommate threw me in the mud outside my Eastern Music Festival dorm.

Walter was much nicer this year. After lessons, when no one else could hear, he'd sometimes give me a heartfelt compliment. Even during lessons, he'd say to the violinist, "Listen to how Jeremy plays that theme." What had happened? Maybe his strictures weren't his only values. I began to sense a need from Walter, a need to have me imagine and invent, to animate his ideas—to help his ideas live free from him.

My attitude went through a profound change that summer. I started to see wisdom in even the most annoying faculty. I played for so many lessons that the ego bruise of a particular hour never lasted. The struggle to satisfy mentors, the pseudo-parental drama—it all went away, leaving only ideas that you encountered, and thought about, like friends.

My most vivid memory of that second Ravinia experience happened in one of the Forums. A formidable Russian pianist named Boris Berman was in residence. A young woman was playing some Brahms, I forget what, when Boris began to speak from his chair. His voice had authority because of its accent, and because of a skill that a friend calls RBS—Russian Bullshit Syndrome—a disease or a genetic superpower that allows Russian people to expound almost any theory and make it sound like the Word of God, if God were cynical and world-weary.

Boris started with a simple observation. He said, "Here, as you see, Brahms writes *dolce*." Yes, yes, I thought, the composer writes such and such.

"And over here," he continued, while I tried not to think of Boris and Natasha from *Rocky and Bullwinkle*, "he marks *espressivo*. Now what does this mean?"

I was pretty sure it didn't mean anything. Both words—*dolce* and *espressivo*—seem to want to drift away from meaning. You ignore them on the page, because you see them so often. Translation doesn't help. *Dolce* becomes "sweet," which in English doesn't have much ring or aura. And *espressivo* means "expressive," a useless placeholder, the kind of word that wants to become another word.

"For Brahms," Boris said, elongating the name in that way people do when they want to invoke greatness, "*dolce* and *espressivo* are opposites. They describe his two halves."

Oh, hello. This was interesting. How could those two namby-pamby words become a life-defining dichotomy? I was shocked to see an unusual look on Walter's face: genuine curiosity. "Boris," he said, "would you care to demonstr . . . ?"

But Boris was already walking semi-regally up to the stage. He shooed the student from the piano; she might have simply vanished, because I don't recall hearing from her again.

"*Dolce* is a sound with overtones," he said. Then he played. The notes floated and hovered. The ring and reverb were as important as the initial attacks. "This is almost like Debussy," he added.

"But *espressivo* is a sound with core." And then again he played, but these notes sank into their initial sounds and made you dwell on the pitch itself, instead of the overtones. Yes, the overtones were still out there, but they were too awed by the import of the main note to present themselves.

That was it. Maybe four seconds of piano playing, in all. But it was a radical revelation for me, how the smallest timbral choices invoked vast and deep dualisms of life, heavy and light, light and dark, individual and mass. The way you controlled your fingers' journey into a key, the degree of attack and release and follow-through, could make a chord feel drawn to the sky or barely able to lift its feet.

Boris also had the perfect pianist's beard and mustache, plus small round Euro-glasses, giving him a Brahmsian-Freudian look. This maximized his delivery. Walter tried to interrupt. Too late. Boris, in the rapture of explanation, was not to be denied. He continued, "Brahms writes combinations, sometimes . . . For example, he writes here *dolce ma espressivo*, sweet BUT expressive," and then from memory Boris played an example—a floating passage with just a shade of sorrow and heaviness in it. "And here *dolce ed espressivo*, sweet AND expressive," and he summoned another ravishing example: some lines *dolce*, some *espressivo*, as if to affirm that the floating and the heavy could coexist. It was miraculous, this control of color on command, each voicing so different from the others, the same piano bent to a rainbow of ends.

Yes, I thought, and that's how you make the instrument tell its best story, with magisterial control, behind the scenes—not in wiggling vibrato, or in wild strokes of the bow, but in subtle changes of speed and finger depth, carried in invisible vectors between the fingertip and the temporal lobe. I wasn't a pianist like that, nor did I hope to be. But I needed to steal some of it, for my own purposes.

{

In Ravinia most things were *espressivo,* particularly the lack of air-conditioning in our dorm. We complained about that on our van commutes—musicians become virtuoso complainers on all our travels; we might as well start early. In the evenings we sometimes made escapes to climate-controlled venues: a blues bar in Wrigleyville, a tapas restaurant in the Near North Side. I discovered goat cheese. The faculty would join us on these expeditions, and we realized they too felt imprisoned by the act of teaching us. It felt like a family from a sitcom: one crazy and astounding pianist who could play anything as long as he could play it as loud as possible; a violinist who practiced so systematically that every phrasing seemed selected by an algorithm; snarky violists who were never as stressed as the rest of us.

I remember several other crucial flashes of teaching. An afternoon where I played the Strauss Cello Sonata for all the strings in a room and Gary Hoffman said that there was nothing to teach, because we had thrown ourselves into the piece with such convincing enthusiasm and love—why should he ruin that with advice? I was pretty smug about that, and the other students grumbled, especially the algorithm violinist, for whom the word "love" had nothing to do with musical excellence. "Yeah, just play with more love," he'd say, while I missed reams of notes in the Schubert *Fantasy.*

Another day I played Bach for Olli Mustonen, the wild Finnish pianist—we were playing one of my new favorite pieces, the C Minor Violin Sonata. It begins with a *siciliano,* a lilting and haunting dance in the minor, with the keyboard playing continuous faster notes in the background. Olli told me that my notes should act not like notes but "like a river," which reminded me of the Ives Trio a couple summers past, and then he explained that articulation was one of the greatest tools while playing Bach.

He then sat and demonstrated a world of varied articulations: the left hand short and the right hand long, the right hand short and the left long, and entrancing versions in between. He seemed to get excited about each of them, finding some divine, rejecting others as ridiculous, and generally he behaved like a tinkerer at his bench, trying to find combinations that accomplished an aesthetic shiver. Sebők hadn't delved deep into Bach's articulation with me, nor had Bill back in New Mexico, except to define a general, acceptable semidetached default, something clean, something good for auditions and competitions. But here was articulation as a dance, a set of almost infinite choices, one of the most essential Bach virtues: how the notes formed and reformed and grouped themselves. As Olli played, I felt the voices begin to allow each other to speak. Articulation was an instrument of thought, a vehicle for conversation, tolerance, transparency.

I also played Bach for the great German cellist Heinrich Schiff, who looked plump and healthy, a golden stein of beer in human form. He said that my slow movement of the G Minor Gamba Sonata was "quite beautiful." We'd worked hard on it. I'd taken my excitement from the Mustonen lesson and inflicted it on this poor Israeli violist—bossing around an Israeli musician is not the easiest thing in the world. When Schiff complimented me, I felt I had used my heart and brain, and found some European virtues, despite my American handicaps.

A few days later, however, in the middle of the Debussy Cello Sonata, Schiff told me I had no clue. He pointed out that Debussy tells you when and how to slow down and speed up and also—so French!—the exact moment to stop. Clear and unambiguous, unlike, say, Romantic Schumann who valued the poetic implications of markings more than their precision. "You cannot treat French markings like German markings," he said. The music coalesced, and acquired a spine. The fandango of the last movement became energized, focused, more strummed.

After that lesson, I had to escape the building and all my fellow musicians. I changed into a swimsuit, grabbed a dubious towel from the floor of my car, and started walking to the lake, which was farther than I thought. My flip-flops were disintegrating. BMWs and Jaguars whizzed by. It was hot as hell.

I had one obsessive thought: all those markings on the page were a force for good. I couldn't believe it. Was this that famous maturity that everyone kept talking about? All my life, markings had been a locus of dread and guilt. Your teacher would point to the score with a scolding finger. You forgot that *diminuendo*! You didn't do that *ritard*! Yet another failure of observation that made you feel like a puppet on strings, a classical emulator, trying to execute everything on the page, not just forests of notes but also inscrutable instructions as to how to shape them.

I dropped my towel on the side of the road. As I bent down to pick it up, I wondered if I'd taken a wrong turn; I wasn't sure of the route to the lake. But in that moment of sweaty uncertainty, I was struck by a vivid image: the written page of music was a treasure map. It had messages from the composer and from the past, telling you just enough to figure out the rest, hints and clues to make the piece live in the present. You didn't obey them because the teacher said so, but because they showed the way.

$$\wr$$

Without knowing or wanting it, I had been planning my escape from Sebők. I'd decided to enter the Munich competition that September—on my own. I had something to offer, I told myself. I needed to step up and be confident. So, during the whole five weeks of "accompanying" labor at Ravinia, I was also squeezing in a couple daily hours of practice on competition repertoire.

Then came six weeks of solo practice in Bloomington. Bloomington has a pleasant late-summer vibe. There is a daily drama of thunderstorms, but mainly you feel a lazy humid continuity and a sense of being abandoned by the busier world. I went off to the quarry to swim, and I grilled hunks of meat that I found on sale at Kroger, but most of the time I just sat in soundproof practice cubicles, and pounded away until there was no chance of a memory slip or any humiliating disaster. The so-called new building, an annex to the main music hive, was full of terrible pianos: almost honky-tonk instruments. You had to lie in wait to try to snatch one of the few good ones. I can see myself in that hallway, lonely and determined, scanning various glass doors, hearing all the other desperate and listless summer practicers, and with a sigh heading back into my room.

Getting to Europe was the same ritual as a year earlier. I got a cheap ticket at the student travel place, booked the same seedy hotel near the Munich train station, drank the same bitter coffee, and had all the Nutella I could stuff in my mouth. But the piano competition was more glamorous and exotic than the duo competition. I got to practice in this Nazi-looking building, in wood-floored rooms you found after ascending the grandest of staircases. You checked out a baroque key from a little panel of female student interns. I didn't understand what it meant when these young women gave me a piece of paper saying "Good luck," with all their lipsticked lips imprinted on the page.

I got through the first round with the Mozart C Minor Sonata and Bach E-flat Minor Prelude and Fugue and Ligeti *Automne à Varsovie*— lots of dark, deep emotion. I played, I believe, Beethoven 109 and Chopin Fourth Ballade for the second round, and passed again. I had momentum. For the third round, I offered a weird pair of pieces: Elliott Carter's Piano Sonata, a great and difficult work, and one that most European judges would not know, and Liszt's *Don Juan Fantasy,* a big silly barn burner—an odd betrayal of the purity of my opening rounds. I remember practicing for the finals, feeling confident, when another pianist knocked on my door, then came in to try to psych me out, saying "You're so sure you will get to the finals?" in a weird and undermining tone. Maybe my fear and suspicion of other pianists, some of whom I'm sure are fine people, goes back to that moment.

Afterward, several audience members came to congratulate me, but the judges felt differently. I didn't get through. A young German woman attendee, however, decided I was the great love of her life, and followed me about the city as I drank gallons of post-traumatic beer. She said I had been robbed. I found this opinion comforting, but then didn't know how to get rid of her. I ran across the American judge on the street, and asked him what he thought. Claude was polite over a sobering coffee and didn't offer any specific advice. The German woman invited herself along to this meeting. After Claude left, she said he was not a serious person, and a true artist like me should not listen to one word he said. He could not judge me, how dare he think he could. I didn't know whether I should make out with her, or if she would strangle me.

}

The return to Bloomington: knocking on the same old door, for my weekly lesson. Sebők had heard from a well-known German judge about my performances. I liked that Sebők cared. But it was unsettling that I could fly all the way to Europe and not escape surveillance. The judge had told Sebők that my Mozart was wonderful. Sebők looked pleased with himself, even more than with me. He had passed something on. "Now, *that* is an accomplishment," he said, "something to be proud of. However," he continued, the same source reported that I seemed tired in the *Don Juan Fantasy*. Well, I thought, who wouldn't? It was a big piece with a lot of octaves. I must have looked crestfallen. If I'd only known I was tired, I could have fixed it, and would now be a famous, world-touring pianist.

"This is not something to be sad about, or to blame yourself for," he said, reading my confused mind. "The real and interesting thing is to ask why it happened." A moment of smoking. "Yes, why," he repeated, "that is what we must explore now." Always why. Something Evelyne said came back to me. She said she wasn't interested in people's wrong notes, but in *why* there was a wrong note, what physical or mental inattention caused it. And when we were reading scores at Ravinia, looking at a mystifying staccato or slur, teachers often asked: Why did the composer write that? I like to ask students that question these days; it rarely occurs to them to reverse engineer the work of the composer, to empathize with their need to communicate.

Sebők and I began to work on the frame of my hand again, to discover what support was lacking, how could I avoid tiredness. But I was still in mourning. It took some weeks to recover my self-esteem and listen to Sebők properly. Evelyne's violist husband, Atar, said the problem was simpler. "Why would you play the Carter and the *Don Juan*, those are terrible choices for a competition," and he too was right.

{

That second-to-last Midwestern year went by in a hurry. Life had comforts, almost too many comforts. A new apartment to myself, and a bread machine. I set it up to make bread every other morning, but it woke me up at 3:00 a.m. when it started kneading. I had to choose between yeast and rest. I had a bay window and a breakfast nook. A conductor lent me his piano so I could practice at home. The toilet fell over and water gushed everywhere, but the piano was spared. Another conductor—with whom I was rehearsing *Falstaff*—asked me again what I was still doing in Bloomington. "We all thought you'd leave a long time ago," he said.

A new competition appeared on the landscape, posted on a faculty door. It was called the National Power World Piano Competition, an impressive mouthful. The prize money was big. My credit card balance was mounting. Also, Princess Diana was going to give out the awards, and a famous British actor was the master of ceremonies. Sebők was supposed to be about not caring about fame, but I wasn't quite there yet.

I created a more strategic program for this competition than Munich. I started again with Mozart and Bach. But I'd meanwhile fallen in love with the "Eroica" Variations of Beethoven, one of the craziest pieces I'd ever seen, and so I threw that in the semifinal round as a big foundation, an accomplishment (if I could pull it off), along with Chopin, Bartók, more Beethoven, and the Elliott Carter for the obligatory post-1945 piece that the judges didn't care about.

Then it came time to choose not one, but two concertos for the finals. This was partly hypothetical, since you'd have to be lucky to even get there.

"How about Rachmaninoff Second?" I asked Sebők, while I was in the middle of all this dithering. He looked at me.

"Many people will play that piece, and have success," he said. "But you are not that kind of artist. You should show them who you are with the pieces you choose."

This felt like the greatest of compliments. And so I ended up putting Beethoven's "Emperor" on the list, and Brahms D Minor. Sebők looked pleased. "Yes, those are who you are," he said.

⸘

I practiced my heart out for the National Power company. I hit the Beethoven "Eroica" first, since I could tell it was a beast. It would take time for it to feel like part of me. I brought it in for a lesson, and Sebők was charming, teasing out the playfulness in each variation. In one variation, the right hand keeps playing some quick fillips, like little ribbits, while the left hand leaps around it, playing one unchanging note in every octave—a B-flat. Sebők said, "You should play this like Ping-Pong." And his left hand danced its way around his right with light and elegant feet, no hurry, always prepared for the next note.

In another variation he encouraged me to think of a street band, something rustic. My staccatos changed and coarsened. Yes, he said. That was better. "Beethoven is quite serious," he said, "even about jokes." We worked awhile on the opening to make sure the reiterated left hand had something to offer, a sense of resistance and stubbornness. Again the philosophical nature of the two hands, Sebők's way of finding meaning and purpose in oppositions.

A couple weeks later, I decided to perform the "Eroica" in studio class, to get the butterflies out. The studio was as usual half-lit, filled mostly with non-American admirers. I had run with Sebők's ideas. I had worked harder than ever and, as I played, felt reasonably confident, nailing licks that seemed chancy in the practice room. The other students gave me warm and generous applause after I finished. Sebők smoked for a while. Perhaps I turned to him looking a bit too jaunty.

At last, coolly and evenly, he said, "You need to learn the difference between character and caricature." The room went silent, absorbing this elegant, lacerating remark.

It got worse. Variation after variation, he demonstrated how I had converted high humor into low slapstick. He seemed to blame me for my enthusiasm for his own ideas. I had been too happy with myself, too in love with my abilities. My joy at being able to play the notes overtook the subtleties. People patted me on the back outside afterward, hugged me, as if I had been the victim of an assault. I tried to laugh it off—after all, it was a great line—but they knew I was stung.

It occurred to me that he was meanest when I felt I had played my best. I grasped the rationale, but I couldn't quite swallow it. Again I wondered, *Doesn't he know how much I love and admire him?* But, of course, he did know.

⁓

So, as the competition loomed, I started to play for other people: Evelyne, of course, but also quite a few times for another faculty pianist named Michel Block. Michel taught the doctoral seminar in "piano literature," a four-semester requirement where we surveyed the vast piano repertoire in blocks: Baroque, Classical, Romantic, Twentieth Century.

The course requirement was simple: prepare an hour-long presentation on some composer or set of pieces. Off we'd go to get recordings and assemble facts. But inevitably, five minutes into our presentation, usually a regurgitation of reference manuals and liner notes, Michel would interrupt and commence a philosophical exploration of his own. His lecture-rants treated music as a mere point of departure. When someone presented on Boulez, he got going for twenty minutes—like Allen Ginsberg narrating *Howl*—with a recurring refrain: *The answer to the question is the question itself.* "Does it matter that we hear the notes? The answer to the question is the question itself" (with a demure smile, as if he knew he was toying with us). "Does it affect us? The answer to the question is the question itself!" (now furious, almost murderous). Which I suppose meant that this music created unanswerable loops about what music was, what purpose it served.

When someone presented on Mozart concertos, and put on a recording by Richard Goode, he also went off his rocker. He started counting in between the beats of the slow movement of K. 488, one of Mozart's most heartbreaking statements, and showed us how each note was placed exactly where it should be. "One two three FOUR five six, one two THREE four FIVE six, everything behaves!" he yelled, counting some more. "Don't you see?" It was annoying how everything seemed placed in an invisible grid. And yet the playing was quite beautiful. "Is this what music-making is, now?" He looked at us. You sensed a vast, almost tragic abyss between his emotional intensity and the jadedness of our grad school selves.

Michel liked me, because sometimes I would raise my hand midrant to mention a novel. So I felt confident asking him for a lesson, and one evening when the school felt quiet and dark, I went into his studio and played through the Chopin Fourth Ballade. I screwed up the coda something fierce. "Oh, that's nothing," he said when I drew his attention to my disaster, "you just pressed too much." What seemed like an unsolvable existential crisis for me was actually a familiar physical problem and solution to him, something that all pianists face, and have to quell, in one way or another—he felt confident I could just deal with it, like you'd drink water when you're thirsty.

But then he suggested there *was* something I really needed, that for whatever reason I'd never been taught. "Martha told me this," he said. Meaning Martha Argerich. I imagined him on a yacht, perhaps, off the Amalfi coast, talking with her about life and piano playing, pursuing ill-starred romances, tossing empty bottles of champagne overboard. "She says if you're not with each top note, each melody note, then your mind has nowhere to focus, and you find yourself at a loss, thinking of everything instead of something." So, he said, just follow from one note to the next. Keep on the path. "Otherwise . . ." and then his face made the expression of going crazy, his eyes swelling, his face puffing, a slight reddening of the cheeks to go with a reddish nose—a lot like his face at the climax of his lectures.

I tried this. It sounded good to be on this path, or any path. But then Michel noticed that some of my melody notes had more core than the others. He sat and started to play a Chopin nocturne. "You know," he said, "it is perfectly possible to play a beautiful melodic line with a pencil." While his left hand kept arpeggiating in that gorgeous Chopin way, he let his right hand stop playing for a moment and pluck a pencil with a nice cushy eraser from the piano's interior. He then resumed the melody with the eraser, guiding the pencil around the nocturne's famous melody. It sounded fantastic, even better than with his fingers. "It works," he said, "as long as the notes aren't too fast," and he smiled at me, savoring the irony of seducing with a schoolroom implement.

It was a trick, of course, but a trick with a moral. If your arm and wrist were supple and well used, then all you needed from your fingers was a certain support, a structural integrity. Also, the pencil didn't press: the pencil had no anxiety, it didn't grab at notes, it was a mere messenger from the arm.

⸮

I flew off to London. I remember the exhausted taxi from Heathrow into town, passing by all those houses so close to the M4, feeling what a weird world it was. They put everyone in a dorm in Islington—not yet a hip neighborhood. I'd brought along a copy of *The Brothers Karamazov*, a cheap thick volume in tiny print, to keep me company in jet-lagged hours, and I remember reading it late at night, nibbling on digestive biscuits, tossing and turning in a student twin bed.

A fellow Sebők student, Silke Avenhaus, was also there, so I felt a certain camaraderie—the opposite of Munich. Quite a few pianists had flown from America; we commiserated about our performances. One night a gang of us walked all the way back from the South Bank to Islington, stopping off at as many pubs as we could. The Thames, the grand avenues, the lit dome of St. Paul's, the impossible postcard beauty of the Parliament building. I felt thrilled and alive, and like I had found London, or London had found me. The competition organizer had commandeered an old rambling building near the South Bank, the county hall—about to be renovated into a Marriott—and in the empty, echoing rooms she'd deposited twenty or thirty Yamaha pianos. It was uncanny, wandering through those halls, filled with dustcloths and ladders and half-removed walls, like a grand estate that had been abandoned, and hearing the gradually dwindling number of us practice our tunes for the next round. We called out to one another, from far away, when we got frustrated or lonely.

I had no trouble in the first round, and played well again in the second. I called home at great expense to tell Evelyne and Atar, who were invested and quite excited. I felt like a real adventurer, negotiating the tube, eating platters of Chinese and Indian food. *The Brothers Karamazov* was a fantastic book, I realized, and I couldn't stop. Packets of biscuits and crisps, epic crumbs in scratchy sheets.

In the third round, I had a few rough "Eroica" Variations, but nothing too bad, and the Carter seemed to go over well. And what do you know—I got through to the finals! The remaining American pianists gave me their best congratulations, and began to phone the airlines to get on the next flight home.

But now, I was truly alone. Just two other competitors, one British, one Russian. Things went downhill. It lost the sense of a pleasant foreign adventure, and felt like a dream in which you are impossibly pressed for time. The Russian and I had to move into a crowded, noisy hotel in Piccadilly Circus. I called my friends at home again. They were even more excited. But now Sebők's decision had come to roost. The judges requested Brahms D Minor in the finals. And maybe because I'd invested so much time and energy in the previous rounds, I hadn't spent enough time on the concerto. Who knew I would be such a success? I hadn't believed it. There was a rehearsal with the Philharmonia Orchestra, and some tug-of-war about tempos. I'm not sure I knew what tempo I wanted the first movement to be. I needed help, guidance, a teacher, or just maybe a hug. But there was no one to hug. The conductor was an enigma; he had to be neutral, and not offer assistance. I was too worried about the skips in the famous solos—one stupid worry that overwhelmed all the others. What a jerk Brahms was to follow up his gorgeous melody with such an awkward development. I resented Sebők for suggesting this piece.

Something was bothering me—so I asked the orchestra to play louder, to give me more support. But the real problem was that I felt naked onstage at the Royal Festival Hall, the biggest hall I'd ever performed in. There is an art to playing in big halls: confidence, a willingness to ignore how small and alone you sound, to believe in the projection of your ideas, and to stick with what you've done before. I didn't have that art. I wanted the room to talk back to me, not face me with a judging expression. My suggestion to the orchestra was a mistake. The orchestra ended up drowning me out, which made me press and strain: a destructive cycle.

Paul Lewis, the now-prominent British pianist, won with a Rachmaninoff concerto, I believe. Again I thought back with bitterness to Sebők's advice. Princess Di gave me third prize, and a kiss on the cheek, as I smiled in front of the big audience as best I could, having lost the night. But I paid off my credit card bill. And I got a picture of myself being kissed by Princess Di, which I faxed to everyone I knew. She and I had the same hairstyle at that time.

At the reception I met all the judges. Many of them congratulated me for my excellent playing throughout and said it was unfortunate I chose the Brahms D Minor, a hard thing to pull off in any situation, not to mention a competition with a minimum of rehearsal. The organizer said they'd done me a favor by asking for the Brahms—instead of the "Emperor," which was much harder—but I wasn't so sure. I remember then feeling adrift, and more alone, that no one really wanted to talk to me—fair enough, since it was hard and awkward work consoling a loser. The hotel room seemed like it might be worse. A familiar sensation for musicians: once the adrenaline of the event fades, that nothing could be sadder than remaining in the city where you've been—a place filled with purpose until that moment; but in an instant, with the fading of the applause, you have become, as elderly people often feel, a burden, a thing to carry to the airport and dispose of.

But just as I was feeling that I must leave the party, the American judge, Herbert Stessin, came over. He taught at Juilliard. He said that I had a beautiful sound and was a beautiful musician and that I should have won, in his opinion. This helped. He told me I should be in touch if I ever wanted to come to study in New York. I wish I could say I reacted with humble gratitude, but I transformed into a diva. I lingered, and had one too many glasses of wine. I thought it was outrageous that there was no car to drive me to the hotel, that they hadn't arranged transport. I marched up to the organizer, a spoiled spectacle, and demanded a car service.

It was hard to tell Evelyne and Atar about this loss, and hear the disappointment in their voices. Sebők felt it was a moral victory, since

I got so far. But the worst part of this loss came a few weeks later, when I visited New Mexico. I told my parents what Stessin had said, that I should have won, and my father said with a sneer, "We read the review, Jeremy. Come on, give me a break." He was referring to an article in a British paper that said I'd had the hardest job of all the competitors, but even considering that, I fell short. That my father would take the side of a random music critic over this judge I had met—a teacher at Juilliard!—and over what little faith I had managed to cobble together about myself; that he wouldn't give me the benefit of the doubt, or allow me this moment at our old dinner table to console myself . . .

When I told this story to Evelyne back in Bloomington, her face darkened and she said, "Oh, of course—he's jealous."

It hit me that she was right. My father had always wanted to be a creative person, a performer, and he pursued all of that too late. He had a subconscious urge or need to make me feel it was impossible. To tell me that I shouldn't get used to the dream. When Evelyne pointed this out to me, some trust in the world vanished. But on the other hand, it was like a marking in the score that I finally understood. I knew why the composer wrote it.

𝄢

My final year in Bloomington, I had my most preposterous apartment, a sprawling basement with tons of mold and spiders and '60s decor. One night I dreamed that it was called "Segovia Ochre." It was located on the road out of Bloomington, toward the airport, neither here nor there. It was harder to throw parties and be a part of the music school world. There were musicology essays, lecture-recitals, Michel's repertoire seminars. An endless array of seeming tasks, giving the illusion of action. I biked to the coffee shop, and to the farmers' market, and had a nice easy life. I made pesto. I think I was happy, I just can't remember. My inability to remember my happiness in my twenties was a major cause of unhappiness in my forties.

My friendship with Evelyne deepened; we played duo concerts. I dated a fellow student pianist, ineptly. I made her watch geeky television, and she broke up with me for being an emotional cipher. I kept trying to earn money through way too much accompanying, and started to scatter my forces, just like at Oberlin.

Lessons began to feel less like progress. Still full of genius, but a tired genius. Sebők tried to give me an important lesson in rhythm using the theme of the last movement of Beethoven's op. 109. The theme is a saraband—a slow Baroque dance in triple time—and Sebők demonstrated how to get a magical lilt: you subtly elongate the second beat and shorten the third, in effect playing the third beat slightly late. It was so flowing and natural when he played it. But the next week, I offered him a limping, drunken saraband; he was not happy. The week after that, I tried to cultivate his reserve, his refinement; then he told me I was playing "like an old man." As I tried to look sublime and philosophical, he said, "I can tell you're concentrating . . . I just don't know what you're concentrating on."

This was a brilliant line, cutting and simple, and I use it all the time with students these days, softening it with a smile, trying to make it clear that I am on their side, trying to be helpful. But for me at that moment it was a boundary. Evil moment, when you doubt the magician's magic, when you wonder if it was more image than insight.

⁊

In Proust's *In Search of Lost Time,* one of the most important elements of the plot is the impasse. He makes a protagonist out of something that seems to be against the grain of the story, of any story, of the idea of story: a whirlpool of loss and waste. He immerses us in unproductive cycles—romantic obsessions, bizarre friendships, social ambitions. It is only when he begins to feel there is no point at all that the point reveals itself.

Since this piano lesson book has taken me so long to write, I doubt I will get around to it, but I've always wanted to write a book about the music of novels. Not literal appearances of musicians in novels, or descriptions of music—everybody likes to talk about that stuff, yawn yawn—but ways in which novels have a long-term musical rhythm. In Proust, the effect of the impasse is a great pause, a dark *fermata,* a sense of frustration, a holding pattern, a style of writing that makes you feel what the author-narrator feels, that art has lost its charms. He is willing to dare you to quit, to stop reading, to make you doubt and even hate him, in order to get the effect he wants. He holds you in that cynical place for an unaccountably long time, and then releases you into an unfolding series of revelations about time and the joys of life. The doubt and the epiphany play off each other like one chord responds to another, chiming back and forth, questioning and answering, inhaling and exhaling.

One of the reasons I never enjoy the music of Shostakovich, although I admire it and think it captures an essential part of the human condition, is that it's all impasse with no release. When there are solutions, they tend to be grudging, tragic, or ambivalent, like the famous ending of the Fifth Symphony that everyone argues about.

Schubert's great final song cycle, *Winterreise,* despite all its allure, is one big impasse too. A kaleidoscope of dead ends. To take just one example, the famous "Frühlingstraum," you have three different mini-songs: an innocent lilting, dancing tune as if from paradise—the dream; then a dark terrified outburst—waking up; then a trance-like tune, almost immobile, its hypnotic beauty laced with sad notes, neither awake nor asleep. It's somehow the gaps between these different musics that you feel the most, an uncrossable divide from dream to reality, or from reality to a less cruel reality. Those three songs can never be reconciled; they just exist in parts of our psyche, haunting one another.

I'm tempted to say that Bach doesn't do impasses. When he encounters a musical or compositional problem, he tends to discover his even more brilliant self in the act of solving it. But as I think about it more, the famous 25th Variation of the "Goldbergs" comes to mind: the far end of the story of human invention, a place where the continuity and unfolding virtuosity are broken into endless shards. People always talk about that one, and I don't think it's just because it's beautiful. Maybe one thing we value about certain pieces is not the obvious mastery, but the sense of doubt they create about their own enterprise.

In Beethoven's last sonata, op. 111, impasse is the central theme. The first movement revisits Beethoven's "C-minor mood," a gestalt that made him famous, that gave him a voice, representing the angst of a whole proto-Romantic generation. But it is fused with a fugal voice from Bach, a sense of the past. This fusion is unsuccessful. The opposed voices and styles don't lock in (the present and past aren't compatible); fugal entries spin off into endless arrays of climbing notes, passages, and sequences, with few if any arrivals. This repetitive quality, the sense of spiraling, retrying the same approach with the same result ("definition of insanity")—it all reminds me of that last, hard year of Sebők lessons.

Beethoven suggests there is nothing to do but start fresh. The second movement of 111 is not in the minor, but in the major, with no hint of the angst of the first, which might as well never have existed. This new theme has serenity, but also a barrenness. It requires patience and time. Then it gradually accumulates things onto itself, variations that are like sublime lessons. These variations teach you about things hidden within the theme, taking rhythmic nuggets and exploring them, accreting them. They add ambivalence and beauty. But all these variations/lessons come with a catch: they obscure the original idea. And it is impossible to know where they are going.

By this time in his life, Beethoven had (to say the least) learned something about story too, about how to make obsessive variations into a narrative—something shared with the "Goldbergs" and Proust— the importance of finding a place where the story falls apart, the importance of making you believe in your doubt. Beethoven saves his best inspiration for this moment of impasse, for the moment where the path is unclear. The music embarks on a series of circular progressions with no knowable end, and when the theme comes back to you it's only because you allowed yourself to be lost.

18. *Rhythm* LESSON THREE

Composers, like performers, have rhythmic fingerprints. One famous example is Johannes Brahms. He was addicted to the hemiola, a rhythm made of two rhythms at war. The term comes from the Greek, meaning "half as much again." A hemiola has two notes in one voice, and three in another, occupying the same duration:

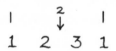

By the laws of mathematics, the second of the two notes arrives halfway in between the second and third of the three notes. This gives the hemiola a meaning, or (in literary terms) a theme: it invokes in-between-ness, drag, difficulty, friction. This in turn connects to Brahms's way with harmony, his love for notes that pull and cling to other notes. Both reflect his complicated place in history: a Romantic who wanted to be a Classic, caught between past and future.

A decade or two after the death of Brahms, another famous rhythmic calling card: the great Igor Stravinsky. He purees time in a blender. He pursues a vendetta against symmetry. He takes a savage pleasure in sending chunks of duration everywhere, throwing accents at unpredictable intervals, slicing beats up with no regard for the listener's sense of stability. As with Brahms, this seems both a personal and a historical reaction. Romantic music is often rhythmically square; along comes Stravinsky with his modern, ironic knife, ripping the comfortable armchairs of Romantic phrases into fragments of fluff, and shredding detested sentimentality while he's at it.

For me, one of the most fascinating rhythmic comparisons in the classical canon is between Mozart and Beethoven, who composed at close to the same time, and using a closely related language, with astonishingly different results. You cannot complain, really, about Mozart's rhythm. He balances stoppage and flow. He knows when to interrupt, when to elide (an underrated virtue), when to gently turn a corner. His greatest gift, maybe, is an ability to create states of suspension, bubbles of what I'd call Apollonian pure time, like the slow movement of the Piano Concerto, K. 467 (*Elvira Madigan*), where it's easy enough to imagine (as Charles Rosen suggests in his great book *The Classical Style*) the shepherd and the nymph, cavorting in some idyllic glade on the side of an ancient urn, their emotions (love, loss, light, dark) frozen in equilibrium, in motion forever.

But if Mozart wrote the ideally timeless, Beethoven managed to write something quite different: music in search of time. Part of this is personality. Mozart, the pragmatic theater composer, assumes time as a precondition of expression. Beethoven, more prone to philosophy, wants to know what time is, what it's made of.

⁊

In 2017, I flew to Minnesota to play Beethoven's Fourth Piano Concerto with the Saint Paul Chamber Orchestra. They usually want me to talk before the concert. So this time I brought (I thought) a special treat: a musicological discovery that people could relate to. I took the stage and picked up the mic. Applause died down.

"Beethoven takes out a sheet of blank music paper," I said in the present tense, a cheap trick to help people imagine that classical music isn't all about plundering the past, that it can live in the now.

"And on the first line, he writes . . ."

With that I plunked out *da-da-da-dum*, the famous opening of the Fifth Symphony. A titter ran through the crowd—laughter of recognition. It's just a rhythm. Once it was a half-formed idea, but now it's almost a prerequisite of existence.

"A little idea, a passing thought he might follow up on . . ." I added, getting more laughter. I told myself not to ham it up, but it was too late.

"On the second line, right below the first . . ." I said, now earnest. This earnestness was not faked or hammed. It occurred to me, right there onstage, that I wasn't exactly telling this story for them. I wanted them to enjoy it, but I also needed to console myself. This musicological fact reassured me then, and still does now, about the possibilities of music, and what it can do for us, and the reasons I stress myself out to play the piano.

"Right below the first . . ." I continued, repeating myself in a slightly higher tone to make sure they got the importance, trying to gain control of the tempo of the talk through rhythmic reiteration, "Beethoven writes another idea, the opening theme of the Fourth Piano Concerto."

I sat down and played, showing how in both passages, the famous and the slightly less famous, it's the same rhythm, the same three notes going to a final, longer note:

one two three one
da da da dum

In the Fifth Symphony, this rhythm represents stormy, angry Beethoven, fighting with fate. But in the G Major Piano Concerto the same rhythm is gentle, playful, and loving, a vehicle for some of the purest happiness he ever wrote. It's not an accident or coincidence. The piece of paper tells us that the idea went two ways in Beethoven's mind—two opposed ways at once, toward tragedy and comfort—and that rhythm was the essence, the link, the conduit.

At the post-concert drinks, I got seated next to the associate principal violinist, an old friend named Ruggero Allifranchini, who you might guess is Italian. We were still in the rapture of the rapturous piece we'd just played. The previous summer, he explained, he'd been talking with the conductor at Mostly Mozart about the beginning of Beethoven's Fifth Symphony.

"I told Louis," Ruggero said, leaning into me with his martini, "and by the way, Louis said this absolutely changed his life—that you should think of a little beat in the middle of the three pickup notes, that there's a hidden beat in there, which gives it . . ." He hesitated, searching for the perfect word in that Italian savoring way, "you know, how you say, a structure." Yes, *structure*, I thought. I didn't buy into his hidden-beat theory, but that word felt important and true.

Beethoven's *da-da-da-dum* has a powerful virtue: it can be chained together, like Lincoln Logs, or Legos:

one two three one / one two three one / one two three one

Repeating the rhythm creates a continuous, unbroken surface— actually an interesting mix of attributes, both continuous and restless. (Restless things are often uneven, with stops and starts.) At the beginning of the Fifth Symphony, Beethoven exploits this duality. He writes a series of rhythms, climbing:

da da da dum

da da da dum

da da da dum

Beethoven stacks vertically, one set of notes higher than the last. Simultaneously he stacks horizontally, through time, from past to future. He's building in (at least) two dimensions. This act, I realized, was so important for him. Ruggero was still talking, but I'd lost his thread. I was thinking that when Beethoven finishes that phrase, you feel something is *held within it.* That stack of notes just barely contains a chord, and all its coiled energy.

I sipped on my martini, and tried to take the advice I give students: Don't just label, always ask why. Why do you build a structure?—and it hit me—for shelter. Shelter, yes! This helped explain so many things: why piano teachers are so obsessed with metronomes, why orchestra committees become prudish. Wayward rhythms can make music seem like a collapsing house. Harmonies can turn from major to minor in an instant; they flicker; they modulate; they act more like water than stone. Melodies are stabler but can be narcissistic, whistling themselves over and over again. But rhythms offer something to hold on to and lean against, a refuge against both change and monotony. Watching dancing friends in a club, I can see that the beat creates a protected space, a force field around them, that lets them let it all out: a structure that at once gives shelter and permits freedom. And what else is music but a space for us to live in, for a while.

⟩

At the beginning of the slow movement of Beethoven's final cello sonata (op. 102, no. 2), the rhythm gives no comfort—the intended effect is shelterlessness. There are a series of quiet, slow statements, each made of seven equal notes:*

one two three four five six seven (wait)
one two three four five six seven (wait)
etc.

There is a structure here: it is the hymn. The notes seesaw. The first four lead in, the last three wrap up. But because it is so slow, and the rhythms are so equal, Beethoven conceals the hymn's consolations. You feel the seven notes plodding in a row and then uneasy silences, waiting without expectation for the next seven: a deathly ticking-off of time.

---

*Some anal-retentive person will doubtless observe that the first statement is eight notes, actually, with a pickup.

In the middle of the movement, we get some relief—salvation in the form of motion, a breeze coming in through the soul's window. But by the end, the rhythm thins out even more than in the beginning. A couple silences make you wonder if the performers have forgotten what is next. At last there's just a chord waiting, a total impasse, like a ship in a deadly calm.

We are rescued from this despair by a party celebrating rhythm, or a roast of rhythm, it's hard to say. It starts with a scale, like a child practicing, and ends with a pair of pairs:

one two
one two

Remember—from the first rhythm chapter—Schnabel/Schubert's *one-two*s? Schnabel played them with an odd equality, to show us the fixed and fateful. But these Beethoven *one-two*s are after the opposite revelation. He writes accents on the second beats so you get

one TWO
one TWO

with the idea of creating an alternate reality, a disputed frame of reference—*I'm the downbeat; no, I'M the downbeat*. An idea arguing with its own premises. Beethoven goes on and on, jabbing into the measures with these accents, his *one*s and *two*s in a continuous exchange, a dizzying shell game:

one TWO
    one TWO
        one TWO

As these beats keep chasing each other over the page of music, like a dog chasing its own tail, you feel Beethoven trying to save rhythm—by destroying it. No beat is settled. The idea passes from deep bass to highest treble; trills cloud everything; and still the game continues.

At last, you round into the final bars. Beethoven writes "ONE TWO," and then again, "ONE TWO," neither of which solves the other. He writes *one* again—but it's on the second beat, if you look at the page. A moment of silence. Then comes a *two,* an emphatic *two,* seemingly the last of many *two*s. But it's actually notated on the first beat! Silence, this time for good. The confused applause begins—what did it all mean? When I play this, I bow and smile, knowing my official work is over, but I can't help feeling that the final downbeat has not yet arrived. It needs to exist, and refuses to exist, and you may feel this elusive arrival in your soul during the fading applause, or hours or days later, or maybe it won't come at all, and you'll have to go back to the practice room to figure out your concept of rhythm all over again, but in the meantime— and I think this is what Beethoven was after all along, an epiphany you can't fit in the program notes or the preconcert lecture—it feels so fucking good to be alive. In that play of rhythm and time, death, so inescapable just one movement earlier, is nowhere to be found.

19. *So You Want to Go to Juilliard*

    SCHUMANN: Sonata no. 1 in A Minor, op. 105, for Violin and Piano

    ELLIOTT CARTER: Sonata (1945–46)

    BACH: Partita no. 6 in E Minor

    SCHUBERT: Sonata in D Major, D. 850

    MONTEVERDI: *"Zefiro torna e'l bel tempo rimena,"* from the Sixth Book of
        Madrigals

    LEON KIRCHNER: Duo no. 2 for Violin and Piano

One thing was clear: I had to leave Bloomington. I called Herbert Stessin, the judge I'd met at the London competition, and told him I wanted to come to Juilliard. It wasn't a want, so much as my sole shred of a life plan. "How old *are* you now?" he asked, in a creaky voice, like my father. I'll be twenty-five in May, I said. Herbert thought the doctoral program was the best and only choice, given my geriatric condition—and it was tuition-free.

Over Christmas in New Mexico, in my childhood bedroom, I composed the last of many overwrought application essays, painting myself as an idealist, rhapsodizing about learning and performance, contextualization, my love of new music and the relevance of— It's exhausting to remember writing that thing. I mailed it off with a check, and received a date for an audition and interview in late February.

Insert countless hours of practicing in a windowless room.

As February began, I realized a concert I'd agreed to play in Indiana conflicted with my audition. I called in a tizzy to shift my Juilliard time slot. The office said no problem. I boarded a commuter jet in Indianapolis, drank a can of ginger ale, ate pretzels, and watched as we came in low over the houses of Brooklyn and Queens. The snaking LaGuardia taxi line could have been labeled ABANDON ALL HOPE. I got out on the corner of 65th and Broadway, lugging my carry-on, feeling that life had become much more inconvenient.

I entered the famous institution, was assigned a warm-up room, and went over the trouble spots. Even after all those international competitions, I was intimidated by the idea of a panel of teachers, and I couldn't help listening to other warmer-uppers, a psychological trap, like looking up symptoms on the internet. At 3:22 or so, I was escorted into the big orchestra room on the third floor, and sat at a piano I had never touched. The faculty were barking at one another—unflattering observations about the last person, and bewilderment about me. "You're auditioning for the *doctoral* program?!?" said the head of the committee. I agreed. A volley of sighing and paper-rustling. The representative spoke again: "This is undergraduate day. Undergraduate auditions are five minutes. Doctoral candidates get fifteen. You're not supposed to be today."

I had practiced my heart out, only to be caught in a procedural dispute, a bit of Kafka. "I rescheduled because of a recital in Indiana," I explained, which sounded frivolous as I heard it out loud. They sighed again and told me to start with what I liked, and, after a moment's shallow breathing, I began to play Bach. In auditions, I had a way of focusing on one or two passages I didn't want to screw up. If I got through them without incident, then I took courage, and began to make music: a terrible way to play the piano, and a worse way to live. I played the E-flat Minor Prelude from Book One of *The Well-Tempered Clavier*, and then a tragic Schubert Sonata in A Minor—unbearable depths of human sorrow, exploited for personal gain.

Juilliard is not a group therapy session. Go ahead, knock yourself out, emote all you want; the jury still must know if you have fingers. There are standards. You have to be able to play fast and loud just to be heard over thousands of other Juilliard pianists practicing Prokofiev and Rachmaninoff. Time pressed. They asked me to play just the ending of Chopin's Fourth Ballade.

"Start from the coda?" I asked weakly, stalling for time. A gnarled passage, a feared reef. How could they be so cruel? I launched in cold, and boy, was it messy. They thanked me. I walked out, sure my future had just evaporated. "Well, at least you made it to the end," Stessin said in the hallway.

I went to the admissions director and explained to her what had happened—the mis-scheduled slot, starting with the coda—like a satire of evil things that Juilliard judges would do to innocent pianists from the provinces. She looked at me—kindly but distracted—and said maybe she could get me a do-over audition the next day.

Excited by this prospect, I called Ravinia friends, went down to the Village, and got colossally drunk. I ended the evening with a double Wild Turkey, a cheeseburger, a chocolate milkshake, boarded the interminable off-peak subway, fell asleep, managed to regain consciousness at 72nd, and woke up the people I was crashing with—husband and wife Darrett and Ingrid, believe it or not, now much further than I along the path to adulthood—unable to solve their forest of deadbolts. Darrett came down in his boxer shorts and opened the door with annoyance, just like the judges at my audition. The next morning, a vision of freshness, I hobbled to Juilliard. The admissions director looked at me with concern and said, "I don't think you should re-audition." A moment of nauseating panic. Then she read out comments from my audition—all positive. I was going to the big city. Why had I been so unsure?

}

Back in Bloomington, at my last lesson with Sebők, he didn't give me a poetic send-off, or koans to treasure. That would have been in bad taste. Whatever he had to say to me, he had already said. He knew that I was looking for success, and we all had to make lives for ourselves. But he distrusted New York. "I could never live there," he said. I felt like he was appraising my chances, wondering if his ideas would take root, or if I would abandon the unpopular process of searching for musical truth. "All the best for your future," he said at last, as he held open the door. He didn't mean that to be brutal, I don't think. I rounded the oval out of his sight and cried in the first empty cubicle I could find.

That night, Evelyne took me out for dinner and listened while I explained what she already very well knew. "It's OK," she said, "you're doing the right thing." This felt harder and deeper than my many romantic breakups. Finding my own way felt like a betrayal. But summer loomed, and after a week, there wasn't time to wallow.

My first stop was the Isaac Stern Chamber Music Workshop, in Carnegie Hall. I'd met a gutsy violinist named Robin Sharp at Ravinia; she and I went as a duo. The seminar was presided over by Stern, of course, but there were numerous other famous faculty: János Starker, the Orion Quartet, the pianists Joseph Kalichstein and Eugene Istomin. The first day, Isaac took us into the big hall, and clapped his hands as if applauding for us or himself. He wanted us to admire the reverberation, to have awe for the august. He gave a speech I cannot quite remember about the nature of art. Then we all moved into the small recital hall and group lessons began. The faculty here were encouraged and even provoked to argue—the opposite of Walter's Forums, and more honest. They interrupted, disagreed, and contradicted themselves, like an object lesson in terrible parenting, while we tried to obey.

This abuse was quintessential New York, I thought. The thrill of the city. I remember saying to myself this was the happiest time of my life. Occasionally one or another of the faculty would take me aside to give me secret tips. Kalichstein showed me how to get effects in the Brahms Violin Sonata (yes, the same sonata, the G Major). Like many people, he thought I tried too hard. It was impossible to find the sweet spot between trying too hard and not trying hard enough. Daniel Phillips told me that I had to voice my chords differently. After that, no one yelled at me for playing too loud. Thanks, Danny! Isaac Stern took me aside near the end and told me to "keep in touch," just like the president of Oberlin had, some years ago. How would I keep in touch with a legend like Isaac Stern? It boggled the mind.

The rest of the summer I was back at Ravinia, hoarding money to afford city life. Then Bloomington again, packing, disposing of comfy kitchen acquisitions, saying goodbye to the Midwest one last time (I thought) in the alluring, soft haze of late summer. In late August, in a rented U-Haul, I pulled up in front of some NYU housing on Bleecker Street, a semi-illegal sublet—like most of New York, I was told. A room in the West Village on the twenty-sixth floor, with a spectacular view of downtown, for only $500 a month. I was a lucky man, and as usual didn't appreciate it.

}

The first Juilliard tasks were regressive, even infantile. New student orientation, name tags, a picnic on the sooty rectangle of granite that served as Juilliard's "quad." The president delivered a lofty convocation. Sarcastic remarks were made. The Twin Towers looked at me every night when I got home to sleep; in the mornings I'd walk to the subway through the Village's beery aftermath.

It's fair to say that Indiana's music school was not perfect, architecturally, and it didn't smell great. But Juilliard was a more formidable enemy of inspiration. The air was compressed and still, the decor was mid-priced-hotel conference room. The layout was two squares surrounding two courtyards, with a few uninteresting asymmetries; dark internal stairwells spit me out at unknown junctures of other floors. Worst of all was floor four, the practice room area. I spent a quarter of each day walking those low-ceilinged halls, passing fellow students on the hunt. The rooms had tinny Steinway grands, with glass screwed on the front to prevent fingernail scratchings. Green curtains deadened the already dead. It's hard to say what color the carpet was. No sense of the outdoors, no life other than the repetition of passages. Maybe it's petty to complain about the decor and amenities of such a premier institution, but you will never meet a more complaining bunch than the Juilliard student body—the brand name incurs buyer's remorse.

After a week, my first lesson with Herbert Stessin arrived. He was quite happy to see me, and yet I had the feeling he'd seen it all before. In place of Sebők's Hungarian accent, a dialect of bagels, laced with complaint. Sebők's long-handled cigarettes, smoked while gazing off into spiritual immensities, were replaced by smelly contraband cigars. Herbert snipped and lit them while you played, at sensitive moments. I took my revenge on my own students years later by opening a can of Coke shortly after they began playing, then burping up the Korean lunch I had just eaten.

Maybe the most noticeable thing about Herbert was the Parkinson's tremor in his hands, which we never discussed. If he tried to demonstrate, he could manage only a few notes before he decided it a waste and gave up. Despite or because of this infirmity, he was always ready with dark humor. I'd say, "You look great, Herbert" and he would say, "Thanks, I have a new embalmer." He had one-liners for every pianistic mishap. If Sebők was competitive (and he was), he kept it concealed. But Stessin was competitive out in the open. We ran across another faculty member in the hall. "Let me introduce you to my enemy," he said, not even half kidding. At Juilliard the faculty were paid per student, a capitalist system with ramifications.

The concerto competition at Juilliard that year was Schumann, a piece I'd played since I was fourteen. I decided to enter right away. What was I here for, if not to make a splash? I brought it in for my first lesson, and launched into the opening burst of cascading chords, followed by Schumann's plaintive miracle of a theme. Stessin was unmoved. "Yes, yes, some good things," he said, in the way an accountant would thank you for last year's tax receipts, and got down to business. Coddling was for suckers. He launched into a mini-seminar about how to play pairs of chords. Instead of up-DOWN, descending on the accented note, he said, why not group from the first note, DOWN-up, so that the accented note was a release? It seemed a lesson against gravity, and against Sebők, but he wouldn't move on until I gave it a real try.

"Didn't anyone ever explain this to you?" he asked.

I got Stessin's motion once—it was strange, less like playing than being played—and not again. At last Herbert, semi-satisfied, let me move on. (The semi-satisfaction of teachers is the profession's defining malaise.)

I was sure that he would be blown away by the way I played what came next—the main theme—but he didn't even say "Some good things." He told me the repeated notes sounded poked out. He hated when the piano revealed its own woodenness. Also, I had forgotten some slurs, and one climactic emphasis. All Stessin's remarks would have been dispiriting enough for my first lesson, but I wasn't catching on. So, he got out a recording of one of his other students playing the same passage, put headphones on me, and made me listen, helping himself to another cigar. I didn't want to know that other pianists existed. But there I was, eyes watering, listening sullenly to a recording of a competitor—was I already thinking in these terms? I'll admit to anger, and pride, and envy, and what are the other seven deadly sins? There was no lust, at least.

After that horrible first lesson, I took Herbert's reverse-gravity idea to a practice room and tried to wrap my head around it. It seemed a waste of time. But—was this possible?—the passage sounded better. My arms worked more efficiently, in cahoots with my hands. After a semester, I realized that this one idea solved a million deadweight moments. It made beats feel less like obstacles.

Sebők believed in solutions that worked for individual pianists—in unique problems and musical limitations. But Stessin had heard thousands of pianists ruin masterworks, and preferred solutions that worked for most everyone, most of the time.

For a few weeks Herbert and I worked on Schumann, and then I played it in Paul Hall for a panel of Juilliard faculty. I wasn't that nervous. The Jeremy Denk of audition day had vanished. A summer with Stern had desensitized me, made me feel I belonged in New York, that I could survive any stress. After some waiting in the lobby next to the security desk, I found that I had won. The prize was to perform in Avery Fisher Hall, with Kurt Masur.

It all seemed to happen so fast, too fast. I'd only been in the city a month and I was already on the stage of Lincoln Center, with a famous conductor. My parents flew out. One twenty-minute meeting with Masur, then forty-five minutes with the orchestra, a thirty-minute dress rehearsal—that was the whole process, comically accelerated after all the consideration and reconsideration of Bloomington. Kurt Masur said my playing was beautiful. My parents came backstage to meet him—an unbelievable thrill, someone from the TV. Apparently a big manager showed up, a man named Byron Gustafson. Dad told me to "keep in touch" with Masur, which—again—what the hell did that mean?

At the post-concert dinner, Dad gave a little speech. He'd been out to Ellis Island that afternoon, and thought about his immigrant parents and grandparents scrimping and saving to make it in the world, and here I was, two generations later, striding onto the stage of Lincoln Center. He was misty and tender and maybe the closest I'd ever seen to being proud, without irony or caveat. He'd realized I just might make it.

⁊

At Indiana, each faculty door had a nameplate, which gave rooms a time and heritage; they were possessed. At Juilliard there were only numbers, like in a hotel, with the implication that rooms were leased by the hour.

One afternoon, mid-fall, some weeks after my big triumph, I knocked at a number. "Normal" Juilliard life had taken over. Stessin had paraded me around the halls for a day or two, a new prize student, then I was back to the rat race: accompanying friends to stay solvent, in between doctoral classes. I was supposed to play the Schumann A Minor Violin Sonata with my roommate Ara. I heard some unintelligible shouting from inside, which I ignored, but moments later the door opened to reveal a stooped figure, with an aggressive grin and a bottle of scotch in his non-door-opening hand. "What were you waiting for, idiot?" he said. He took a swig. This room, like my teacher's across the way, reeked of cigars. I learned later that Harvey Shapiro (the famed cello professor in front of me) was Herbert's supplier.

I walked in and sat at the piano. Ara slouched on an armchair, kibitzing. Harvey was finishing up another lesson. Despite his ninety years, he was flirting with a young Korean cellist—one of a million lawsuits waiting and deserving to happen. She left; we started in on Schumann. First he focused on making Ara feel terrible about the way he was playing. There is no greater pleasure in a chamber music coaching than the coach blaming all your problems on somebody else. Then we got to the second movement, where adult turmoil drops away to reveal a curious, smiling child.

This innocent melody is a chain of flowing notes, with only one moment of stoppage, like a stone in a stream. Equality can be a problem. Variations in rhythm emit signals—places to go, places to scurry away from—but sameness requires finesse. Harvey listened, uneasily. "For the life of me," he said, "I can't figure out what the *fuck* is going on." He went after Ara some more, shaping the contour, tweaking vibrato. Still it wasn't right. "Goddammit," he said, and in desperation he started to play. It was one of the most angelic sounds I'd ever heard. An older timbre, an older way of thinking, different from Sebők's or Starker's, more like recordings I'd heard of Fritz Kreisler, but without the scratches and clicks. It seemed impossible that this music-making could exist in the present. I started to play along with him—as if I could possibly have something to offer!—and he turned on me, in a rage. "You. You. *You're* the actual bastard who's ruining the fucking phrase."

The pianist only controls the rhythmic position of one note in this melody. But it's the only note without another note right after it. To express this importance (and my own importance), I'd waited a moment to play it. "Why are you fucking waiting?" he yelled in my face, coating my cheeks and lips with a fine film of scotch-scented saliva. I thought of *Patton*, my father's favorite movie. We played it again, pause-free, and it was great. Harvey smiled. "You bastard, you rat bastard, all this time," he said, shaking his head. This was Juilliard? "Have a drink," he said, handing me the bottle, and I drank.

}

A week or two later I encountered Robert Mann, another legend, then in his final years as leader of the Juilliard Quartet. My friend Indira and I brought in a Beethoven violin sonata. Mann was an amazing teacher, a consummate musician, and a bloodhound who sniffed out your fatal flaws. That was his favorite hobby: to find the tendency that will ruin your musicianship, and proclaim your doom.

We'd rehearsed once. Mann listened, his face a cipher. But half a second after the last note, he erupted: "You guys think you can come here without having really rehearsed, and play a BEETHOVEN SONATA?" He had figured out that people asked me to play because I could read things fast and we wouldn't need much rehearsal. But when I had to play under pressure, my ease vanished. Unconsidered voids appeared.

Soon Mann found my other tragic flaw. He was suspicious of beauty for its own sake. His playing could be described as rough—he was oriented toward expression, not seduction. (Or maybe: the seduction of truthful expression.) Mann made a number of preliminary complaints about my overpedaling, but then his tone got deeper and darker. "Jeremy," he said, "the problem with you is you're afraid of silence. You don't even like to play staccato"—we started playing again, and he stopped us right away for another example: "Like there, why are you so scared of the release of the note . . ." He sat down. "You'll never be a real musician if you can't deal with rests." (This brought back lessons from Mona when I was six.) He was right, of course; my urge was to connect, always to connect. Like someone who won't stop talking, who won't let anyone else in to speak, or even take a moment to breathe.

On the other pole from Mann was the legendary teacher (and power broker) Dorothy DeLay. I hadn't had any contact with her—she had a ready-made crew of staff pianists—but I was desperately curious. Students waited whole days for lessons in that lounge, and those lessons might not materialize, or if they did, not until one in the morning, after she had ordered Chinese takeout. She was enormous, gluttonous, magisterial; she could bestow careers. Which Mann, for all his intelligence and culture, could not.

So when my friend Neil asked me to play the Brahms G Major Sonata for her, I said yes. I was hoping DeLay would be dazzled by my knowledge of the piece, and that she would take notice of me—an absurd plan, if I'd known the first thing about her. As we played the first movement, she offered a few remarks to Neil and only one to me. "You really like music, don't you?" she said. It didn't sound like a compliment.

The second movement, despite all its beauty and complexity, went by without incident.

But she was displeased by our third movement. "Now," she said, "what do you think: Is this movement happy or sad?" This kindergarten question was an unexpected blow. She didn't care about all the subtleties and shades, my many years of thought, my diligent parsing of the song and poem in Musicorda. Neil hesitated: "Umm." "Don't you think, Ms. DeLay," I said, interrupting, "that it's more complicated than that, maybe it's a bit of both?"

Her eyes landed on me. I had the sense of a dragon, disturbed in its lair. "Well, it is the last movement, isn't it?" she said, brightly but with an edge. *What does that even mean? I thought. Is she toying with me?*

"But Brahms marks *Allegro molto moderato* . . ." I observed. A strange turn of events: I was presuming to teach Dorothy DeLay. Which of us was out of our depth?

"Now Itzhak told me, when he was playing these with Barenboim"—if I was going to invoke the authority of the score, DeLay was going to refer to the authority of actually famous people—"that Danny really wanted to play a certain tempo and Itzhak had to convince him to go a bit faster. And if you think about the audience, really, they need a new energy . . ."

She was trying every possible maneuver to tell me that we played too slow. For all I know, she was right. But as she spoke, with a tone combining motivational speaker and preschool teacher, I realized I'd found it, the perfect and absolute anti-Sebők, the antidote to years of Bloomington idealism. It was all that Juilliard promised and gave and took away. Was it calculating to say that in a big hall, in view of an audience, circumstances punished nuance and knowledge and rewarded a bold, simple stroke? It felt like a violence and a useful truth.

{

One day in February, just six months into this new life, I got a call from Henry Upper, an assistant dean at Indiana University and, in a way, an old friend. Henry was wondering if I might come back to audition for an open faculty position. Faculty! I was overwhelmed by the idea of joining so many legends. I'd be elevated to legend status by association, and could skip the process of being discovered and playing concerts, which I'd forgotten was my whole goal to begin with. Plus: a salary.

I flew out to Bloomington, at their expense. The central part of my audition was to teach a master class. I was twenty-five; this was the first public class I'd ever taught. I put on a stuffy suit and returned to the stage of the MAC, the venue where I'd accompanied *Carmen* and *Don Giovanni,* and where I heard Sebők and Starker not really rehearse. There they all were, the faculty I had dreaded, people who had been sitting in judgment over my juries and recitals . . . Strangest of all, Sebők, the god I'd torn myself away from, was now just a quiet and genial panelist.

A student played the Bartók sonata. A surreal choice: one of the first pieces I'd played for Sebők, back in 1990. I listened, then translated Sebők into my own language, while he watched. I tried to make her play the piece with joy instead of anger. I told her about the buoyant offbeats that had changed my life. After a few nervous minutes, an inner momentum took over and I was just thinking about music. Sebők said afterward that "I was a force for good." I couldn't quite process that compliment. A week or two later I got a call from the dean of the music school, Charles Webb, offering me the job. It was in some ways too much to imagine. How could I turn down such an opportunity and tenure track, at such a tender age?

Back in New York, I told everyone the news. Friends were hesitant to weigh in. Stessin thought it was a prestigious offer, and he knew a musician's life was hard—he didn't push me one way or the other. I dithered. I didn't want to abandon New York or the doctorate. But by some miracle, all the classes I needed for my second and final Juilliard year were on Wednesdays. I could fly to the city once a week for my classes, and otherwise be six days a week in residence in Indiana. A stupid proposition, but doable; yet another attempt to do it all.

"But," the librarian and doctoral den mother Jane Gottlieb said in her book-crammed windowless office, an office that would drive most souls to despair, "you just got here, you just got your start in New York. Why are you going back?" A central question, and it was odd that a librarian was the only one who posed it to me, point-blank. But I got myself an apartment in Bloomington, furnished it with a futon and a couch and not much else. Was this a promotion or a retreat?

}

My new teaching load was eighteen hours a week. There were no exceptions, not even for the famed Menahem Pressler, pianist of the Beaux Arts Trio, who had every reason to slack off. But no: Pressler had a little fold-out chair under his piano for naps in between lessons. That's how devoted, or insane, he was. Because I was the most junior faculty member, I had to take whatever I was assigned, an array of what we called "secondary pianists": music education majors who required lessons for their degrees, or composers, or other people for whom the piano was a vehicle and an obligation.

I'd equipped my apartment with a twelve-cup coffee maker monstrosity, which I would hit hard before biking in to campus. I'd run down the stairs to my basement studio—with rows of clanking ceiling pipes and a bit of sun coming in through high windows. I believed each lesson was a moment to come to grips with great issues of music and life. So, no matter their skill level or aspiration, I treated each student as if they were a young Vladimir Horowitz.

Some of my students really got into this approach. One young woman wanted to be a choral conductor. She wore exclusively plaids, with an emphasis on reds and greens, and stared at me through thick glasses. She couldn't have been nicer. We worked ever so hard on her Haydn sonata. I told her that the character was constantly in flux, and that surprise and humor were essential to the style. It didn't occur to me that our ideas of humor might be incompatible.

"*Subito forte,*" I said, urging her to play louder.

She added the tiniest emphasis, almost unnoticeable.

"No, more, it's supposed to be a surprise!" I went on, quivering in my swivel chair, cups of coffee coursing through my system.

She did a bit more, maybe, if you squinted with your ears. I couldn't take it. "No, no, no, WILDDDDDDDDD!" I offered, leaping out of the chair and screaming the word in her face. She flinched, then decided I was well-intentioned, and smiled. By the end of a half hour, I'd gotten her up to a solid *mezzo forte,* but she would go no further. She had faith that God would make the music funny, while I felt God helped those who helped themselves.

This aspiring choral conductor played in studio class, at the end of months of work. She came to the reappearance of a theme—a theme we'd heard before, in another key. She played the right hand in the new key, but the left hand in the old, creating a terrifying twenty seconds of dissonance. On her face, you saw an awareness that something was wrong, along with a complete failure to know what it was.

"That was amazing," I said dryly, after she finished. "I couldn't do that if I tried."

This was me trying to be nice—and yet it all came out sarcastic. *Oh God, no, I'm not becoming my father so soon.* So I tried to backpedal ("We've all been there"), but it was too late, she looked crushed. I realized that while I'd been working on expressive subtleties, we should have been exploring fundamentals of harmony, her sense of place, her ability to feel her way around chords, like you know your way around your bedroom in the dark.

Another memorable student was appropriately named Sherene. A sorority girl, but not frilly—a tomboy, used to holding her own with the guys. She was always hoarse, from chugging beverages and screaming over sound systems. I was envious. She was enjoying life far more than I ever had.

Sherene reacted better to the word "WILD," and thumped loudly when you got after her. But every phrase was a knife plunged in the heart of nuance. I had to reach back to my lessons with Lillian and teach Sherene about classical phrasing, the little tapers, the differences between dissonances and releases. Even that was too much, I realized. First, I had to establish the basic proposition that some notes in a melody should be more or less than others.

"Dude," she rasped, "how do you tell what's a dissonance?" I felt a deep desire to return to my futon and curl up in a ball. But actually, it was a good question.

I worked on one Haydn phrase with Sherene for an entire hour.

"That note a bit more," I'd say. It took five minutes for her to get that. I could hear her thinking, *Ugh, now I see what classical music is, and why I've never liked it.* After mind-bending effort, she was able to play that one phrase more or less in a listenable way, with contour and aspiration. "Dude, no one's ever tried so hard with me. What's up with that?" she asked, smiling. This gratitude and awareness made me feel a wash of tenderness. We both were trying our best! We both knew it was futile, and yet affection ran both ways.

I had one composer student who played the most beautiful opening of Beethoven 109 I'd ever heard; everything else he played was a disaster. How was that possible? Another composer refused to observe the markings on the score. "Dude," I said, taking my rhetorical tips from Sherene, "you're a composer! You above all should know the composers want you to read what was written." But he looked at me with youthful mockery, and the next week I had to tell him the same things, and I felt myself growing prematurely old, knowing that with each week of repetition, it was ever less likely that he would do what I asked.

$$\wr$$

You could call it a continuous culture shock, teaching five days a week and then flying Tuesdays to New York for doctoral courses and piano lessons—and meanwhile trying to build a performer's future. I remember sitting in the Pittsburgh airport one morning, at the wrong gate, not knowing whether I was going to New York or back to Indiana. Both student and teacher roles felt like pretend.

But that scattered year was the most important of my career. I was selected winner of the William Petschek Award at Juilliard, which gave me a solo recital debut in Alice Tully Hall. Stessin croaked, "Finally someone who deserves it wins," a compliment crusted in bitterness. He and I began preparing. He told me to play only repertoire I loved, and so I ended up with a hardcore program that no normal audience would want to hear: the E Minor Partita of Bach, the Elliott Carter Sonata (old standby), and the D Major Sonata of Schubert. These were pieces I could spend a lifetime on, I felt, and I hoped they made a statement.

And in the late fall, I was lying on my second futon on West 98th Street, a new semi-illegal sublet, sleeping off my travels, when the phone rang. "Hello, my name is Susan Wadsworth. Is this Jeremy?"

"Yes . . ." I replied, and before I could say anything, she asked, "Why aren't you applying?" She wasn't a big believer in niceties.

"What do you mean?"

"I heard your tape," she said, by way of explanation.

"What tape?"

"You have to apply for YCA," she continued, impatiently. She was referring to her management competition, Young Concert Artists. The tape she meant was with a violinist I'd met at Ravinia, playing the little A-minor Beethoven Sonata.

"But you're too old," she said, like Herbert and my father. "Why did you wait so long?"

I wanted to tell her that I'd never completely believed in myself, and needed to discover things, and acquire technical confidence, and study with Sebők until I knew what music was for . . . but it didn't seem like she or the city of New York would have the patience for this.

"I don't know," I said.

She also encouraged me to pick repertoire that was distinctly me, and come audition in January. Herbert got involved in the project. He liked the way I threw myself into the Wagner "Liebestod" transcription. I was obsessed with the irreverent Beethoven Sonata, op. 31, no. 1, and also the quite different pleasures of the Schumann *Fantasy*, the way that the surging waves of passion fall apart, reconstruct themselves into intimate expressions, and then fall apart again.

A few months later, on the stage of the 92nd Street Y, I played Wagner and Schumann and a bit of Beethoven, and though I got tangled in Beethoven's evil second theme, the judges forgave me and I won. Which meant I would have a manager, and would be booked for paying concerts—a life I had always thought semi-imaginary. My girlfriend and I went down to our old Mexican standby in the Village, and I called Stessin from a pay phone in the flush of margaritas and victory. "You did it," he said, several times. He had been too nervous to go to the actual audition. The pay phone was in the basement, in a hallway that reeked of urinal cakes, but I could hear the sound of my progress in his overjoyed voice, more real for him than it was for me—a kind of music.

}

The Alice Tully recital, my debut, was in April. In February and March, I listened to dozens of recordings of the E-minor Partita: Schiff, Gould, Tureck, every famous Bach person. I decided that many of those recordings were boring, and I had to fix the boring world. I wondered whether the last movement should be in eighth notes or crazy triplets. Stessin encouraged me to be jazzier. He loved a wild Bach. He told me to rush less and pedal less—excellent advice, still good since the age of six—but then he let me develop a vision and try to find all my possibilities. Over martinis (his favorite) after one lesson, he said, "You'll find your way of playing Bach eventually, if not now." But I needed it now! "That's not the way it works," he grunted.

Stessin had nothing to say about my Elliott Carter. He said it sounded great, I should play it just like that. But the Schubert was different. Here he found a world of technical and musical dissatisfaction, and begged for crisper rhythms, better shaping, and on and on. The last movement, my favorite, was the puzzle. Almost too silly to be taken seriously, and yet, of all the movements, the most perfect.

Because of my Oberlin Mahler obsession, I knew there was a strong connection between this piece and the last movement of Mahler's Fourth Symphony, a song about children in heaven, playing with the Saints:

We enjoy heavenly pleasures
and therefore avoid earthly ones.
No worldly tumult
is to be heard in heaven.

Both the Mahler and the Schubert have rough and light parts— pratfalls, crashes, mini-dramas—evoking running and colliding toddlers, meltdowns and tantrums. But surrounding all that is a guiding rhythm, a lilt, a sense of being rocked or cradled, creating a haunting, dual perspective of age and youth.

One afternoon, Stessin (adult) and I (still more of a child than anything) wrangled our way to the middle section of this rondo. It's a folk tune with bits of wistful minor, just the sort of music that a Viennese street band, without classical inhibitions, would inhabit perfectly. The pianist has to multitask. You have to be the cello laying down the bass, and the rustling viola, and the sweetly harmonized chorus.

One more time, one last time, we took it all apart, like a car engine, and put it back together. First, the left hand: uncomfortable staccato bass notes. Stessin told me to "get over it." He made me work on my left thumb's viola rustle: "Come on, you're still too young to be that lazy." Then off to the right hand, to make sure the melody formed a line, and to tease out the inner voices, especially one sad and persistent B-flat. At last—but before I could think about it all too much—he made me play the parts together. And it happened, that rare miracle in piano playing, where all you're doing is pressing keys down, but the result all feels up. Gravity was reversed. We were no longer having earthly concerns.

Stessin leaned over the piano as if he was going to consult the music, but instead turned to smile directly in my face; his spotted, owlish face beamed. "That is it, you got it," he said with disbelief and delight. He put his trembling hand on my shoulder, then tousled my hair like a son. What a complicated joy that must have been: provoking me into doing something he could never do again.

{

The debut approached. My parents flew out to hear me: a big production, a full day's travel with my mom's ever-deteriorating bones and muscles. My dad said, "It would be considerate if you'd get some gigs closer to home." He gave the trademark frown again, marking the joke that is not a joke.

I remember feeling well prepared, and not more nervous than usual. I ate a big pizza backstage just before I went on, a new tradition and superstition. I thought pizza was a good-luck charm. But it didn't prevent a significant snafu: I forgot to acknowledge the great Elliott Carter in the audience. I had to apologize after intermission. After my Schubert, I played for an encore the trusty "Liebestod," which was the opposite of Schubert, although both pieces drifted off into eternity. And then came a reception, and lots of loving friends, and my girl-friend, and some charming congratulations from other faculty members—a happy night, all in all.

A day or two later, I got a decent review in *The New York Times*. It said my Bach was full of interesting ideas, maybe too many in a row. Fair enough! My Carter was compelling. And it was coy but kind about the Schubert. All in all, a good showing for such a difficult, serious program. The big manager—saintly Byron Gustafson—introduced himself backstage, and that was the most important thing, as people explained to me later. Stessin said, "The Schubert was a rough draft, but there were good things," just like any other lesson—but I could tell he was satisfied. A couple weeks later, Stessin and I had our last session. Life as a piano student, in the official sense—almost the only life I'd known—was over.

⁂

Back in Bloomington, my huge squadron of students congratulated me on my review, which was posted up on the School News bulletin board in the main lobby. It was near the end of the semester and hard to concentrate. I coached them for their juries, trying to look happy while they limped through their Haydn sonatas.

In May, I threw a party in my almost-unfurnished apartment, to celebrate quite an array of events: the end of a semester, their hard work, my debut, my first year as a teacher, the end of my piano lesson torments, everyone passing their juries, me signing with Byron Gustafson and a big management firm. Evelyne brought over folding chairs. My students got me a present. It was big but light, and beautifully wrapped. They stashed it next to my hideous bargain couch. After a drink or two, and lots of awkward conversation, one of my shyest Korean students said it was time. I started ripping at a corner. I thought I was prepared for any gift they could bring. But they'd gone to Target and bought a

24-pack of Kleenex, to have in the studio for all the hundreds of times I'd made and would make them cry.

I looked at Evelyne, hoping for a smile. But all I got was a piercing stare. The room was quiet. After all the piano lesson suffering I'd been through, had I come up with no better, no more creative response than to inflict it on the next generation? At last I said, "Oh, I'm so sorry."

}

I passed into professional life, still teaching but also playing a fair number of concerts. My career was respectable; or anyway, I was happy with it. A few years with a smallish number of solo recitals and concertos, and tons of chamber music. But in late spring of 2001, Juilliard sent me a stern letter reminding me that I had to finish my degree, or else.

The final assignment of my endless musical education was a doctoral document. Juilliard wouldn't go so far as to call it a dissertation. I hemmed and hawed on a topic; but at last, I proposed to write a manifesto about the evils of musical education. My committee of music educators took this personally, to my surprise. They told me they would give me some leeway but it would need to be good. My thesis was that Musical Form should be taught using more verbs and fewer nouns—basically, more creative writing than chemistry.

It is impossible to underestimate the lack of system I brought to this enterprise—as with most of my enterprises. My first task, I decided, was to make a list of pieces I loved. Love was the key to conquering my doctoral committee. If only I could make them love music as much as I did! This list was random—mostly pieces I'd just heard, like the slow movement of one of the Razumovsky Quartets of Beethoven, a miraculous unfolding statement in E major. I bought reams of index cards, more than anyone could use in a lifetime. (I still have packs of them in my closet, stacked alongside an artificial skeleton.) I'd pull one out, throw it down on my desk, scribble an observation—"a line going up," or "the harmony shifts"—and then follow the consequences of this fact for a little while. Maybe this idea meant something, maybe it didn't. Trust the process. New card.

When my apartment got too hot, I scooped up my cards and headed to Central Park. I found a spot in the middle, full of hills and hidden nooks, and climbed to the top of one forbidding rock, sheltered by greenery, the perfect aerie for knowledge. I heard miscellaneous sounds from time to time, but no one could be seen. It was my third day in a row. I had the score of a Monteverdi madrigal, *"Zefiro torna e'l bel tempo rimena,"* open in front of me, when a young man climbed up the rock and stood maybe ten feet away. I ignored him. I thought it was self-evident that I was studying, but after a minute or so I looked up and he was making an unmistakable gesture. Never before had mind-sex collided with body-sex in such an obvious way. Putting my head down to consult Monteverdi, I waited quite a self-conscious while for him to decide to leave, while my heart beat away, a third party.

It took me some months to admit what had happened (though I'd done nothing at all). But I was no longer comfortable working there. I stuck to the Great Lawn. Later, my friends laughed at me. Didn't you know you were in the Ramble, they asked, a famous place for cruising?

{

By fall, I had all my "great thoughts" and now needed a semblance of structure to dump them in. The doctoral deadline was imminent. My pile of index cards resembled a trap or a labyrinth. The landline rang—fate? It was a non-musician friend I'd met—let's call him Danny—I preferred non-musicians, in those days. "Hey, I'm going to a party in Brooklyn," he said. "Do you want to come?"

At thirty-one, I was beginning to feel too old for Brooklyn—but I'd been working so hard! So I sat on the 2 train for an hour and wandered Park Slope and at last found Danny in a pre-war apartment, tipsy and talking to a young woman. Loud music coming from nowhere I could see, every surface covered in used Dixie cups.

Danny's friend knew him from the world of graphic design. They were in the middle of a deep conversation about fonts, which segued into an ethical exploration of arrangements of objects and ideas in general. I butted in.

"You know, my doctoral committee just made me change my title." My audience didn't seem riveted.

"I'm writing about Musical Form, but they made me change the word to 'Design.'"

"Yeah," Danny said, "it sounds like they don't know what design is."

I didn't either. How could design have ethics? They returned to fonts. I looked around the crowd of twenty-somethings that knew one another, and then gave up. It was too loud. My ideas weren't interesting enough to scream, and maybe the whole doctoral enterprise was a ridiculous bother. I'd embarked on an exciting Brooklyn adventure only to find that classical music was irrelevant, and—in a related development—Danny was focused on someone else, who spoke a different language, and belonged to the moment.

Tuning out the party and my little storm of emotions (such as they were), I did the only thing I could think to do. I started going over the bit of writing I'd been doing that afternoon—an analysis of the Monteverdi madrigal "*Zefiro torna.*" I felt I'd written down all the details, and that I knew everything there was to know about the piece, but hadn't found the point.

The madrigal was a setting of a Petrarch poem, about spring and awakening desire. The music begins with a dance—the dance of nature. Except for one rogue breeze, the words and notes conform to rhythmic patterns like the seasons.

When the poem pivots to the self—"but for me"—Monteverdi shifts every musical element at once. The rhythm moves from dancing triple to mourning duple. The melody stops leaping and starts sighing: a deep sigh, passed from voice to voice. Monteverdi's design tells us there is no common ground between the speaker and his surroundings. The world may be spring, but within this person there are no seasons.

As we come to the final three lines, Petrarch's poem reminds us of nature:

and the songs of little birds, and the flowering fields,
and the virtuous acts of noble women

And Monteverdi brings back his dance for two brief phrases, like when you're looking at a Renaissance painting and your gaze shifts from the figures in the foreground to the receding hills and trees of the background. Musical Form—I mean Design—allows him to refer and gesture. But (Petrarch continues) these beauties of nature

are for me a desert and wild, savage beasts

For Petrarch, this is more or less one image. But for Monteverdi it is two. On "desert" Monteverdi writes plain chords, music about the idea of emptiness. After that comes the fullest thing you can imagine, a passage so crammed with dissonance that you can hardly believe it.

We've absorbed the contrast between individual and nature. But now, within the individual, the music makes you see a second abyss, between something dead and something only painfully alive. In the last forty seconds or so, Monteverdi expresses this inner suffering, far more searing than the previous sighs, ripping apart the three-minute piece and its pretensions to lightness, and even the way that desire can seem natural—"it's just spring." No, whatever desire you find in the last forty seconds of this madrigal, it's not natural. You feel human intervention all over it, and Monteverdi's mastery, climbing up a few notes as you expect, then disclosing running notes in the middle, making the dissonances on the outside seem even worse— they radiate a combination of pain and pleasure. You want them to stop and you never ever want them to stop. If you wanted to explain "dissonance" to someone, I would choose this example. You drink these dissonances, and when you're done, spring's universal desire seems pale. The purpose of Monteverdi's design is to make you forget his own beginning, to almost annihilate it in the memory, to make it impossible to hear anything other than this suffering, the individual destroyed by love.

}

Danny's friend went home, and the two of us ended up half-sitting, half-lying against a wall, watching people dance. The music got yet louder. "Let's bounce?" he said. The car service took forever to arrive, as we'd forgotten where we were. We climbed in and he gave his address, and as we rumbled toward the Brooklyn Bridge through funneling roads his hand found mine. Unfamiliar hair. He asked if I wanted to crash at his place, and there was little to do but say yes.

His mattress was on the floor. We fumbled with each other before falling asleep, to no particular result, and then I woke up with a crushing hangover and a radiant happiness. Danny was already up and fidgeting. I got up on my knees, then gave up and lay back again. He toasted some bread, and brought me a slice. We were both being kind to each other, thoughtful and considerate. His kindness was horrible because I could tell it was forced. My kindness was real, but also horrible, because it was all about preventing Danny's further discomfort.

He suggested we go to Barnes & Noble. "They'll have coffee," he said. Yes, I supposed that was true. He wanted me to disintegrate into my component molecules and never reappear. Nonetheless we got dressed, stumbled into Barnes & Noble, bought coffees, and browsed the stacks. Danny called me over to look at a book on design by one of his idols. And at that moment, feeling that standing up was an untenable position, I remembered, incredibly, that I had a lesson with Mitsuko Uchida (a rather famous pianist I'd met at the prestigious Marlboro Music School) in just a few hours. I'd just read a passage in Ishiguro's *The Unconsoled* when the main character suddenly remembers he has a concert—a nightmare, like much of that novel—but this was happening to me in real life. I was supposed to play for one of classical music's few true gods on East 79th Street, and I had to get back to the Upper West Side first, to change and shower. It wasn't clear how I had forgotten this big event, or why I'd en route decided to drink uncountable drinks and participate in a misguided sexual awakening.

I remember the taxi back to my place, the city still in morning light. Everything, even the grayest buildings, looked green. When hungover, some people crave fatty foods—I can't get enough metaphor. To me, this greenness was obviously a symbol, it was tenderness, tinting everything, even a homeless man in filthy sweatpants sitting and laughing against a wall, and then a woman with a coffee cup, licking the dripping edges. Everyone was going, and I was going by them. A universal motion, a giant spring dance of desires.

A rush of cleaning at my apartment. Tooth-brushing. Befuddled warming-up. I was going to play one of the most austere and tragic pieces in the world for Mitsuko—again, Bach's last Partita, in E minor. I taxied again, now more nauseatingly, over to the East Side, and said hello to the charming Adele Moskowitz, her host. I sat at the brown piano with a sweeping view of Central Park and tried to play. Mitsuko did not say much. She seemed disappointed, but she couldn't understand about the index cards, or my evening, or how beautiful the world had become.

When the lesson was finished, eighty-year-old Adele, sixty-year-old Mitsuko, and just-becoming-sober I—an unlikely trio—piled into a taxi at the corner of 79th and Madison. A few minutes later, we all got out at the 92nd Street Y for a Musicians from Marlboro concert. And there, after semi-sleeping through the first half, I heard the Schumann F Major Trio, played by Richard Goode (another famous pianist, another idol) and two other younger string players. The music was bounding along until a moment, in the second theme, where Goode hesitated ever so slightly just before one note. The way he hesitated stunned me. That was it, the tenderness I'd seen all over the city, and which I'd been waiting all day to recapture, since failing to find it in Danny's eyes. Yes, yes: some joys make you want to rush into them, while others make you want to hold off, as if happiness were a pool you were testing with your toes. I tried to explain this revelation to Richard Goode (with some redacted elements) at the post-concert reception, which didn't go over well.

⁊

By June of 2002, my doctoral document had been written and approved and given an award, despite one quite hostile member of the committee. My father came to commencement. An excited graduating student kissed Kevin Spacey, who was receiving an honorary doctorate. Then Dad wanted some bonding time. We installed a bookshelf. I wanted to dazzle him with my new cooking prowess, so we went to Zabar's, Citarella, Murray's Cheese—everywhere packed, endless queues. Dad quipped, "So the city that never sleeps is mostly standing in line." Then the two of us cooked osso bucco and risotto in my tiny below-market apartment, a place I had no idea would be my home for twenty-three years. It was sweet and absurd.

The next morning, my father went off to LaGuardia, and I had a few weeks on my own in New York. I decided it was high time, as a newly minted Doctor, to get my Love Life in order. Danny hadn't made me rethink any premises. I'd filed that night away under miscellaneous. Friends encouraged me to create a profile on something called "nerve dot-com," which I did, and I met a twenty-something woman from Brooklyn down on Cornelia Street for dinner. In her profile, she said she enjoyed browsing through Ricky's, which she explained was a makeup store. This didn't dissuade me, though I'd never dated a girl who wore makeup. We had a lovely, unmemorable conversation. I was a perfect gentleman and took a taxi home. I went online and, several hours later, maybe two in the morning, kicked a random guy out of my bed and apartment with relief and fear and self-disgust.

A week later, I drove up to the Marlboro Music School, in the rolling near-mountains of southern Vermont, and there *you* were, staring back at me in the dining hall at lunch. The look was direct and unashamed. I filed this away, too, for a week or so. Most of my attention was consumed with a new piece by the eighty-something composer Leon Kirchner, a sort-of-sonata for violin and piano. It was clear that this piece was a struggle, representing so much love, so much of Leon's life's work, and I could see, measure by measure, all the detail of its resolutions and non-resolutions, a tortured accumulation of dissonances. Even if the whole story didn't make sense, it was incredible to follow its thinking. I kept wanting it faster, to feel the urge and the frenzy, as if putting Leon's overconsidered life on fast forward, just like I'd always wanted to learn faster than I could. The violinist was furious at me for pushing her. Leon worked with us for hours and hours in humid Marlboro rooms. He described his wife, who had just died of cancer, as a "rare butterfly," and there were in the middle of the piece certain fermatas, moments where the harmonies did in fact hover, and alight, as if discovering themselves. I felt those, and felt all the intensity of Leon trying to create a work that would make his life land. One day, I played a few bars of Janáček after rehearsal. He looked more crestfallen than usual. "Oh," he said, "I never wrote anything as beautiful as that one phrase."

It happened, I think, that same evening. My mind was still in the emotions of Kirchner's piece, trying to solve its puzzle, and there you were (again) in the coffee shop, as beautiful as anyone I'd ever seen. We drank a few beers, talking, as if just joshing around. But then, down the hill on the way to our dorm, a couple hours later, we were making out. A flutist ran across us. He snarked, "I guess you're not totally straight," and this seemed irrelevant, I didn't care who saw or who knew. I didn't have to come out; I was already way, way out. We left him and walked along a dark gravel road—snippets of music, summer, nature, night. I asked what you wanted. You said, "Everything." And so, that whole summer, we swam in the pond, took quiet long walks in the woods, hiked Vermont's mountains, and everyone asked me if I was OK. I had never been better. I think I played the piano; I just don't remember.

My body had been waiting for me all that time, waiting for my mind to find it. It wasn't the Monteverdi madrigal; I was, in that magical period, allowed to be both individual and nature, the sigh and the dance.

Coda (TRANSITIONS)

PLAYLIST

MENDELSSOHN: *Variations Concertantes*
LISZT: *Spanish Rhapsody*
MOZART: Concerto in C Major, K. 503, recorded by Jeremy Denk and the
Saint Paul Chamber Orchestra

In 1999, while I was still procrastinating on my doctoral document, Sebők died. When I heard the news, I was in my apartment in New York, on the floor, crammed between my bed and an IKEA media stand, watching—of all things—*Felicity*. It felt like a warning not to waste my life and my time. I flew back to Indiana and attended some memorial events. Evelyne and I were now roommates and friends; she'd left her husband and was giving me informal lessons on the frame of the hand, which saved me through my early concertizing years, help-ing me feel like I could survive whatever piano I found in whatever dry concert hall. We listened to Starker and Sebők's recording of Mendels-sohn's *Variations Concertantes,* where Sebők's wit and tenderness and reserve are all at play, along with a stunning and subtle virtuosity. We marveled at Sebők's early disc of the Liszt *Spanish Rhapsody*—what could be, and kind of is, a vapid showpiece. He shaped the minor-key chaconne to a dark, thundering climax, then gave the ensuing Spanish dance a castanet clarity. Its lesson was more or less the same as the first private lesson I had with him: you could ennoble anything, depending on the choices you made.

I chose, a couple years later, in 2002, to quit teaching for the time being. It was too soon; my teaching was a disservice, both to me and to my students. Evelyne gave me a couple thousand dollars to make me braver. She knew I needed nudging. (Where would my life be without her? Hard to say.) I added her funds to a small hoard I'd saved and moved to New York full time, to finish what I had theoretically started. There were a few years of financial anxiety, but I had crucial assists from friends, fellow musicians, presenters, and random believers. I became, inarguably, a concert pianist.

Sebők's influence would reassert itself, here and there, unpredictably. On one of my tours, in the late 2000s, I found myself sitting at a post-concert dinner with Joseph Schwartz, my Oberlin teacher. I hadn't seen him since 1997. We were at an Applebee's in Florida, near Sarasota, the only place open. We exchanged summaries of our lives, and then, just when the conversation was flagging, out of nowhere he said, "Do you remember that Bach gigue Sebők played at Oberlin?" Yes I did, I said, and found myself tearing up. I couldn't believe that, twenty years later, in this land of traffic lights and strip malls, we were both still carrying the memory of those two minutes of Bach.

Not long after that, I have a vivid memory of playing a recital in Philadelphia, in their wonderful then-new recital hall, the Perelman Theater. I lifted my arm confidently to play a passage. A flurry of wrong notes rang out. I had a moment of panic, a quick intake of breath, and was beginning a litany of self-blame when I heard a voice in my head with a quaint Hungarian accent: "The problem with you is that you're a perfectionist." I played more freely; there suddenly seemed to be more options. After the concert, trying to smile as people offered compliments, I was still in my head, comparing this Sebők moment to Bill Leland, and all his nitpicky reminders in the black lesson notebook.

Leland had been right to remind me that there was no end to the details one could strive for, but Sebők was also right—the desire for perfection could be a deadly weakness. Living comfortably in that paradox, without even knowing it, is part of being a musician. There's a labyrinth of voices inside your head, a counterpoint of self-awareness and the remembered sayings of your guides and mentors, who don't always agree. Sometimes you wish you could go back to ask your teachers again to guide you; but up there onstage, exactly where they always wanted you to be, you must simply find your way. They have given all the help they can; the only person who can solve the labyrinth of yourself is you.

𝄐

In December of 2017, after four or five of my most visible, busiest touring years to date, I rented an Airbnb in New Mexico, on the shore of Lake Abiquiu—Georgia O'Keeffe country. To get there, I had to drive through a herd of cattle; the dark beasts parted like the Red Sea as I puttered ten miles an hour through their sacred space. Every minute or two, the lake and sun and hills reshuffled themselves into another version of astonishing, and I felt I had to leave the car to take a picture; the herd didn't like that, and stirred uneasily. I was exhausted by the time I arrived. The nearest restaurant was forty-five minutes away. There was a hot tub. At 6,500 feet, the air was cold and clear, a conduit for absolute silence. Night came on fast, and with it fields of stars, and no other lights except the ones you turned on in the house to feel less alone.

Like most of my non-concert trips, this one was booked impulsively, with a dubious mix of motivations. The flight would finally give me long-desired Diamond status on Delta. But my deeper thought was, *I don't care about anybody or anything,* because of all the stupid death that happened that year, and because certain guys who shall remain nameless had screwed with my head over long periods of time. I wanted to take revenge for my solitude with more solitude.

Once settled in the Airbnb, though, I realized I hadn't thought any of it through. I had to practice. There was no piano. I hadn't looked for a piano, or wanted it. Maybe this was deliberate self-sabotage. Dates for a recording with the Saint Paul Chamber Orchestra—Mozart's great Concerto in C Major, K. 503—were coming up soon. They had been set long ago. I drove off to the gas station/local store and while checking out tried to ask, as casually as possible, "Umm, weird question! Do you know of anyone with a piano around here?" and the lady said, well, there's a woman named Madeline who teaches kids.

And so I sought the services of a neighborhood piano teacher once again, some forty years after my first. Madeline was gracious. (Mona Schneiderman, Madeline Williamson . . . a coincidence of names.) She welcomed me into her light-filled home, introduced me to her packs of dogs, and brewed me tea. I didn't know what to say. I sat at her piano for a few hours each day, as long as I could stand it. My attitude was not tip-top. Occasionally, I felt I would rather be crucified while listening to Donald Trump read Dante aloud than practice the piano another minute. But each day, I found more in the music, or at least not less: a stubborn value that wouldn't vanish. This sensation started with a particular passage in the last movement of the Mozart, a rondo.

&

Rondos require passages of return, like houses require hallways. Often these transitions, like hallways, are innocuous. They tend to have scales or arpeggios rather than melodies—unmemorable notes you have to practice, rather than notes you whistle or sing. A lot of noodling, to give the impression of traveling, of getting somewhere.

Mozart wrote plenty of elegant and deferential lead-ins, but sometimes he decides he'd rather write something spectacular. He puts unnecessary magic in a functional spot. It's rare and foolish for me to attempt a sports metaphor, but here goes. Imagine you're sliding toward home plate, and it's obvious that inertia is about to carry you to your goal, but while this is happening, as you are sliding and surrendering to inevitability, in that un-holdable moment you realize something eternal about existence, something much more important than *I'm about to score a run*—something about the nature of games, maybe, the reasons why we play them, the deep emotional niche they fill in our lives. That's what Mozart's greatest transitions are like.

This particular passage has three ingredients. Number one, the piano has a series of up-and-down gestures:

But these small loops all serve a longer process (ingredient two)—

—a scale that descends, note by inevitable note, a bird gliding to the ground. In these two ingredients, a conversing microcosm and macrocosm, and two types of travel: looping amble and purposeful flight.

But then comes the third ingredient, the renegade. Every beat or so, not exactly regularly, Mozart switches between major and minor. It's like putting time under a strobe light—

light dark light dark light dark

—and for me the effect lies between uncanny and ravishing. The switches to minor are strange—*Why are we suddenly sad?* But the reappearances of major feel even more unsettling—*Why are we happy again?* Ingredient one fills the space with action. Ingredient organizes space in a direction. But the third complicates space, asking *Where are we?*

In the mornings, because the high desert brought on insomnia, I'd be up at 4:00 or 4:30. I'd go out to the hot tub and sit naked in the dark, waiting in the amniotic water without laptop or phone. At a certain point, I'd lose faith that the sun would rise. I warned myself not to fall asleep and drown in the tub. But then there it was: an imperceptible brightening at one end of the sky.

The vast sky became small potatoes as the complex edges where it met the land came alive. The long angle of the light was the hero. The rim of cliffs around Ghost Ranch started first, with a paleness, the whitish rock declaring itself awake; and then this foundation gathered into itself a family of pinks and oranges and reds, enough beauty in that corner of the spectrum for a lifetime's contemplation. Meanwhile, on another edge of the valley, a cliff with more piñon trees had a calmer response: only a few garish pinks emerged from the forested mass, peeking out from boulders. Time passed in the form of light. I thrashed around in the tub trying to not miss any of these amazing mini-events, turning my head from one end of the compass to another. I wanted to become an all-seeing eye. Was it more beautiful two minutes earlier or now? I don't know why I was judging and rating. Why do I care that something is more beautiful than something else?

You never wanted it to end, and you never wanted to go anywhere else, until a certain too-clear moment when you knew it was over, and you couldn't be there anymore. I got out of the tub, dripping, shivering, and ran barefoot over the rocky path back to shelter. Inside was warmth and petty concerns. Why didn't they have robes? I typed a seemingly polite but peevish note to the Airbnb owner. I googled "health effects of long hot tub soaks." Meanwhile, I kept trying to hold in my mind those in-between colors. I wanted to live in the transitions.

⁂

Later in the rondo of 503, it becomes necessary for Mozart to write another transition—to return to the act of return. We've come to the middle of the piece. Half in the past, half in the future. We're in the throes of a love sextet between the piano and the winds. It is full of yearning, even though the melody is quite basic, made of three repeated, descending notes:

three blind mice

What makes this melody transcendent and not idiotic is that the chord changes on each middle note, on "blind." (We call those notes "passing tones"—an eloquent label.) Those magical changing chords are mostly seventh chords, like the ones in the second Harmony chapter, chords that live between the desire to resolve and the desire to be prolonged. A middle section, about middle notes and middle chords.

To escape from this section, Mozart writes a transition like no other. He breaks the singing symmetry with a small stumble, a syncopation like the glitch of a broken record, as if to say *Let's try that again.* As time is added, retracting and retracing the past, the chords shift beneath our feet, sending us into an unknown future. Mozart becomes an unreliable narrator. We travel in the dark without rail or track, like the famous boat scene in *Willy Wonka and the Chocolate Factory,* singing "There's no earthly way of knowing which direction we are going." The winds still sing "three blind mice," but now desperately, over tragic harmonies.

Just when dark seems to have won, Mozart switches gears again: six long measures of blinding light, rising in the major (!). At this juncture, as the winds ascend, I begin to feel a pressure, and not just an intense need to resolve. For me this pressure reflects a sense that this master-piece is "too full," that it's trying to contain two pieces, sunny major and tragic minor, elated and terrified, normative and uncanny, and the act of trying to stuff these contradictions into a single narrative leads to these outbursts, overflows, moments of pouring over.

At last the orchestra goes silent, and the pianist takes over with a mere thread of notes, a gossamer double scale. The pianist inches down ...

... to a certain point, then turns back around, as if having missed its object, as if having gone past the exit ...

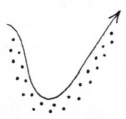

On the way back up, without warning, we find that we are there. The old theme appears—a rabbit pulled from a hat. The crisis is not solved, but merely dissolved.

As I practiced this passage, I stared out a large glass opening to a peculiar New Mexico vista: the Rio Chama drifting by. In the desert, all water looks improbable. Silty snowmelt coming down from the Rockies. The endless, evaporating sun shone off it. Caught between the music and this sight, my brain started up an involuntary bookkeeping, a checklist of loss: the death of my father a couple years past, who loved New Mexico and all its complex bloody history, who drove and mocked me and made me feel it was never enough and still loved what I did; more recently my mother, in what felt like a dream, losing her ability to breathe while I was selfishly away concertizing in the endless sun of Finland; and last, in the most underhanded turn of events, opening my laptop on a concert afternoon in Arkansas to discover on the internet the death of my friend Michael, for whom I'd nursed a decade of bitterness about the impossibility of our ever being what I wished we would be.

While my mind was against my will counting to three, there I was, practicing a little nursery rhyme theme of Mozart's in the sunshine, with a feeling I recognized to be happiness. Back when I was twelve, and my mother was deathly ill, music had no consolation to offer—it felt fake. But now, after all those losses and teachers and time, it felt like one of the few dependable realities. I kept playing the transition, over and over, while Madeline bustled in the kitchen. She couldn't help interjecting "That's quite some tempo you're taking!" I laughed; probably she wanted me to put on the metronome. But I was too busy trying to sort out the truth of this passage. Mozart prepares the return of this theme with unprecedented inspiration. He goes to the ends of the musical earth to bring us home. And yet, after all that, it still feels like an accident when you find yourself back on solid ground.

Acknowledgments

First, I must thank all my teachers, and apologize. I've already exploited them once in my life! And here I've done it again. I made a semi-conscious decision to depict many of them as I saw them, back then, in all my confusion and inexperience. So—sorry to Norman for the conspicuous bad breath, and to Greg for the mole, and to Larry for the wheedling, etc.: all partly caricatures. I hope the most lasting impression is affection. My deepest regrets go to Joseph Schwartz. We were the wrong match at the wrong time, and I couldn't tell the story without making that evident. But he is and was a wonderful pianist and teacher, and deserves far better.

Then I must give thanks for the well-tested patience of my editor, Andy Ward, whose enthusiasm for this project still boggles my mind. He would write back in ecstasy when he got excited, and with a kind, furrowed brow when he got worried. And my consummate agent, Elyse Cheney, who met with me after my *New Yorker* piece about Leland and Sebők. I will never forget that meeting. She lay back in her chair while I mumbled incoherently, and I felt afterward that I could dream this book into whatever form it took.

Many other devoted people at Random House too: Kaeli Subberwal and Marie Pantojan, who processed dilatory edits and gave me some nice feedback that made me feel less insane, and Lawrence Krauser, who did an intense copyedit, catching mistakes, asking me to clarify, researching darker corners of my past. London King has worked so hard on publicity. Madison Dettlinger has been helpful with my social media incompetence. Lucas Heinrich designed the fabulous cover (heartbreaking to choose just this one beautiful option from his many proposed possibilities), and Simon Sullivan—who didn't even know about my font fetish—made the text look so elegant. Such a lovely inspiration to put rests in the pauses.

Then there's Leo Carey at *The New Yorker,* who patiently shuffled my two six-thousand-word pieces through his rigorous process, and sat up with me late one night when I was on tour in South Carolina, and I stared at a sad plate of takeout and he stared at whatever book was in his cubicle, until we found a word to fix the final sentence of the piece, the one about the labyrinth that finally found its way to Oprah's website, which somehow made the piece hang together. Leo is a great lover of music and words, and I've never met anyone more dedicated to his work, no matter how exhausting and frustrating it might be.

Bouquets of thanks to all my distinguished sample readers: the composer John Adams, the novelist Edward Docx, the wonderful musicologists Peter Burkholder and William Cheng, my dear longtime friend Eileen Brickner, Anya Grundmann from NPR, my brilliant English professor David Walker, who did so much for me over many many years, Paul Keene from the Barbican, my late composer unrequited love Michael Friedman, and two music-loving super-gay friends from Seattle, Zach Carstensen and James Urton, who gave me the straight dope.

}

Many great teachers and lessons got cut from this book. One I regret is the music history professor James Hepokoski, a force at Oberlin when I was there. I loved the lingo and style and insights of his old-school musicology lectures and essays, and some of that is in this book. But, now that I look back at it, I have to think of another, quite different influence: the great Susan McClary. Like idiots, we all made fun of *Feminine Endings* when it came out in 1991, for being so wild in its imagery, and yet now I can see how vital it was. My chapter on harmony and sex wouldn't exist without her influence.

I fell in love with a wonderful but odd book of essays by Brian Blanchfield called *Proxies,* and that really loosened me up to write the interlude chapters. And I have to again thank Andy for introducing me to the recent book by George Saunders, where he unpacks Russian short stories.

{

This book ends when I am not yet truly established in a career. But it wouldn't exist without the hordes of people who helped pave my way to playing for more and more audiences. They are curiously elided over in the book ("I became a pianist, bit by bit")—the text is long enough already!—and maybe here I could thank some of them. First I should mention the great conductor Michael Tilson Thomas, who saw something in me (a shared love for Ives, an affection for composers' self-destructive tendencies). He made a lot of things possible. And Susan Wadsworth, of course, the founder of Young Concert Artists (and Monica Felkel, who worked with me at first), and Bettie Buccheri, a well-connected legend in Chicago, who heard me at the Ravinia festival and started recommending me around. She led me to another benefactor: Byron Gustafson, sadly passed away of ALS, who brought me on at ICM Partners (now Opus 3). Byron was unbelievably patient and did an immense amount; then his protégé David Baldwin, along with a great publicity team at 21C, especially the charming Albert Imperato. NPR's *Performance Today* made me their Artist in Residence. Scott Nickrenz kept hiring me at the Gardner Museum. Then, so many people to thank: Hanako Yamaguchi and Jane Moss at Lincoln Center; Kristin Lancino, Judy Arron and then Jeremy Geffen and Clive Gillinson at Carnegie Hall; Chad Smith, who gave me crucial opportunities with the LA Philharmonic; Esa-Pekka Salonen; Tom Morris, who got me involved with Ojai; Hanna Gaifman and now Amy Lam at the 92nd Street Y; and, maybe most faithful of all, the people at Marlboro and the Philadelphia Chamber Music Society: Tony Checchia (who believed in me when it was a pretty dubious proposition), Miles Cohen, Mitsuko Uchida, Richard Goode. Perhaps it was through the latter that I ended up under the wing of Robert Hurwitz, at Nonesuch Records— not enough gratitude could be expressed about that. And likewise to my current managers, David Foster and Adelaide Docx!

The generosity of the MacArthur Foundation is also worth mentioning.

❧

My friends Mike Nicholas and Matt Lipman, combined with some alcohol, helped me survive the pandemic and keep cheery between
bouts of writing. As did my devoted and sweet partner, Vince Tseng—
among infinite other things he cooked and cleaned and let me be for
hours upon hours, to obsess. My friends Hyon Chough and Maurice
Singer in California gave streams of encouragement.

Maybe the most archaeological thank-you goes to Anya Grundmann, who told me back in 2006 to start blogging. She reminded me of
my love for writing, and said I had a thing for connecting the unlikely.
She suggested I might find a specific voice if I let myself pursue those,
and anyway why not try to be happy, doing what you're good at? My
friend Evelyne Brancart, whom I've already thanked in the narrative,
gave me the same lesson, in different ways.

To Donna Herron, my high school orchestra teacher, and Bill Leland, and Mona and Lillian, and all the other teachers who do what
they do against all odds, trying to make musicians hear better, and become the best versions of themselves: Thank you. And, of course,
Sebők. Thank you for saving me. Maybe one last essential thank-you to
his wife, Vica, who would occasionally take me aside with a look, concerned and gentle, to make sure I knew that Sebők had hope for me,
despite the last mean thing he said. "He likes hearing you play," she
said, an unimaginable compliment. We all need a Vica.

Appendix AN ANNOTATED PLAYLIST

1. *The Earliest Lessons*

SAINT-SAËNS: Symphony no. 3 in C Minor (*Organ*), second movement

Camille Saint-Saëns is not in fashion at the moment (unlike the next composer on this playlist, Mahler, whose alienation is still relevant). Saint-Saëns was a prodigy, and had a prodigy's problems. He lived a long time, surveying much of Romanticism—he died at eighty-six—but often reverted to facile, ingenious, clever youth. Life was a little too easy for him, perhaps.

This orgiastic symphony occupies the same thematic territory as the Mahler to follow: Faith versus Doubt. The first movement is mostly human restlessness. It connects without pause to the slow second movement, where the organ begins to stand out. (The organ is connected to the superhuman, the divine.) We hear a long, spun-out, paradisiacal, hymnic theme, with occasional reminders of our agitated, doubting theme from the movement before.

We get a short break to cough and fidget in our seats, and then the third movement starts up: a good old-fashioned scherzo, with a charming interlude. Just when you think you are about to hear the interlude a second time, a Bach-ian rewrite of the hymn appears. Saint-Saëns (like so many of us) invokes Bach as a symbol for God and Truth. When my father's favorite organ chord comes in, signaling the last movement, you really feel that the Hosts of Heaven have appeared. Campy and kitschy, sure. But also fantastic. Just the sort of thing I tend to look down my nose at now, to my regret.

MAHLER: Symphony no. 1 in D Major (*Titan*), first and fourth movements

Warming up in the dressing room, I'll hear a knock at the door. An artistic administrator enters with an apologetic expression, explaining that my Mozart concerto will have twenty minutes less rehearsal because the orchestra is running over, rehearsing their Mahler symphony. Almost always Mahler!—occasionally Bruckner, Shostakovich, Tchaikovsky.

So my opinion of Mahler these days has resentment baked in. I loved him epically around ages nineteen and twenty, and did a Mahler winter-term project on the college radio station, interspersing the symphonies with overheated personal commentary (surprise, surprise). Mahler is a world, and once you believe, he consumes you. He battles with death, ephemerality, love, alienation, loss, limits, and limitlessness.

I grew up with the Bruno Walter and Columbia Symphony recording and I think I was lucky—it's a beautiful performance. If you want a nerdy thrill, compare Mahler's opening to the opening of Beethoven's Fourth Symphony. An honorable theft: reshaping, modernizing.

Notice how the first dark, mysterious descending pair of notes (a falling fourth) gradually morphs into the upbeat of the happy-go-lucky main tune. In the meantime, it also becomes a bird call. This one pair of notes splits into three meanings: the supernatural world, the natural world, the voice of humanity.

The first third of the first movement is one arc of awakening, from darkness and hesitation into the walking tune, which accumulates ever more abandon. After that climax, again we come back to a preternatural stillness, where all the sweep has died, with the cellos hauntingly going over phrases. I know how I felt listening to that moment, my mind stilled. To escape from this mourning monotony back into the joy of nature, Mahler writes a masterful modulation, creating a sense of deep change within.

I am often annoyed that the last movement takes so long (the symphony is quite concise for Mahler up to this point!), but it's hard to argue with its impact. He again begins by copying Beethoven (the last movement of the Ninth Symphony) for a cry of the wounded soul. Gradually the torments die away, revealing a love theme that won't let go, a lesson in How to Extend a Melody. The struggles of counterpoint, often finding dead ends, surrender to the last burst of triumph. You may feel somewhere in those twenty minutes that the finale jumps the shark. But that's how you know you're listening to a Romantic symphony.

CLEMENTI: Sonatina in F Major, op. 36, no. 4

Clementi (1752–1832) was a generation older than Beethoven, but lived four years longer: he saw the whole Classical heyday. He represents a lot of the period's strengths and shortcomings.

I say enough about this piece, and the curse of Sonatinas, in the chapter itself. I even feel a bit bad about it. To atone, I'll tell you that he wrote quite a number of fascinating sonatas—not for students—full of adult invention. Among the most well known is the Sonata in F-sharp Minor; there you find some exploratory aspects of Haydn, in phrases that are constantly reinventing themselves, and even a bit of Scarlatti—unusual keyboard textures that engage the ear, with a bit of Spanish flair. The Sonata in F Minor, op. 13, no. 6, is also worth your time.

The Clementi Society website alleges that some of the later pieces are "on a par with late Beethoven and Schubert," which, umm, I can't quite agree with.

2. Harmony, Lesson One

RAVEL: Piano Concerto for the Left Hand

There are chapters in this book about harmony, melody, and rhythm; I regret that I haven't covered color or texture, such important joys of music. Anyway, a lot of what there is to learn about color can be found in this one piece, maybe coupled with another Ravel masterpiece, *Daphnis and Chloe*. Ravel's music affirms the very French premise that color is not decoration, but expressive essence, as deep as any harmonic progression. Color is the quality of the sound—I suppose you can also call it "timbre," but I think "color" captures it more, the painterly, the part of music that most calls out to the other senses, to smell, touch, taste . . . Sometimes a coloristic emphasis can make the music feel like it wants to vanish, evaporate in a cloud of smoke—but here, in the Left Hand Concerto, you feel a tremendous strength.

The opening cadenza (which I talk about in the chapter) is a miracle of piano writing, but it's a mere trifle in comparison to the last cadenza, a tour de force that implies two or maybe even three hands at work. The understanding of the piano and the human hand that this requires! I remember a live video of an early performance with Leon Fleisher (who'd recently lost his right hand to focal dystonia) in an outdoor venue—pretty astonishing, but I can't locate it anymore. There is also a lovely performance from the BBC Proms with Jean-Efflam Bavouzet, who yelled at me once for having the piano at Bard College brightened.

MOZART: Concerto in F Major, K. 459

A great and underplayed piece, full of wit. The march theme of the first movement is almost too simple, and the movement is largely mono-motivic: an obsessive, Beethovenian situation. It requires that the pianist and orchestra play with great imagination: each new harmonic setting of the main idea (a march) has to evoke a different nuance, articulation. I feel like, for instance, Radu Lupu with Zinman is beautiful but a bit too serious for me, like many recorded performances of this piece. Mitsuko Uchida is a bit cheekier!

MOZART: Sonata in C Major, K. 545, second movement

I heard Mitsuko Uchida play this as an encore several times, and decided to steal it for myself. I recommend her recording. (Full disclosure: I also have a recording on my album *c.1300–c.2000*, where this piece appears as a shorthand or stand-in for the idyllic, pastoral Classical period itself.)

K. 545 is subtitled "Sonata Facile," and it is ubiquitous in children's recital programs. Mozart is writing for students, like Clementi, and yet manages to cast a spell. How can you teach, and still be transcendental?

SCHUBERT: Impromptu in F Minor, D. 935, no. 1

My first experience of this piece (one of my great loves) was tied up with an intense infatuation-crush I had on a barista at my favorite coffee shop in Indiana. I performed it in concert one Sunday Bloomington afternoon, then ran off for a midafternoon cappuccino to have my usual brief chat with her. When I arrived, she was sweeping the deck with a strange expression, gazing off into space. I was too cowardly to approach, and the next day found that she had left town for mental health reasons, and would not be returning. There was an element of fate, and a braid of comedy and tragedy.

Schubert begins with an oddly non-melodic statement: a descending scale creating an outburst, followed by a sad, soft reply. (Very few recordings wait quite enough time for this reply, IMHO.) It happens again, and we get the same soft reply, more or less, and then we are off, on the train of Schubert, of Vienna, an endlessly ambiguous train with elements of the dance and song and lilt, with occasional kicks and grace notes at the ends of bars that feel like they're trying to stop the train—but it keeps on.

The passage I refer to in this chapter happens roughly 2:45 minutes in, depending on the performance. (2:45 is from Radu Lupu on Decca/YouTube.) I would call this the "heart" of the piece, where we find its inner life. It starts in the minor, but gradually finds the major, of course.

It's hard to say what performance I recommend. Schnabel first made me fall for the piece, and yet his recording is a mess, rushing sloppily, even at certain points inexpressive. Many great performances are out there (Uchida, Lupu, Perahia). I feel like none of them capture my (possibly un-capturable) dream for this piece: a subtle tension between the two impulses, the desire to continue the story and the constantly altering states of mind we visit, the pull of tragedy and tenderness against the rhythm.

SCHUBERT: Sonata in B-flat Major, D. 960, second movement

What can you say about this movement that hasn't already been said? The sense of leave-taking (written in Schubert's last month of syphilis-afflicted life), the rhythm of a funeral march merged with the meter of a dance. Perhaps the most affecting moment for me is not too far in, where the music has built itself up to a tragic arrival, and then suddenly we shift harmonies to E major—the quintessential Schubert modulation, combining ravishing beauty and transgressive instability. I recommend Mitsuko Uchida. Her modulations are unbeatable. If you want to watch the ballet of the hands (as discussed in the chapter), there is a video with Brendel, with a quite different interpretative stance.

BEETHOVEN, Sonata in C major, op. 53 ("Waldstein"), third movement

To appreciate the beginning of the last movement, start at least as far back as the beginning of the second movement—reaching musical questions with deflecting, mysterious answers. The music becomes lyrical, but only for a while: darkness gets deeper and more persistent toward the end. The right hand reaches up and up, but the left hand keeps insisting on two bass notes. The last movement appears as more or less the solution to all this cross-hand struggle.

There is a controversial pedal marking in this last movement. Beethoven instructs you to leave the pedal down for long stretches, blurring chords. I recall sitting in an Indiana University faculty committee, next to Karen Shaw (a formidable pianist and teacher, but not the friendliest of colleagues). She looked over at me and asked: "Why would Beethoven ever write that ugly pedaling?" I stared at my feet, resisting the urge to scream. I suppose this is just the sort of moment a pragmatic pedagogue is going to dislike. It violates the contract of classical piano playing, but it has a profound purpose. Like the ending of the first movement of the Schumann *Fantasy,* or certain moments in Haydn (a *pianissimo* section in the first movement of the famous C Major Sonata), this blurring suspends the rules. For a moment, there is no correct or incorrect.

Many pianists don't honor this marking. They blather on about how the piece was written for an older piano, and the effect doesn't translate to the modern piano. Bullshit. Schnabel does it, and it sounds fantastic, like a dream, like melody emerging out of the dream of harmony, or vice versa.

But there are a million great recordings. Go nuts.

3. Forty Days and Forty Nights

MOZART: Viennese Sonatina no. 1 in C Major, K. 439B, first movement

A sonata in miniature, a perfect sandbox for a child to begin to think through Mozart, to understand the gestures. Not many "adult" recordings. In the last movement, a small episode in minor tells you the real, complicated Mozart is there, somewhere.

CHOPIN: Waltz in A Minor, B. 150, op. posth.

Ignaz Friedman is often my go-to guy for Chopin, but he didn't record this particular waltz. He did record another A Minor Waltz, though—op. 34, no. 2—with matchless elegance and care. Don't hesitate. Life's too short not to hear this performance. He has a way of investing the singing tone with tremendous center, and then letting the tone go faint, finding the inner *mezza voce,* and even another fainter sound within that one, voices within voices like a nesting doll. As we strain to hear these refinements, he draws us in, making the listener into an accomplice and confidant. Similar skill can be heard in Sokolov's live performance of "my" waltz, from Amsterdam in 2005.

CHOPIN: Prelude in D-flat Major ("Raindrop")

Friedman plays the "Raindrop" too, rather faster than I used to. I'm sure my twelve-year-old self mooned over the rhythm. One of the joys of Chopin melodies are free whorls that appear from time to time, either groups of seven or fifteen or nineteen notes, which cannot be played exactly in time. They come from the world of vocal cadenzas, of singers making up passages on top of what's written, and yet you feel Chopin's little cadenzas are both improvised and immutable.

DEBUSSY: Arabesque no. 1

This piece is from 1891. In a few years, Debussy will be in full revolt against the grand story of classical style, undermining foundations of harmony and strictures of form, incorporating Asian traditions (gamelan, among others) into a new paradigm. But here he is, starting out, tenderly, with just some arpeggios up and down, taking on one of the most old-fashioned Western tropes: a chord progression. Converting counterpoint into pleasure. Intimacy and simplicity as a rebuke to all overheated German Romanticism—refusing to take Wagner's bait.

This Arabesque occupied an interesting place in my education: it made me feel more confident about the pedal. Somehow Debussy's pedaling rules came naturally to me, more than any other composer's.

The Arabesque's innocence contains deep feeling, but none of the torment of the Chopin Prelude, or the languid melancholy of the waltz. You don't beat your breast in Debussy, or faint. For a start, why not listen to the great Debussy pianist Gieseking?

MOZART: Concerto in A Major, K. 488, first movement

This piece was composed in 1786, just before *The Marriage of Figaro*—in Mozart's absolute prime, and you feel it.

If you don't know your way around the first movement of a classical concerto, don't fret. Here's how it will happen. The orchestra presents all the musical ideas once. The pianist sits around like an idiot (actually, originally the pianist played along . . . a lost tradition). At last the pianist comes in, and we hear all these ideas again, but now in the form of dialogue, with the piano's more pointed articulation and array of possibilities. The piano is not just a new timbre, but a new personality.

When the orchestra has its next big solo, we've entered a new section—the development. All bets are off. New keys. Often more drama, and a clever or suspenseful bridge back to the opening. Then, we hear everything a third time (!). A solo moment for the pianist—an opportunity to show off. The orchestra shuts the pianist up at last, and closes us out.

It sounds like a lot of repetition, and it is. And yet the sequence of ideas, and the constant play of contrast, conceals it. At its best, it is like hearing a wonderful story told from three perspectives. The dialogue between the various themes; between lyrical themes and virtuoso passagework; between the orchestra and piano, of course; and, in the development, between what the themes are and what they might be.

There is a special, and especially Mozartian, treat in this first movement. At the beginning of the development (four minutes and change in), we come to a stop for a second, and the strings lay down (I think "lay down" is better than "play" because it suggests trying to create possibility, rather than stating something) a new theme, something unheard and unheard of. This theme has some particularly gorgeous harmonies. The chords suggest Bach chorales (to me, at least), but the melody is hardly staid: it sweeps through octaves, around and about.

This new theme is a "mistake," according to the so-called rules of sonatas. The development is supposed to play with ideas we've already heard, not step off into terra incognita. But this mistake is just what the piece needed. We've heard many ideas so far that fold in, or laugh, or sigh elegantly—but none that soars.

After the orchestra plays this soaring theme, and the piano decorates it, the clarinet (with its special timbre) takes it up, a third time, in the minor. This theme, so new to our world and so full of life, gets haunted immediately by darkness, and you realize that some of the wistfulness of the previous music is finding an outlet—like when you need to talk through an issue you've been keeping under wraps, cloaked beneath irony or nonchalance. The winds become the soloists, obsessing over the new theme as they reveal this current of sadness.

This new "mistake" theme makes one more cameo, toward the end of the last section (about eight minutes in). The pianist gets to play it alone, so all its counterpoint can be heard, in its purity and Bachitude (not a word, but who cares?). Then the winds join in (so much meaning in this act of joining in), and a new sequence emerges out of it, as if the leaping of the melody needs to stretch its own boundaries. By this point we've heard this "new" theme so many ways: as a loving string chorale, as a piano arabesque, as an ever-changing cry of the heart from the winds, then pure and contrapuntal, lastly ecstatic. A story within the story, which almost seems to encompass all the rest.

The playing is so thoughtful and expressive in Richard Goode's recording with the Orpheus Chamber Orchestra. It's always interesting to listen to Clara Haskil.

And if you're after historical versions, why not try the brilliant Robert Levin's, with fantastic ornaments?

4. Harmony, Lesson Two

GOUNOD: "Ave Maria" (sung by Barbra Streisand)

BACH: Prelude in C Major from *The Well-Tempered Clavier,* Book I

I will not attempt to recommend a recording of this Prelude. Anyway, it's a part of the cultural consciousness; you already know it, even if you don't. It is amazing how variable performances of this icon can be. This piece has no "definitive" version. It also has stubborn, intractable interpretative problems. Because the pattern repeats, you tend to fall into a rut rhythmically—it can sound like a broken record or, if you add too much rhythmic sauce, a cluster of seasick chords. You have to ask yourself how much personal expression to put in, and how much to let the notes "speak for themselves." The piece becomes a litmus test, a rite of passage.

NINA SIMONE: "Just in Time," from the Tomato Collection

My lovely former English professor at Oberlin directed me to this passage from Max Wilk's book *They're Playing Our Song:*

> [Adolph Greene and I] were talking to Jule, and said, "Wouldn't it be nice to have something in the show like an old Youmans tune, where there's two notes, but the bass keeps changing and moving under the notes, making different harmonies and moving a melody." Very simple. Jule went to the piano and started playing a simple thing—*da,* dee *dah.* He asked if that was what we meant, and we said absolutely!

"Jule" means Jule Styne, the composer. I like that this kind of tune is a type, a "Youmans," a well-known songwriting practice. And I like the idea that it's "very simple," because what Nina Simone wrings from this simplicity is so rich and complex.

5. Moments of Truth

STRAVINSKY: *The Rite of Spring,* introduction

In conservatory music history classes, you tend to focus on three key modernists: Debussy, Stravinsky, Schoenberg—three faces of the same dissatisfaction. But there are more nostalgic modernists too: Janáček, Ives, Mahler. A fertile period, from 1890 to 1920. So much to destroy, and so much to create in the rubble.

There are too many great recordings for me to recommend any one. Anyway, it's a conductor's world. Savagery meets beauty; sheer strength of conception; one marvel of color and orchestration after another; and rhythm, rhythm, rhythm. The punk-rock part that I sang at music camp, thinking I was such a rebel, comes about three minutes in.

MOZART: Concerto in A Major, K. 488, third movement

The theme I love most in this movement is just a scale (about three minutes in), rising an octave and a half, then taken up in the winds . . . the pure joy of rising, over a folk drone. It's almost impossible to play that idea with enough sweep and release.

So often, orchestras want to get polite at the end of Mozart rondos—because Mozart is "supposed" to be polite—but Mozart was a theater composer, and from my experience of theater composers, there is nothing more important than to make the ending stick. This ending is one of Mozart's best. In a rare turn of events, the piano keeps playing almost to the end, driving the conversation (still that rising scale, the same one from my favorite theme), aiming toward a blaze of glory and trying to prevent orchestral inertia, one of the most powerful forces on earth.

BEETHOVEN: Sonata in C Minor, op. 13 ("Pathetique"), first movement

I think it's fair to consider Beethoven both a tormented genius and a cynical master of self-branding, since he found a "sound" and used it to great advantage. In his first published set of pieces, three Piano Trios, you have a brilliant comic piece; a more pastoral, meandering piece in the major; and at last—the work that defined him—a restless masterpiece in C minor. In the biz, we call this Beethoven's "C minor mood." Especially in the last movement, each phrase seems to spill over onto the next—the impulse of the composition is breathless, endless.

He was twenty-seven years old when he returned to the C minor mood for the "Pathetique," with no inkling of deafness or the other afflictions he would acquire (he started losing his hearing the next year). It was, and remains, a big hit— embers of Romanticism, breaking through the molds of Classicism.

Even now, it's thrilling, the throughput, the sense of continuous perpetual motion (so different from the whorling, exploratory phrasings of Haydn, or the back-and-forths of Mozart), the Big Line. In Mozart and Haydn, you have outbursts of virtuosity, but nothing so sustained, so extreme or extravagant. It's partly the threat of destroying the piano and pianist that makes it so great.

The introduction is a mini-opera, a lesson in concise scene-setting. First stern, tragic rhythms. Then what seems like a love theme (based on the same rhythm). This is cut short. The love theme tries again, is cut short again (melodrama!), then again, yearning, up, up, up . . .

I mean, do you even need to ask? Listen to my man Artur Schnabel, at least for the intro. He gets messy later, but if this bothers you (and yes, I'm judging you for being bothered) you can switch to Richard Goode.

BEETHOVEN, Sonata in C Major, op. 53 ("Waldstein"), first movement

This piece feels like an extension of the "Pathetique" but in the land of the major key (another storm, but a storm of light). Again, sheer motion, with only occasional respite: a chorale that appears intermittently. No slow intro this time—right into the drama.

The opening is feared by pianists for its virtuosity, for the triple demands of playing fast and crisp and soft. Most recordings don't sound soft enough to me, I'll admit, but that's so subjective. Fast can be overdone. Richard Goode once said a performance he heard was so fast that it sounded like a "vacuum cleaner," which made me laugh and think of another great Beethoven story. Ferdinand Ries played a bit of the "Tempest" Sonata and Beethoven was listening and scolded him for messing up. So Beethoven sat down to demonstrate, and it sounded, in the words of Ries, "like someone was cleaning the piano." Heh. All teachers know the dangers of demonstrating, and the feared look of disappointment on your student's face when you fuck up worse than any student would.

Goode's recording is plenty fast, and thrilling.

MOZART: Sonata in A Minor, K. 330, first movement

Sonatas in the minor key are comparatively rare for Mozart and Haydn, and special. The two Mozart Sonatas in minor are both more "orchestral" than the others—much of the typical piano tinkling is gone. The music is more austere and angular.

All throughout this movement (written in the summer of 1778, in Paris; Mozart was twenty-two) you feel the drive of the march, the feeling of having to continue, and then hesitations.

For me, there are two crucial interpretative questions. First, I find a strange desperation in the march, an unresolvable dissonance and protest. (Those insistent chords in the left hand!) And then, right afterward, a total absence of all that: a listlessness, or emptiness. I listened to twenty formidable recordings and didn't find these things. This is me being an ass, I realize. Some pieces just are greater than their performances. Maybe my favorite version (the angriest) is Malcolm Bilson on fortepiano. In the softer parts, I just wish it was on a more mellifluous modern piano (Malcolm will hate my saying that!).

SCHUMANN: Concerto in A Minor, first movement

The minor key is not rare for Romantic composers; they love to mourn and wallow.

We burst onto the scene, only to find ourselves in a fit of melancholy. The main theme is played by the oboe, then reheard in the piano—two timbres, two ways of thinking about phrasing, breathing, freedom. At the top of this tune you find a high note, an A, on a dominant seventh chord (a chord "explained" in Harmony, Lesson Two). Somehow Schumann discovered a way to use this chord, to suspend it in the middle of phrases as an instrument of unrequited longing.

You could say this piece is in sonata form, and it kind of is, but I think it's more accurate to say that it looks at sonata form with respect, and decides to go its own possibly self-destructive way, like a young person making college decisions.

The piece has two standout highlights: the quiet slow section in the middle, where we hear the main theme, now over rippling arpeggios in the piano. What had seemed sorrowful is now blissful—coital or postcoital. And then, of course, the cadenza, where the piano takes the energy of the orchestra, winds it down, ruminates, and then builds back, in waves, to the most stunning return. The coda is the kind of audience-pleasing ending (yet with integrity) that Schumann didn't often find a way to write. It's very hard to recommend a recording of this piece; it's so personal. The orchestra is so interwoven. Try Argerich, Lipatti, Rubinstein, Richter, Myra Hess.

6. Harmony, Lesson Three

BACH: Fugue in B Minor from *The Well-Tempered Clavier,* Book I

I say enough about the construction of this piece, perhaps, in the chapter. I recommend Edwin Fischer, who is often criticized as a "Romantic" because he uses pedal and sometimes doubles bass notes. But I find his approach musically pure and selfless in many other ways—in some of the most important ways. You feel lost in his account (in a good way). But I recommend you listen to great harpsichordists—Pierre Hantaï, to take one example. Do not bother with Glenn Gould on this one—it's a travesty, the work of a spoiled man-child, like peeing on a monument just because you can.

SCHUBERT: "Auf dem flusse," from *Winterreise*

If you don't mind being depressed, the song cycle *Winterreise* is one of the treasures of the classical canon, a summation of Schubert's long habit of spelunking through the uncanny. It was written in his last year of life (January 1828, I think) and only shortly after Beethoven's death. I grew up with Fischer-Dieskau and Gerald Moore, but there are so many shattering performances.

To dig deep, I recommend Ian Bostridge's great book *Schubert's Winter Journey: Anatomy of an Obsession,* a book I wish I had written. He is also one of the work's foremost interpreters. He was, alas, quite prickly when I interviewed him at the 92nd Street Y. We got in an argument about whether *Winterreise* is actually a sad piece. Schubert himself called these songs "truly terrible."

JOPLIN/CHAUVIN: "Heliotrope Bouquet"

Whose ragtime to listen to? On the internet, I find some mechanically inspired quickstep recordings—a bit heartless, to my ear. And then the famous Joshua Rifkin, a participant in ragtime's Renaissance—quite slow. In between, you find a version by William Bolcom from an album entitled *Heliotrope Bouquet*.

This represents a perpetual argument about ragtime. Should it be fast and cheeky or slower and sung? Some rags seem to me more like tunes and others more like dances; most live in between.

If I had to say what I love about ragtime, it's charm. The structure is formulaic. The chords stay pretty close to home (although this one is an exception!). There are many limitations. But the limitations, clichés, and formulas become a kind of petri dish for elegance, for the cleverness of harmonic interpolation and diversion, what you might call dimples of musical invention.

CHOPIN: Ballade no. 4 in F Minor, op. 52

No matter how beautifully you play the opening of the Fourth Ballade, it will never be enough. So Chopin gives you a second chance. This is the moment I discuss in the chapter; it arrives roughly halfway through the piece.

Allow me to present a formal accounting of what leads up to this moment, and bore you to tears:

1. brief intro
2. melancholy main theme, obsessively repeated, escalating to a tragic climax
3. lyrical slow theme, becoming a waltz
4. mid-waltz, fragments of the melancholy theme begin to weave their way back into the story

The sad theme appears sad for a few bars, then does a wild U-turn into an ecstatic climax. Every pianist will agree: this is one of the best moments of the piece. It's there, where all expectations are mixed, and the keys are wandering and there is no solid sense of a "section"—that's when Chopin brings back the intro and everything makes sense (symmetry and inevitability, mixed with the ravishingly unexpected).

Chopin slides up one half step (to A major) for this intro return. This is the opposite motion from "Auf dem flusse." Opposite from Schubert in direction, but also in meaning. Chopin doesn't just slide; he "earns" his modulation. He's not after Schubert's violation but revelation. As in many of the greatest modulations, it creates the sense of a hallowed space, a new territory that has been made available for hearing and feeling.

For recordings, maybe try Argerich, Rubinstein—it's shocking how different this piece feels under different hands. I've never heard a recording that seemed right in the opening bars.

7. *The Real World*

BEETHOVEN: **Sonata in F Minor, op. 57 ("Appassionata")**

I always yell at young pianists to play in tempo in the first movement, but it's not entirely their fault. Beethoven makes it difficult to feel a tempo, or any steady thing. Yet there is a drive behind the story, a continuous suspense. Those two forces (disruption and drive) are at war. You have to be willing to risk it all.

In the second and third movements, a different breath appears. The feeling of falling apart vanishes. The second movement has all the serenity and soothing continuity that the first lacked, and it gradually fills itself in, over a series of variations, with ever faster notes, into a luminous climax. Moving from rich bass up to heavenly treble.

To me, the great Barenboim (in a live performance on YouTube) has lots of feeling in the second movement, but (in my humble opinion) maybe too much for the process, for the bigger growth. By the time the fast notes arrive, they don't feel to me like they come out of the joy of what preceded. Richter, live from Leningrad, gets the weirdness of the variations, but not much of the playfulness. I might choose (not that we have to choose) Richard Goode.

BEETHOVEN: **Symphony no. 7 in A Major, first movement**

Maybe one of the most effective ways to begin a piece—one that Brahms used often—is to present a musical idea, then let it unravel a bit. Just a bit! Then, once you've laid your trap, you let your idea come back a second time, with a new depth, with the addition of another layer. You reel us back in. It's a premature recapitulation, a way to find recurrence even in the act of birth.

For me, the spell of this performance was tied up in hearing the winds of the Cleveland Orchestra, so I recommend the classic Cleveland Orchestra and George Szell recording. Savor the almost violent short nature of the string chords at the beginning, against the held wind notes. And then the big sweep, when the theme returns with running scales in the strings underneath.

CHOPIN: *Berceuse*, op. 57

Here again, as with the Ravel Left Hand Concerto: sound and color. Check out Ignaz Friedman (fast, evanescent, kaleidoscopic, dazzling) and Rubinstein (more conventional, and gorgeous).

SCHUMANN: Toccata in C Major, op. 7

You have two imperatives at war here. Young Schumann wanted to write a big virtuoso piece, possibly "the hardest piece ever written." Meanwhile, there's all this generous Romantic feeling in him, bubbling out.

Chopin had a great sense of how to make the piano less of a clunky instrument, how to thin out the middles, how to let the trebles radiate, and make the basses offer pillowy support. Schumann, for the most part, didn't have this skill. He liked to fill out the middles of his harmonies. This piece is crammed with harmony to the gills, more than you can play. And so many notes, almost no time to sing.

I don't recommend this piece for most young pianists. But the young Gilels could sure play the hell out of it!

8. Melody, Lesson One

BRAHMS: Trio in B Major, op. 8, first movement

This piece has an interesting backstory. Brahms composed it when he was nineteen, and probably couldn't believe his luck. I mean, who could? What a tune! He got a minute or two in—it was going swimmingly—and began to choke. He couldn't figure out how to go on, let alone construct a Big Important Piece. He composed a second theme: a dark mirror-image of the first, with none of its charm or logic. He imagined he was "developing" the idea, but instead stopped it in its tracks. Things got even more desperate about two-thirds of the way through. He decided to add a fugue, based on the ghostly rewritten theme—the equivalent of being mid-coitus when your geometry professor knocks on the bedroom door. In short, Brahms stumbles around for fifteen minutes of laborious composition, just trying to live up to his one minute of flowing melodic inspiration.

Later in Brahms's life, his publisher invited him to revisit some older works. He discarded the entire first movement, and all its shadowboxing, except for the melody. This melody was precious to him—as it is to me. He wanted to do justice to the idea, and rescue youthful brilliance from inexperience. And so he did. In this later version the second theme is far more concise and eloquent than the fugue theme, with a haunting aspect that balances out the feverish, extroverted opening. The hot-mess transitions are all gone, and the return of the opening theme is a miracle of elision (older, wiser Brahms finding a passage back to his youth).

You can listen to any number of recordings of the later, "real" version, including the early Beaux Arts Trio. Steven Isserlis, Joshua Bell, and I recorded this early version of the Brahms Trio on our album *For the Love of Brahms*. It sounds pretty OK, considering how much we argued about it.

BEETHOVEN: **Quartet in C-sharp Minor, op. 131, first movement**

I often rail against Romantic composers writing fugues—something to do when they've run out of ideas. But here, the form fuses with the austerity of the idea and the sense of a dark obsession. It creates a spell; it has no whiff of the school-room.

This is true late Beethoven, from the 1820s: when his friends began to feel he'd gone off the rails. He had, and hadn't. For this piece, he created a unique narrative form, a chain of seven movements (five main parts and two interludes) connecting to and also disrupting one another, including this tragic fugue; then slipping up a half step to an unearthly dance (paradise?) in D major; a long, ornamented slow set of variations (another sort of paradise); a hilarious, self-interrupting scherzo (Beethoven again allowing the comic and the sublime to interpenetrate); and finally an incisive finale that revisits the conflicting notes of the fugue, and doesn't quite resolve them.

This is among musicians' favorite pieces, but probably not audiences'. Too many dark mysteries that decline to explain themselves. My friends in the Brentano Quartet have a wonderful recording.

9. Motivations, Pure and Otherwise

SCHUMANN: *Symphonic Études, op. 13*

The Cortot recording is justifiably famous.

MICHAEL DAUGHERTY: *Snap!*

As with Clementi, I must apologize. I found a performance of *Snap!* on YouTube (likely not our Oberlin Contemporary Ensemble performance, because the beginning sounded rhythmically competent). And what do you know? It's a clever and well-composed piece.

I think one of the many obstacles to my enjoyment of Daugherty's music was that my Oberlin self thought that New Music should be dissonant and serious and unlistenable. The more unlistenable it was, I felt, the better it was. I'd learned just enough history to know that classical music had a progression ever since Bach toward more and more dissonance. To turn back to nicer harmonies was to sell out, to abandon classical music's "high ground," to allow classical music to merge with "popular music"; and since everyone had always bullied me about how I loved classical music ("gay" music) and told me I was silly not to love popular music, I regarded popular music as an enemy and oppressor—which I still to some extent do, despite knowing that this opinion is silly in many ways.

SHOSTAKOVICH: **Cello Sonata in D Minor, op. 40**

For an account of Shostakovich's life and woes, go to Alex Ross's *Listen to This*, or any number of biographies. A fascinating creative life under totalitarian repression (a compositional career from the 1920s through the '70s); a man whose talent made him the symbol of a nation, and also therefore its victim. A voice that tried to tell truth while censors made it impossible; who straddled the line and survived Stalin (barely) because of the talent, and because of music's semantic flexibility, because one person's triumph is another's tragedy.

The slow movement of this piece is a great lament. (Admire the skill it takes to create a long musical sentence with so many phases of arrival, so many different catharses.) You have the sense that Shostakovich's "true" voice appears here. But it's impossible to know what Shostakovich is specifically lamenting. The last movement is both witty and tragic, carnivalesque, evoking the violent antics of commedia dell'arte puppets. You might find it interesting to hear a live recording with Shostakovich himself at the piano, with Daniil Shafran.

BRAHMS: **Cello Sonata in F Major, op. 99, first movement**

Darrett and I didn't agree on much, but we both loved a recording by Truls Mørk at Oberlin, and I still love it today. This kind of cello sonata, written in the prime of Brahms's life, is quite far from the old world of Beethoven cello sonatas. It takes a symphonic, wrestling approach, despite just two players on stage. The pianist often rumbles, like an orchestra. Every idea aspires to be more than it is. I also recommend, for your happiness, that you listen to my teacher György Sebők and János Starker play the first movement of the E Minor Sonata. There you'll find a more intimate Brahms, grand but not grandiose.

10. Melody, Lesson Two

BEETHOVEN: **Sonata for Piano and Cello in A Major, op. 69, first movement**

Egad, not more Beethoven! I recommend you don't get too used to any one recording, but flip back and forth. In the old days I loved the Jacqueline du Pré recording with Barenboim, a true Romantic version, with everything taken to the limit. She makes you experience the theme as a Shakespearean protagonist.

11. Self-Destruction and Self-Salvation

SCHUMANN: *Dichterliebe*

I would opt for recordings with the most poetic and imaginative pianists (but of course I would). I especially love the old Cortot/Panzéra recording, quite different from expectations of vocal timbre and interpretation today. Panzéra sings with French restraint and precision. Meanwhile, Cortot plays with copious and brilliant rubato, the rhythm bending around the aching pull of the notes.

Dichterliebe is, you might argue, the Ultimate Romantic Piece. It provided source material and a model. One famous instance: the third movement of Mahler's Second Symphony (approaching the endgame of Romanticism) is based on the *Dichterliebe* song ("Das ist ein Flöten und Geigen"). In this song, the narrator overhears the sound of his beloved's wedding music, a kind of klezmer waltz. Music becomes the message-bearer of his loss. Mahler, fifty-some years later (1890s), responding to the klezmerish-ness and the sense of an endless circling dance (arguably also a dance of death), freely extrapolates this tune into a massive unfolding, branching folk scherzo (Second Symphony, third movement). Then Luciano Berio, seventy years or so after that (1960s), composed one of the greatest postmodern masterpieces out of Mahler's scherzo—a quote of a quote (of a quote). He layers many other texts about texts on top of Mahler, already so layered, and so also on top of the Schumann, a giant stack of hip classical in-references. With the result that this minute and a half of music—a symbol of Music That Is Not for You, a dance about other people's dances, full of alienation, allure, and self-replication—has a life of over 125 years.

BRAHMS: Sonata no. 3 for Violin and Piano in D Minor, op. 108, first movement

Many recordings are miked very close on the violin, making this piece sound like the Tchaikovsky Violin Concerto, which it is not. Try a bunch; I can't say I found one that is my soulmate.

The prevailing ethos of the first movement is *hovering*. The opening theme wavers, hesitates, starts, stops, fades into silence. A transition explodes; lots of Brahmsian density; at last we get to sing and soar. But then in the development we come back to the dark hovering: an endless pedal point.

The theme I'm talking about in the chapter comes about a minute and a quarter in, depending on the performance, and it comes again later, and if you don't recognize it the second and third times, that's on you. Not a single performance I found does the beautiful markings that Greg taught me—alas, there are some complicated things even the greatest musicians choose to ignore.

SCHUBERT: Sonata in B-flat Major, D. 960, first movement
Schnabel.

MESSIAEN: *Oiseaux Exotiques*
Messiaen, an emblematic mid-twentieth-century modernist, was the favorite composer of grad school students for presentations, because there was always so

much to talk about without having to really think or do much research. Messiaen was a devout Catholic (five minutes on that)! Messiaen loved Indian music, and used non-retrogradable rhythms (ten minutes)! Messiaen loved birds (and how)! He thought specific chords were specific colors (five to ten minutes, listing)!

God, I used to dread those presentations.

Anyway, this piece, written in 1955, is a bird love letter. The Hindu mynah bird. The American wood thrush. I especially enjoy what must be one of the most obstreperous, stubborn birds ever—the Himalayan laughing thrush—played by the whole ensemble (*brrrk-brrrk-brrrk-brrrk-brrrk*, ad infinitum). You could definitely imagine this bird pooping on your head, with glee.

I recommend Messiaen's wife, Yvonne Loriod. She plays with warmth. Her radiant wood thrush is at 2:20 on YouTube.

BRAHMS: Concerto no. 2 in B-flat Major, op. 83

I recommend the early Gilels recording (with Reiner, and János Starker playing the famous solo), or the legendary Edwin Fischer with Furtwangler.

BACH: Partita no. 1 in B-flat Major, Gigue

I mean, Sebők's performance of this is available here and there. I'm not sure all of his recordings capture his unique musicianship, and I know he felt the same way. I often recommend Perahia's Bach also, and of course Angela Hewitt, András Schiff, etc.

This is a unique piece, a gigue like no other (the same is true of the gigue in the Sixth Partita). After all the foundational simplicity of the rest of the B-flat Partita, after all its restraint and pastoral charm, this movement is quite cheeky. It ends not by grounding but by hurling us into the air. Bach is never so profound that he can't also smile, or, put another way: his smiles are as profound as his sighs and frowns.

12. Melody, Lesson Three

VERDI: *Falstaff*, Act I, Scene 2

I fell in love with *Falstaff* when I was fourteen, watching it on PBS, and it's never lost any of its charms. I recommend Tito Gobbi as the title character, with Karajan, a famous recording. Don't just put the CD on. You must listen with the text! Give it your full attention. Or watch a video version with a translation.

"*E il viso tuo . . .*" are the words at the beginning of the passage I analyze in this chapter, but listen from the beginning of Scene 2—it's not that long, and it boasts some of the lightest, swiftest comedic writing imaginable.

13. *"Nothing Is Done, Everything Is Done"*

CHARLES IVES: Trio, S. 86

Ives's CliffsNotes summary is the ideal program note:

> First movement, a short but serious talk, to those on the Yale fence, by an old professor of Philosophy; the second, the games and antics of the students ... on a Holiday afternoon ... the last [movement], a remembrance of a Sunday Service on the Campus which ended near the "Rock of Ages."

In other words, campus memories in three zones: academic, fraternity, church.

Most people don't get the old philosopher quite right for me in the first movement—the half seriousness, the academic turgidity mixed with the sublime. A pompous fanfare appears in sort-of C major, mixed with disrespectful blue notes ... When the cadence comes at the end ("Amen"), that's a quintessential Ives joke: "Oh, so all you soft-eared audience lemmings want a proper ending, here you go, and screw you."

Gilbert Kalish is one of the great Ives interpreters, and so I recommend you listen to his recording with a no-name cellist, Yo-Yo Ma, and Ronan Lefkowitz.

MOZART: Sonata no. 14 in C Minor, K. 457, first movement

Here's a music-historical observation for you: in most works of Bach, there are few silences. I believe there's not one rest in the entire "Goldberg Variations," for instance (except obviously for breaks between variations, which then become very important decisions): anytime one hand stops, another is playing. There might be an exception or two that proves the rule—so sue me.

But here, fifty years after the "Goldbergs," as you can hear, the silences between the phrases are absolutely essential "notes," intangible presences and doorways in which the emotion of one idea passes to the emotion of the next. One of my favorite moments in the first movement is a little inquisitive idea, cut off. The silence is met with a gentle, elegant reply. The question is repeated—silence—then unleashes a wild torrent. Elegance and collapse find themselves in curious symmetry.

I also love the fraught silence before the recapitulation. The music whittles itself down to just two notes and enigmatic chords. An excellent trick: collapse and disintegration of the story at its most crucial juncture. In the classic sportscast version of Beethoven's First Symphony with Peter Schickele, he makes this point brilliantly and deftly, without my excess verbiage.

Really enjoying a live performance by Kristian Bezuidenhout on fortepiano. The rage is there, the uncertainty, the tenderness. He really milks the rests, too! Lots of rubato. And there's Mitsuko Uchida, of course, if you like more well-behaved, but still expressive, interpretations.

BARTÓK: Piano Sonata (1922), first movement

The first movement of this sonata has so many events, tumbling upon one another, that it's hard to appreciate its intricacy and cleverness. Even the most interesting recorded performances (for instance, Kocsis) can sound dour. The opening segment of the piece is more or less in E major (for me, one of the "happier" keys), but it almost never sounds like that. I couldn't find a Sebők recording of this piece. But he recorded the Dance Suite, and there you can hear his approach. Not too violent. At the end of each movement of the Dance Suite comes a lyrical refrain, and he plays this folk tune hauntingly, just like I remember in class. It grabs the ear; you say to yourself, "*Now, at last,* I hear the notes."

CHOPIN: Fantaisie in F Minor, op. 49

My theory is that Chopin had plenty of fantasy built in; when he told himself to be fantastical, he overthought it. This piece, with its various odd leaps from idea to idea, reminds me of a golfer trying to escape from a sand trap.

I feel as though this piece also resists being recorded. An obsessive YouTube person collected five or six versions in one video. None of them did it for me. This made me feel far less bad about massacring the work in my youth.

Maria João Pires, live and messy, had something. She made me (almost) believe.

BRAHMS: Sonata no. 1 for Violin and Piano in G Major, op. 78

I think a *Guardian* survey from 2001 is right to suggest that there's no "definitive" recording. Sebők recorded it with the famous Arthur Grumiaux—certainly worth a listen; some good stuff in there, but it feels mismatched.

This sonata is a distillation of Brahms's lifelong nostalgic message. States of being born too late (a would-be Classical composer in a Romantic age), or being too full of longing and duty to cope or act. Basically Anthony Hopkins in *The Remains of the Day*.

The opening theme—a waltz in the making—is amazing but impossible. Josef Suk's opening sounds to me too monumental, architectural, not enough breath and intimacy. Perlman with Ashkenazy is gorgeous but sounds like a reverie from the beginning, as if we've skipped all the steps, entering early retirement. A minute and a half (Rubinstein/Szeryng) into the first movement, you get another, more soaring waltz theme. Three minutes in (also Rubinstein/Szeryng), you get yet another: this one is more flirtatious, sticking to a few chromatic notes. Three sides of a waltz: tender, soaring, charming.

Who plays the last movement well? You have to decide for yourself. Every so often, both players abandon any melody and just play rain, for a measure or so. Performers should change sound more for this, and they never do. Imagine you're having all kinds of emotions (a life's worth) and then for a moment you shut down your inner voice, and just listen to the rain. The rain is the frame of reference, and a friend, and the idea of falling, and time, and an emblem of sadness, all at once. But—I think to myself with annoyance in the audience, listening to the violinist do all kinds of fancy vibrato and slides—the rain itself should not have feelings.

14. Rhythm, Lesson One

COPLAND: Sextet

A charming piece: young American gay Communist Copland, 1933, fresh from his time in Europe, from studies with the famed counterpoint master Nadia Boulanger and encounters with Stravinsky. This is before Copland became Copland; money was still tight; he was "finding his voice."

I found a lovely performance by the Vanbrugh Quartet on YouTube, with tons of rhythmic vitality and also the occasional telltale split second of uncertainty. There are two kinds of rhythmically hard pieces: the ones where the audience can tell you are not together, and the ones where they can't. Unfortunately, this piece is the former.

MOZART: *The Marriage of Figaro*, Act I, Scene 1

So many magisterial recordings of this. I grew up, and fell in love, with Solti and Frederica von Stade and Lucia Popp. I still think it sounds good. But I had great pleasure listening to the opening of the more "historically informed" Gardiner performance.

Notice how the charming counting of the opening scene gradually transitions into more menacing numbers (*ding ding, dong dong*), as Susanna finally has to explain the facts of life to Figaro.

MOZART: *Don Giovanni*, Act I, Scene 1, just after the duel, from "Ah, soccorso!"

I found the *one-two-three* excellent on an old video performance from Covent Garden (Colin Davis, Kiri Te Kanawa, Thomas Allen, etc.). The Commendatore is stabbed at 9:50. The counting starts up at 10:00, and winds down at 11:15. Don Giovanni's high note at 10:35 or so, a lament's lament—how can you complain about opera when it does stuff like that? But people love to complain about opera.

A joke appears right after this most transcendent of passages: Don Giovanni asks Leporello if he's there, and Leporello asks Don Giovanni which of them is dead, the Don or the Commendatore. Just the sort of wicked, brilliant thing that Mozart is best at; the quick transition from deep tragedy to farce.

VERDI: *Falstaff,* Act III, from *"Uno ... due ... tre ..."*

The counting moment happens about an hour and thirty-seven minutes into Karajan/Gobbi (on YouTube).

SCHUBERT: **Impromptu in A-flat Major, D. 935, no. 2, recorded by Artur Schnabel**

Listen to the whole set with Schnabel while you're at it.

15. More Europeans!

MOZART: **Concerto in C Major, K. 415**

I'd recommend a live performance with the masterful Uchida and the Salzburg Camerata, which you can find on YouTube, or the famous set (which I grew up on) with Murray Perahia and the English Chamber Orchestra.

But I must say, even the most beautiful recordings I've heard fail to capture Sebők's Puckish quality in the first entrance. Some are plain and lyrical, some insist on emphasizing the redundant C.

Think about that moment in *Don Giovanni,* slipping from loss and death into a joke. That's just the kind of valuable life insight that we lose when we over-prettify Mozart. Perahia's last movement (rondo) theme is funnier than most, and the orchestra is a bit more rambunctious than most. When Mozart wants to party, why not let him?

BEETHOVEN: **Sonata in F Minor, op. 57 ("Appassionata"), second movement**

Refer to earlier note (p. 349).

BEETHOVEN: **Sonata no. 3 in A Major, op. 69, for Piano and Cello, third and fourth movements**

I'd recommend a beautiful performance by Paul Tortelier and Éric Heidsieck. The third movement is quite short. You could call it an introduction, but I think better to call it a vision, a lyrical ideal. Beethoven only rarely wrote these sorts of melodies that live a perfect, isolated, untroubled existence. He doesn't develop this tune at all (unlike the first movement's master class in development); he just lets it appear, exist, and vanish.

I could never get my left hand to go fast enough in the last movement. Come to think of it, much of my life has been trying to get my left hand to go faster and my right hand to go slower.

MENDELSSOHN: Sonata for Cello and Piano in D Major, op. 58, third
   movement, recorded by János Starker and György Sebők

Obviously, listen to Starker and Sebők.

A sonata from the high-water mark of Romanticism (1843). It's hard to make a
hymn work in a classical piece (unless you're Bach), but this is one of the success
stories.

Many Mendelssohn pieces present an idea, A, that has a certain way about it;
a second idea, B, that behaves quite differently; and then a synthesis, C, where B
becomes the accompaniment for A or vice versa, resolving the contradiction.
Here, after you're done focusing on Sebők's ridiculously beautiful arpeggios, listen to how the cello continues to play once the chorale has returned. Have faith
and doubt merged? Do they comfort each other?

16. Rhythm, Lesson Two

CHOPIN: Étude, op. 25, no. 9 ("Butterfly"), recorded by Ignaz Friedman

If you don't know the Chopin Études, congratulations, you've been living in a
bubble. He composed two sets of twelve: two grand and consummate demon-
strations of technical and compositional abilities.

I bet you've not often heard these Études played like Friedman does. I especially love his C Major Étude, and the "Double Thirds" (the G-sharp Minor
Étude). Friedman's favorite pianos had a light action, and he could be fleeter than
us modern pianists manage. It's all aerodynamic, at least until Friedman decides
that the bass line needs to be boisterous, and then he approaches the world of
stride or ragtime pianists, with a wonderful swagger down to the bottom and up
to the chords.

17. The End of the Line

BACH: Sonata no. 3 in G Minor for Gamba and Keyboard

I recommend Anner Bylsma's recording with Bob van Asperen—such fabulous
musicians. I walked up to Anner at Marlboro once, quite tipsy, to tell him how
much I loved his Haydn performance (so much freer than many other more
"American" Marlboro performances), and he gave me a very Sebők/European
look and said, "Oh yes, you're the young man who likes things," and turned away
to order a beer.

The Bylsma/Asperen recording is with organ, which works really well to my
ear (mellower than harpsichord!). Their first movement is an imitation of a con-

certo, with intricate solo passages and big repeated unison passages, where two players pretend to be an orchestra. The second movement is a kind of limit piece for Bach. It seems to ask *What is the melody?* and *Do we even need melody?* There are recurring ideas in the bass, getting things going, but most everything else seems invented on the spot, a few eloquent notes in the keyboard, fillips of ornament in the viola, attempts to take over that never last.

The last movement, only three minutes long, a jewel of counterpoint and dance, is my favorite. Bylsma plays the fugue subject (which starts with a bunch of repeated notes) quite fast, and so the triplets that come eventually are crazy fast—the organ hoots and scrambles. But all is quelled when we get to the "second theme." You'll know it when you hear it (at 10:50 or so). Bach writes simply one word there, *"cantabile,"* which means singing—a rare moment of Bach stepping in to tell you what to do. For a Romantic or even a Classical composer to write *cantabile* is like, whatever. But in the context of reticent Bach, that one word is everything.

BACH: Sonata no. 4 in C Minor for Violin and Keyboard

You could spend a lot of time trying to pierce the mystery of the two slow movements of this sonata, the first and third. I know I did. It was my favorite piece for a couple months. The first movement is a *siciliano,* a dance in dotted rhythms (long-short-long) that often inspires Bach to incredible things. What was it about that rhythm? The unevenness, the sense of floating?

Try Isabelle Faust with Kristian Bezuidenhout. Their first movement is beautiful and stylish. I think in my dream performance the keyboard would be a bit more in its own world, less deferential, only occasionally trying to "be with" the violin.

In the third movement you may hear a similarity to the famous hit "Jesu, Joy of Man's Desiring." Triplets in the keyboard; devotional tune above. Bach is unusually specific about dynamics. He writes a series of calls and responses, loud and then soft. A piece about echoes. At first the soft phrase is the same music as the loud, a literal echo. But gradually (as in life's memories) the echoes become more complicated, more of a translation, refracted by time and other needs.

I'll admit I find Faust/Bezuidenhout's third movement too fast, and also the harpsichord can't do the echoes. Sad. That's kind of the point?! Just one of many occasions where you feel Bach would have preferred the modern piano (even more hate mail expected). On YouTube as part of a Melbourne Bach marathon, I found a beautiful performance of this movement with a couple young musicians, Grace Wu and Laurence Matheson. No fucking around. Simple, gorgeous. The burden of time was lifted. Don't overthink it. I realize there's some irony to my saying that.

LIGETI: *Automne à Varsovie,* **from Études, Book I**

I will shamelessly recommend my own recording on Nonesuch, as well as Pierre-Laurent Aimard's version live from Carnegie Hall, which you can find googling about. His ending is just awesome.

BEETHOVEN: Variations and Fugue in E-flat Major, op. 35 ("Eroica")

One of Beethoven's most brilliant piano works—not an audience favorite. It's from the early middle period, as he's searching for his more epic voice.

You can regard this work as just a study for the last movement of the more famous "Eroica" Symphony. Yes, Beethoven takes the same idea and follows the same path for a while, but then he goes after piano-specific pleasures. He demands every kind of keyboard technique, in quick-fire succession. Arpeggios and scales, leaps and hand crossings, canons with the two hands chasing each other (like the "Goldberg Variations"), one famous variation with an orgy of deliberate wrong notes. At last the stage opens up for two slower variations, one in the minor, the second an endlessly unfolding major, a kind of super-aria.

I often think of a microscope in these Adagio variations of Beethoven's, where he looks down at his theme in unbelievable detail, magnifying the smallest event to the nth degree. At the same time that he slows the action down, he creates a sense of sweep. Chords now feel like columns, or poles of a planet: vastly separated, but tied by powerful unseen forces.

It's hard to know who to recommend. Try Emanuel Ax's recent lovely recording! Brendel's recording is funnier and wackier than I'd remembered, so I'll suggest that too.

BEETHOVEN: Sonata no. 32 in C Minor, op. 111

One of the greatest and weirdest of all pieces. Try Goode, Uchida, Kempff (and there is a Denk version somewhere out there). The ecstatic state of the last movement is so different for everyone. How slow should it be? How do you hear the famous boogie-woogie? How do you reconcile it with the rest?

One reason I don't spend much time with pianists is that they get obsessed with certain notorious piano problems: for instance, the trill at the end of this piece. For me, if you get that far and I'm still interested, if you managed to create in me an altered mental state, if the theme's beauty can still be felt within the madness of its variations, if time itself surrenders to the allure of pure sound, then I'm happy, and who gives a fuck about the trill.

18. Rhythm, Lesson Three

BEETHOVEN: **Concerto no. 4 in G Major, op. 58, first movement**

Again, Schnabel! London Phil, conducted by Malcolm Sargent, 1937, HMV. He's so good, and not too reverential. Playfulness isn't smothered by classical purity.

BEETHOVEN: **Symphony no. 5 in C Minor, first movement**

You don't really need to listen to this, do you?

BEETHOVEN: **Sonata for Cello and Piano in D Major, op. 102, no. 2, second and third movements**

I think you have to hand it to Jacqueline du Pré and Daniel Barenboim for daring to play the slowest, deadest slow movement possible: it truly feels like the end of the line, and that the piece is about to disintegrate, and yet it doesn't. I don't usually have patience for this kind of approach (as the reader has already learned), but here it pays off (and how!). When, in the slow movement, they get to the last two utterances in the major key, both Barenboim and du Pré break your heart; beautiful simplicity and depth of feeling.

Their last-movement fugue is great too. Clean, transparent, witty, and still full of forward energy and wildness, slipping perfectly from a more poised *three* to a sweeping *one,* the joy of rhythm, the very thing I was trying to write about, yes I feel so happy listening to it, and resentful of the fact that I have to write more playlist notes instead of cavorting off into the sunshine. OMG they go so crazy at the end!!!!

19. So You Want to Go to Juilliard

SCHUMANN: **Sonata no. 1 in A Minor, op. 105, for Violin and Piano**

What do Schumann's pieces want? They often begin, as this one does, in the middle of uncontainable desire, here a darkly circling theme in the violin, going over certain notes, hearing the emotional distances between them, looking for a way out. Piano replies; violin replies in the major; but still . . .

Schumann does not write the clear climaxes of Rachmaninoff (for instance), or even Brahms. I feel like this connects to his personality: a refusal to bound his desires, or give them a specific goal, at the risk of trivializing or falsifying them. In the course of a Schumann piece, you have to find transitions between desires—from urgent, to ever so slightly less urgent, to mysterious need.

At the end of the first movement, a relatively simple solution: the coiled energy releases in a virtuoso outburst. The final chords are almost savage.

The second movement is a different form with a different solution. Childlike and innocent music. A dark vision in the middle. Then the child again, awaking from the fears of night.

Gidon Kremer and Martha Argerich are vivid. As an exercise in time travel, try listening to Busch/Serkin. Once your ears adjust to the "old recording" vibe, you may find something to treasure there, to the way they listen to the harmonies. No one is quite innocent enough in the second movement, to my ear.

ELLIOTT CARTER: Sonata (1945–46)

I'd recommend an old performance by Beveridge Webster, a lovely pianist who taught at Juilliard. It's not the cleanest version (OK, catastrophically messy) and the piano is out of tune, but it has deep feeling (despite the difficulty), sweep, and rubato . . . also color!

In the first movement, slow austere harmonies alternate with wild, rapid riffs. In the second, a much longer austere, singing section frames a brilliant jazz fugue.

Paul Jacobs's fugue (middle of the second movement) is cleaner than Beveridge's, but sounds like a fugue. It's often nice to make people forget they're listening to a fugue.

BACH: Partita no. 6 in E Minor

This piece lasts a half hour, if you play all the repeats, and is one of Bach's grandest, most audacious keyboard creations. The opening movement, the Toccata, is a free improvisation framing a fugue. Both the free and the fixed parts play with the same fundamental ideas—a falling half step, and a descending four-note thing—musical symbols of sadness.

I remember Leon Kirchner singing the opening arpeggio to me with a pained look—eyes up, mouth pulled down. One of the messages of this movement is the nobility it gives to sorrow. It creates constant tension between falling and rising (even in its first idea, the arpeggio rising to a sigh that falls away), and this has emotional resonances—the admission that there is always falling, always loss, even obsessive loss; but also the assertion of rising against it.

A partita is a collection of dances. The typical set is:

Allemande (slowish, duple)
Corrente (faster, triple)
Sarabande (slow, triple)
Free Dances (gavottes, minuets, etc., mostly medium speed)
Gigue (fast, triple)

It's fair to say Bach takes these existing templates as a point of departure and a site for experiment—something to emulate and something to transcend. The Allemande is, as usual, full of ideas passing from voice to voice, and no real single melody. The Corrente is all demonic or devilish syncopation, with the right hand almost always "off" from the left. You get an unexpected interpolation: a brief Air, lighter and simpler, perhaps to recover. Then the goddamned Sarabande, one of the most ornamented he ever wrote, where the sigh returns with a vengeance, finding itself in all the voices, at the ends of long spiraling, curling phrases. Not just undanceable, but seemingly unknowable. Then comes a Gavotte—again relief.

At last, the weirdest, most abstruse of all. A Gigue, in four instead of three by some mutation, living a double life as a fugue, leaping and hopping about. As it goes along, you have to fit in little mad fillips of rhythm. It has intellectual aspects, but also sheer life force.

So many amazing recordings. Try the live video of Murray Perahia, perhaps. I will also recommend the one I made when I was too young to make it, on Azica Records, which you can find. I wish I had played a little slower. Just a little more breathing. Six percent maybe. So close!

SCHUBERT: Sonata in D Major, D. 850

I recommend (surprise!) Schnabel. But also Richter. Richter (live) was the performance that transfixed, that made me feel I *had* to play the piece. But Schnabel is better at the Viennese lilt. Russians are not famous masters of lilt. Most young pianists, when I tell them it needs more lilt, ask me what lilt is. I've almost given up.

MONTEVERDI: *"Zefiro torna e'l bel tempo rimena,"* from the Sixth Book of Madrigals

Madrigals are often overheated. In a way, it's hard to imagine a more emotionally rich and intense and bite-sized genre in all of so-called Classical Music. It has elements of a string quartet—conversational, two or three or four or five voices, etc. All the voices represent one voice; they are all facets of the inner life of the speaker of the poem.

I recommend, if you can find it, the Rooley-Consort performance of this madrigal. For me, their ending is the most overwhelming.

LEON KIRCHNER: Duo no. 2 for Violin and Piano

This piece has many beauties in the details; each measure is obsessively crafted. But what is the big story? You can find a recording of me and Ida Levin from Marlboro in the summer of 2002, in the spell of perpetually unsatisfied Leon. So many musical sentences spilling over one another, and only a few moments of true repose—those are my favorites.

Leon rewrote the piece a year or so later for solo piano, partly because Ida and I never stopped fighting about the tempo, and partly (I think?) because he was late on some solo piano commissions. And one beautiful Sunday afternoon, in the old, high-ceilinged library in Beacon, New York, I played my dream version of that piece. Leon went nuts; he loved it too, and asked me: "Why don't you always play like that?"

You can find this performance on YouTube, as part of a compilation of Leon's solo piano music. Unfortunately, toward the middle, someone has a coughing fit. Around ten minutes in, when I start heading for the climax, it sounds pretty good if I do say so myself, and then the piece dissolves (to the extent it was ever cohesive) into fragments of music heard, lost, remembered. By twelve minutes we're in a blissful F-sharp major—and that would have been lovely, but Leon insisted on stacking more dissonance and longing onto that. Of course he did.

Coda (transitions)

MENDELSSOHN: *Variations Concertantes*

Yes, there are amazing variation sets that become worlds, like Bach's "Goldbergs" or the Brahms Handel or Rzewski's *The People United*. But consider this piece, a mere eight minutes in length, and one of the most perfect ever written. I love the way the variations twist and turn, slipping in and out of virtuosity, never plodding too much in the mud in that way that certain variations do (I'm looking at you, Brahms!).

Sebők and Starker are almost businesslike in the opening, as if they don't want to let the sweet tune cloy. But then the games begin. Listen to Sebők starting at 53 seconds or so: the slight unevenness of his notes. (Furtwangler: "The key to musicianship is the almost imperceptible variability of the tempo.") Sebők takes the reins again around 1:45 for a beautiful cadence. Listen to him smile through his short chords between 2:50 and 3:30; then be a full-fledged storm at 4:45, etc.; and then, when after darkness and tempest, and after Starker lands on his held note and waits for his lifelong friend to come in, Sebők takes a little tiny bit of time on some parts of the theme (5:53). A liberty that he permits himself. This moment of permission always brings me to tears: his noticing of beauty, his assertion of the importance of noticing beauty, but also the continuous reminder: not too much, never too much.

The way Sebők plays the final arpeggio! WTF. That's a piano lesson. He once told me that the secret was to play fast notes but with slow key-speeds: the notes come quickly, but the fingers enter the key relatively slowly. A nice paradox.

LISZT: *Spanish Rhapsody*

There hasn't been much Liszt in this book, and I suppose I don't always love Liszt, because he couldn't distinguish that well between his best and worst inspirations. But Sebők loved and transformed Liszt. As of this writing, I couldn't find the old recording of him playing this piece (though it certainly exists!). Hopefully you might come across it. But if you're not in a sleuthing mood, you can easily hear his Liszt Sonata, which has all the hallmarks—a classical approach, a command of the keyboard, clarity, a desire to find integrity.

MOZART: **Concerto in C Major, K. 503, recorded by Jeremy Denk and the Saint Paul Chamber Orchestra**

Read my liner notes for the record, please? I worked hard on them.

About the Author

JEREMY DENK is one of America's foremost pianists. Winner of a MacArthur "Genius" Fellowship and the Avery Fisher Prize, Denk is a member of the American Academy of Arts and Sciences. He returns frequently to Carnegie Hall and has appeared with renowned ensembles including the Chicago Symphony, New York Philharmony, and Los Angeles Philharmonic. His recordings have received critical acclaim, including reaching #1 on the *Billboard* classical charts and featuring on many best-of-the-year lists. His writing has appeared in *The New Yorker, The New Republic, The Guardian,* and *The New York Times Book Review.* Denk graduated from Oberlin College, Indiana University, and the Juilliard School. He lives in New York City.

About the Type

This book was set in Arno, an expansive neohumanist type-
face family designed by Robert Slimbach and released by
Adobe in 2007. Arno's letterforms are based on fifteenth-
and sixteenth-century Italian typefaces, including those
of the Venetian calligrapher and printer Ludovico degli
Arrighi.